'The third edition of *International Organization* provides a comprehensive survey of the history of international organizations (IOs) and a careful analysis of mainstream theories relevant for modern IOs. Beyond its theoretical merit, a major strength is the instrumental value of this text for explaining the policy-making process in IOs. The authors also include a meaningful discussion of many contemporary international issues on the agenda of different IOs.'

—**Houman Sadri, University of Central Florida, USA**

'Despite the lack of world government, world affairs are remarkably stable and predictable, owing to international organizations functioning as the great stabilisers of global governance. Their work affects ordinary citizens on a daily basis. They have been the backbone of the post-war liberal world order that is currently under challenge from emerging powers while also increasingly contested by its own creator. At this critical juncture, the third edition of this highly regarded textbook elucidates the workings and impacts of international organizations across a broad range of areas, such as security, trade, finance, development, human rights and the environment.'

—**Ramesh Thakur, Australian National University, Australia**

'An outstanding textbook that presents much of the best recent research on international organizations and at the same time remains highly accessible. Comprehensive and very well structured, it will be of great help to instructors in a wide range of educational programmes.'

—**Mathias Koenig-Archibugi, London School of Economics, UK**

'This third edition of *International Organization* is written in an accessible style, helping those who are not already experts in the field to get to grips with the subject. Building on the legacy of Volker Rittberger, the new author team have made some major changes to this new edition that will ensure students from various disciplines can learn about the foundations of the international political system and their main actors in a concise way. Compared to other books in this area, this text offers students a succinct overview of the topic and valuable references for gaining a deeper understanding of international organizations.'

—**Wolfgang Gruber, University of Vienna, Austria**

'At this moment of crisis for the liberal international order, the third edition of this brilliant textbook offers an indispensable guide to how international organizations are created and maintained, how they operate and with what consequences. Written in a cogent and easily accessible style, and offering a rich array of contemporary examples, this book provides an essential and comprehensive primer for anyone wishing to learn the basics of international organization in theory and practice.'

—**Mette Eilstrup-Sangiovanni, University of Cambridge, UK**

'Comprehensive and well researched, the book provides a valuable introduction to international organizations. The emphasis on the institutional aspects of international organizations is a major strength compared to other textbooks. The book presents theories in an accessible way and offers concepts and typologies that are useful in teaching.'

—**Johan Christensen, Leiden University, the Netherlands**

'I have been anxious to see a new edition of this textbook. Students get not only the nuts and bolts of international organization, but also the historical setting for the creation and functioning of international institutions and the theories that help make sense of it all. The clarity of presentation, broad scope and firm grounding in the academic literature will appeal to both newcomers and those ready to dig deeper into the subject.'

—**David Kinsella, Portland State University, USA**

'This book provides an excellent overview of the literature and debates that relate to international organizations. The authors provide a clear and engaging account of the conceptual and historical foundations for different types of international organizations and address key theoretical questions on the emergence, internal decision-making and substantive policy impact of IOs.'

—**Zeynep Bulutgil, University College London, UK**

'In the 20th century, international organizations have added a new dimension to diplomacy and world politics. National governments, whether democratic or autocratic, have no choice but to engage with this world of IOs. Scholars and students need to study it, and this book provides an excellent starting point. This textbook stands out among the competing volumes for various reasons. It is comprehensive. It deals with IOs as a global phenomenon and covers a much wider range than most other works. It offers an accessible way to analyse IOs. The book's effective methodological input/output logic helps to open up the black box of conversion-roles performed by IOs in world politics. It covers five major issue areas (peace & security, trade & development, finance & monetary relations, the environment, and human rights), and does so from both a global and a European perspective – an obvious, but seldom applied practice in textbook.'

—**Jaap de Wilde, University of Groningen, the Netherlands**

'The updates and extensions in the third edition have made this excellent volume even more compelling as the main textbook for courses on international institutions. A must-read for students, scholars and practitioners of international organizations.'

—**Ulrich Sedelmeier, London School of Economics, UK**

INTERNATIONAL ORGANIZATION

Third Edition

Volker Rittberger,
Bernhard Zangl,
Andreas Kruck and
Hylke Dijkstra

 macmillan
international
HIGHER EDUCATION

 RED GLOBE
PRESS

Second edition published 2012
Third edition published 2019 by
RED GLOBE PRESS

Red Globe Press in the UK is an imprint of Springer Nature Limited, registered in England, company number 785998, of 4 Crinan Street, London, N1 9XW.

Red Globe Press® is a registered trademark in the United States, the United Kingdom, Europe and other countries.

ISBN 978–1–137–61005–8 hardback
ISBN 978–1–137–61004–1 paperback

This book is printed on paper suitable for recycling and made from fully managed and sustained forest sources. Logging, pulping and manufacturing processes are expected to conform to the environmental regulations of the country of origin.

A catalogue record for this book is available from the British Library.

A catalog record for this book is available from the Library of Congress.

Contents

List of Figures

List of Tables

List of Boxes

List of Acronyms

AOSIS	Alliance of Small Island States
ASEAN	Association of Southeast Asian Nations
ATTAC	Association for the Taxation of Financial Transactions and Aid to Citizens/Association pour la Taxation des Transactions Financières et l'Aide aux Citoyens
AU	African Union
BCBS	Basel Committee on Banking Supervision
BRICS	Brazil, Russia, India, China and South Africa
CAC	Codex Alimentarius Commission (FAO)
CAP	Common Agricultural Policy (EU)
CCOL	Coordinating Committee on the Ozone Layer (UNEP)
CDF	Comprehensive Development Framework (World Bank)
CFCs	chlorofluorocarbons
CICC	Coalition for the International Criminal Court
COP	Conference of the Parties
COPA-COGECA	Committee of Professional Agricultural Organisations and the General Committee for Agricultural Cooperation in the European Union (EU)
COREPER	Committee of Permanent Representatives (EU)
CSCE	Conference on Security and Co-operation in Europe (see OSCE)
DFID	British Department for International Development
DG	Directorate-General (EU)
DSB	Dispute Settlement Body (WTO)
DSU	Dispute Settlement Understanding (WTO)
ECB	European Central Bank (EU)
ECE	Economic Commission for Europe (UN)
ECF	Extended Credit Facility (IMF)
ECHR	European Convention for the Protection of Human Rights and Fundamental Freedoms (Convention on Human Rights)
ECJ	European Court of Justice (EU)
ECOSOC	Economic and Social Council (UN)
ECU	European Currency Unit (EU)
EESC	Economic and Social Committee (EU)
EFF	Extended Fund Facility (IMF)
EFSF	European Financial Stability Facility (EU)
EFSM	European Financial Stabilization Mechanism (EU)
EMS	European Monetary System (EU)
EMU	European Economic and Monetary Union (EU)
ESA	European Space Agency

ESM	European Stability Mechanism (EU)
ETUC	European Trade Union Confederation
EU	European Union
Europol	EU Agency for Law Enforcement Cooperation
FAO	Food and Agriculture Organization (UN)
FCL	Flexible Credit Line (IMF)
G7/8	Group of Seven/Eight (leading industrial countries)
G20	Group of 20 (industrialized and emerging-market countries)
G77	Group of 77 (developing countries)
GAB	General Arrangements to Borrow (IMF)
GATS	General Agreement on Trade in Services
GATT	General Agreement on Tariffs and Trade (WTO)
GCF	Green Climate Fund
GDP	gross domestic product
GEF	Global Environmental Facility (UN)
GOIC	Gulf Organization for Industrial Consulting
HCFCs	hydrochlorofluorocarbons
HFCs	hydrofluorocarbons
HIPC	Heavily Indebted Poor Countries (IMF)
HRC	Human Rights Council (UN)
IAEA	International Atomic Energy Agency (UN)
IBRD	International Bank for Reconstruction and Development (World Bank) (UN)
ICAO	International Civil Aviation Organization (UN)
ICC	International Criminal Court
ICJ	International Court of Justice (UN)
ICRC	International Committee of the Red Cross
ICTR	International Criminal Tribunal for Rwanda (UN)
ICTY	International Criminal Tribunal for the Former Yugoslavia (UN)
IDA	International Development Association (World Bank)
IEO	Independent Evaluation Office (IMF)
IFC	International Finance Corporation (World Bank)
ILO	International Labour Organization (UN)
IMF	International Monetary Fund (UN)
IMO	International Maritime Organization (UN)
INC	Intergovernmental Negotiating Committee
IPCC	Intergovernmental Panel on Climate Change (UN)
IRENA	International Renewable Energy Agency
ISAF	International Security Assistance Force (Afghanistan)
ITO	International Trade Organization
ITU	International Telecommunication Union
IWC	International Whaling Commission
MDGs	Millennium Development Goals
MIGA	Multilateral Investment Guarantee Agency (World Bank)
NAB	New Arrangements to Borrow (IMF)

NAFTA	North American Free Trade Agreement
NASA	National Aeronautics and Space Administration
NATO	North Atlantic Treaty Organization
NDC	Nationally Determined Contribution
NGOs	non-governmental organizations
NIEO	new international economic order
NPT	Nuclear Non-Proliferation Treaty (UN) (Treaty on the Non-Proliferation of Nuclear Weapons)
ODP	Ozone Depletion Potential
OECD	Organisation for Economic Co-operation and Development
OHCHR	Office of the High Commissioner for Human Rights (UN)
OIC	Organization of Islamic Cooperation
OIHP	International Office for Public Hygiene
OPEC	Organization of the Petroleum Exporting Countries
OSCE	Organization for Security and Co-operation in Europe (see CSCE)
PRSP	Poverty Reduction Strategy Paper (World Bank)
R2P	responsibility to protect
RCF	Rapid Credit Facility (IMF)
SAP	Structural Adjustment Programme (IMF)
SBA	Stand-By Arrangement (IMF)
SCF	Standby Credit Facility (IMF)
SCSL	Special Court for Sierra Leone
SDGs	Sustainable Development Goals
SDRs	Special Drawing Rights (IMF)
SQP	Small Quantities Protocol (IAEA)
SRSG	Special Representative of the Secretary-General (UN)
TEU	Treaty on European Union
TFEU	Treaty on the Functioning of the European Union
TPRB	Trade Policy Review Body (WTO)
TRIPS	Agreement on Trade-Related Aspects of Intellectual Property Rights (WTO)
TTIP	Transatlantic Trade and Investment Partnership
UN	United Nations
UNCLOS	United Nations Convention on the Law of the Sea
UNCTAD	United Nations Conference on Trade and Development
UNDP	United Nations Development Programme
UNEP	United Nations Environment Programme
UNESCO	United Nations Educational, Scientific and Cultural Organization
UNFCCC	United Nations Framework Convention on Climate Change
UNFPA	United Nations Population Fund
UNHCR	United Nations High Commissioner for Refugees
UNICEF	United Nations Children's Emergency Fund
UNIDO	United Nations Industrial Development Organization
UNIIMOG	United Nations Iran–Iraq Military Observer Group

UNITAR	United Nations Institute for Training and Research
UNMIK	United Nations Mission in Kosovo
UNMOVIC	UN Monitoring, Verification and Inspection Commission (Iraq)
UNSCOM	United Nations Special Commission
UN WOMEN	UN Entity for Gender Equality and the Empowerment of Women
UPR	Universal Periodic Review
UPU	Universal Postal Union (UN)
USA	United States of America
WFP	World Food Programme
WHO	World Health Organization (UN)
WMO	World Meteorological Organization (UN)
WTO	World Trade Organization
ZOPA	zone of possible agreement

Preface

The liberal world order is under attack. It is not only challenged by emerging powers such as China, India and Brazil; stunningly, the liberal world order, which was built and sustained by US leadership in the twentieth and early twenty-first centuries, is increasingly contested by its own creator. The United States under President Donald Trump is turning against international institutions such as the North Atlantic Treaty Organization (NATO), the World Trade Organization (WTO) and the Paris Agreement on Climate Change. International organizations have been the backbones of the post-war liberal world order. Therefore, at this moment of crisis for the liberal order, it is timely to reflect on the conditions for the creation, the workings and the impact of international organizations. This textbook aims to give an overview of international organizations, and their causes and decision-making procedures and the consequences of these. Better understanding how and when international organizations are created and used, how they actually work, and how we can evaluate their contribution to international cooperation in a range of areas, such as security, trade, finance, development, human rights and the environment, is now more important than ever before.

For the third edition of this textbook the author constellation has changed. Volker Rittberger passed away in 2011. He was the initial author of this book's first German-language edition in 1994. But afterwards, when he was successively joined by Bernhard Zangl for the second German edition in 1996 and Andreas Kruck for the fourth German edition in 2013, he was still the intellectual engine of the book. He was also the driving force behind an English translation which appeared in its first edition in 2006 (with Bernhard Zangl) and its second edition in 2012 (with Bernhard Zangl and Andreas Kruck). We are extremely grateful to Volker Rittberger for all the energy he devoted to the project over all those years and his tireless intellectual guidance and stimulation. We sincerely hope that he would like what we have done with this third edition in English. For this edition, Hylke Dijkstra has joined the team of authors. With Bernhard Zangl and Andreas Kruck progressively withdrawing, he will become the lead author for future editions. For the third edition, Hylke Dijkstra has taken the lead in revising the manuscript and worked on the majority of the chapter revisions.

This edition's revisions have sought to improve *International Organization* in several ways. First, we have revised the chapter structure to make the length of the chapters more balanced, expanding on topics in some chapters while cutting unnecessary slack in others. As a result, we believe the book will be more informative and easier to use in class. Second, we have aimed to make the text more accessible, particularly for undergraduate students. Third, we have put considerable effort into streamlining, systematizing and simplifying the book's account of international organizations as political systems in Part II and using this approach more consistently in Part III. Fourth, we have updated relevant data and added recent examples throughout the book. Finally, reflecting more recent research and the new author constellation, we have put more substantive emphasis on the interaction between member states and international secretariats, underlining that international organizations are both member state-driven entities and bureaucracies. We hope that readers of this textbook will find these revisions, as well as the approach that has characterized this book over several editions now, useful.

We dedicate this edition to the memory of Volker Rittberger.

Bernhard Zangl, Andreas Kruck and Hylke Dijkstra
Munich and Maastricht, August 2018

1 Introduction

International organizations are a relatively new phenomenon in international relations. They first emerged during the nineteenth century and became ever-more important over the course of the twentieth century. Today, international organizations are involved in nearly all issue areas – from A, as in **A**rms Control, to Z, as in **Z**ones of Fishing. General purpose international organizations such as the United Nations (UN) or the European Union (EU) cover many different topics, while task-specific organizations such as the International Labour Organization (ILO) or the European Space Agency (ESA) specialize in specific issue areas. Some international organizations, like the UN, have a near universal membership. Others restrict membership on the basis of criteria such as geography, economy, culture or religion; examples include the EU, the African Union (AU), the Organization of the Petroleum Exporting Countries (OPEC), the Organisation for Economic Co-operation and Development (OECD) and the Organization of Islamic Cooperation (OIC). All these international organizations contribute to establishing and implementing norms and rules which guide the management of transnational, cross-border problems, such as climate change, the proliferation of weapons of mass destruction or international terrorism. It is thus no exaggeration to say that it is difficult to understand contemporary world politics without referring to international organizations.

International organizations are, however, not only for diplomats, or for academics to study. Ordinary citizens are also confronted on a daily basis by the work of international organizations. In the wake of the global financial and economic crisis, the International Monetary Fund (IMF) and the EU, including the European Central Bank (ECB) and the Eurozone group, have become familiar to even the most casual newspaper readers. In recent years, the work of some international organizations has also become fiercely contested. The World Health Organization (WHO) was criticized when it failed to bring the Ebola pandemic under control. Through a referendum, British voters decided to leave the EU. US President Donald Trump decided to quit both the Paris Agreement on climate change and the United Nations Educational, Scientific and Cultural Organization (UNESCO). The fact that ordinary citizens pay attention and that the work of international organizations has increasingly become contested is perhaps the best evidence of their significance: international organizations are no longer technical agencies; they have actual influence on people's lives.

The international organizations mentioned so far only represent a fraction of the approximately 330 international *governmental* organizations existing at present (Pevehouse et al. 2004), not to mention around 37,500 international *non-governmental* organizations (NGOs) (Union of International Associations n.d.). Figure 1.1 provides an overview of how the number of international

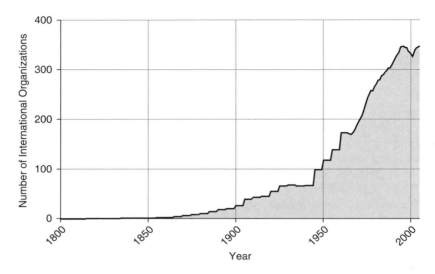

Figure 1.1   Total number of international organizations since 1800
Source: Based on data from Pevehouse et al. (2004).

organizations has developed since the beginning of the nineteenth century, show-ing a significant increase after the Second World War ended in 1945. Indeed, the post-war period can be characterized as an era of growing institutionalization of interstate relations. The number of international organizations has stabilized in more recent years. Yet the overall number of international organizations does not tell us everything. Since the end of the Second World War, there have been increases in the political significance of, financial resources assigned to, and num-ber of civil servants working for international organizations. The growth in the number and significance of international organizations are discussed throughout this book.

This first chapter starts, however, with a seemingly simple question: what are international organizations? The answer, however, is not straightforward. The chapter puts forward a definition, which requires international organizations to have three or more states as members, a plenary meeting at least every ten years, and a permanent secretariat and correspondence address (Pevehouse et al. 2004). As such, international organizations differ from other international institutions, such as international regimes (which do not have a secretariat) or NGOs (which do not have states as members). Yet even when we follow this restrictive definition, we are still left with approximately 330 international organizations of many shapes and sizes. The chapter therefore also introduces a typology that conceptualizes these international organizations along three different types:

- *Task-specific* international organizations address a limited set of problems, while *general purpose* international organizations have a wide policy scope.

- *Programme* international organizations focus on setting norms and rules to address problems, while *operational* international organizations implement those norms and rules.
- *Centralized* international organizations have the authority to address problems themselves, while *decentralized* international organizations rely on the authority of their member states.

After discussing what international organizations are, this chapter asks how we can study them. It suggests three big questions:

- Why are international organizations created?
- How are decisions made and implemented within international organizations?
- How do the decisions and activities of international organizations affect international cooperation?

WHAT ARE INTERNATIONAL ORGANIZATIONS?

International organizations are obviously of practical importance. But how can they be conceptualized? Surprisingly, the term 'international organization' became part of scientific and everyday vocabulary only relatively recently. During the nineteenth century, expressions such as 'international public union', 'international office' or 'commission' were commonly used. A very early example is the Rhine River Commission, which was founded in the aftermath of the Congress of Vienna (1814–15). Its task was (and remains) to facilitate and coordinate the navigation of international traffic on the Rhine. Even today, we cannot simply determine an international organization by its name: the World Trade *Organization* (WTO) is clearly an international organization, yet the International Atomic Energy *Agency* (IAEA) is an international organization as well. It is therefore important to provide a definition of international organizations which distinguishes them from other forms of governance, such as international regimes or NGOs.

As a starting point, it is important to point out that international organizations are a specific sub-category of international institutions. *International institutions* can be defined as 'persistent and connected sets of rules (formal and informal) that prescribe behavioral roles, constrain activity, and shape expectations' (Keohane 1989: 3). International institutions are a very broad category. For instance, the 'nuclear taboo' (Tannenwald 1999) – states refrain from using nuclear weapons even if they can – is also an international institution. After all, it is an example of a persistent informal rule (a norm), which constraints the use of the most powerful weapon and shapes expectations between states. Yet the nuclear taboo is clearly not an international organization: it does not have a building, it does not have member states, nor a budget or staff. Instead it is part of the nuclear non-proliferation regime, which also includes the Treaty on the Non-Proliferation of Nuclear Weapons and the IAEA – all different sorts of international institutions aimed at reducing the threat and use of nuclear weapons.

> ## Box 1.1 International institutions, international regimes and international organizations
>
> *International institutions* are 'persistent and connected sets of rules (formal and informal) that prescribe behavioral roles, constrain activity, and shape expectations' (Keohane 1989: 3). *International regimes* are 'implicit or explicit principles, norms, rules, and decision-making procedures around which actors' expectations converge in a given area of international relations' (Krasner 1983: 2). *International organizations* have three or more states as members, hold a plenary meeting at least every ten years, and have a permanent secretariat and correspondence address (Pevehouse et al. 2004).

So what are international organizations? And how can we distinguish them from other international institutions? In this book, international organizations are defined as having (1) three or more states as members, (2) a plenary meeting at least every ten years, (3) and a permanent secretariat and correspondence address (Pevehouse et al. 2004). It is important to discuss these three elements of the definition in greater detail:

- *Three or more states as members*: International organizations can be distinguished from, for instance, NGOs due to the fact that their membership predominantly consists of states. So while the Universal Postal Union (UPU) is an international organization with 192 member states, the International Committee of the Red Cross (ICRC) is not as it does not have states as its members. This part of the definition also makes international organizations *multilateral* (three or more states as members) rather than *bilateral* (two states as members).
- *A plenary meeting at least every ten years*: International organizations can be distinguished from ad hoc international conferences because they have a regular plenary meeting. So when the international community organizes, for instance, a donor conference for Afghanistan or Syria, these are normally one-off events. Such conferences are therefore not international organizations. The ten years requirement is a minimum to be defined as an international organization. In many international organizations meetings are organized much more frequently, for example in the EU where ministers meet almost every week. Some scholars therefore feel that a more restrictive definition, requiring more regular meetings, is appropriate. For instance, Volgy et al. (2008) have proposed a plenary meeting every four years, though note that most international organizations have a plenary meeting every year.
- *A permanent secretariat and correspondence address*: International organizations can be distinguished from regular international conferences or regimes because of a higher degree of institutionalization in the form of a permanent secretariat and correspondence address. Or, to put it differently, 'international organizations are palpable entities with headquarters and letterheads, voting procedures, and generous pension plans' (Ruggie 1992: 573). A secretariat can,

however, be a modest affair. A single member state may, for instance, make a few diplomats in its foreign ministry available for secretarial support. This is why several scholars suggest a stricter definition. Hooghe et al. (2017), for instance, suggest that the secretariat should consist of at least 30 civil servants. As a result, they only identify 76 international organizations (compared to the 330 of Pevehouse et al. 2004).

While scholars debate the exact definition of international organizations, they largely agree that international organizations consist of states, are continuous and permanent. As its title suggests, international organizations are also the topic of this book. While we recognize their importance, we do not focus on NGOs, such as Amnesty International, Greenpeace or Transparency International, or multinational companies such as General Motors, Amazon or Citigroup. These actors may be involved in the work of international organizations, but they are not the topic of this book as such. Still, this leaves us with a wide variety of international organizations which are not necessarily always comparable. The EU, for example, may not have much in common with the Gulf Organization for Industrial Consulting (GOIC). And comparing them is a bit like comparing apples and oranges: both fruits are round and of similar size, but they have a different colour, taste and texture. The bigger challenge therefore is to create a typology of international organizations. We argue that international organizations can be classified according to their scope, function and centralization.

First of all, it is important to distinguish between *task-specific* international organizations and *general purpose* international organizations (Lenz et al. 2014). They differ in terms of their scope (Koremenos et al. 2001). Whereas task-specific international organizations focus on one or a limited number of issue areas, general purpose international organizations address a range of issue areas (see Table 1.1). The underlying rationale of both groups of international organizations is different (Lenz et al. 2014). Task-specific international organizations are problem-driven – that is, a group of states want to address a problem in a specific issue area. For instance, the founding states of the Rhine River Commission wanted to solve navigation problems on the Rhine. General purpose international organizations, on the other hand, are community-driven: a group of member states, which share a purpose, set up an international organization to address a range of problems. For instance, the EU facilitates cooperation between states on the European continent. As such, general purpose international organizations tend to

Table 1.1   Types of international organizations (scope)

Type	Task-specific	General purpose
Scope	Few issue areas	Many issue areas
Examples	IAEA	AU
	IMF	EU
	World Bank	UN
	WTO	

Table 1.2   Types of international organizations (function)

Type	Programme organization	Operational organization
Function	Setting norms and rules	Implementing norms and rules
Examples	ILO	IAEA
	UN	IMF
	WTO	World Bank

have a smaller membership (Lenz et al. 2014: Figure 2). Many of the international organizations with universal membership, on the other hand, are task-specific.

Secondly, international organizations can be distinguished with regard to their main function (see Table 1.2). *Programme* organizations deal primarily with programme formulation – that is, they determine the norms and rules to address international problems. The WTO, for example, sets the rules concerning global trade. The ILO sets international labour standards. The UN General Assembly adopts many resolutions concerning human rights. *Operational* organizations, on the other hand, concentrate on implementing those norms and rules. This includes both the monitoring of compliance by states with agreed norms and rules and actual implementation activities by the international organizations themselves. The IAEA is an example of the former. It 'verifies through its inspection system that States comply with their commitments ... to use nuclear material and facilities only for peaceful [i.e. non-military] purposes' (IAEA n.d.). The World Bank is an example of an operational international organization engaged in capacity-building. It had more than US$60 billion in 2017 in outstanding loans, grants and investments in support of development assistance across the world. Operational organizations indeed often have large budgets.

Finally, international organizations can also be distinguished according to the degree to which authority has been centralized within them (Table 1.3; Koremenos et al. 2001). The centralization of authority is about its pooling in decision-making and the delegation of tasks to international organizations (Hooghe & Marks 2015). In *decentralized* international organizations, the member states make decisions by consensus and they are themselves in charge of implementation. An example

Table 1.3   Types of international organizations (centralization)

Type	Decentralized organization	Centralized organization
Authority	Consensus decision-making and implementation by states	Majority voting and implementation by international organizations
Examples	NAFTA	EU
	North Atlantic Treaty Organization	IMF
	OPEC	World Bank

is the North American Free Trade Agreement (NAFTA) between the United States, Canada and Mexico. While there is a NAFTA Secretariat (making it an international organization) and a dispute-settlement mechanism, the actual delegation of tasks is minimal, and decision-making is by consensus. The same goes for OPEC. In *centralized* international organizations, on the other hand, states make decisions through majority voting and delegate the implementation of decisions to the secretariat, agencies and other organs of the international organizations. The IMF and World Bank are two examples of international organizations with extensive majority voting, whereas the EU member states have delegated much of the implementing authority to the EU institutions.

HOW CAN WE STUDY INTERNATIONAL ORGANIZATIONS?

It is important to define international organizations and classify them. Yet scholarship is not merely about systematic description. In this book, we raise three big (research) questions. The purpose is to make sense of the rapid increase in the number of international organizations since the nineteenth century. We also want to know how international organizations work; and, finally, how they affect international cooperation. These questions are introduced below and answered in Parts I–III of this book.

Why are international organizations created?

As mentioned earlier, international organizations first appeared in the nineteenth century and they have become particularly numerous since 1945. To put it differently, international organizations have not always been around. While evidence exists of diplomatic relations going as far back as 2550 BC (in Mesopotamia, modern-day Iraq) and, more recently, appearing in the modern state system which developed after the Treaties of Westphalia (1648), international organizations are very much a contemporary phenomenon. This raises the question of why states did not create international organizations earlier – or, in other words: what triggered the creation of all these international organizations over the last 200 years? It is fair to say that something must have changed in the international system. Was it the 'first wave' of globalization between 1870 and 1914, which required new forms of international governance to facilitate the rapidly increasing trade volumes? Was it about the prevention of future war following the millions of casualties from the two world wars of the twentieth century? Was it about the awareness of cross-border environmental problems which became a key issue on the international agenda in the 1970s? Or was it mainly about American hegemony in the post-war and particularly the post-Cold War period?

Understanding the changes that motivated the creation of international organizations is only the first step. We also need to know why states considered that international organizations could better address international problems than could other forms of governance. To go back to the definition, what is it precisely about multilateral cooperation (between three or more states), with regular meetings and permanence in the form of a secretariat, that makes international organizations better equipped for today's problems than other international institutions? Why not simply address cross-border problems on an ad hoc basis, as they come along, only with the involved states? Chapters 2 and 3 provide detailed answers to these questions. Chapter 2 focuses on the main international relations theories and how they regard international organizations. Chapter 3 provides a historical overview of the creation and development of international organizations.

How are decisions made and implemented within international organizations?

After we have studied why international organizations are created, the next logical question is: how do international organizations work? To answer this question, we can no longer treat international organizations as 'black boxes'. Rather than simply saying 'the EU does this' or 'the UN did that', we need to look inside international organizations and study the actual 'machinery'. Which actors set the agenda and propose new norms and rules? Which actors call the shots and make the important decisions? Do all member states have an equal say, or are there more powerful member states, such as the five permanent members of the UN Security Council? Is implementation delegated to the secretariat or a specific agency? We argue in this book that international organizations are political systems. That means that all international organizations have their own constitutional and institutional structures as well as their procedures and practices. These structures, procedures and practices determine which actors within international organizations can make and implement decisions. As such, the political system of each international organization facilitates the process of policy-making. At the same time it also constrains the different actors in that it tells them which procedures to follow.

While it is important to understand the constitutional and institutional structures of the individual international organizations and their procedures and practices, this is not the whole story. It is also important to know what the actors want to achieve in the context of an international organization. What are their interests and preferences? For instance, in the (failed) Doha Development Round – the multinational trade negotiations under the WTO – the Western countries wanted lower trade barriers including for services. The developing countries, on the other hand, wanted access to Western markets to sell their agricultural goods. Such preferences by the member states are '*inputs*' into the political system of an international organization. How such preferences are precisely channelled through international organizations and result in decisions is what we call the '*conversion process*'. The decisions, in turn, result in the '*output*' of international organizations, which includes policy programmes as well as operational activities. Chapter 4 discusses the constitutional and institutional structure of international organizations. Chapter 5 focuses on input, while Chapter 6 discusses conversion and Chapter 7 analyses output.

How do the decisions and activities of international organizations affect international cooperation?

After we know how decisions are made and implemented, we need to pay attention to the actual outputs of international organizations. What is the substance of the policy programmes by various international organizations, such as the UN, EU or IMF? To what extent does the UN Charter limit aggressive behaviour by states? What type of rules govern the EU's internal market? Why can the USA not discriminate between French and Indian products under the WTO framework? What is the role of the IMF when countries have payment problems? What commitments have states made in terms of addressing climate change and global warming? And how important is the Universal Declaration of Human Rights? In addition to all these international rules and norms, we argue that particular attention should be paid to their actual implementation. International organizations have developed a whole range of operational activities that help states further specify rules and norms. In some cases, policy implementation is actually delegated to international organizations themselves. International organizations also have an important role to play in monitoring implementation as well as adjudicating between disputes among the member states and imposing sanctions on non-compliant member states. Indeed, we argue that operational activities have a significant impact on the effectiveness of international cooperation among states.

In Chapters 8–12, we address the outputs of international organizations and the effectiveness of this output across different policy areas. Chapter 8 focuses on questions of peace and security. It highlights the policy programme of the UN which restricts the use of force and the operational activities that the UN has developed: pacific settlement of disputes, peace enforcement and peacekeeping. We also address questions of nuclear arms control under the Treaty on the Non-Proliferation of Nuclear Weapons. In Chapter 9, we focus on trade and development. We address how the output of the WTO and EU have resulted in increased trade among the member states. We also focus on the World Bank and its role in providing development assistance and loans. In Chapter 10, we pay particular attention to finance and monetary relations. We study the changing role of the IMF as well as EU monetary policy and the role of the ECB. The focus of Chapter 11 is on the environment. We contrast the outputs of the member states in the case of the ozone layer regime with more recent climate change policies. Finally, Chapter 12 is about international human rights. We discuss the negotiations of a policy programme in the UN following the Second World War and some of the operational activities developed by international organizations, including the International Criminal Court.

Discussion Questions

1. How do international organizations differ from other international institutions?
2. Which types of international organizations can be distinguished? Please provide several examples.

Further Reading

Abbott, Kenneth W. & Snidal, Duncan 1998. Why states act through formal international organizations, in: *Journal of Conflict Resolution* 42: 1, 3–32.
Pevehouse, Jon, Nordstrom, Timothy & Warnke, Kevin 2004. The correlates of War 2 international governmental organizations data version 2.0, in: *Conflict Management and Peace Science* 21: 2, 101–19.
Ruggie, John Gerard 1992. Multilateralism: The anatomy of an institution, in: *International Organization* 46: 3, 561–98.

Part I Theory and History of International Organizations

2 Theories of International Organizations

In this chapter, we look at several theories of international organizations. International organizations are complex. They often have many different member states which all have specific preferences. They also have different constitutional and institutional structures. The day-to-day practice of an international organization can indeed be a mystery to anyone who has not been familiar with that specific international organization for a long time. The purpose of theory is to structure and simplify such complexity. This allows us to identify patterns, trends and causal relationships *within* an international organization, but also *across* international organizations. For instance, by studying regional integration in Europe (the European Union (EU)), we may also be able to say something about the prospects of regional integration in Africa, Asia or Latin America (the African Union (AU), Association of Southeast Asian Nations (ASEAN) and Mercosur). The aim of theory is therefore to generalize and to put the daily practices into a broader context. By developing and then applying theories, we can better explain and occasionally predict developments in international organizations.

In the area of international relations there are three dominant theories (Table 2.1). *Realist theory* stresses the importance of power: the power of states is largely based on their military capabilities, such as the number of soldiers and weapons. International organizations are, for realists, simply forums where states diplomatically fight out their conflicts. *Institutionalist theory*, on the other hand, is problem-driven. It argues that states – as a result of globalization – increasingly face cross-border and international problems. States cannot solve those problems, such as global warming or international terrorism, alone. International organizations help them to address these problems collectively. They facilitate the process of cooperation between states. Finally, *constructivist theory* argues that international problems are not simply 'out there', but that they are 'socially constructed'. The perception of problems matters. For instance, only relatively recently we started to

Table 2.1   Theories of international organizations

Realist school	Institutionalist school	Constructivist school
Realism	Federalism	Normative idealism
	Functionalism	Transactionalism
	Neo-functionalism	
	Interdependence analysis	
Neo-realism	Neo-institutionalism	Social constructivism

pay attention to human rights in international relations; previously human rights were simply perceived as domestic matters. These three theories not only suggest different reasons for why international organizations are created, but also provide us with alternative explanations for how international organizations are designed and what the effects of international organizations are.

THE REALIST SCHOOL

While realist theory is occasionally traced to the political philosophers Thucydides, Machiavelli and Hobbes, our starting point is *classical realism* as introduced by E. H. Carr (1939) and Hans Morgenthau (1948). This theory claims that the state is the primary actor in international politics. In realist analyses, other actors such as non-governmental organizations (NGOs), multinational companies or international organizations are left out or are assigned a secondary role. Realists also do not distinguish between different types of states – for instance, democracies or autocracies. The only thing that matters are *the differences in the power of states*. Classical realists hold that it is an important part of human nature to strive for power. Accordingly, they assume that international politics is characterized by the continuous quest for power by all states, just as national politics is characterized by the quest for power of competing politicians and parties (Morgenthau 1948). In other words, domestic and international politics are two different manifestations of the same phenomenon: the struggle for power.

Importantly, different moral, political and social conditions prevail in domestic and international spheres (Morgenthau 1948). In national politics, the struggle for power between politicians and parties is constrained because the state has a monopoly on the use of force. In international politics, the struggle for power between states can escalate into violence, because there is no supranational authority capable of constraining states. In other words, 'wars occur because there is nothing to prevent them' (Waltz 1959: 232). Classical realists also note that all states are responsible for their own survival. Because states cannot trust other states to come to their rescue, every state has to provide for its own security. They can do so through maximizing their (military) capabilities. Consequently, states are caught in a situation known as the security dilemma (Herz 1950): the efforts of one state to enhance its security by enlarging its capabilities are perceived by other states as threatening. This leads to a vicious circle of distrust, competition and strife for power. Since this struggle for power is automatic, the best way to avoid a large-scale war is to establish an 'equilibrium' or balance of power (Morgenthau 1948). Weaker states can team up and form temporary alliances against powerful states.

According to realist theory, international organizations are of little help in addressing this power struggle. International organizations cannot change human nature. They also cannot transform the anarchical structure of the international system, in which states constantly have to maximize their own capabilities in order to survive, into a hierarchical structure. Rather, for classical realists, international organizations are used by powerful states to implement their power politics more effectively and to pursue their self-interest. International organizations are only established when it is in the interest of powerful states. Similarly, international organizations can only succeed – and indeed survive – if they have the support of powerful states.

Classical realism has been replaced by *neo-realism* since the late 1970s (Waltz 1979; Gilpin 1981; Grieco 1988; Mearsheimer 2001). Whereas classical realism was informed by history, philosophy and most prominently the experience of the two world wars, neo-realism is considered to be more 'scientific' in its approach. Through logical reasoning, neo-realism can explain to us 'a small number of big and important things' (Waltz 1986: 329). For instance, contrary to classical realism, neo-realism does not assume that that all humans are 'evil'. Rather, neo-realism claims that the anarchical structure of the international system requires states to pursue a security-oriented policy of maximizing capabilities and autonomy in order to survive (Waltz 1990: 29–37). As a result of the absence of an overarching monopoly of force in the international system, there is no guarantee of survival for states. Therefore, states have to ensure their survival themselves. States that do not orient their policy according to this 'self-help' imperative will inevitably perish (Waltz 1979: 79–101).

As the anarchical structure of the international system requires states to maximize their capabilities, international organizations are largely ineffective. From a neo-realist perspective, long-term interstate cooperation is almost impossible to achieve. Even if cooperation results in gains for those states that do cooperate, there is always the risk that today's friend may become tomorrow's enemy (Mearsheimer 1995: 11). States must therefore ensure that other states do not benefit *more* from cooperation in international organizations than they do themselves (Grieco 1988). This makes long-term international cooperation hard to achieve, as cooperation always takes place against the backdrop of mistrust and cheating. Sustained cooperation in international organizations is only possible, according to neo-realists, if one of the states concerned possesses such superior power that it can afford to tolerate the relative gains of other states (Keohane 1980). In other words, Western cooperation since the Second World War was only possible because the omni-powerful USA allowed its allies substantial gains of cooperation as well. This is, however, the exception and not the rule.

As international organizations are instruments of powerful states, their design will also reflect the interests of those states (e.g. Krasner 1991; Gruber 2000; Drezner 2007). From a realist perspective, the decision-making procedures of international organizations will thus be set up in a way that privileges the most powerful member states, for instance by giving them a disproportionate share of voting rights or special voting rights. Examples are the system of weighted voting in the International Monetary Fund (IMF) Governing Board and the World Bank, which still favour Western industrialized states and in particular the United States. Or consider the United Nations (UN) Security Council: the five most powerful countries insisted that they would have a veto to stop the Security Council doing anything to hurt their interests. In many international organizations we therefore find skewed decision-making procedures that promote rather than mitigate imbalances in power.

While realists have traditionally not paid much attention to international organizations, more recent scholarship uses power-based explanations to uncover how international organizations favour strong states. Scholars have studied, for instance, the informal channels through which states can assert their power: when international organizations deal with crisis situations, strong states often take a lead role (Stone 2011). Powerful states are also good at lobbying the permanent secretariats of international organizations, because of their informal contacts, and placing their own nationals in senior positions (Urpelainen 2012; Kleine 2013; Dijkstra 2017; Parízek 2017). In other words, they often use international organizations and the permanent secretariats to exert power over weaker states (Manulak 2017). Along similar logics, powerful states are interested in bringing on board non-state allies. They may favour opening up international organizations to like-minded NGOs (Sending & Neumann 2006). While such power-based explanations go beyond neo-realism in its purest form, they are relevant in understanding the design of international organizations (see below).

THE INSTITUTIONALIST SCHOOL

The institutionalist school includes a wide variety of different theoretical approaches. The common theme in institutionalist theories is that states try to address *international and cross-border problems* through the creation of international organizations. Many institutionalists share the realists' view of an anarchic international system. In contrast to realists, however, institutionalists view cooperation through international organizations as a way of taming the struggle for power. In international politics, according to institutionalists, the interests of different states are usually neither mutually exclusive nor harmoniously in agreement. Instead, states have a common interest in reaping joint gains from cooperation while, at the same time, each individual state has some incentive to refrain from cooperation (Keohane 1984, 1989). Neo-institutionalism notes that as a result of globalization, states have become ever-more interdependent and their relations ever-more complex. This often leads to problems that no state can master alone. Given the problems caused by interdependence and mutual vulnerabilities, even powerful states must depend on other states' renouncing self-help strategies in order to establish stable cooperative relationships within the context of international organizations (Keohane & Nye 1977).

Federalism is the oldest theoretical perspective within the broader institutionalist school (Friedrich 1968). It draws on the historical example of the creation of confederate and federal states, such as the United States, Germany or Brazil. Federations can bring different states together in a common order, yet each state nevertheless maintains its identity. Federations are normally created through a conscious decision by political elites with the support of mass movements. Examples of federal states can serve as blueprints for some international organizations, such as the EU. Another perspective is *functionalism* (Mitrany 1933, 1966). For functionalists, international organizations help interdependent states to overcome cross-border problems. The evolution of modern society and globalization is, in this respect, the main cause of international organizations:

technological progress creates interdependent relationships between states, which causes problems that can only be addressed through international organizations. The development of international organizations is therefore a gradual process rather than a conscious decision by political elites. Mitrany (1933, 1966), for instance, noted that increased cooperation between states in one issue area will tend to 'spill over' into other issue areas as well.

Neo-functionalism abandons the premise that increasing transborder interdependencies lead almost automatically to an increasing role of international organizations (Haas 1964, 1968). While it underlines that technological and economic developments drive political integration, it also argues that political integration drives further interdependencies. Neo-functionalism was inspired by the process of European integration. It assumes that the creation of an international organization (the EU in this case) starts a dynamic process requiring further integration. In this view, an international organization, which was established to solve specific problems arising from the interdependence in one issue area, creates new interdependencies in bordering issue areas. This, in turn, results in incentives for member states to delegate the task of dealing with the resulting problems to the same organization. The international organization itself – following its political agenda – is thus also a driving force for further integration.

While the theory of neo-functionalism was inspired by the process of European integration, the *interdependence* approach (Nye & Keohane 1971; Keohane & Nye 1977) originally focused on the prominence of multinational companies in world politics. It notes that relations between different states no longer solely take place at the governmental level (for instance between two diplomatic services). Indeed it points out that relations operate through multiple channels, including direct interactions at the societal level (for instance between two companies in different countries). This whole web of interactions leads to increasingly complex interdependence across state borders. The problems caused by such new sorts of interactions are addressed by the growing number of international organizations. Different from functionalism, interdependence theory recognizes that the creation of international organizations is, to a large extent, dependent upon the prevalent balance of power between states. In this context, power is understood as issue-specific power. For instance, if states need each other equally in a specific issue area, the design of international organizations will reflect such equality. If, however, some states are more dependent on cooperation than other states (which might have alternatives to cooperation), the distribution of institutional power within international organizations will likely be asymmetric.

While all these theories provide important insights, *neo-institutionalism* – also known as neo-liberal institutionalism – has become the most prominent institutionalist theory (Keohane 1984; Abbott & Snidal 1998; Koremenos et al. 2001). It provides what is considered the 'standard explanation' of why states establish international organizations. In addition to explaining institutional creation, it can also explain why international organizations are designed in different ways. Beyond the design of international organizations, neo-institutionalism is furthermore increasingly used to examine the day-to-day operation of international organizations. Because of the prominence of this theory, we will discuss it at greater length.

The starting point of neo-institutionalism is that international institutions can help states to cooperate successfully in the pursuit of common interests when these interests are neither totally aligned nor mutually exclusive. While achieving such common interests yields significant benefits for all states involved, there is often a risk that individual states defect from joint cooperation in order to reap extra gains. Even if states genuinely want cooperation, they may still fear that other states might secretly abandon cooperation. To address this challenge, states can decide to organize their cooperation 'through' international organizations (Abbott & Snidal 1998; Keohane 1989). International organizations provide stable and permanent forums for cooperation, which reduce uncertainty among states and improve states' expectations of one another (Hasenclever et al. 1997: Chapter 3). They can also reduce the transaction costs of cooperation, such as the preparation and completion of contracts and the monitoring and enforcement of contract provisions (Coase 1960). International organizations thus remove various obstacles to cooperation. States, therefore, have an interest in establishing and maintaining them (Keohane 1984: 80).

One way to illustrate the need for international organizations is through the so-called 'Prisoner's Dilemma'. In the Prisoner's Dilemma, the two interacting players have strong incentives to defect from cooperation, but are thereby likely to end up both in a worse situation than if they had cooperated (see Table 2.2). International

Table 2.2   The 'Prisoner's Dilemma'

		Player B	
		Cooperate	*Defect*
	Cooperate	1/1	10/0
Player A			
	Defect	0/10	5/5

10 = ten years in jail; 0 = prisoner goes free. Each player prefers defection, while the other cooperates, to mutual cooperation. However, both consider mutual cooperation more beneficial than mutual defection. The worst outcome for each player is to cooperate while the other defects.

Note that both players always have an incentive to defect in order to increase their payoff. In the absence of international organizations this will most likely result in the suboptimal equilibrium outcome (defect/defect), which leaves both players worse off than the Pareto-optimal cooperative solution (cooperate/cooperate). The Prisoner's Dilemma models the situation of two suspects arrested by the police. As the police have insufficient evidence, they offer each of the (separated) suspects the same deal. If one testifies (*defects* from the other) for the prosecution against the other and the other remains silent (*cooperates* with the other), the betrayer goes free. The silent accomplice will receive a full ten-year sentence. If both remain silent (cooperate), both prisoners are sentenced to only one year in jail for a minor charge. If each betrays the other, each receives a five-year sentence. The dominant strategy of each prisoner will be to betray the other (defect) because, independently of what Player B does, Player A is better off when employing a defective strategy. The Prisoner's Dilemma game can be applied to a wide range of phenomena in international politics, including arms races or trade protectionism (see Chapters 8–11).

organizations help to address this dilemma. They can provide reliable information about the other parties, thereby reducing mutual uncertainty. Furthermore, due to the permanent nature of international organizations and their continuity, states are more likely to cooperate because they know they will meet each other again.

Neo-institutionalist theory thus provides an explanation for why states prefer to cooperate within the framework of (formal) international organizations as opposed to ad hoc cooperation. It also provides strong insights into how cooperation within international organizations is organized. Two closely related concepts are important in this respect: *legalization* of cooperation (Abbott et al. 2000) and the *institutional design* of international institutions (Koremenos et al. 2001). The first thing to know is the extent to which states decide to 'legalize' their cooperation. Legalization consists of three elements. The first element is *obligation*: are states legally bound by their commitments to other states? While states often make binding commitments within international organizations, just as often they issue non-binding joint declarations of intent. The second is *precision*: do cooperation agreements leave states room for manoeuvre? For an international organization as important as the North Atlantic Treaty Organization (NATO), the North Atlantic Treaty is remarkably short with only 14 articles. Even its cornerstone, Article 5 (an attack against one member state is an attack against all), is not very precise. The final element is *delegation*: do states grant authority to third parties for the implementation of agreements and dispute settlement? An interesting example is the authority of the World Trade Organization (WTO) Appellate Body. If states have a trade dispute, for instance over state aid, they can turn to these judges who independently adjudicate over conflicts under the WTO rules. By distinguishing between these three elements of legalization, it becomes possible to identify strong international organizations with binding and precise rules and delegated authority, and weaker ones with non-binding and non-precise rules and without delegated authority.

The concept of institutional design takes this discussion forward. Koremenos et al. (2001) explain why international institutions 'are organized in radically different ways' (p. 761). They therefore wonder why there is such great variation in how international organizations look. They put forward five dimensions of institutional design. First, which *members* are included in international organizations? Do international organizations have a universal membership, such as the UN, and allow all states in or do they have clear restrictions on membership, for instance in the case of the EU or AU? Second, what is the *scope* of international organizations? Do they deal with all sorts of policies (general purpose) or only a limited number of policies (task-specific)? Third, to what degree is policy-making *centralized* in international organizations? Have states delegated authority to third parties, such as international secretariats or courts? Fourth, how are international organizations *controlled* by their member states? Do member states take decisions by consensus or through majority voting? Finally, how much *flexibility* do international organizations have? Can they adapt to new circumstances? Do they have 'escape clauses'? These dimensions of institutional design have been studied in great detail over the last two decades (e.g. Hooghe & Marks 2015). They also form the basis for the typologies of international organizations put forward in the introduction of this book (see Chapter 1).

Of all the different elements in the design of international organizations, the centralization and delegation of authority has been researched most.

Principal-agent theory, a variant of neo-institutionalist theory, sheds more light on this design feature (Hawkins et al. 2006; Pollack 2003; Tallberg 2002a). It provides an answer to the question of why states sometimes delegate certain tasks and authority to third parties within international organizations. According to principal-agent theory, the relationship between the member states of an international organization and its supranational bodies – i.e. permanent secretariats, technical agencies, dispute-settlement units, and the like – can be understood as the relationship between a principal and its agent. A principal–agent relationship is defined by a contractual arrangement which provides for the delegation of certain policy functions from a principal (e.g. the EU member states) to an agent (e.g. the European Commission). This conditional and revocable grant of political authority empowers the agent to act on behalf of the principal in order to produce outcomes desired by the principal (Hawkins et al. 2006: 7; Tallberg 2002a: 25).

From the perspective of principal-agent theory, states create and sustain different kinds of international organizations with varying degrees of 'supranational' authority in accordance with the functions these agents are supposed to perform for the member states (Hawkins et al. 2006: 13–23; Pollack 2003: 20–24; Tallberg 2002a: 26). In this view, there are incentives for member states to delegate a good variety of functions to the organizations' supranational bodies. Member states may, for instance, not always have all the relevant *information and expertise* at their disposal that are necessary to perform a certain task. In particular, when the task is very complex and/or technical in nature, principals may delegate it to an *expert agent* that is specialized in this field (Hawkins et al. 2006: 13–15; Pollack 2003: 23, 28–29). Member states may also delegate *agenda-setting competencies* to an *agenda-setting agent* to 'avoid endless cycling among alternative policy proposals' (Pollack 2003: 24) that might occur in a system where all principals would retain agenda-setting rights for themselves. As discussed above, member states may find it attractive to delegate *monitoring of compliance* with international obligations, in some cases even *sanctioning* of non-compliance, to third parties such as supranational bodies. Furthermore, supranational bodies can help to solve problems of *incomplete contracting* among principals. In this case, the tasks of 'filling in' and specifying incomplete (or unclear) international agreements are delegated to agents. Through delegation of authority, states can thus make cooperation within international organizations both more credible and more efficient.

Despite all these advantages of delegation, member states will ensure they eventually keep control over their agents. Principal-agent theory underlines that member states need to control their agents through the use of material and immaterial incentives (carrots and sticks). This is necessary because supranational agents are actors that have preferences of their own which may diverge from the preferences of their principals (the member states). As a result, supranational agents may behave opportunistically and minimize the effort they exert in the implementation of tasks on their principal's behalf. Or alternatively they may shift policy away from their principal's preferred outcome and towards their own preferences. In order to avoid a loss of agency, member states employ selection and control mechanisms and may sanction 'runaway bureaucracies' (Alter 2008: 34; see Pollack 2003: 39). However, control and sanctioning mechanisms are themselves costly, and too much control may undermine the very advantages of delegation (Kiewiet & McCubbins 1991: 27). Member states thus have to make trade-offs between efficient policy-making, the cost of exerting control, and the potential loss of control (Dijkstra 2016). They often prefer to err on the side of caution: they typically delegate too few tasks rather than risking a loss of control.

While principal-agent theory puts forward an elegant model of the relationship between the member states and the supranational agents in international organizations, it is often also criticized for being too simplistic. Scholars have therefore tried to further specify the model. They have, for instance, analysed how conflicts between the member states themselves affect the delegation of authority in international organizations. While some scholars have shown that a divided group of member states is less likely to delegate as they do not want to lose control over policy (e.g. Hawkins et al. 2006: 20–21), other scholars have found that divided member states delegate more authority, precisely because they do not trust each other (Green & Colgan 2013: 477–78; Hooghe & Marks 2015: 317). Yet other scholars have examined how supranational agents play groups of states out against each other (Chorev 2012). Finally, some scholars argue that like-minded states and supranational agents team up against other groups of states (Dijkstra 2017). In other words, how relations between the member states and supranational agents play out depends to a large extent on the specific issue area and context.

Finally, drawing on *resource exchange theory*, institutionalism may also offer an explanation as to why many international organizations in their institutional design have become much more open towards non-state actors, including towards other international organizations or even NGOs. The argument is that few international organizations possess the necessary resources to address all relevant problems within their scope themselves. For example, NATO might have the military resources to enforce the peace in a civil conflict, but it does not have the civilian resources to build the peace after its intervention. It therefore needs the help of other actors, such as the EU and the UN. International organizations may also anticipate that by working with NGOs and civil society actors, and granting them access to policy-making, they will be better off than relying solely on their member states. Resource exchange theory argues that international organizations will open up to non-state actors if states consider the goals and strategies of these actors as compatible with their own goals *and* are dependent on these actors' immaterial or material resources (such as knowledge, expertise, legitimacy, or financial means) for organizational goal achievement (Tallberg et al. 2013; Biermann & Harsch 2017; Pfeffer & Salancik 2003 [1978]). The higher the essentiality and the lower the substitutability of non-state actors' resources, the more pronounced will be international organizations' openness or even inclusiveness towards them.

THE CONSTRUCTIVIST SCHOOL

Different theories provide different explanations about international organizations, mainly because they have different views on how actors behave and the international system is structured. Realism and institutionalism generally agree that states are rationalist actors which make constant cost-benefit calculations about survival and cooperation in an anarchical international system. They merely draw different conclusions regarding the likelihood of cooperation between states and the usefulness of international organizations in strengthening such cooperation. The constructivist school, however, differs fundamentally from these two theories. It notes that key aspects of international relations, such as 'anarchy', which realists and institutionalists take for granted, are actually 'socially constructed' and can therefore be transformed (Wendt 1992). In other words, the whole structure in which international relations take place is not a 'natural fact', such as gravity or the shape of the globe, but something resulting from social practice.

The starting point of constructivism is the reflexive concept of action, according to which state and societal actors follow not only the rationalist 'logic of expected consequences' (Coleman 1990; North 1990; Shepsle 1997), but also the 'logic of appropriateness' (March & Olsen 1989). Actors try to pursue their interests, but they do so within the framework of existing norms and rules. For instance, as human beings we refrain from engaging in robbery not only because we fear the consequence of being caught, but mainly because we have internalized the norms and rules that forbid engaging in robbery. In this view, norms and rules are not only part of institutional structures that constrain the action of actors, but they actually constitute and determine actors' interests and even their identities. Going beyond the purely anarchical understanding of the international system, by introducing an ideational concept of structure, has far-reaching consequences for the way in which international organizations are conceived. We begin by looking first at the older normative idealism of the nineteenth and early twentieth centuries, before introducing social constructivism and in particular theories of bureaucratic culture which, for the past few years, have enjoyed ever-growing attention in the context of international organizations.

Normative idealism can be seen as a radical alternative to realism (Kant 1991 [1795]; Wilson 1917/18). Its starting point is the premise that not states but societies – or people(s) – are the central actors of international politics. To normative idealists, human beings are moral actors who can differentiate between good and evil, true and false, and so on. Societies therefore not only orientate themselves towards power and survival, but they are also guided by their ideals, values and norms. While different societies might have different ideals, normative idealists hold that societies can find some common normative ground. One key observation of idealist thought is that democratic societies, which share a number of ideals, rarely go to war with one another (e.g. Doyle 1986). International organizations help stabilize the common ideals and values of different societies. US President Woodrow Wilson (1856–1924), for instance, advocated the creation of a League of Nations after the First World War. This would contribute to the creation of a worldwide public opinion reflecting the common values and norms of different societies. Wilson was convinced that such a worldwide public opinion would always favour a legally constituted peace over war and would be able to maintain peace even when individual states wanted to go to war. Thus normative idealism views international organizations both as the representatives of an order of values and as the advocates of the norms which constitute this order.

While normative idealists are convinced that world peace arises from liberal societies whose norms and values are represented and fostered by international organizations, *transactionalism* holds that intensive interstate and inter-society transactions and communications lead to the creation of 'security communities' in which the threat or use of force between states becomes unthinkable (Deutsch et al. 1957). Such communities differ according to the degree of integration of their members. An amalgamated security community, to which formerly independent states belong (e.g. the USA), is more closely integrated than a pluralistic security community in which member states remain formally independent but are nevertheless closely linked through an international organization (e.g. NATO). Transactionalism attaches considerable importance to the density and quality of communication and transactions across borders in the creation of security communities. This density presupposes, inter alia, a compatibility of core values. It is these tightly woven relations which give rise to a 'mutual responsiveness' between the participating states and societies, engendering security communities supported by international organizations (Deutsch et al. 1957).

Transactionalist arguments have been picked up and expanded by social constructivist scholars of security communities (Adler & Barnett 1998). Such accounts of security communities emphasize the emergence of mutual trust and collective identities out of positive experiences with cooperation, intensified dialogue and social learning. As states come to identify with one another and develop a sense of community, they develop 'dependable expectations of peaceful change' (Adler & Barnett 1998: 30). From that perspective, international organizations do not only facilitate cooperation, but also contribute to socialize states into common values and norms which are constitutive for a collective identity.

Social constructivism follows the tradition of the older idealist and transactionalist schools in some important aspects (Adler & Haas 1992; Wendt 1992, 1999; Risse 2000). To be sure, it has shed the normative mantle of idealism, and at least some constructivist authors do not tire of emphasizing that many social constructs (including undesirable ones) are solid as a rock and may not change easily. Nonetheless, similar to older idealist and transactionalist approaches, social constructivism emphasizes that social actors do not only act rationally according to their selfish interests, as in realism and institutionalism. Instead, their actions are also informed by shared values and norms. Thus social actors not only ask what gains they may derive from their action ('interest orientation'), but also what is expected of them on the basis of the ideals, values and norms of their society ('norm orientation').

Social constructivism therefore stresses that the creation of international institutions in general, and of international organizations in particular, depends on whether there is a consensus over values and norms. International organizations are likely to emerge whenever the values and norms they represent are widely shared in the participating societies (Risse 2000). Furthermore, social constructivists draw attention to the importance of cognitive agreement when it comes to the creation of international organizations: different societies need to perceive cooperation problems in a similar manner. Wherever there are fundamental differences in the perception of the problems at hand, it is particularly hard to set up a successful international organization. The creation of effective international organizations is therefore only likely when the participating societies share a basic perception of the problem (Haas 1990, 1992a; Parsons 2003: 1–33).

In contrast to realism and institutionalism, when analysing the creation of international organizations social constructivism focuses on the role of social groups (as well as individuals) that function as norm entrepreneurs seeking to persuade states to agree on and adhere to specific norms (Finnemore & Sikkink 1998). Out of altruism, empathy or ideational commitment, norm entrepreneurs call attention to political issues and try to convince states to embrace new norms within the context of international organizations. Thus social constructivists attribute key roles to non-state actors in promoting social norms, as well as to epistemic communities and advocacy networks. Epistemic communities – transnational networks of recognized, issue-specific experts (for instance environmental experts) – help in the formation of cognitive agreement (Haas 1992a: 3), whereas transnational social movements and advocacy networks are especially significant for the formation of consensual norms. Members of epistemic communities share causal beliefs and those of advocacy networks hold common principled beliefs (Keck & Sikkink 1998; Thakur et al. 2005). 'Principled beliefs' refer to ideas that express specific values on the basis of which individuals and collectives can differentiate between good and evil, just and unjust. 'Causal beliefs', by contrast, define ideas about the relations between cause and effect on the basis of which one can differentiate between true and false (Goldstein & Keohane 1993: 9–10).

From a social constructivist perspective consensual values and norms are not only important for the creation of international organizations, but also for how international organizations are designed. Many constructivists argue, for instance, that there is a growing stock of global norms and blueprints of what 'proper' international organizations should look like (Archibugi et al. 1998). For example, the increasing openness or even inclusiveness of international organizations towards civil society actors is seen as reflecting the diffusion of a global norm of democracy. Similarly, accountability, transparency and legitimacy are increasingly demanded from international organizations. This ranges from accountability of peacekeeping funding in the UN to competitive elections for the European Parliament.

Like normative idealism, social constructivism underlines the dual role of international organizations. On the one hand, international organizations reflect the values and norms on which they are founded. On the other hand, they influence the values and norms of participating societies. As they influence the way in which state representatives and their societies think about the world, they – so the argument goes – do not only impact on their behaviour, but also on their interests and identities. International organizations may shape the action of states depending on the configuration of their interests, but they can also, through the values and norms embedded in them, influence the interests and identities of states and thus, ultimately, the structure of the international system (Wendt 1999).

Three specific mechanisms can be distinguished through which international organizations may influence the values and norms of their members' societies. First, international organizations offer organizational platforms for NGOs that, as norm entrepreneurs, seek to persuade states to adhere to global norms such as human rights. If NGOs can argue that a state infringes norms to which it has committed itself through membership of the relevant international organization, it may be possible to mobilize social groups in support of these norms. The state is then compelled by internal forces to behave in a manner commensurate with the values and norms embedded in the relevant international organization (Klotz 1995; Katzenstein 1996). Second, international organizations can be seen as sites where persuasion and discourse within negotiations among states may lead to shifts in actors' interests. From this perspective, international organizations provide (or fail to provide) conditions under which, sometimes through the inclusion of NGOs, states can be convinced by the 'power of the better argument', even if it is advanced by traditionally weaker actors (Deitelhoff 2009). Third, the secretariats of international organizations themselves promote the respective values and norms by engaging in persuasive communicative action with member states and by supporting those NGOs, and the social groups represented by them, which espouse these values and norms. In this view, international organizations also act as 'teachers of norms' (Finnemore 1993).

Importantly, social constructivism claims that international organizations also have their own bureaucratic authority. Theories of *bureaucratic culture* note that the power of international organizations is not only based on the functions delegated to them by states, but derives from their own expert or moral authority (Barnett & Finnemore 2004; Hurd 2007). Such authority allows international organizations to frame – for states and non-state actors – what are relevant political problems and propose appropriate solutions to these problems. International organizations develop a distinct life of their own. While not negative about international organizations' performance per se, theorists of bureaucratic culture do reject idealist notions of the effectiveness of international organizations and point to bureaucracies' dysfunctionalities and resistance to reform (Barnett & Finnemore 2004; Weaver 2008). They wonder how an international organization such as the IMF, created to help countries with failing economies, made recessions worse on a number of occasions. According to constructivists, one needs to account for the resilience of bureaucratic cultures to understand why international organizations sometimes do things contrary to what their founders had intended. For instance, in the IMF a bureaucratic culture exists that strongly prioritizes macroeconomic theory and models. This has persisted even in the face of unsatisfactory policy outcomes.

One of the most recent constructivist advances in studying international organizations is *practice theory* which focuses on the smallest unit of analysis: how politics in international organizations is conducted, in practice, on an everyday basis (Adler & Pouliot 2011). Practice theory goes beyond abstract theories, such a realism or institutionalism, that are concerned with 'big things' such as anarchy and the nature of cooperation. Instead it focuses on micro-level patterns in daily behaviour. As Adler-Nissen and Pouliot (2014) note, '[w]hile IR [international relations] theories may help identify *who* pulls the strings of multilateral diplomacy, they are less useful to understand *how* strings actually get pulled' (p. 890). Practice theory therefore takes, just like realism, power seriously in international relations. Practices may, for instance, reveal underlying patterns of power. At the same time, perceptions and implicit claims of authority are critical in international organizations. Newcomers may find out that, contrary to their preferences, 'things are done' in a certain way within a specific international organization (Adler-Nissen & Pouliot 2014: 893). Furthermore, despite formal rules on the equality of states within many international organizations, diplomats tend to be well aware of an informal 'pecking order' in international relations (Pouliot 2016). Diplomats from small states, such as Peru, will not claim a seat at the head of the table or repeatedly raise their voice in discussions, even if they are formally equal. This brings us back to the logic of appropriateness stressing appropriate behaviour.

OTHER THEORETICAL APPROACHES

We have discussed realist, institutionalist and constructivist theories of international organizations in quite some detail because these three schools of thought reflect well-established and widely applied theoretical approaches to international organizations. However, there are other theoretical perspectives on international organizations, including critical, neo-Gramscian, feminist and 'green theory' approaches.

Critical theories reject outright any idealist conceptions of international organizations. Instead, they conceive of international organizations as reflections and vehicles of not only material, but also immaterial power structures. International organizations are thus the expression of hegemonic ideas, values and interests. International organizations tend to reproduce these prevailing social constructs – at the expense of materially and discursively weaker actors – through their rules and activities. As the hegemony of prevailing social constructs frequently is contested, international organizations may also turn into sites of discursive struggle over 'adequate' norms and ideas. Other critical perspectives point out that since there can be no 'us' without a 'them', the potential of international organizations to contribute to the establishment of common identities beyond the state has an important (and inevitable) flipside: the social construction of 'an Other' that is excluded from the community (Linklater 1990, 1998; see also Neumann 1996). In this view, international organizations, just as with any social order, are based on, and inextricably involved in, mechanisms of inclusion and exclusion, differentiation between insiders ('good' members) and outsiders (non-members or 'bad' members), and resulting discriminatory treatment.

For *neo-Gramscian theorists* (see Cox 1981, 1983; Strange 1996; Van der Pijl 1998), following in the footsteps of the Italian philosopher and communist politician Antonio Gramsci, it is mainly transnational political-economic elites that use international organizations as vehicles for the reproduction and stabilization of a neo-liberal world order. From that perspective, international organizations are created if there is a transnational elite consensus that international organizations are conducive to the advancement of the neo-liberal hegemonic project. In their design, decision-making processes and outputs, international organizations are skewed towards the realization of the ideas and interests of transnational corporate and political elites (see Gill 1989). Thus, from a neo-Gramscian perspective, the stabilization of a neo-liberal world order, as well as its concomitant negative effects on workers and politically and economically weak social actors, are important problematic effects of international organizations. Scholarship on international organizations should therefore contribute to unveiling the institutional and ideological power biases in and of international organizations.

Feminist theorists (see Tickner & Sjoberg 2010; True 2013) argue that gender must be introduced as a category of analysis into the study of international organizations in order to shed light on how they deal with and are engaged in global gender politics. From a feminist perspective, the policy choices and activities of international organizations are often shaped by stereotypical ideas about gender and masculinity/femininity. International organizations produce gendered policy choices, which may harm women disproportionately, not least because women are underrepresented in international organizations' decision-making processes. While international organizations can also promote gender-emancipatory discourses, norms and eventually law, feminists stress that more often than not international organizations tend to reproduce prevailing gender images, for example by reifying, in Security Council resolutions, gender-based expectations of women as 'passive victims' of violent conflict (Tickner & Sjoberg 2010: 202; see Shepherd 2008).

Green theory approaches are a very recent addition to the range of theoretical approaches to international relations and international organizations in particular. Critical of allegedly state-centric, rationalist and 'ecologically blind' mainstream realist and institutionalist approaches, green theorists, of both critical International Political Economy and normative cosmopolitan wings, analyse the role of international organizations in promoting or hindering global environmental justice and articulate alternative avenues for 'greening' international economic organizations such as the World Trade Organization (WTO) (Eckersley 2010: 265–73; Falkner 2012; see Paterson 2013). Scholars also discuss the implications of the Anthropocene era for international institutions (Biermann et al. 2012; Dryzek 2016; Young 2017). While each of these other theoretical approaches provide logically coherent perspectives on what international organizations are and should be, they are not the main focus in this book. We will mention them where relevant, but the wide diversity of theories – in particular the category of 'other theories' – makes it impossible to do justice to all of them (see Burchill et al. 2013; Dunne et al. 2016; Weiss & Wilkinson 2018 for a more detailed treatment).

CONCLUSION

Each of the contemporary manifestations of the three main theories of international organizations that we introduced in detail – neo-realism, neo-institutionalism and social constructivism – claims to explain the causes, design and effects of international organizations (see Table 2.3). In this respect, the three theories compete with one another. At the same time, the creation of sustained patterns of cooperation in and through international organizations, such as the EU, the WTO and the IMF, but also the UN, Organization for Security and Co-operation in Europe (OSCE) and NATO, provide a significant challenge to realist theoretical

Table 2.3   Three contemporary theories of international organizations (IOs)

	Neo-realism	*Neo-institutionalism*	*Social constructivism*
Structure	Material: anarchy	Material: anarchy and interdependence	Immaterial: distribution of ideas, values and norms
Actors	States	States, secretariats	States, secretariats, NGOs, individuals
Causes of IOs	Hegemon able to bear coopera-tion costs	Transnational problems require cooperation	Cognitive agreement; shared perception of problems
Effects of IOs	No independent impact	Facilitating cooperation to reap joint gains	Change of political actors' identities, interests and policies; reproduction of domi-nant norms and ideas
Design of IOs	Procedures biased in favour of the most powerful	Depends on cooperation problems; states delegate authority, but ultimately remain in control	Shaped by global norms and bureaucratic cultures; high degree of bureaucratic authority

approaches. While realism can undoubtedly explain 'a small number of big and important things' (Waltz 1986: 329) in international relations and urges us to take power seriously, it is not the strongest theory to analyse everyday developments in international organizations. It can explain why international organizations fail or why powerful states may ignore them, but not necessarily why international organizations succeed and how they make policy. In this sense, much of the current scholarship on international organizations is informed either by institutionalist or constructivist theories.

While it is attractive to compare theories and present alternative explanations, this assessment is, nevertheless, only partially justified because the theories oper-ate on the basis of different assumptions. It is therefore necessary to contextualize each theory in order to evaluate its validity adequately. Neo-realism may well help to explain security policy in the Middle East better than neo-institutionalism or social constructivism. In that particular region of the world, international politics does not yet appear to be marked by complex interdependencies and compat-ible values. Instead it corresponds to a mainly anarchic self-help system, so that international organizations such as the UN are only partially effective. However, the EU's internal market policy or the WTO's international trade policy suggests a very different situation. In this case, neo-realist explanations fare worse than those of neo-institutionalism or social constructivism. For the EU with its largely compatible values, social constructivism may offer the better explanation, whereas neo-institutionalism is more suited to studying the WTO, whose complex interde-pendencies have so far not been conducive to a congruence of values as we have seen in the EU.

Discussion Questions

1. Why do states create international organizations? Discuss the reasons from the perspectives of three different theories of international organizations.
2. How much leeway do international secretariats enjoy from their member states? Discuss this question with reference to different theoretical approaches and illustrate your answer with empirical evidence.
3. How do the three different theoretical schools, mentioned in this chapter, explain the design of international organizations?

Further Reading

Barnett, Michael N. & Finnemore, Martha 2004. *Rules for the World. International Organizations in Global Politics*, Ithaca, NY: Cornell University Press.

Hooghe, Liesbet & Marks, Gary 2015. Delegation and pooling in international organizations, in: *The Review of International Organizations* 10: 3, 305–28.

Koremenos, Barbara, Lipson, Charles & Snidal, Duncan 2001. The rational design of international institutions, in: *International Organization* 55: 4, 761–800.

Mearsheimer, John J. 1995. The false promise of international institutions, in: *International Security* 19: 3, 5–49.

3 History of International Organizations

This chapter provides a historical perspective on how international organizations were created and how they developed over time. It starts with the Peace of Westphalia of 1648 and ends with the intention of the Trump administration to withdraw from the Paris Agreement on climate change by the end of 2020. The chapter, however, does not provide a chronological list of events. Rather it seeks to explain where international organizations come from and how they change in response to important developments in world politics. It therefore uses the three theories – realism, institutionalism and constructivism – outlined in the previous chapter to give context and meaning to the history of international organizations.

Our starting point in this chapter is neo-institutionalist theory. This approach notes that international organizations emerge when *complex interdependencies* prod states into international cooperation to further common interests (the 'problem condition'). We have identified six important issue areas in international relations, which have caused problems for states over the last four centuries. Indeed, in none of these six issue areas have individual states been able to address all challenges themselves. For instance, no individual state can solve the problem of climate change alone, thereby creating incentives for cooperation through the framework of international organizations. The six issue areas are:

1. war and power politics;
2. international commerce;
3. global economic crises;
4. human rights violations;
5. developmental disparities;
6. environmental degradation.

Institutionalist theory provides a strong answer to why we have seen increased cooperation among states including in the context of international organizations. Yet the emergence of international organizations depends not only on the mere existence of complex interdependencies themselves, but also on the *collective understanding* that these interdependencies lead to problems which can only be overcome through cooperation within international organizations. The constructivist theories, indeed, tell us that cooperation only occurs when international issues are perceived as problems and it is recognized that international organizations can make a useful contribution (the 'cognitive condition'). Finally, from realist theory we know that the presence of a *powerful state*, willing to bear the costs of the creation of international organizations, is also often a requirement for cooperation (the 'hegemonic condition'). We therefore propose that international organizations are most likely to be created when each of the three conditions are met at the same time.

WAR AND POWER POLITICS

The modern system of sovereign states dates back at least to the Peace of Westphalia of 1648. These treaties ended the Thirty Years War (1618–48), which was one of the most destructive wars in European history, between the Catholic Habsburg alliance and much of the rest of Europe. They marked the start of a new period in international relations characterized by the 'balance of power' between the great European powers. In this anarchic self-help system, where all states had to look after themselves, a 'security dilemma' was inherent: when one power became too dominant, it became a threat for the other powers. Some observers recognized – for instance in the theoretical treatises of the Abbé de Saint-Pierre or Immanuel Kant – that this 'problem' could be addressed through international organizations standing above the states. Yet the idea that international organizations could contribute to stabilizing international relations by curbing the resort to violent means of self-help was insufficiently shared by states themselves. Moreover, no hegemonic power existed that could have helped to create such international organizations.

The situation changed after the Napoleonic Wars (1803–15) and the Congress of Vienna of 1814–15. The major European states assumed joint responsibility for securing peace and reducing prospects of conflict. They installed a consultation mechanism to facilitate peaceful conflict resolution and they established a canon of clearly defined rules and customs for diplomatic intercourse. This consultation mechanism was called the 'Concert of Europe'. It is generally seen as an important forerunner of today's international organizations (Armstrong et al. 1996: 4, 12–15; Taylor & Groom 1988: 8–9; Jacobson 1984: 31, 34). The Concert system was an inward-looking security institution (Wallander & Keohane 1999). Its task was not to deal with external threats, but to guarantee security within the European system. With the exception of the Crimean War (1853–56), it contributed to the absence of continent-wide wars between the great powers for much of the nineteenth century. For instance, it helped to settle the Belgian, Greek and Italian revolutions that took place between 1821 and 1848. While it could not prevent the Franco-German War of 1870–71, the Berlin congresses of 1878 (convened to discuss the Balkan question) and 1884–85 (to settle the Congo question) were of particular significance. Afterwards, the system rapidly disintegrated and its fate was sealed with the outbreak of the First World War in 1914 (Osiander 1994).

The Concert of Europe was a consultative mechanism for states. During the nineteenth century, however, non-governmental actors also increasingly became involved in questions of war and peace. Most famously, the Swiss businessman Henry Dunant wrote about the horrors he had seen at Solferino in 1859, where wounded soldiers were left dying on the battlefield. He then lobbied Europe's leaders to promote the norm that wounded soldiers should be cared for. This resulted in the first Geneva Convention of 1864 and the creation of the International Committee of the Red Cross – a completely neutral international non-governmental organization (NGO) charged with taking care of the wounded regardless of the side they were fighting for. There were other attempts at international organizations. As the consultative Concert declined in importance, various NGOs lobbied for a 'world peace organization' (Chatfield 1997). While negotiations on arms control agreements and an all-encompassing international peace organization largely failed (Armstrong et al. 1996: 11–12; Dülffer 1981), states created, as part of the Hague Peace Conferences of (1899 and 1907), the Permanent Court of Arbitration to resolve disputes arising from international agreements (Table 3.1).

The creation of international organizations became a significant topic of discussion after the First World War. The war had brutally exposed the problems of an anarchical international system (the problem condition). It was widely recognized that questions of war and peace could no longer be addressed in an ad hoc consultative mechanism such as the Concert of Europe. Instead, a more permanent and institutionalized solution in the format of an international organization was required (the cognitive condition). Furthermore, it was critically important that the USA intervened in the First World War as an outside power, albeit relatively late in 1917, thereby tilting the balance in favour of the allied powers. This gave the USA an aura of hegemony and considerable authority over how the post-war system would look (the hegemonic condition). The convergence of the problem, cognitive and hegemonic conditions resulted in the creation of the League of Nations as part of the Paris Peace Conference (1919–20).

The League of Nations' main task was to strengthen international security worldwide, not just among the major powers in Europe (Gill 1996). For the first time, states pledged to ban the use of force in international politics – albeit with

Table 3.1   War and power politics as a stimulus for international organizations

Security threat	International organizations (or institutions)
Napoleonic Wars (1803–15)	Concert of Europe (1815–1914) The Hague Peace Conferences (1899/1907)
First World War (1914–18)	League of Nations (1919–46)
Second World War (1939–45)	United Nations (1945)
East–West confrontation (1947–89)	North Atlantic Treaty Organization (1949) Warsaw Treaty Organization (1955) Commission on Security and Cooperation in Europe (1975)
New wars and transnational terrorism (1990–present)	United Nations (since 1990) North Atlantic Treaty Organization (since 1991) Organization for Security and Co-operation in Europe (since 1994) African Union (since 2002) European Union (since 2003)

certain limitations. In order to implement this ban, which was further strengthened by the Kellogg–Briand Pact of 1928, systems for the peaceful settlement of
disputes and for collective security were set up. In many ways, the new organization was a continuation of the Concert of Europe, but now also included smaller
states and had permanent institutions. Its principal body was the Assembly,
in which every member state had one vote. The Assembly met in Geneva once a
year in September. In addition, the League of Nations had a Council composed of
permanent members and non-permanent members elected by the Assembly. The
permanent members were initially Britain, France, Italy and Japan, and later also
included Germany and the Soviet Union. The idea was that the Council continued
to uphold the tradition of the Concert's consultative system, thus maintaining
its great power orientation. The Council met 107 times between 1920 and 1939.
A final innovative element was the permanent secretariat in Geneva consisting of
international experts, who were completely impartial with respect to the competing national interests. Their job was to prepare the agenda and keep the machinery
running.

The League of Nations did not change the anarchical international structure and
it left states' sovereignty untouched. The organization was supposed to embody 'a
world conscience' and help to strengthen the position of the 'general public' across
all member states. According to US President Wilson, this would prevent the governments of member states from going to war, because governments were answer-
able to the people. Relying on this idealistic belief, the League of Nations stood by
as Japan expanded aggressively in Asia (1931) and Italy in Abyssinia (1935). Most
significantly, it did not respond to the aggression of Nazi Germany in the 1930s.
The League of Nations also never had sufficient 'buy in' from its member states.
While US President Wilson was a key proponent of the League of Nations, the
USA did not join as a member state, after the US Senate failed to approve membership. Japan and Germany withdrew from the League of Nations in 1931 and 1933,
respectively. The Soviet Union – founded in 1922 and suspicious of the League of
Nations all along – joined only in 1934 after Germany's withdrawal. It was expelled
in December 1939, as the Second World War was underway, for aggression against
Finland (Archer 2001: 14–34; Armstrong et al. 1996: 33–61).

After the Second World War, a new solution for the prevention of interstate
war seemed imperative. The structural problem of sovereign states facing a security dilemma had persisted (the problem condition). There was a consensus that
this structural problem was to be solved by the establishment of a new and strong
international organization (the cognitive condition). Furthermore, the United
States was deeply committed to stabilizing peace by means of international organizations (the hegemonic condition). Like its predecessors, the United Nations (UN)
also emerged on the basis of a victorious war coalition (Luard 1982; Osiander
1994). In 1945, the UN Charter was negotiated by 50 states in San Francisco.
Today UN membership stands at 193 states.

The UN security system is based on a general ban on the use or threat of force
among states as determined by Article 2(4) of the Charter with the exception of
self-defence (Article 51). The member states undertake collective measures against
any state that acts as an aggressor, and they further attempt to re-establish peace.

The Security Council, as the principal security organ of the UN, bears primary responsibility for the maintenance of international peace. The Security Council determines the existence of any threats to, or breaches of, the peace and in addition, according to Chapter VII of the Charter, responds to acts of aggression with non-military or military enforcement measures (Armstrong et al. 1996: 62; Malone 2007; Price & Zacher 2004). Importantly, compared to the League of Nations, only the permanent members of the Security Council (China, France, Russia, the United Kingdom and the United States) have a veto over all substantive decisions. This ensures the 'buy in' of the great powers. Furthermore, the role of the UN Secretary-General was expanded beyond that of an impartial neutral civil servant: the Secretary-General needs to 'bring to the attention of the Security Council any matter which in his [or her] opinion may threaten the maintenance of international peace and security' (Article 99), even if this means confronting member states.

During much of the Cold War, the role of the UN in ensuring security remained effectively blocked. Within the Security Council, the USA and the Soviet Union used their veto to protect their own interests and allies (Malone 2007; Roberts 1996). As a result, the UN could often not directly act against aggressor states. Instead it had to appeal to states to voluntarily renounce or terminate the threat or use of force. One of the innovations was the use of peacekeeping missions to facilitate ceasefire agreements. The UN would deploy 'blue helmets' to monitor whether conflicting parties were obeying their own agreements. Peacekeeping required the consent of all states involved. It was therefore different from peace enforcement, in which the UN would forcefully intervene into conflicts. Secretary-General Dag Hammarskjöld famously referred to peacekeeping as 'Chapter Six and a Half' of the Charter – a bit more than the pacific settlement of disputes (Chapter VI); a bit less than peace enforcement (Chapter VII). While UN peacekeeping was modest during the Cold War, it helped to stabilize regional disputes and to avoid escalation in which the two superpowers (USA and Soviet Union) would need to choose sides (UN 2004; Urquhart 1995: 575).

The end of the Cold War in 1991 put renewed attention on the Security Council. Whereas the five permanent members had used their veto 279 times between 1945 and 1990, since 1990 they have only used their veto sporadically (Malone 2007: 121; Roberts 1996: 316). The UN reacted, for instance, forcefully to Iraq's invasion and annexation of Kuwait (1990) by authorizing a military response, thereby acting in the spirit of the Charter (Taylor 1993). Furthermore, the UN became increasingly involved in a growing number of so-called 'new wars' such as those in Somalia (1992–95), Bosnia (1992–95), East Timor (1999) and Kosovo (1998–99), as well as in the global fight against 'new terrorism' (since 2001) (Kaldor 1999). During the 2000s, this resulted in a very significant increase of UN peacekeeping deployments to almost 100,000 blue helmets in 2018. The mandates of UN peace operations have also become both more robust and more complex, to deal with the variety of new security challenges (Doyle & Sambanis 2006; Fortna 2008; Karlsrud 2018). These twenty-first century peace operations are driven by a strong convergence of the problem condition (many new (intrastate) wars), the cognitive condition (that UN peacekeeping is the most (cost-)effective solution), and the hegemonic condition (the USA favouring such robust types of missions).

While the UN has primary responsibility for peace and security, the UN Charter emphasizes the importance of regional organizations in maintaining peace (Chapter VIII, and specifically Article 52). As with UN peacekeeping, the importance of regional organizations has really taken off since the end of the Cold War. The African Union (AU) has a large-scale operation in Somalia and there is a joint UN–AU peacekeeping mission in Darfur, Sudan. The North Atlantic Treaty Organization (NATO) – even though not a formal peacekeeping or regional organization (see below) – has provided a stability force in Bosnia (1995–2004) and Kosovo (1999–present day). The European Union (EU) has also deployed a number of peacekeeping missions since 2003. And the Organization for Security and Co-operation in Europe (OSCE) has become specialized in sending small-scale civilian peace-support missions across Eastern Europe and Central Asia. The OSCE's main role – originally as the Conference on Security and Co-operation in Europe (CSCE) – since 1975 Final Act of Helsinki had been to act as a sort of regional UN on the European continent with the goal of avoiding East–West confrontation. The full burden for peace and security therefore does not fall entirely on the UN, but also involves a range of international organizations.

Throughout the centuries, we have thus witnessed an increasing institutionalization of how we organize collective security. Rather than organizing ad hoc peace conferences in the context of the Concert of Europe, we now have institutionalized forums such as the UN Security Council where ambassadors from conflicting parties can meet directly. Such institutionalization is, however, not limited to international organizations providing collective security. We have also seen an institutionalization of (military) alliances. Alliances used to be ad hoc and depended on the flavour of the day. For instance, a variety of different coalitions fought against Napoleon (1803–15). Nowadays alliances such as NATO have been turned into permanent international organizations, themselves tasked with providing collective defence against outside aggressors on a permanent basis.

During the Cold War, as noted above, the most prominent international organization was not the UN. In Europe, the international organizations dominating questions of peace and security were NATO (1949–present day) and the Warsaw Treaty Organization (usually referred to as the Warsaw Pact) (1955–91) (Wallander & Keohane 1999). The main responsibility of NATO was and remains the protection of all its member states against military aggression. NATO was founded by the USA, Canada and Western European countries in 1949 as an immediate response to the Berlin Blockade (1948–49) by the Soviet Union and the rigged elections in Central and Eastern Europe (late 1940s). Interestingly, NATO was originally founded as a traditional alliance. It was not until 1951 – in response to the Korean War (1950–53) – that a Secretary-General was appointed, the International Staff was created and US General Eisenhower started to develop a permanent command structure (initially from Hôtel Astoria on the Avenue des Champs Elysées in Paris). The idea of a permanent and institutionalized alliance was certainly innovative. It was the result of a strong convergence of the problem condition (Soviet aggression), the cognitive condition (that bipolarity in a nuclear age required new forms of defence), and the hegemonic condition (the unquestionable role of the USA as a guarantor of Western Europe).

As the Cold War came to an end, observers were quick to predict the end of NATO. The realist Kenneth Waltz (1993) infamously predicted that 'NATO's days may not be numbered, but its years are' (p. 76). The mistake of Waltz and other realists was to consider NATO as like any other temporary alliance instead of a more permanent international organization. They underestimated the investment that NATO allies had made in the organization, including setting up top-notch military machinery and a command structure (Wallander 2000). Furthermore, NATO was not just the 'winner' of the Cold War, it became also the 'saviour' of the Western Balkans in the 1990s when it successfully intervened in Bosnia in 1995 and Kosovo in 1999 to prevent further bloodshed. Over the decades, NATO had also become the permanent forum to discuss transatlantic (security) relations. Generations of diplomats and military officers had grown up with NATO, had gone together to NATO war colleges, and had 'internalized' the idea of NATO being the cornerstone of Western security. Furthermore, NATO has proved able to adjust to the new post-Cold War challenges, including the wars in the Balkans, the 9/11 terrorist attacks and the operation in Afghanistan, as well as renewed Russian aggression in Eastern Europe and the Caucasus.

When mentioning NATO, it is important to also pay attention to the Warsaw Pact as an international organization. It was officially established in 1955 as a reaction to West Germany joining NATO. Yet it also served to buttress the Soviet Union's control within its sphere of influence. It was meant to reinforce the signatories' military and foreign policy cooperation as well as their readiness for defence. In the case of an armed attack on any member state, an automatic duty of mutual assistance existed. Until 1975 this duty was geographically limited to Europe. In the course of the treaty's extension in 1975 the words 'in Europe' in Article 4 were deleted, thereby extending the treaty to the Asian part of the former Soviet Union. Besides the Warsaw Pact, various other bilateral agreements on assistance and the stationing of troops existed between its members. In the wake of rapprochement with the West at the end of the 1980s, the Soviet Union loosened its hold on its allies and, after the breakup of the local Communist parties' monopoly of political power, allowed the Eastern Bloc states to choose their own defence. As a consequence, the Warsaw Pact was disbanded on 1 July 1991.

INTERNATIONAL COMMERCE

The Industrial Revolution, which lasted from the 1760s to the 1840s, led to the creation of many international organizations in the nineteenth century. Due to the Industrial Revolution – resulting in increased production, better transport and multinational companies – the interdependencies between states increased dramatically. Global trade and commerce took off rapidly in what is often referred to as the 'first wave' of globalization. This created strong incentives to harmonize all sorts of standards for transport, communication, social regulation and intellectual property (the problem condition). These challenges were clearly recognized by contemporaries (the cognitive condition). The United Kingdom, as the most industrialized state at the time, was willing to sustain common standards (the

Table 3.2   International commerce as a stimulus for international organizations

Area of expansion	International organizations (one example)
Standardization of transport regulations	
River navigation	Rhine River Commission (1815)
Railways	International Union of Railways (1922)
Maritime navigation	International Maritime Committee (1897)
Air transport	International Civil Aviation Organization (1944)
Weights and measures	International Bureau for Weights and Measures (1875)
Standardization of communications	
Telecommunication	International Telegraph Union (1865)
Post	Universal Postal Union (1878)
Internet	Internet Corporation for Assigned Names and Numbers (1998)
Standardization of social regulations	
Health	International Office for Public Hygiene (1907)
Food and agriculture	International Institute of Agriculture (1905)
Working conditions	International Social Conference (1890)

hegemonic condition). The convergence of these conditions meant that a spectacular number of international organizations were created across different issue areas (Mangone 1975: 67–92; Weber 1983: 15–59) (See Table 3.2).

Transport

Early in the nineteenth century international organizations were set up to guarantee the freedom and security of international trade routes. For instance, river navigation still provided the most common means of transport for international trade. As trade volumes increased, this created an increasing demand for international standards of river navigation. One key example is the Rhine Navigation Act of 1815. In this treaty, the countries along the Rhine agreed to set up a special administration, the Central Commission for the Navigation of the Rhine, to develop navigation standards. The Rhine River Commission, which still exists with its secretariat in Strasbourg consisting of a dozen civil servants, was one of the first international organizations as we define them today. It has more than three member states, meets on a regular basis and has a permanent secretariat (Mangone 1975: 68–73; Weber 1983: 19–21; see also Chapter 1). The Rhine River Commission set the example for other river commissions, for instance for the Elbe in 1821, the Weser in 1823, the Meuse in 1830, the Danube in 1856 and the Congo in 1885 (Groom 1988: 11–19; Weber 1983: 21–24).

Maritime navigation further developed during the nineteenth century, which led to a standardized set of rules for international merchant shipping. The use of steamships, for instance, required clear rules for marine navigation to avoid collisions. The International Regulations for the Prevention of Collisions at Sea were therefore adopted in 1889, based on existing British maritime law (Luard 1977: 44–62). Throughout the twentieth century, the international maritime traffic regime and institutional arrangements had repeatedly been changed. Since 1982, the International Maritime Organization (IMO) has had responsibility for many aspect of maritime navigation.

Technological advances created a need for international regulation in other areas of transport too. The first international organizations for rail transport were founded in the mid-nineteenth century and for air transport in the early twentieth century. These were formalized in 1922 with the International Union of Railways (UIC) and in 1944 with the International Civil Aviation Organization (ICAO). Moreover, international organizations were established to standardize weights and measures, because international transport was handicapped by the multitude of national systems in existence. An example is the foundation of the International Bureau for Weights and Measures in Paris in 1875. This organization also acts as the keeper of two platinum standards for the metre and the kilogram.

Communication

Communication technology also went through a revolution in the nineteenth century – with the inventions of the telegraph, telephone and radio. These 'modern' means of communication required international regulation as well. For instance, through the telegraph, multinational companies could establish a quick line of communication, and major powers could communicate directly with their colonies. Interconnecting national telegraphic networks, however, required a set of common rules to standardize equipment, states to adopt uniform operating instructions and common tariff and accounting rules. After a multitude of conventions between different European states, the International Telegraph Union was founded in 1865. It finally became the International Telecommunication Union (ITU) after the Second World War. The ITU is responsible for the whole of the telecommunications spectrum: telegraph, telephone, radio, new information technologies, the allocation of frequencies and setting of fees. It enjoys universal membership (Luard 1977: 27–43; Mangone 1975: 74–77; Weber 1983: 24–27, 53).

Harmonizing the postal systems across countries proved more difficult. Individual states had fiscal interests and the postal system represented a lucrative business. While there was a clear industrial and economic need for a faster, standardized, safer and cheaper cross-border postal system, it was not until 1874 that a treaty set up the General Postal Union (later the Universal Postal Union (UPU)). Significantly, the basic regulation of the UPU treats the territories of all member states as a single postal area, operating on the principle that the sender country's postal system determines and keeps the revenue. The treaty of the UPU has been extended several times in accordance with general technological advances. Today, the UPU is the world's largest international organization in terms of membership and geographical extent (Luard 1977: 11–26; Weber 1983: 27–28).

Social regulation

The rapid increase in international transport and cross-border movement also resulted in international cooperation on public health. Starting with regular international sanitary conferences in the mid-nineteenth century, an International Sanitary Code was adopted in 1880 which called for the creation of health inspection commissions, especially at ports. In the Americas, a Pan American Sanitary Bureau was, furthermore, established in 1902, whereas in Europe an International Office of Public Hygiene (OIHP) was created in 1907. The OIHP, a direct forerunner of the World Health Organization (WHO), gathered and disseminated public health information. By comparison, WHO's activities today are far more comprehensive, covering the full gamut of public health activities such as the fight against epidemics, the establishment of hygiene guidelines to wipe out certain diseases (such as malaria and smallpox), vaccination and immunization, and the training of medical personnel in developing countries (Basch 1999; Lee 2009; Hanrieder 2015).

International commerce and the growing speed and safety of international transport also had consequences for food and agriculture. The development of sectoral world markets in agriculture had significant effects on traditionally influential producer groups as, for example, in the case of cereals. Continuous information about developments on world markets was required in order to manage suitable national protection mechanisms for domestic markets, producers and consumers. This was an essential precondition for the creation in 1905 of an early warning system in the form of the International Institute of Agriculture, a precursor of today's Food and Agriculture Organization (FAO). Created in 1945 as a UN Specialized Agency, the FAO attempts to improve world nutrition through increased production and improved distribution of food products (Marchisio & Di Blase 1991: 3–22). In addition, together with the WHO, in 1963 the FAO created the so-called Codex Alimentarius Commission (CAC), which defines international food standards to protect consumers from harmful food products (Hüller & Maier 2006).

In the late nineteenth century, the mitigation of the negative consequences of industrial expansion for the living and working conditions of industrial workers were also recognized as a public responsibility with an international dimension. As early as 1890, an international social conference was held in Berlin to discuss harmonizing national labour laws. The aim was to prevent and eliminate distortion of competition between countries because of different laws. A private initiative with official support led to the creation of an international bureau in 1901: the International Association for Labour Legislation, based in Basel. It was responsible for providing information on new developments in national labour legislation and the elaboration of international treaty proposals for specific employment protection measures. For example, a convention was signed prohibiting night-time work by women.

The International Labour Organization (ILO), established in 1919, was an initiative by Western European trade union leaders which endeavoured to give legal force to stronger labour standards. The ILO features a tripartite representation of governments, employee and employer organizations in its decision-making bodies. After the Second World War, the ILO was incorporated into the UN system. Besides developing international standards in labour and social law, it has also implemented programmes to fight unemployment (Weber 1983: 38–42, 84–86). Moreover, the ILO is heavily engaged in attempts to curb child labour, to fight forced labour, to battle against discrimination at work and to guarantee the freedom of association for trade unions, as well as employers' associations (Dirks et al. 2002; Hughes & Haworth 2010).

GLOBAL ECONOMIC CRISES

With the expansion of the world markets during the nineteenth century, a need emerged for international organizations to protect open markets and trade in times of economic crises (the problem condition). This need had been widely recognized as early as in the Long Depression of the 1870s and 1880s as well as in the Great Depression of the late 1920s and early 1930s (the cognitive condition). However, with the declining hegemony of Britain after the First World War, the structures of a liberal economic order collapsed. The world economic crisis which started in 1929 destroyed any hope of the order's resurrection. Led by Germany, almost all states turned to a policy of increasing tariff barriers, devaluing currencies and introducing non-tariff trade barriers. This led to an escalating spiral of protectionism. Between 1929 and 1932, the volume of world trade decreased by 30 per cent (Madsen 2001: 848; Parker 1967: 101–10; Van der Wee 1984: 389–427). It was only after the Second World War that a liberal economic order could be re-established with the help of US hegemonic leadership (the hegemonic condition). This included the creation of various international organizations, such as the International Monetary Fund (IMF), the World Bank, and the General Agreement on Tariffs and Trade (GATT)/World Trade Organization (WTO). See Table 3.3.

Trade relations

In the spring of 1946, the UN Economic and Social Council convened a conference on a World Trade Charter, which concluded with the adoption of the Havana Charter. Its aim was to create an International Trade Organization (ITO) that would guarantee free trade. However, the Havana Charter failed, as US President Truman never submitted the Charter to the US Senate for approval, fearing that the Senate would reject the proposals because of a perceived infringement on American sovereignty. Yet, in April 1947, at the same time as the deliberations for a World Trade Charter were taking place, the USA had begun to negotiate with 23

Table 3.3   Global economic crises as a stimulus for international organizations

Crisis	International organizations
Trade order	
Long Depression (1878–91)	British hegemonic power adopts the principle of free trade with limitations
Great Depression (1929–32)	General Agreement on Tariffs and Trade (1948)
Neo-protectionism (1970s and 1980s)	*Global* World Trade Organization (1995)
	Regional European Union (since 1987) North American Free Trade Agreement (1994) Association of Southeast Asian Nations (since 1993)
Financial order	
Long Depression (1878–91)	Britain keeps the gold standard and free convertibility
Great Depression (1929–32)	International Monetary Fund (1944)
Collapse of the Bretton Woods system (1971–73)	Reformed International Monetary Fund (1978)
Great Recession (2007–12)	Reinvigorated International Monetary Fund (2010) Reformed European Union (2011)

states in Geneva for the mutual dismantling of trade barriers. In a protocol, they agreed to a reduction of trade barriers and to the temporary coming into force of some parts of the Havana Charter on 1 January 1948. This was called the General Agreement on Tariffs and Trade (GATT). It would become the core of the international trade order.

The contracting parties committed to liberalizing trade relations by reducing trade barriers. They agreed to abolishing import quotas and to lowering import tariffs. Moreover, the GATT prohibited discriminatory treatment between trading partners. This would, for instance, avoid a situation in which the USA would apply different tariffs for New Zealand than for the Netherlands. Each state thus had to concede 'most favoured nation' status to all the other states. Only trading partners within a recognized free-trade area or customs union, such as the EU or North American Free Trade Agreement (NAFTA), could be given favourable treatment (Jackson 2004). During the existence of the GATT (1948–94), the contracting parties successfully reduced the average tariffs on goods from 40 per cent to 6.4 per cent (Senti 2000).

While the GATT was successful in targeting tariffs, many countries started to apply hidden forms of protectionism through what is called non-tariff trade barriers during the 1970s and 1980s. These range from domestic subsidies (state aid) to anti-dumping measures (selling products under cost price) and bureaucratic customs and administrative entry procedures. Such non-tariff trade barriers were hardly regulated under the GATT and they therefore presented a clear problem to global trade (the problem condition). When the USA, burdened in the 1980s by a growing trade deficit, recognized the problem (the cognitive condition), it took the initiative (the hegemonic condition) and put, among other things, the topic of non-tariff trade barriers on the agenda of the Uruguay Round of the GATT (1986–94). This major negotiation initiative, consisting of a series of high-level conferences, eventually gave rise to a new international trade organization: the WTO (Braithwaite & Drahos 2000: 178–81).

With the creation of the WTO, international trade regulations were transformed insofar as they now covered not only trade in industrial products (as under the GATT), but also trade in services (the General Agreement on Trade in Services, or GATS) and the protection of intellectual property (TRIPS). This wider coverage of regulations is reflected in the institutional structure of the WTO. Beneath the highest decision-making body of the Ministerial Conference (formerly the Assembly of the contracting parties), there is the General Council which presides over three other councils: the Council for Trade in Goods (formerly the GATT Council), the Council for Trade in Services (GATS Council) and the Council for Trade-Related Aspects of Intellectual Property Rights (TRIPS Council). As an organization the WTO also has a secretariat and a Director-General, both of which already existed prior to 1995 under the old GATT (Senti 2000). A Trade Policy Review Mechanism was furthermore established and the existing Dispute Settlement Procedures were strengthened considerably (Jackson 2004; Zangl 2008).

Whereas the WTO is the main international organization for trade at the global level, there are also a multitude of regional free-trade areas and customs unions. The EU is perhaps the most famous example. The six original member states (Belgium, France, Germany, Italy, Luxembourg and the Netherlands) formed a customs union in which all internal tariffs were removed and replaced by a common external tariff. While the customs union was completed by 1968, the global neo-protectionism and non-tariff barriers gave rise to the ambition in the 1980s to establish a genuine EU single market. In North America and South East Asia regional trade organizations have also been created. Through NAFTA, the USA, Canada and Mexico formed a free-trade area in 1994. The member states of the Association of Southeast Asian Nations (ASEAN) have also formed such a free-trade zone (Feske 1999: 549). While the EU has abolished all internal tariffs, agreed on common external tariffs and made great strides towards eliminating non-tariff barriers to trade, NAFTA and ASEAN are still stuck at a lower stage of integration (Krugman & Obstfeld 2008: Chapters 10 and 11).

Monetary relations

Following US leadership after the Second World War, a new monetary order was also established based on the Bretton Woods Agreement of 1944 (Helleiner 1994). The Bretton Woods Agreement required states to guarantee the free convertibility of their currencies and to maintain a stable exchange rate with the US dollar. It was the responsibility of the IMF – one of the key Bretton Woods institutions together with the World Bank (see below) – to oversee the implementation of this monetary regime. In addition, the IMF was meant to be a 'currency buffer' by granting loans to states with temporary balance-of-payments deficits.

After a difficult start, the Bretton Woods system began to function in the late 1950s. Yet in the late 1960s the first crisis symptoms appeared. The unexpected growth in international trade and the increased private and public demand for money raised questions about the gold standard – that is the arrangement whereby central banks across the world could exchange their dollar holdings for gold (at a fixed rate of US$35 per ounce). At first, the IMF tried to stabilize the liquidity of global markets, yet in 1971 US President Nixon removed the gold backing of the dollar and thereby destroyed the system of fixed exchange rates (in the words of US Treasury Secretary John Connally: 'The dollar is our currency, but it's your problem'). A reform of the IMF statute in 1978 took account of the new realities of the world currency system. However, the IMF membership remained committed to avoiding erratic fluctuations of exchange rates. The IMF was there-fore given the task of supervising exchange rate policies. In addition, 'special draw-ing rights' (SDRs) were introduced as a new reserve currency, but they have failed to challenge the continued dominance of the US dollar (Braithwaite & Drahos 2000: 115).

A new challenge for the IMF came as a result of the debt crises of many devel-oping countries in the 1980s, such as the Latin America debt crisis. The IMF sustained debtor countries in order to keep them creditworthy, thereby averting a possible collapse of global financial markets (Helleiner 1994: 175–83). The IMF became a crisis manager. It provided not only financial but also political support while insisting that debtor countries comply with their loan conditions. While the IMF's political and market power was increasingly questioned, espe-cially after the Asian financial crisis of the 1990s, the IMF once again played a key role during the most recent global financial and economic crisis ('the Great Recession', 2007–12). Together with the EU, the IMF helped bail out Eurozone countries, such as Greece, Ireland and Portugal. This resulted in a reinvigoration of the IMF, whose borrowing capacity was increased tenfold in 2010. For the EU, it resulted in an extensive package of Eurozone reforms aimed at reducing the future risk of sovereign debt crises.

HUMAN RIGHTS VIOLATIONS

By the second half of the nineteenth century the idea of a democratic constitu-tional state began to assert itself in Western Europe and North America. This gave rise to the consensus that sovereignty and internationally supervised human rights protection were not mutually exclusive. However, despite the noteworthy advocacy activities of early transnational antislavery and women's rights move-ments in the late nineteenth century (Keck & Sikkink 1998: Chapter 2), and the

Geneva Convention of 1864, human rights (for civilians) remained mostly an issue of domestic politics. The situation changed after the Second World War. The enormities of the Nazi and fascist regimes demonstrated the 'moral interdependence' between states and societies (the problem condition). They also led to the recognition that some international guarantees for the protection of human rights were needed (the cognitive condition). In addition, the USA, as the most powerful state, was willing to convince the community of states to accept such international guarantees for the protection of human rights (the hegemonic condition).

Protection of universal human rights

In 1941, British Prime Minister Churchill and US President Roosevelt adopted the Atlantic Charter, which included Roosevelt's doctrine of the four basic freedoms: freedom from want, freedom from fear, freedom of expression and freedom of religion. The Preamble of the UN Charter adopted in 1945 similarly emphasized the importance of human rights. In 1948, the international community took this commitment further, adopting the Universal Declaration of Human Rights which called for civil, political, economic, social and cultural rights. Subsequently, the UN Commission on Human Rights, which was established in 1946, was tasked to codify the rights enshrined in the Universal Declaration into international law. This led to tough negotiations, as the member states of the liberal West, the Communist East and the growing number of developing countries from the South held conflicting values in relation to human rights. It finally resulted in the adoption of the International Covenant on Civil and Political Rights (the Civil Pact) and the International Covenant on Economic, Social and Cultural Rights (the Social Pact) (Donnelly 2006) in 1966. It took another decade before the Covenants came into force.

Through the Civil Pact, the UN provides individuals with many liberal rights against abuse of power by the state. They include the right to life, liberty and security of the person, to protection against discrimination, to protection from torture and slavery, to equality before the law, to the protection of privacy, to freedom of thought, conscience and religion, to freedom of expression, to the protection of the family, and to vote in elections based on universal and equal suffrage. The rights embraced by the Social Pact include the right to be free from hunger and to an adequate standard of living, to work and to enjoy just and favourable conditions of work, to leisure, holidays and social security, and to education. Despite their significance, the mere codification of human rights in the Civil and Social Pacts was not going to lead automatically to compliance. Therefore committees of experts were established to check the reports that states have periodically to submit regarding human rights. A similar practice is in place for the various other UN Human Rights Conventions negotiated since the 1960s. The Commission on Human Rights and its Sub-Commission on the Promotion and Protection of Human Rights were empowered in 1967 and 1970 to undertake specific investigations of a state's human rights practices, with or without the permission of the state concerned.

Since the end of the Cold War, various additional institutions have been established to address human rights violations. For instance, the Office of the UN High Commissioner for Human Rights (OHCHR) was established following the World Conference on Human Rights in Vienna in 1993. The Human Rights Council (HRC), a standing committee of 47 member states, was furthermore set up in 2006. It uses three procedures to monitor states' human rights policies, including Universal Periodic Review (UPR), Special Procedures and a complaints mechanism. This work is strongly supported by human rights NGOs, especially Amnesty International and Human Rights Watch. These NGOs, along with many others, have been granted consultative status which gives them the right officially to take part in meetings of the HRC.

These human rights developments have taken place outside the realm of the UN Security Council. Yet, since human rights questions are often related to issues of war and peace, the Security Council has also carved out a role for itself. In the 1960s and 1970s, it had already interpreted massive human rights violations of the apartheid regimes in Rhodesia (now Zimbabwe) and South Africa as threats to international peace and security and decided to impose sanctions. Following the end of the Cold War, the Security Council started more actively intervening in states' domestic affairs if they committed massive human rights violations (Chayes & Chayes 1995: 47). The UN peace missions to Somalia, Cambodia and Haiti in the 1990s were justified by such violations. In the 2000s, these practices gave rise to the norm of a responsibility to protect (R2P). The norm holds that sovereign states have a responsibility to protect their own citizens. Yet when they are unwilling or unable to do so, it becomes the role of the 'international community of states', that is of the Security Council, to take over this responsibility (International Commission on Intervention and State Sovereignty (ICISS) 2001; United Nations General Assembly 2005). The Security Council made implicit reference to R2P in 2011 when it authorized member states 'to protect civilians and civilian populated areas under threat of attack in [Libya]' after it reiterated 'the responsibility of the Libyan authorities to protect the Libyan population' (Resolution 1973: preliminary paragraph 4 and operational paragraph 4).

In addition, in the 1990s the Security Council introduced the practice of setting up war crimes tribunals following the outbreak of brutal ethnopolitical conflict in the former Yugoslavia and Rwanda (see below). These tribunals, in turn, provided the blueprint for the international community to set up an International Criminal Court (ICC) with the authority to bring alleged war criminals to justice. The Rome Statute, setting up the ICC, was signed by 120 state representatives in 1998. The Court itself is based in The Hague and began functioning in 2002. In addition to examining possible instances of war crimes, the ICC has indicted various high-level individuals, including the Ugandan rebel leader Joseph Kony, the Sudanese president Omar al-Bashir, and the Libyan leader Muammar Gaddafi. While various indicted individuals remain at large, the Congolese vice-president Jean-Pierre Bemba was convicted to an 18-year sentence and a case is ongoing against the former President of Ivory Coast, Laurent Gbagbo.

Regional protection of human rights

While human rights are often said to have universal character, they are also addressed at a regional level. Especially in Europe, a remarkable set of institutions for the protection of human rights has emerged. The European Movement, consisting of important politicians and civil society actors, born at The Hague Congress of 1948, drafted a European human rights charter and demanded oversight by European courts. It thus contributed decisively to the foundation of the Council of Europe in 1949 and the signing of the European Convention on Human Rights (ECHR) in 1950 (Grabenwarter 2005; Keller & Stone Sweet 2008). Civil society actors were also decisive in the elaboration of the European Social Charter of 1961 and the negotiation of numerous additional protocols to the ECHR.

The main difference between the global human rights institutions and the regional human rights regime in Europe is not the interpretation of human rights norms, but the institutionalized procedures for implementing them (Moravcsik 1995). Monitoring in the European human rights system is based on three routes similar to those of the UN: the states' duty to report, complaints by states and complaints by individuals. The striking feature of the European human rights regime is, however, that ordinary citizens have direct access to the European Court of Human Rights in Strasbourg. Once all national legal instruments have been exhausted, individual citizens can launch a complaint with the European Court. While the large majority of cases are deemed inadmissible (out of the tens of thousands submitted every year), for the cases that did go to the (Grand) Chamber, the Court found at least one violation of the Convention in 85 per cent of the cases in 2017. Most cases were against Russia, Turkey and Ukraine. While compliance with the court judgments remains a challenge (particularly in those countries), it is extraordinary for ordinary citizens to have access to an international court.

At the regional level, several international courts have also been set up to deal with human rights violations. The International Criminal Tribunal for the former Yugoslavia (ICTY) (1993–2017) was set up by the Security Council to address the war crimes committed in the conflicts in the Western Balkans in the 1990s. It followed the examples of the temporary Nuremberg and Tokyo tribunals set up after the Second World War. While the ICTY has been criticized for its slow proceedings and excessive costs, it has indicted 161 high-profile persons and has sentenced 90 persons for war crimes. These include, among others, Bosnian Serb leader Radovan Karadžić and General Ratko Mladic, both convicted of genocide. The ICTY was closed in 2017. The Security Council has also set up the International Criminal Tribunal for Rwanda (1994–2015), which performed similar functions to the ICTY, albeit at a lower intensity and with less high-profile exposure. Beyond war crimes, another regional human rights court is the African Court on Human and Peoples' Rights established in 2004. These regional courts also set the example for the ICC which addresses human rights violations at the global level (Table 3.4).

Table 3.4   Human rights violations as a stimulus for international organizations

Violations	International organizations
Second World War: human rights violations during Nazi and fascist reign in Europe	*Global* United Nations Commission on Human Rights (1946) United Nations Universal Declaration of Human Rights (1948) *Regional* Council of Europe (1949) European Convention on Human Rights (1950) European Court of Human Rights (1959)
After the end of the East–West conflict: continuing human rights violations	*Global* United Nations High Commissioner for Human Rights (1993) International Criminal Court (1998) Human Rights Council (2006) *Regional* Reformed European Court of Human Rights (1998) International Criminal Tribunal for the former Yugoslavia (1993–2017) African Court on Human and Peoples' Rights (2004)

DEVELOPMENTAL DISPARITIES

Decolonization in the 1940–60s led to a further demand for international organizations. Despite their newfound political independence, economic dependencies of decolonized states on their former colonial powers persisted. These dependencies of developing countries in Africa and Asia went hand in hand with global socioeconomic disparities. This North–South divide had the potential to undermine the world economic order, which created an incentive to reduce these disparities with a view to stabilizing the global economic order (the problem condition). In the Cold War context, demands from the South could not be easily rejected either. As a result, as soon as the international community grasped these disparities (the cognitive condition), under the leadership of the USA (the hegemonic condition), it took the initiative in building international organizations that could reconcile the South with the existing economic order. Two types of international organizations emerged: those to administer funds for financing development and those to sustain economically fair structures favourable to developing countries. See Table 3.5.

Table 3.5   Developmental disparities as a stimulus for international organizations

Disparity	Organization
Shortage of available resources in developing countries	World Bank Group: International Bank for Reconstruction and Development (1944); International Finance Corporation (1955); International Development Association (1960). United Nations Development Programme (1966)
Structural dependence of developing countries	United Nations Conference on Trade and Development (1964) United Nations Industrial Development Organization (1966)

Financing development

The most significant international organizations to address disparities in economic development between the South and the North belong to the World Bank Group, comprising the International Bank for Reconstruction and Development (IBRD) – generally referred to as World Bank – and its subsidiaries, the International Finance Corporation (IFC) and the International Development Association (IDA) (Marshall 2008).

The World Bank makes loans at market rates to governments, their subordinate authorities and, exceptionally, to private enterprises. These loans are always linked to a specific project agreed to by the Bank and intended to stimulate private, and especially foreign, direct investment. The Bank gives technical assistance to recipients on the preparation, running and implementation of the project. A small part of the Bank's financial resources comes from the member states. For the rest the Bank taps the world's capital markets. The contributions of the 186 member states are based on their economic capacities and determine their number of votes in the main decision-making bodies of the Bank. The Bank makes loans to the tune of US$20 billion each year.

Compared to the World Bank proper, the IFC and the IDA have a somewhat different lending profile. The IFC only provides loans to the private sector in less-developed countries for projects aimed at raising the productivity of the borrowing country. As with the World Bank, these loans are made available at market rates. Approximately 80 per cent of the IFC's resources come from the international capital markets. The remaining 20 per cent are borrowed from the World Bank. The activities of the IDA are more oriented towards comprehensive economic and social development goals. It provides concessional assistance to the poorer developing countries, generally in the form of interest-free long-term loans, with repayment periods of 35 to 50 years being quite common. Its contributions can truly be called development aid. The IDA is thus more of a fund administrator than a bank, in contrast to the IBRD and the IFC. Its resources have to be replenished repeatedly to make approximately US$13 billion-worth of loans a year.

Beyond the World Bank institutions, the UN Development Programme (UNDP) is also engaged in financing development. Compared to the World Bank institutions, its agenda is more strongly influenced by the interests of the developing countries, which form the vast majority of UN members. The main activity of UNDP is technical assistance, including the financing of pre-investment activities. In contrast to financial assistance by the World Bank institutions, technical assistance generally means sending experts, granting scholarships for training or further education, and sending equipment or other forms of aid in support of these objectives. UNDP's financing of development projects takes the form of non-repayable grants. In total, UNDP had a budget of about US$4.9 billion in 2017.

Development and trade

In the wake of decolonization, the developing countries brought their own political agenda to the UN system. They insisted on creating international organizations within the UN system to change global economic structures, allowing them to catch up with developed countries. The most important of these is the UN Conference on Trade and Development (UNCTAD), a subsidiary organ of the UN General Assembly, created in 1964. While Western industrialized countries saw the GATT as the institutional centre for international trade policy, developing countries were determined to discuss trade policy in the context of UNCTAD. Following the successful conclusion of the Uruguay Round and the establishment of the WTO, the rationale of UNCTAD has repeatedly been questioned. Many developing countries have joined the WTO.

The UN Industrial Development Organization (UNIDO) also came into being at the insistence of developing countries. Formed in 1966, it became a UN Specialized Agency in 1986. This means that within the UN it has sector-specific competencies in the area of industrial development for developing countries. During the early 1990s, UNIDO entered a serious crisis. Leading member states questioned not only the effectiveness of the organization, but also its right to exist. In 1996 the USA withdrew from the organization, resulting in a decrease of the budget by US$60 million. In response to this crisis, UNIDO went through a successful reform process, streamlining its programmatic focus and increasing its overall effectiveness. In 2004, the British Department for International Development (DFID) ranked UNIDO the most effective specialized agency in the UN system.

ENVIRONMENTAL DEGRADATION

Environmental problems, such as air and water pollution, have always been side effects of industrial production. The state, however, was at least in principle capable of dealing with these problems by introducing and enforcing legislation on environmental protection. But in the age of nuclear power plants, the diminishing ozone layer and global warming many of these environmental problems transcend national borders and can therefore not be resolved by one state alone. In order to mitigate these cross-border problems, the international community of states must act collectively (the problem condition). The resulting demand for international organizations led to their creation mainly in issue areas in which public awareness was bolstered by non-governmental environmental organizations (the cognitive condition), with hegemonic leadership provided by the USA (the hegemonic condition). See Table 3.6.

To facilitate cross-border environmental protection, states have created a number of international regimes. They have passed the responsibility for ensuring compliance either to existing international organizations or to new organizations created for the purpose (Biermann et al. 2009). This has therefore resulted in an expanded scope of the mandates of several international organizations to cover environmental protection activities. The World Meteorological Organization (WMO), for instance, went beyond its initial concerns with meteorology and data exchange to also take environmental questions into its purview after the hole in the ozone layer and global warming had been discovered (Newell & Bulkeley 2010; Parson 1993). Similarly, the IMO was given the task of sustaining efforts at reducing pollution of the high seas (Mitchell 1994). Since 1959 various conventions have been concluded to ban, for example, the dumping of substances such as radioactive waste in the high seas. The UN Economic Commission for Europe (ECE) has achieved impressive results in the formation and implementation of the acid rain regime in Europe (Levy 1993). The EU was given competencies for the protection of the environment in 1987 (Lenshow 2010).

Beyond the establishment of specific international regimes for the protection of the environment, states were willing to confront international environmental problems within the more encompassing context of the UN, which in turn has increasingly shaped domestic environmental agendas. Meeting in Stockholm in 1972, the UN Conference on the Human Environment led to the establishment of the UN Environment Programme (UNEP), providing the UN with a special organ to deal with environmental questions. UNEP consists of a Governing Council of 58 state representatives elected by the UN General Assembly, and a small secretariat with its seat in Nairobi (Chasek et al. 2010). UNEP is responsible for coordinating the environmental activities of states and international organizations to promote

Table 3.6   Environmental problems as a stimulus for international organizations

Problem	*International organizations*
Cross-border environmental degradation	*Creation of new organizations:* United Nations Environment Programme (1972) International Renewable Energy Agency (2009)
	Extension of international organizations' mandate: International Maritime Organization World Meteorological Organization United Nations Economic Commission for Europe European Union (since 1987)

better regional and global environmental protection. In the beginning, its role was more that of a coordinator and catalyst; more recently it has evolved into an actor with its own programmes.

UNEP has made an impact. International negotiations, under UNEP, have not only shaped domestic environmental agendas and promoted the establishment of national ministries for the environment (Buzan et al. 1998: Chapter 4; De Wilde 2008): UNEP also made a substantial contribution to, for instance, the Vienna Convention for the Protection of the Ozone Layer in 1985 and its formalization in the Montreal Protocol of 1987. UNEP played a key role in preparing the Rio UN Conference on Environment and Development in 1992 and the Johannesburg Earth Summit in 2002. In addition, UNEP developed important activities to combat climate change caused by the greenhouse effect. A landmark success was the signing of the UN Framework Convention on Climate Change (UNFCCC) in 1992 and its elaboration in the Kyoto Protocol in December 1997. Under the framework of the UNFCCC, states also negotiated the Paris Agreement on climate change signed in 2016. The Paris Agreement was interesting not just for the clear presence of the problem and cognitive conditions, but particularly for its American and Chinese leadership. An important question is whether the hegemonic condition will continue. In 2017, the Trump administration announced its intention to withdraw from the Paris Agreement by the earliest possible date (November 2020).

CONCLUSION

How can we make sense of this historical account of international organizations? In this chapter, three relevant conditions have been identified, which help to explain why states create international organizations. First of all, states need to encounter a cooperation *problem* (problem condition). Second, they need to *recognize* that they cannot address this problem alone, bilaterally, or in an ad hoc manner: they need to recognize that they can most effectively address it through the creation of international organizations (cognitive condition). Third, since international negotiations are complex and involve many competing interests, the creation of international organizations is most likely if a *powerful state* is truly committed and nudges the other states into international cooperation (hegemonic condition). When all the three conditions are present, the creation of international organizations may prevail.

This chapter has provided many examples of the creation and development of international organizations across different policy areas. It has shown that industrialization and globalization since the nineteenth century have posed many cross-border *problems*, which states have addressed through international organizations: from the Rhine River Commission (addressing cross-border transport) to the GATT (lowering tariffs) and UNEP (dealing with pollution). It is important, too, that certain problems, such as human rights violations and poverty, are no longer *recognized* as purely domestic affairs but, indeed, also as international problems which need to be addressed through international organizations: from the ICC (addressing war crimes) to the World Bank and UNDP (providing funds for development).

Finally, the chapter has made clear that the commitment and 'buy in' of the USA and its post-war Western *hegemony*, in particular, have been critical: from the UN Security Council (as the main forum for questions of peace and security) to the promotion of liberal values in the areas of trade, human rights and development.

These developments across the six policy areas, discussed in this chapter, are also reflected in the total number of international organizations as they have developed since the early nineteenth century. In the introduction of this book, we have provided a graph that shows how the total number of international organizations has dramatically increased over time (Figure 1.1). In particular, we saw sharp increases after the Second World War ended in 1945. The post-war period can be characterized as an era of growing institutionalization of interstate relations. Apart from a whole range of *new problems* that states needed to address (decolonization; environment; 'new wars'), there was also strong *cognitive support* that international organizations provided the answer. Indeed, it was often understood that problems were previously not effectively addressed as a result of weak forms of international cooperation. Especially in the years following the Second World War, this resulted in strong international organizations, such as the UN, the Bretton Woods institutions and NATO. This institutionalization of cooperation was not only supported by the USA as a *hegemon* willing to incur some cooperation costs; indeed, intensive Western cooperation was seen as the best remedy to keep the Soviet Union at bay.

While the extent of international cooperation has increased dramatically during the post-Cold War era – inspired by continuous US leadership – it is also remarkable that the total number of international organizations has stabilized in more recent years (Pevehouse et al. 2004). It is worth reconsidering the three conditions, in this respect, to see whether they can also explain why we have not seen the creation of more international organizations in the last two decades. In terms of the *problem condition*, we would expect that once cooperation problems have been solved, states will disband the international organization. Examples include the war crimes tribunals for the former Yugoslavia and Rwanda. At the same time, there are also currently so many international organizations that we can wonder whether we have reached a maximum. Creating new international organizations tends to be expensive. Increasing the scope of existing international organizations may therefore be a better way of addressing new problems that arrive on the international agenda (Jupille et al. 2013). We have also seen the creation of many international NGOs, which may also address problems and which are often supported directly and indirectly by states and international organizations. International NGOs can, in this respect, be alternatives or substitutes for traditional international organizations.

In terms of the *cognitive condition*, the trust in the ability of international organizations to actually address problems has also decreased. Whereas in previous decades increased institutionalization and the creation of more international organizations was seen as the solution to cooperation problems, currently international organizations face a lot of criticism in terms of their effectiveness and legitimacy. In some cases, such criticism has resulted in member states leaving international organizations, including the EU, ICC and UNIDO. Finally, in terms of the *hegemonic condition*, it is questionable whether the USA is still willing to bear a disproportionate amount of the costs of sustaining a liberal system of global governance. Part of the success of many international organizations is that they have dramatically expanded their membership. China's accession to the WTO in 2001 is an obvious example. The flipside of the coin is that with more members, the ability of the USA to control international organizations diminishes, which may result in less 'buy in'. Two centuries of international organizations have, however, shown us that their development does not necessarily follow a predictable path. We should, therefore, be cautious in making predictions about how international organization will develop in the future.

Discussion Questions

1. What conditions explain the development of international organizations in the last two centuries? Choose a specific issue area to illustrate your argument.
2. To what extent does the creation of international organizations differ per policy area? Are international organizations used similarly in the area of security as in trade?
3. How will international organizations develop without the strong support of a hegemon, such as the USA? Give examples of different policy areas.

Further Reading

Reinalda, Bob 2013. *History of International Organizations. From 1815 to the Present Day*, London: Routledge.

Part II Policy-Making in International Organizations

4 International Organizations as Political Systems

We conceive of international organizations as political systems. Political systems convert inputs into outputs (Easton 1965). Based on developments in the international environment, political actors formulate demands and provide support for international organizations (inputs). International organizations convert these inputs into decisions and activities (outputs) directed towards the international environment. For instance, when the Gaddafi regime behaved aggressively against its own citizens in Libya in 2011, France and the United Kingdom demanded an international response (input). This provided input for the United Nations (UN) Security Council, which adopted a resolution authorizing the international community 'to take all necessary measures ... to protect civilians and civilian populated areas' in Libya (Resolution 1973: paragraph 4) (output). Similarly, when the economic and financial crisis started in 2007 and it became clear that some Eurozone countries, such as Greece, could no longer pay their bills, the international community demanded action from the European Union (EU) and International Monetary Fund (IMF) (input), which drew up bailout packages to help out indebted countries (output). International organizations, such as the UN, EU and IMF, thus convert inputs into outputs. See Figure 4.1.

In this book we argue that *the process* through which international organizations convert inputs into outputs significantly affects how outputs eventually look. In other words, what happens *inside* international organizations matters (the grey box in Figure 4.1). By acting through international organizations, member states can therefore expect different outputs than when they act outside the framework of international organizations. Yet the argument goes further. The way international organizations are designed, in terms of rules, scope, membership and so

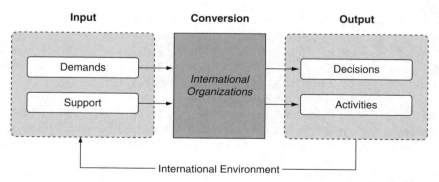

Figure 4.1 The political system of international organizations

on, also affects what outputs eventually look like. The reality that the UN Security Council has five permanent members with veto rights significantly affects the number and substance of its resolutions. The fact that the EU member states have delegated tasks in many policy areas to the experts of the European Commission makes a difference for EU output. If two international organizations are designed differently, they will convert exactly similar inputs into two different outputs.

This chapter and the next three chapters discuss the different aspects of the political system. This chapter focuses on the *constitutional structure* and *institutional structure* of international organizations. Just as in football the size of the field greatly affects the players' tactics, the same can be said about international organizations. The structure of international organizations determines how states negotiate and make policy within them. Therefore we should first analyse the structure ('the box' itself) before we can study how states and other actors pursue their interests within international organizations. While the constitutional and institutional structure determine the venue and set the fundamental rules of the game, it is important to understand that they themselves have also been subject to intensive negotiations by the member states. Yet once the constitutional and institutional structure are agreed, they provide the overall framework for policy-making. After this chapter about the structure of the political system of international organizations, Chapters 5, 6 and 7 focus respectively on the input dimension, conversion process, and output dimension.

THE CONSTITUTIONAL STRUCTURE OF INTERNATIONAL ORGANIZATIONS

Despite the anarchical structure of the international system, international politics is not devoid of legal rules and norms. Besides the general principles of international law (e.g. *pacta sunt servanda* (agreements must be kept)), there are two primary sources of international law: international treaty law and customary international law. The international treaty law is of great importance for the creation of international organizations. In general, international organizations are set up by a treaty between three or more states. Such treaties are frequently negotiated at diplomatic conferences before being signed and ratified. For example, the founding treaty of the UN (the UN Charter) was drawn up and signed in 1945 by representatives of 50 countries who had convened in San Francisco for the UN Conference. However, international organizations can also be established by the decision of an existing international organization, if this right was granted in its founding treaty. For example, the UN can create new subsidiary organs through resolutions of the General Assembly (Jacobson 1984: 84–86; see also Johnson 2014). The UN Conference on Trade and Development (UNCTAD) (1964), United Nations Industrial Development Organization (UNIDO) (1966) and UN Entity for Gender Equality and the Empowerment of Women (UN WOMEN) (2010) are examples of organizations established in this way within the UN system.

A founding treaty normally outlines the organization's mission and membership, establishes its various organs and determines the allocation of competencies between these organs. It thus acts as a sort of 'constitution'. While international organizations do not fully compare to sovereign states, they are clearly 'constituted' through their founding treaties. These founding treaties vary considerably in terms of their ambition and precision. For example, the EU treaties are very detailed and ambitious, covering almost 400 pages (see the consolidated version of Treaty on European Union (TEU) and Treaty on the Functioning of the European Union (TFEU)). Besides general statements about the EU's mission and institutional structure they also contain policy programmes (such as the freedom of movement of persons, services and capital, Articles 45–66 TFEU) and clauses authorizing the formulation of further policy programmes. The UN Charter, by contrast, is both less detailed and less ambitious. It is only 20 pages (excluding the Statute of the International Court of Justice (ICJ)). Although the Charter contains statements about the UN's general mission and its organizational structure, it hardly defines any policy programme which could be implemented without further elaboration.

Constitutions of international organizations are subject to formal and informal change. Formal changes can occur either through a procedure prescribed in the constitution itself or through a new (complementary) treaty signed by the member states. Informal changes occur on the basis of customary international law (Seidl-Hohenveldern & Loibl 2000: 217–29). Yet, just like constitutions of countries, the founding treaties of international organizations tend to be hard to amend. For example, the UN Charter requires that amendments (a) are adopted by two-thirds of the members of the General Assembly and (b) are ratified by two-thirds of the members of the General Assembly, including all permanent members of the Security Council (UN Charter, Article 108). This has only happened five times, in 1965, 1968 and 1973. These amendments were about increasing the membership of the Security Council and Economic and Social Council (ECOSOC) as a result of the increased overall UN membership after the period of decolonization.

Often, formal constitutional changes in international organizations have to do with the expanded scope or membership of the organization. The founding treaties of the EU, for instance, have been amended through, among others, the Single European Act (1987) and the Treaties of Maastricht (1993), Amsterdam (1999), Nice (2003) and Lisbon (2009). All of these changes had to do with further European integration, strengthening the EU institutions, and creating more flexible decision rules (Christiansen & Reh 2009). In addition, the EU has amended its founding treaties to allow for the accession of 22 countries between 1973 and 2013. The constitutional structure is also affected by the withdrawal of the United Kingdom: the withdrawal from the EU by a member state requires the negotiation of a withdrawal agreement that specifies the arrangements for withdrawal as well as the likely future relationship between the exiting member state and the EU.

Since formal changes to constitutions of international organizations are difficult to achieve – often requiring supermajorities, consensus and domestic ratification – informal constitutional changes play an important role. The legal source of such informal changes is not the international law of treaties, but rather customary international law. It can be defined as 'general practices' in international relations which are accepted by states as law (Statute of the ICJ, Article 38(1)(b)). States can,

for instance, adopt certain working methods within the international organizations, which get reinforced over time and therefore become a 'practice'. In some
cases this can go against the letter of the treaty. For instance, the UN Charter
states that 'Decisions of the Security Council ... shall be made by an affirmative
vote of nine members *including the concurring votes of the permanent members'*
(Article 27(3), emphasis added). This implies that the five permanent members
cannot abstain. After all, an abstention is not a concurring vote, and therefore formally equals a veto. The five permanent members, however, quickly decided among
themselves that they should have the possibility to abstain. They did not decide
to formally amend the UN Charter, but rather created a new informal practice.
Following decades of precedent, it is now customary international law that the permanent members can also abstain.

THE INSTITUTIONAL STRUCTURE OF INTERNATIONAL ORGANIZATIONS

The description of institutional structure is often an important part of the founding treaties. About half of the chapters and articles of the UN Charter deal with the
six UN organs (Chapters III–V, X, XIII–XV). Similarly, Articles 13–19 of the TEU set
out the EU institutions and much of the rest of this treaty discusses institutional
details. Yet despite the fact that the institutional structure features prominently
in most founding treaties, international organizations vary widely in terms of how
their institutions look. As noted in Chapter 1, international organizations should
have, at the minimum, a plenary meeting of three member states at least every ten
years, as well as a permanent secretariat and correspondence address. Many international organizations, however, have a much more elaborate structure. To allow
for the comparison between international organizations, this chapter discusses six
different types of 'organs' (or institutions) (Amerasinghe 2005; Jacobson 1984:
86–93; Klabbers 2009; Seidl-Hohenveldern & Loibl 2000: 112–16). While a few
international organizations, such as the EU, have all six organs, many international
organizations only possess two (plenary meeting and a permanent secretariat).
The six different types of organs are:

1. a plenary organ representing all state (and, if applicable, non-state) members; for
   example a general conference, a general assembly or a council of ministers. The
   plenary organ is normally the international organization's highest authority;
2. an executive council or board to manage and supervise day-to-day business.
   The executive council usually consists of a limited number of state (and, if
   applicable, non-state) members elected by the plenary organ;
3. a permanent secretariat with administrative staff led by a secretary-
   general, a director-general or a commissioner responsible for expert advice,
   implementation and external representation as well as administrative tasks
   such as conference management;
4. a court-like body or a court of arbitration in cases of disputes among members,
   or between the administrative body and another organ or a member;

5. a parliamentary assembly of elected representatives or delegates from national parliaments that debates, reviews and, in certain cases, approves of the organization's policies;
6. an organ representing civil society organizations and/or other private actors or sub-national, regional or local administrative bodies.

Plenary organs

The plenary organs of international organizations are based on the principle of member states' sovereignty. All states therefore have their own representatives within the plenary organs. They act according to their governments' instructions. Despite the increasing role that non-state actors play within international organizations, in most plenary organs, such as the UN General Assembly or the EU Council of Ministers, only governments are represented. A long list of 'non-member states, entities and organizations' have a standing invitation to participate, for instance, in the UN General Assembly as observers, but they are not formal members and do not have voting rights. The plenary organs are frequently at the centre of international organizations' decision-making. They are normally the international organizations' highest authorities (Figure 4.2).

The policy-making procedures in plenary organs vary considerably. While in some international organizations the plenary organs take decisions by consensus (e.g. the ministerial councils of the North Atlantic Treaty Organization (NATO)), other international organizations have majority voting (e.g. UN General Assembly). Yet even when it comes to majority voting, there is a wide variety among the plenary organs in terms of the number of votes required for reaching a decision and the weighting given to the votes of different members. The number of votes required can be situated on a continuum ranging from the principle of near unanimity to that of a simple majority (50 per cent + 1). The closer the procedure in the plenary organ is to the principle of unanimity, the more arduous and time-consuming it is to reach decisions (Lister 1984: 7–11; Tsebelis 2002). Sometimes decisions cannot be reached at all. It is also important how many votes

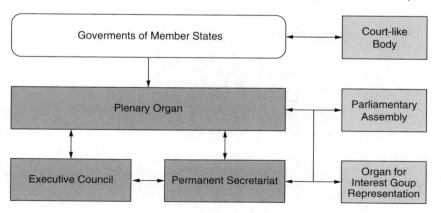

Figure 4.2   The institutional structure of international organizations

each member state has. While in the UN General Assembly each state has one vote, in the plenary organs of the EU, IMF and World Bank votes are weighted. In giving powerful states more voting power, chances are smaller that powerful states will simply disregard decisions made by a majority of smaller states. The weighting of votes can be based on the population of member states or their economic power.

When it comes to policy-making procedures in plenary organs, there is an important balance between the efficiency and legitimacy of decision-making. In the EU, for instance, for reasons of quick and efficient decision-making, member states have over time moved away from consensus decision-making towards qualified majority voting in most policy areas. At the same time, there is the risk that states which are outvoted do not consider the decision legitimate and will not implement it domestically. In many international organizations, states will therefore negotiate until they have a consensus even, if the formal rule is majority voting. A good example is the UN General Assembly: while decisions can be taken by 'two-thirds majority of the members present and voting' (UN Charter, Article 18(2)), most decisions are actually taken by unanimity. If there is no unanimity, implementation and compliance with the decisions of the General Assembly becomes a real issue of concern. For instance, the General Assembly regularly votes on resolutions sponsored by Arab countries aimed against Israel. While such resolutions get adopted, because they have a two-thirds majority, they also get ignored by Israel, the United States, and other countries voting against.

As noted, the plenary organ of the UN is the General Assembly (Figure 4.3). It convenes at least once a year from September to December for a regular session. All

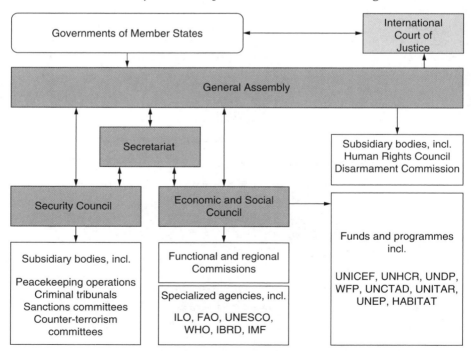

Figure 4.3   The institutional structure of the United Nations (UN)

member states are represented, with one vote each. The General Assembly starts off with a high-level 'General Debate' which involves a week of speeches by national leaders and their foreign ministers. In the months after, much of the work gets done in the six committees of the General Assembly in which all states are represented. The General Assembly is chaired by a president, who is elected every year. The General Assembly examines and approves the organization's budget, determines the members' contributions and elects, in conjunction with the Security Council, the UN Secretary-General and the judges of the ICJ. Furthermore, it can voice an opinion on practically all problems of international politics in the form of legally non-binding resolutions. As every state has one vote in the General Assembly, it is politically the domain of 'the South'. For instance, the Group of 77 (G77), which is the main coalition of 130+ developing countries, already has a two-thirds majority and is therefore a key actor in the General Assembly.

The plenary organ of the EU is the Council of the EU (often referred to as the Council of Ministers) (Figure 4.4). It consists of the member states' ministers and meets in ten different configurations, such as the Foreign Affairs Council, Agriculture and Fisheries Council, and Economic and Financial Affairs Council. The Foreign Affairs Council consists of the foreign ministers, whereas the Agriculture and Fisheries Council consists of agriculture ministers. All these Council configurations are chaired by the six-monthly rotating presidency: every six months another member state is in charge and presides over the Council meetings. The exception is the Foreign Affairs Council, which is chaired by the High Representative of the Union for Foreign Affairs and Security Policy. The High Representative is appointed for five years and also serves as Vice-President of the European Commission. Another interesting formation is the Eurogroup. This is, in fact, an informal body where the ministers of the eurozone area member states discuss matters relating to the euro. It often meets back-to-back with the Economic and Financial Affairs Council. The Eurogroup, even though it is an informal body, has a permanent president.

While the Council of the EU is the formal plenary organ and the EU highest law-making authority, it actually operates under the European Council. The European

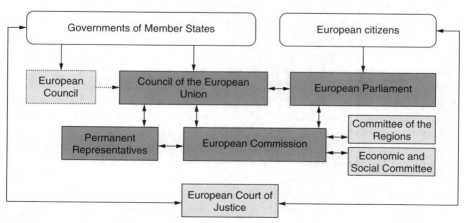

Figure 4.4   The institutional structure of the European Union (EU)

Council, consisting of national leaders, defines 'the general political directions and priorities' of the EU (Article 15 TEU). As such, it is critically important (and has become even more important over the last decade) but it does not engage in actual EU law-making. Decision-making procedures in the Council of the EU vary widely across policy areas. According to the so-called 'Ordinary Legislative Procedure', the Council is the co-legislator together with the European Parliament (see below; see Chapter 6) and takes around 80 per cent of decisions with qualified majority: 55 per cent of the member states need to vote in favour and these member states need to represent 65 per cent of the EU population (Article 16(3) TEU). In practice, however, many decisions in the Council are reached unanimously or by consensus (Heisenberg 2005; Hayes-Renshaw et al. 2006; Häge 2013; Novak 2013).

When reviewing plenary organs we also need to mention the Board of Governors of the IMF and the World Bank. The Board of Governors includes a representative from each member state, typically the minister of finance or head of the central bank. The Board of Governors of the IMF and World Bank hold one joint Annual Meeting once a year. The decisions are based upon weighted voting and are taken with a qualified majority. In both international organizations, approximately 5.5 per cent of the votes are distributed equally among the member states (so-called basic votes). The remaining 94.5 per cent of the votes are distributed based on the contribution that member states make to these organizations. IMF members get one vote for each quota of 100,000 Special Drawing Rights (SDRs), whereas votes in the case of the World Bank are calculated on the amount of share capital. This weighted voting right gives Western industrialized countries, and especially the USA, a decisive influence. In the case of decisions such as the replenishment of capital and change of quotas, which require a qualified majority vote (85 per cent), the USA and the member states of the EU (acting collectively) have de facto veto rights. For instance, the USA has respectively 16.52 per cent and 16.89 per cent of the votes in the IMF and World Bank.

Executive councils

Executive councils of international organizations meet more frequently than the plenary organs. Indeed, some meet in permanent session. Their main task is to supervise the permanent secretariat of the organization and to take on the implementation of policy programmes decided by the plenary organ. Executive councils are often smaller than plenary organs. Many executive councils are composed of a limited number of member states' representatives elected by the plenary organ. In some inclusive organizations such as the Global Fund to Fight AIDS, Tuberculosis and Malaria, the executive council (or rather the 'board') is formed by representatives of state and non-state (civil society and/or business) constituencies. Moreover, some executive councils have a mixture of permanent and non-permanent members. The UN Security Council, for instance, has five permanent members and ten non-permanent members. In the Governing Body of the International Labour Organization (ILO) the ten major industrial countries are similarly permanently represented. Where members are elected, often the larger, politically and economically important countries are more regularly chosen, for instance in the Executive Board of the UN Development Programme (UNDP). In addition, the allocation of seats on governing bodies or executive councils often has to satisfy principles of fair regional representation. For instance, this holds for the election of the members of the Security Council and of ECOSOC.

The division of competencies between the plenary organ and the executive council is of major importance for the decision-making process of international organizations. Sometimes, the executive council is given important competencies. This makes decision-making quicker and more efficient, because the number of participants is limited. Yet it makes compliance by the members of the organization not represented on the executive council more difficult. The effects of keeping the major decision-making competencies within the plenary organ are the reverse: decisions may be easier to implement, but reaching them is often much more arduous. Also, when the plenary organ fails to take a decision, further negotiations may have to wait for the next session (which could be in 12 months). Hence the question of a sound distribution of competencies between the plenary organ and the executive council is a key topic of debate.

The system of governing bodies and executive councils in the UN system follows a functional differentiation. The Security Council, for instance, is responsible for all questions pertaining to international peace and security. ECOSOC, on the other hand, deals with economic, social and cultural problems of international politics. Yet the competencies of ECOSOC, which can only make legally non-binding decisions by simple majority, are rather modest. It functions mainly as a coordinating body for different UN Special Organs and Specialized Agencies. The 54 members, 18 of whom are elected annually by the General Assembly for a three-year period, meet two to three times a year (Rosenthal 2007; Taylor 1993).

The UN Security Council, by contrast, has far-reaching competencies. It can, according to Chapter VII of the UN Charter, pass legally binding resolutions, including resolutions about military operations and sanctions. Such resolutions are binding not only on UN member states but also on non-members and even on individuals. Groups such as al-Qaeda or private companies such as North Korean banks can be the targets of legally binding Security Council resolutions, as can be individuals such as state or rebel leaders indicted by the International Criminal Court (Joseph Kony) or leaders of terrorist groups (former associates of Osama Bin Laden) who have been violating UN Charter principles. Of the Security Council's ten non-permanent members, five are elected each year by the General Assembly for a two-year term. The election follows a geographical distribution: three states from Africa, two from Asia, two from Latin America and the Caribbean, two from the 'Western Europe and Others' group and one from Eastern Europe. Decision-making in the Security Council depends partly on the issue under consideration. While decisions on procedural matters require a majority of nine of the total of 15 permanent and non-permanent members (Article 27, paragraph 2 of the Charter), decisions on all other matters require the same majority but can, in addition, be vetoed by any one of the five permanent members (Article 27, paragraph 3). Since, in practice, most matters the Security Council has to deal with are not considered 'procedural' but rather 'other matters', this extends the right of veto to each of the permanent members on nearly all questions (Bailey & Daws 1998: 250–52; Malone 2007).

Due to their limited membership, various regional organizations, in contrast to global organizations, can do without executive councils. For example, the Council of Europe does not have an executive council in addition to its plenary organ, the Committee of Ministers. The EU, on the other hand, does have executive councils. The range of its tasks cannot be managed by the Council of Ministers alone. Thus the Committee of Permanent Representatives (COREPER) assumes the responsibilities of an executive council and deals with day-to-day business. It meets at least once a week in order to coordinate relevant policies and to prepare the agenda for Council meetings. In addition, the EU has a number of other executive councils, including the Political and Security Committee for foreign and security issues, the Special Committee on Agriculture, the Economic and Financial Committee, and the Trade Policy Committee. These committees are formally different from the Council of Ministers and have their own set of competencies defined in the Treaties. This makes the EU different from, for instance, NATO's North Atlantic Council which is a single body that can meet at different levels (ministers and ambassadors).

Permanent secretariats

A permanent secretariat with administrative staff is a necessary part of the institutional structure of any international organization (as per the definition of international organizations, see Chapter 1). Since the secretariat, also called 'bureau' or 'commission', often has a building, a figurehead, a press department and serves as the main contact point, it is frequently mistaken for the international organization as a whole. This is not the case: the European Commission is not the same as the EU and the IMF Staff is not the same as the IMF. Also, in some international organizations, there is a permanent secretariat as well as a separate secretariat for the plenary organs and executive councils (e.g. European Commission and General Secretariat of the Council of the EU). Unlike the members of the plenary organs or executive councils, the people on the secretariat staff are normally not representatives of member states' governments. They are therefore independent of instructions from the governments of their countries of origin (in small international organizations, one of the member states may provide secretarial services which are then often based in the ministry of foreign affairs). Some permanent secretariats only provide technical services in the preparation for meetings of the plenary organs or executive councils. However, in many of the larger international organizations, permanent secretariats have become sizeable bureaucracies that frequently exert independent influence on policy-making in international organizations (Barnett & Finnemore 2004).

The UN Secretariat's staff members are recruited on the basis of ability and suitability, as well as political-geographical distribution. UN personnel constitute an international civil service and are not allowed to follow instructions from their countries of origin or other member states. That said, officials from high- and low-income countries are overrepresented across the UN system, while officials of middle-income countries are underrepresented (Parízek 2017). The Secretary-General presides over the Secretariat and is elected by the General Assembly for a period of generally five years on the recommendation of the Security Council.

The Secretary-General can exert influence on decision-making in the General Assembly and the Security Council. Formally, the Secretary-General has the duty to bring to the attention of the Security Council all matters affecting peace and security (Article 99 of UN Charter). The Secretary-General, with support of the Secretariat, does so by writing formal reports on a daily basis. These reports contain concrete policy options for the Security Council and the General Assembly. He/she has also a considerable media profile and can draw attention of the international community to certain conflicts simply by visiting a country or holding a press conference (Chesterman 2007).

The European Commission, the administrative staff of the EU, is one of the largest and strongest permanent secretariats. It has extraordinarily wide competencies. Across most policy areas, the European Commission is the only body that can submit draft proposals for legislative acts to the Council. Therefore the Commission is the engine of law-making in the EU. Besides its involvement in law-making, the Commission also monitors the application of European laws in member states and can, in case of their non-compliance, file lawsuits before the European Court of Justice (ECJ) (Jönsson & Tallberg 1998; Wallace 2010: 70–75). The head of the Commission is the President, who is nominated by the national leaders and approved by the European Parliament, subject to hearings, for a five-year term. The same goes for the other commissioners, one for each member state. One of the Vice-Presidents of the Commission also holds the position of High Representative of the Union for Foreign Affairs and Security Policy. He/she is in charge of the European External Action Service, a separate permanent secretariat within the EU, which resembles an EU diplomatic service with 130+ EU embassies across the world. It is important to note that members of the Commission are independent from the governments of their state of origin.

The Commission's staff is organized into departments known as 'Directorates-General' (DGs) and 'services'. Each DG operates in a specific policy area and is headed by a Director-General who answers to one or more commissioners. Across the European Commission, there are more than 30,000 officials who run the EU on a day-to-day basis. They get recruited through an open competition (concours) and are formally independent from the member states. Contrary to various international organizations, where members of staff are appointed on a temporary contract basis, European Commission officials normally have a job for life. This further signifies their independence from the member states and gives them additional autonomy. First and foremost, they serve the 'European interest' (see further Chapter 5).

Courts of justice

Some international organizations have courts of justice or court-like bodies as part of their institutional structure. Their task is to decide on disputes between the members of the organization, between the organization and its members or between organs of the organization. Sometimes they can even decide on disputes between individuals, the organization and/or its member states. In some international organizations these bodies function as supranational courts in which independent judges exercise compulsory jurisdiction. This means that the court has automatic authority to deal with a dispute: the disputant states do not have to first accept the court's authority. The Appellate Body of the World Trade Organization (WTO) is a case in point. In other organizations, however, these bodies can hardly be regarded as standing above the parties; they may not be able to exercise compulsory jurisdiction and the judges may be politically dependent state representatives. Usually these bodies are meant to support intergovernmental efforts at dispute settlement through political compromise rather than to adjudicate disputes and appoint a 'winner' and a 'loser' (Keohane et al. 2000; Zangl 2008).

The ICJ in The Hague is the relevant body for the UN and the ECJ in Luxembourg settles disputes for the EU. While the 15 judges of the ICJ are elected separately by the UN Security Council and the General Assembly, with an absolute majority required in both organs, the judges and advocates-general of the ECJ are appointed unanimously by the EU member states. In practice, each EU member state proposes one judge of its nationality. The political independence of the judges is guaranteed in both courts. However, the ICJ's capacity to decide in cases of a legal dispute between states is rather limited, because the court does not have compulsory jurisdiction. The ECJ, by contrast, can exercise compulsory jurisdiction. Hence, no member state that has been charged with violating its commitments under EU law can prevent the court from ruling. Through binding rulings the ECJ asserts the supremacy of EU law over national law and implements it in conjunction with the courts of the member states. The ECJ thus has competencies that are comparable to those of national administrative and constitutional courts (Alter 2001).

Parliamentary assemblies

Some international organizations, such as the EU, the African Union (AU), the Council of Europe, the Organization for Security and Co-operation in Europe (OSCE) and NATO, have parliamentary assemblies. Their function is to provide legitimacy for the intergovernmental organization's decision-making process. Parliamentarians represent the input of citizens. However, the competencies of, as well as the representation in, these assemblies vary considerably. While since 1979 the members of the European Parliament have been elected directly, the members of most other parliamentary assemblies are delegated by member states' national parliaments – that is, a select group of parliamentarians from each national parliament meet as part of the parliamentary assembly of the international organization. The European Parliament has generally accrued major rights (Rittberger 2005). It is now the co-legislator on most EU policy areas and has the right to appoint and dismiss European Commissioners. The parliamentary assemblies of most international organizations play a much more modest role.

Since the European Parliament has such exceptional powers for a parliamentary assembly, it is important to elaborate further to put them in context. The role of the European Parliament has gradually developed over time, partially due to a general understanding that the EU has a 'democratic deficit' and partially through precedent. The introduction of the co-decision procedure in the Treaty of Maastricht (1993) was important. The role of the Parliament as the 'second legislative organ' beside the Council was further affirmed by the Treaty of Amsterdam (1999), the Treaty of Nice (2003) and the Treaty of Lisbon (2009). These treaties allowed the European Parliament to exert influence through the ordinary legislative procedure, which is used in the large majority of policy dossiers. In addition, the European Parliament has used its various competencies to further increase its power. For instance, it threatened to exceptionally use its power to dismiss the full Santer Commission in 1999 following a corruption scandal involving one of the Commissioners, after which the full Commission resigned. Since this 'triumph' of the Parliament, it has used this precedent to hold tough hearings with all Commissioners prior to the appointment of the full Commission. These hearings regularly lead to individual Commissioners getting blocked. The European Parliament has also used its budgetary powers to further increase its profile.

Representation of non-governmental actors

So far, we have mainly focused on the institutional structure of what can be called traditional international organizations. Many of the relevant international organizations such as the UN, the WTO or NATO are still relatively closed organizations that cater for their governmental member states. However, the representation of non-governmental actors in international organizations has significantly increased since the end of the Cold War (Tallberg et al. 2013). Inclusive organizations such as the Global Fund have been created in which state and non-state actors are members of the plenary organ and/or the executive council (usually called 'board'). In addition, most international organizations have tried to increase their legitimacy by opening up for a more or less formalized participation of non-state actors. For that purpose, they allow for non-governmental actors' consultative status and have created organs and procedures for the representation of civil society groups, business actors, or regional and local administrative bodies. However, the opportunities that these organs and procedures offer to non-state actors in terms of effective participation in decision-making vary considerably (Tallberg et al. 2013).

Within the UN, ECOSOC is an open intergovernmental body that provides formal access for NGOs. According to Article 71 of the UN Charter and ECOSOC resolutions 1296 (1968) and 1996/13 (1996), NGOs can be granted consultative status (Alger 2002). The Committee on Non-Governmental Organizations of ECOSOC examines NGOs' applications. Currently, more than 4000 NGOs such as Amnesty International, Greenpeace, and Transparency International enjoy consultative status in ECOSOC. They are allowed to make oral or written statements in ECOSOC sessions and to submit proposals for the agenda of ECOSOC sessions and its subsidiary organs (Schulze 2002). Besides participating in ECOSOC meetings, NGOs can also take part in global conferences convened by the UN. This enables the UN to take the interests articulated by non-governmental actors into consideration. In the area of protection of the environment and of human rights, NGOs have become remarkably influential participants in global conferences held under the auspices of the UN.

Within the political system of the EU, the European Economic and Social Committee (EESC) is the main organ in which NGOs can formally present their concerns in hearings before the Commission, Council and Parliament. Such formal representation comes in addition to the informal lobbying of the other EU institutions by NGOs and business associations. In addition, the Committee of the Regions established in 1993 by the Treaty of Maastricht gives regional and local authorities some access to decision-making in the EU. Its members aim to aggregate regional and local concerns at the European level and to channel these into EU decision-making. The EESC and Committee of the Regions must be consulted by the Commission, the Council and the Parliament in areas such as education, employment and the environment. Despite their formal position in EU policy-making, neither the EESC nor the Committee of Regions has really been able to significantly influence policy output.

CONCLUSION

This is the first of four chapters that analyse international organizations as political systems. Political systems convert inputs into outputs. This is also a useful conceptual approach to understand policy-making by international organizations. The argument in this book is that *the process* through which international organizations convert inputs into outputs matters. Different international organizations may convert the same inputs into different outcomes. This chapter has focused on the constitutional and institutional structures of international organizations. Picking up again on the football analogy referred to at the start of this chapter, the constitutional and institutional structures of international organizations can be compared to the field and the fundamental rules of the game. They provide the setting for actors to make policy within international organizations. If different international organizations have different constitutional and institutional structures, they are also likely to convert inputs differently into outputs. The founding treaties or 'constitutions' shape policy-making by outlining the organization's mission, establishing its organs and determining the allocation of competencies between them. Focusing on institutional structure, we have introduced six typical organs of international organizations and how they shape the process of policy-making.

This chapter has largely focused on the political systems of international organizations as more or less fixed entities. This makes sense: if today a certain input reaches an international organization – for instance a recent conflict is brought to the attention of the UN Security Council by the member states or the Secretary-General – such input is converted into an output on the basis of the constitutional and institutional structure as it is in place at this time. In other words, at least in the short term, the constitutional and institutional structure is fixed and stable. Through various examples, this chapter has, however, also hinted at the fact that the constitutional and institutional structures of international organizations develop over time and are subject to change. Indeed, states put in a great deal of attention when they design the constitutional and institutional structures (Abbott et al. 2000; Koremenos et al. 2001). They make careful trade-offs, for instance, in voting rights between the sovereign equality of the member states on the one hand and the need to recognize the special role of the great powers within international organizations.

Because the design of the constitutional and institutional structures is often a matter of compromise between the founding states, they tend to be hard to change. It is therefore not a surprise that the five permanent members of the Security Council are still the same ones as when the UN Charter was negotiated in 1944–45. It is also not a surprise that the leadership positions in the IMF and World Bank are always divided between Europe and the United States. At the same time, there have been several changes in the constitutional and institutional structures of international organizations over the last decades. China, India and some of the other emerging countries have lobbied hard, with some success, for more representation in the international organizations (Zangl et al. 2016; Lipscy 2017). Furthermore, while NGOs were largely excluded from policy-making during the Cold War, many international organizations now formally consult them and in several instances they have become formal power holders of their own.

The perspective of political systems assumes that international organizations are the 'focal institutions' (Jupille et al. 2013) where international problems get addressed. In other words, when states and other international actors face certain problems, they turn to the relevant international organization. This perspective is not concerned with international cooperation and conflict outside the framework of international organizations. It can thus not explain why international actors may sometimes act 'through' international organizations and at other times address their problems in an informal ad hoc manner (Abbott & Snidal 1998; Vabulas & Snidal 2013). Furthermore, while this perspective is very helpful to understand how states fight out their conflicts, and how dissatisfied states change their support and demands of international organizations, it is less appropriate to explain why states challenge the political system as such. For the hostility of the Trump administration towards international organizations or the British decision to withdraw from the EU (challenges to the political system of international organizations), we need to return to the three conditions why states create (and join) international organizations in the first place (see Chapter 3). In other words, the political system perspective is most effective in explaining how international organizations address problems as they come along on a day-to-day basis.

Discussion Questions

1. How do constitutional and institutional structures affect policy-making in international organizations? Use a concrete example to illustrate your answer.
2. To what extent does the choice of voting procedures involve a trade-off between the probability of reaching decisions and the effectiveness of implementation? How can this tension be resolved?
3. Can the political systems of international organizations be compared to the political systems of countries? Argue in favour or against.

Further Reading

Easton, David 1965. *A Framework for Political Analysis*, Englewood Cliffs, NJ: Prentice Hall.

Hix, Simon & Høyland, Bjørn 2011. *The Political System of the European Union*, 3rd edn, Basingstoke: Palgrave Macmillan.

Tallberg, Jonas, Sommerer, Thomas, Squatrito, Theresa & Jönsson, Christer 2013. *The Opening Up of International Organizations: Transnational Access in Global Governance*, Cambridge: Cambridge University Press.

Weiss, Thomas G. & Daws, Sam (Eds) 2007. *The Oxford Handbook on the United Nations*, Oxford: Oxford University Press.

5 Input: Actors' Demands and Support

In the previous chapter, we discussed the constitutional and institutional structure of the political system of international organizations – the venue and the fundamental rules of the game. In this chapter, we focus on the actors by discussing the input dimension. While the venue and rules affect how the actors play the game, and can put certain actors at a disadvantage, they do not determine the ultimate score. We therefore also need to analyse the actors' motivation, commitment and behaviour. Following the discussion of the constitutional and institutional structures, we therefore focus in this chapter on the actors relevant to international organizations. On the basis of their interests and values, actors formulate their preferences towards international organizations and they provide support (input). For instance, when scientific research showed in the 1970s that certain greenhouse gases had a negative effect on the ozone layer, most states developed preferences on how quickly they wanted to reduce those greenhouse gases (input). The administrative staff of the United Nations Environment Programme (UNEP) with support of environmental non-governmental organizations (NGOs) pushed for a policy programme for the protection of the ozone layer (input). Communities of experts furthermore made additional scientific evidence available (input). All these inputs were converted through negotiations into output: the adoption of the Montreal Protocol on Substances that Deplete the Ozone Layer in 1987.

In this chapter, the main focus is therefore on five different types of political actors operating within international organizations. We discuss who they are, what they want, and their resources to achieve their preferences. It is important, in this respect, to distinguish the political actors from the institutional structures they

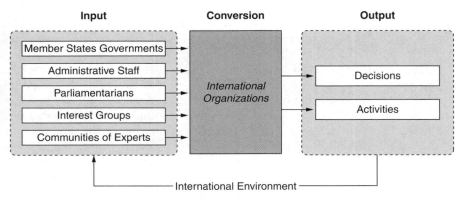

Figure 5.1   The political system of international organizations (input)

have at their disposal. For instance, a founding treaty (constitution) may establish a permanent secretariat (institutional organ), but this does not automatically determine whether the administrative staff within the secretariat will behave as a political actor, on the basis of which interests and values, and how it will leverage its resources to exert political influence over the output. Similarly, international organizations may have a formal platform (institutional organ) for NGOs and other interest groups to provide their input, but this does not determine what the actual input from NGOs looks like. In this chapter, we therefore study five different groups of political actors:

1. member states' governments;
2. administrative staff;
3. parliamentarians;
4. interest groups;
5. communities of experts.

GOVERNMENTS OF MEMBER STATES

The member states in most international organizations are represented by their governments, either through ministers in the plenary organ or ambassadors and diplomats in the executive councils. Most of the inputs in international organizations – and often the most important inputs – therefore come from the governments of the individual member states. It is critical to stress the word 'government', because the interests and values of governments do not necessarily align with the interests and values of the *entire* member state. For instance, the inputs of the USA to international organizations over the last two decades have differed considerably depending on whether the Republican or Democratic Party held the presidency: the Bush and Trump presidencies have been much more sceptical of global environmental cooperation than the Clinton and Obama presidencies. The preferences pursued by member states may therefore be affected by elections and the composition of the government. That being said, the USA remains an exception. The input provided by most member states is more stable and less affected by the government composition. Yet it still matters whether member states have left-wing or right-wing governments for issues such as trade, development cooperation or counter-terrorism.

Because the USA has played such an important role, as a hegemon, in establishing international organizations (see Chapter 3), it is important to discuss its foreign policy traditions. When it comes to international cooperation, liberal internationalism or 'Wilsonianism' immediately comes to mind. According to this foreign policy tradition, the pursuit of liberalism abroad, including the promotion of democracy, human rights and free trade, is the best guarantee for world peace. For US President Woodrow Wilson the origins of the First World War could be traced to the oppression of nations in the Austrian-Hungarian Empire and the secrecy with which states negotiated international treaties and military alliances. Wilsonianism in US foreign policy has had its ups and downs, but has left a strong mark on international organizations, including through the creation of the United Nations (UN), the Bretton Woods institutions, US support for European integration after 1945 and the promotion of global human rights norms, as well as environmental cooperation.

While liberal internationalism has been a significant tradition in US foreign policy, it stands in contrast to equally important traditions of isolationism and non-interventionism. The Monroe Doctrine of 1823, for instance, stated that the USA would not interfere in Europe's wars, while demanding at the same time that the European states would stay out of North and South America. While it may seem odd to associate the United States with non-interventionism, with its recent military adventures in Afghanistan, Bosnia, Iraq, Kosovo, Libya and Somalia, the US public traditionally remains rather sceptical of liberal interventionist missions (Jentleson & Britton 1998). And the fact that the US acts internationally does not mean that it acts through international organizations. Both US Presidents Bush and Trump have been sceptical of international cooperation, from questions of international security to support for the climate change regime, or diplomacy with Iran, North Korea and Cuba.

US input for international organizations has therefore fluctuated from general support for the overall system of global governance (in the Wilsonian tradition) to specific support for issues that benefit the US in particular (Mead 2002). In general, however, international organizations are regarded by the USA as a means to an end rather than an end in themselves. They can help the USA achieve its interests and values, but the USA does not hesitate to go unilateral whenever it believes this is required. It is also significant that the USA goes to great lengths not to be bound by international organizations. It did not join the League of Nations as a member, it does not deploy its own troops in UN peacekeeping missions, and it withdrew its signature from the Rome Statute of the International Criminal Court in 2002 exactly to avoid that its leaders and soldiers would be tried for war crimes. The USA also does not hesitate to withdraw its support for international organizations, through cutting funding and even leaving, if it disagrees with the adopted policies. Because the USA is the largest donor in many international organizations, paying sometimes as much as a quarter of the budget, it can use its resources to support or undermine international organizations.

Europe's three largest states – France, Germany and the United Kingdom – traditionally put stronger emphasis on multilateralism and international organizations than the USA. For them, global governance can be an end in itself. France and the United Kingdom jealously guard their permanent membership of the UN Security Council and take a particularly active role in supporting the work of the Security Council. At the same time, they also consider themselves major powers by the virtue of their nuclear weapons; this is formally recognized under the Non-Proliferation Treaty. Through the framework of the European Union (EU), they have also focused on strengthening the 'rules-based global order' (European External Action Service 2016: 8). While Brexit presents a British challenge to the EU, there is no evidence of the United Kingdom reducing its support for other international organizations. Germany traditionally has a strong attachment to international organizations as part of its post-war legacy. This includes strong support for international organizations, such as the UN and EU. At the same time, being one of the principal donors of many international organizations, Germany has also been keen to increase its influence. Furthermore it actively uses its financial power within international organizations, including by insisting on zero or limited budgetary growth.

Russia has long been sceptical of the independent role of international organizations in world politics. For Russia, international organizations are foremost venues where national interests are defended and power politics is played out. Ever since Joseph Stalin demanded a veto in the Security Council in 1945, Russia has keenly used this institutional power to block all sorts of undesired resolutions. Russia has, in this respect, an ambiguous attitude with regard to international law. During the post-Cold War period, it has insisted on the UN Charter stipulating that questions of peace and security need to be addressed in the Security Council (where it has a veto). In New York, it has also upheld the non-interference norm including, for instance, by vetoing more than half a dozen Western-sponsored resolutions on the civil war in Syria since 2011. At the same time, Russia has not shied away from breaking international law when it comes to conflicts in its own neighbourhood. Its annexation of Crimea in 2014, for instance, was unprecedented in the post-Cold War era and a very blatant disregard for international law.

While China regularly sides with Russia in the UN Security Council, particularly when it comes to non-interference in the domestic affairs of other UN member states, the preferences of China towards international organizations are actually very different. The People's Republic of China was originally deeply sceptical of international organizations. In 1945, China had been granted a permanent seat on the Security Council, but the seat was occupied by Taiwan for two decades (1949–71) following the Chinese civil war. China has also long opposed international human rights regimes that affect its internal policies, including after the Tiananmen Square protests of 1989. In more recent decades, however, China has largely turned into a supporter of international organizations (Johnston 2007). Importantly, it became a member of the World Trade Organization (WTO) in 2001. Its membership has contributed to tremendous economic growth in China, and China is generally seen as a moderate voice in this organization (Hopewell 2015). China has furthermore become a key player in the climate change negotiations. It is also the only permanent member of the Security Council that regularly contributes troops to UN peacekeeping missions. Over the last two decades, China has discovered that global governance can be greatly beneficial and as such it has become a crucial stakeholder in maintaining international organizations (Ikenberry 2008, 2011).

While the permanent five members of the Security Council are actors of their own, many countries actually try to act within international organizations through regional groupings or special coalitions. The EU itself is a prime example. On many dossiers within international organizations, the member states of the EU vote as a block or even speak with one voice through representatives from the European Commission and the European External Action Service (Jørgensen 2009). Yet there are many more regional groups. The G77 of 130+ developing member states is a critical group when addressing economic and social issues. Through its sheer size, it can determine the outcome of UN General Assembly resolutions. Similar things can be said about the Non-Aligned Movement or the Organization of Islamic Cooperation. In the field of climate change, the unlikely coalition of 38 small island developing countries, many of which are at serious risk of flooding, has become a relevant political actor. One of the main challenges, however, for regional groups and special coalitions is their internal coherence. Sometimes it can be more difficult for them to agree internally than it is for them to subsequently agree with other groups.

A final new set of states are the emerging countries and particularly the BRICS (Brazil, Russia, India, China and South Africa). Emerging countries have long tried to increase their weight in international organizations. For instance, Brazil and India have been key political actors in the WTO ever since the start of the Doha Round in 2003 (Narlikar 2004; Narlikar & Tussie 2003; Odell 2006). And, at least in some issue areas, China and Russia are perhaps not even emerging countries, but rather established powers with a permanent Security Council seat and nuclear weapons. Yet in Durban, South Africa in 2013, the BRICS made a powerful collective statement demanding a larger say in international organizations. The summit declaration was a *tour d'horizon* with input for many of the world's international organizations. It notably called 'for the reform of International Financial Institutions to make them more representative and to reflect the growing weight of BRICS and other developing countries' (paragraph 13). What made, however, this BRICS statement stand out was the establishment of a 'New Development Bank' (paragraph 9), a parallel institution to the World Bank and Asian Development Bank, run entirely by the BRICS. It was a clear signal to the existing, Western-dominated international organizations: if you do not take our concerns seriously, we will create new institutions.

The governments of the different member states thus have varying interests and values (Figure 5.1). And depending on the issue, preferences can differ tremendously. The USA, France and the United Kingdom have been keen to establish UN peacekeeping missions around the world, but have been reluctant to make their own soldiers available. The BRICS may want a larger say in policy-making in international organizations, but they generally oppose international organizations infringing on the sovereignty of their members. It is therefore difficult to make general statements about what each state precisely wants in each area of global governance. Furthermore, governments change in countries and many governments make up their mind only once faced with developments in the international environment. Yet once governments have defined their preferences on an issue, the question is how they go about achieving them. They have various resources to influence and support the policy-making process in international organizations.

A first resource is material power. Countries around the world listen to the USA simply because it has military and economic power. This extends to its role in international organizations. For all the sovereign equality of international organizations, ultimately some states are more equal than others, and this particularly goes for the major powers. In crisis situations and moments where policy-making within the international organizations really matters, all eyes turn to the major powers (Stone 2011), whether the USA in the UN Security Council, France and Germany in the EU, or China and the USA when it concerns climate change. The major powers are also often able to exert influence in areas where they may not have obvious resources. For instance, while American fishing companies are not engaged in whaling, the USA can nevertheless be regarded as one of the most influential members of the International Whaling Commission (IWC) (Zangl 1999). And many non-permanent members of the Security Council vote along with the USA, because they know this may result in more development aid and more favourable treatment at the International Monetary Fund (IMF) and World Bank (Kuziemko & Werker 2006; Dreher et al. 2009a, 2009b). The USA has indeed control over issue-transcending resources and can link negotiations across several international organizations (Keohane & Nye 1977: 3–47).

A second resource is the expertise and administrative capacity that states have. This is often issue-specific (Keohane & Nye 1977: 3–47; Baldwin 2002: 180). Due to its expertise in nuclear technology, for instance, France is a major actor in the issue area of nuclear reactor safety. In deliberations about international standards of reactor safety within the International Atomic Energy Agency (IAEA), French diplomats are therefore particularly influential. The importance of expertise and administrative capacity cannot be overstated. With so much going on in all international organizations across the world, it is hard for most member states to keep up. For instance, the ten elected members of the Security Council are not necessarily able to assess the exact consequences of a specific clause in a resolution authorizing a peacekeeping mission in South Sudan; and yet, they are expected to vote on exactly such resolutions. This strengthens the position of those Security Council members that do have expertise about the situation in South Sudan or the capacity to find out (Dijkstra 2015).

A third resource is the support (or 'buy in') of member states in international organizations. Through their financial contributions and their supply of information and personnel they provide the support which enables international organizations to carry out their tasks. The dependence of international organizations on the financial contributions from member states is especially obvious because hardly any international organization has its own financial resources (see Goetz & Patz 2017). In the case of the UN system, the financial resources are divided into 'assessed' (that is, compulsory) and voluntary contributions (Graham 2015). In some international organizations – such as inclusive organizations – member states are less dominant in terms of providing inputs. The Bill and Melinda Gates Foundation, for instance, also makes a contribution to the Global Fund. Yet states are usually the key political actors formulating demands on, and offering support to, the organization. It is important to elaborate on the support of member states as it provides a concrete input to international organizations.

In most international organizations the size of national contributions reflects the 'ability to pay' based on the wealth of each of the respective countries. Accordingly, the USA, Japan and China provide the biggest financial contributions to the UN. The US contribution to the UN's regular budget for 2018 amounted to US$591 million (22.0 per cent of the total of US$2.69 billion) in addition to US$1.9 billion for the UN peacekeeping budget (28.5 per cent of the total of US$6.8 billion). The Japanese regular contribution was US$260 million and its peacekeeping contribution was US$658 million. The Chinese regular contribution was US$213 million and its peacekeeping contribution was $US697 million. In the EU, the biggest financial contributions in 2016 came from Germany followed by France with 27.5 billion and 21.1 billion euros (19.1 per cent and 14.6 per cent), respectively, out of the total member states' contributions of 144.1 billion euros.

It goes without saying that the size of member states' financial contributions can have a crucial effect on their influence within international organizations. In other words, states try to convert their financial support into a source of influence. This has been evident, for instance, in the IMF and the World Bank, where the major Western donors have largely shaped policy programmes in the postwar era. On the other hand, when major contributors turn their backs on international organizations, these organizations get into major financial trouble. The USA, for instance, withdrew from the UN Educational, Scientific and Cultural Organization (UNESCO) in 1984, accusing it of excessive politicization and lack of budgetary restraint, and again in 2018 as a result of Palestinian accession to UNESCO. Similarly, it withdrew from the United Nations Industrial Development Organization (UNIDO) in 1996 because it dismissed this organization as ineffective and viewed its advocacy of public sector responsibility for industrial development with suspicion. In both cases, the USA deprived these organizations of its contributions, which made up sizeable proportions of their overall resources. In a similar way, since 2002 the USA has refrained from providing financial contributions to the UN Population Fund (UNFPA) in protest over UNFPA's endorsement of China's population policies. This has severely compromised the viability of UNFPA's projects. More generally, the Trump administration has complained about UN budgets overall and has made an effort to reduce them. This coincides with less support for the UN system.

Although states adjust their support according to whether their demands are met, withdrawing from an international organization or holding back 'assessed' (compulsory) financial contributions is not how states usually behave. Normally, states make their demands through their delegations or permanent representatives to the organization. In most cases such demands are voiced in the plenary organ or executive councils, since that is where the member states' representatives have the right to vote. This holds especially for far-reaching demands: nothing beats making a big statement during the UN General Assembly's General Debate in September or European leaders making their demands at European Council meetings. For the less important demands of day-to-day politics, it is unlikely that member states' concerns will be addressed by delegations or permanent representatives to the plenary organ. In such situations, matters are raised in committees, working parties or with the relevant department of the permanent secretariat.

ADMINISTRATIVE STAFF

While most inputs to international organizations come from representatives of the member states, there are several other political actors that provide considerable input to policy-making as well. It is important to pay particular attention to the administrative staffs of the permanent secretariats. Although their power is formally quite small, their contributions are nevertheless very real (Barnett & Finnemore 2004; Biermann & Siebenhüner 2009; Jacobson 1984: 118–23; Mathiason 2010; Eckhard & Ege 2016). Secretariats provide planning documents for military operations in the UN, EU and NATO (Dijkstra 2016). IMF officials visit indebted countries to verify whether policy is properly implemented. The Intergovernmental Panel on Climate Change (IPCC) issues reports on the effects of climate change, which subsequently inform policy. States have also recognized that the administrative staff of international organizations can be an important ally when developing policy (Manulak 2017; Dijkstra 2017). Member states are thus keen to invest in the administrative staff and to make sure that their nationals are well-represented (Parízek 2017). They also lobby the administrative staff heavily (Urpelainen 2012; Panke 2012).

The influence of international organizations' administrative staffs, especially their executive heads, stems mainly from their location at the centre of the policy-making process. As a result, administrative staffs often have an information advantage over member states. This information advantage can come from studies, reports and proposals that members of administrative staff are asked to prepare, or which they themselves initiate, to inform policy-making within the organization. In addition, their central position lends a secretariat's leadership a remarkable influence as an agenda-setter. Frequently, the administrative staffs of international organizations (co-)determine the agendas, thus influencing the decisions to be taken. Where member states' interests are not clear, the administrative staff's influence on policy-making can grow very rapidly to the point where it is not only playing the role of agenda-setter but also that of policy entrepreneur (Pollack 2003).

The extent to which tasks are delegated to the administrative staff varies significantly across international organizations (Hooghe & Marks 2015). In the case of the EU, the European Commission exceptionally has the exclusive right of legislative initiative. The Commission alone can initiate and table legislation. This right of initiative has been critical with respect to implementation of the internal market and in the creation of economic and monetary union. The Commission, under its then president, Jacques Delors, gave the internal market idea, later agreed upon in the Single European Act, a decisive launch with its White Paper in 1985, while Delors's ideas about economic and monetary union found their way into the Treaty of Maastricht (Ross 1995; Sandholtz & Zysman 1989). Through its monopoly on proposing new legislation the Commission possesses a special control over input.

In the UN, too, a considerable agenda-setting power can be ascribed to the administrative staff, with the Secretary-General at its apex. Under Article 99 of the UN Charter, the Secretary-General is tasked to bring all matters to the Security Council that affect questions of peace and security. Successive Secretary-Generals have interpreted this function as a right to travel around the globe and engage in mediation and conflict prevention. The administrative staff in the UN Secretariat has also played a critical role in developing peacekeeping doctrine: from Dag Hammarskjöld's original focus on peacekeeping to the Agenda for Peace (UN-Doc. A/47/277) proposed in 1992 by Boutros Boutros-Ghali, the keynote Brahimi report of 2000, and the High-Level Independent Panel of Peace Operations (HIPPO) in 2015 (Weinlich 2014). Even when the member states decide on policy, the officials in the UN Secretariat can give it extra spin. For instance, the administrative staff turned the lengthy and dry Millennium Declaration of 2000 into eight concrete Millennium Development Goals (MDGs) with clear targets. This logic was then also followed with the Sustainable Development Goals (SDGs).

Also beyond the EU and UN, we see a significant footprint left by the administrative staffs of international organizations. In the IMF, for instance, the administrative staff has considerable expert authority in the area of macroeconomics. While the Executive Board formally can amend staff proposals, for instance on loans with borrowing countries, in practice this almost never happens (e.g. Martin 2006: 143). The Executive Board relies, in this respect, heavily on the expertise of the IMF staff. NATO provides another example, where the Secretary-General actually chairs the North Atlantic Council. As such, the Secretary-General can determine the agenda and the procedure with which NATO takes decisions. In the World Health Organization (WHO), the administrative staff has been able to play member states from the North out against member states from the South, thereby furthering its agenda (Chorev 2012).

Given their rational-legal, delegated, moral and expert authority (Barnett & Finnemore 2004), an important question is what the preferences of administrative staffs are. While there is almost always some sort of goal conflict between some of the member states and the administrative staffs of secretariats, it is more difficult to make general statements on what administrative staffs actually want. In the literature on bureaucratic politics, many scholars make relatively simple assumptions about motivations of administrative staffs of international organizations, such as their desire to maximize their budget or institutional power (Vaubel 1996; Vaubel et al. 2007; Pollack 2003). The reality is more complicated (Trondal et al. 2010). For instance, high-level officials may focus on increasing operational budgets, as it gives their organization more relevance in the outside world, rather than fighting for the administrative budgets that actually pays for staff (Dunleavy 1985). While many officials in the secretariats will undoubtedly prefer to expand their own bureaucracies, in reality the administrative staffs of international organizations are still relatively small. For instance, only around 600 officials in the UN Secretariat are responsible for the deployment of nearly 100,000 peacekeepers (Dijkstra 2016).

Apart from budget maximization, we can identify three goals which are shared across most administrative staffs. First, the administrative staff tends to be pro-cooperation, wanting member states to reach viable agreements that benefit the international organization as a whole (Beach 2004). Officials in UNEP, for instance, are keen to see more cooperation on environmental protection. Second, the administrative staff tends to value policy effectiveness based on its technical expertise. The IMF Staff has a preference for economic considerations (Martin 2006: 142) and the WHO Staff focuses on medical and scientific evidence (Cortell & Peterson 2006: 266–67). Finally, the administrative staff is, like most political actors, guided by a desire to avoid uncertainty. Officials in the administrative staff know very well that in case their international organization fails, they are first in line to receive the blame. They will be cautious in the risks they take on and insist on achievable policies and adequate resources to fulfil the delegated functions (e.g. Barnett & Finnemore 2004; 130–35). This can put secretariats on a collision course with the member states, which may demand as much value possible for money or are looking for a convenient scapegoat.

The initiatives – the demands of the administrative staffs of international organizations – are for the most part addressed to the member states of the organization or the plenary organ in which they take decisions. Thus the agenda-setting phase of the policy-making process can be described as the interplay of initiatives between the member states and the administrative staff. While the administrative staff represents the collective interest of the organization, each member state mainly looks after its individual interest. The initiatives of the administrative staff of an international organization will mostly be directed towards strengthening the authority of the organization, while those of member states are of various kinds.

PARLIAMENTARIANS

Although generally less effective than representatives of member states' governments and the administrative staff, parliamentarians can also formulate demands for or lend some support to the policy-making processes within international organizations. Apart from the democratic control of their governments through their own national parliaments, their main forums for influence are the parliamentary assemblies that some international organizations have. Their most important input, within these parliamentary assemblies, is to increase the legitimacy of policy-making. In fact, parliamentary assemblies are often created in order to reduce the so-called 'democratic deficit' of international organizations, which is considered a consequence of policy-making being dominated by government representatives (Rittberger 2009; Zürn 2000). Indeed, sometimes governments actually use their privileged position in international organizations to insulate themselves from national parliaments. Governments benefit from the fact that policy-making procedures in international organizations are complex and not very transparent. Also national parliaments are confronted with policies made in international organizations on a 'take it or leave it' basis. In such circumstances national parliaments are unable to provide democratic legitimacy. To compensate for this gap, international parliamentary assemblies are created to provide additional legitimacy (Rittberger 2005).

While it is not always obvious that parliamentarians in parliamentary assemblies are actually able to provide additional legitimacy, the perception that they represent the 'voice of the people' makes it hard for the member states and administrative staffs of international organizations to completely ignore their demands. In other words, their perceived legitimacy is the main source of influence. The European Parliament, in particular, has repeatedly been successful in bringing its concerns onto the agenda of the EU. For example, the revitalization of the common market programme in the 1980s was partly due to pressure from the European Parliament to deepen European integration (Corbett 2002; Sandholtz & Zysman 1989).

Moreover, the European Parliament can rely on power resources other than its perceived legitimacy to influence EU policy-making. With the coming into force of the Single European Act in 1987, and in particular the Treaty of Maastricht (1993), the European Parliament was given the institutional power to block decisions made by the Council of the EU. The Treaties of Nice (2003) and Lisbon (2009) have further enlarged its legislative powers (see Chapter 4). Hence it has become an indispensable player in EU policy-making, and neither the Council nor the Commission can ignore the Parliament's concerns. Moreover, the European Parliament's power to bring a vote of no confidence against the Commission, as well as its power to withhold approval of the budget, have enhanced its role in the EU's policy-making process. It must be emphasized, however, that, owing to the far-reaching consequences of these measures for the EU as a whole, the European Parliament will withdraw its support from the Commission only in exceptional situations.

If we accept that parliamentarians in political assemblies provide relevant input to the work of international organizations, it is important to ask what parliamentarians actually want. Beyond generic interests, such as more influence for their political assembly and to be taken seriously by the government representatives and administrative staff, it is difficult to pinpoint precise preferences. The European Parliament is said to be largely pro-European integration even though there is some left–right politics ongoing during the debates in Brussels and Strasbourg (Hix et al. 2006). The European Parliament has also given several national politicians a platform and resources. For instance, the National Front has had great difficulty in getting elected in the French presidential system, and has used the European Parliament (which has a proportional electoral system) as its base. Yet the European Parliament is and remains an exception. In many parliamentary assemblies, such as the ones of NATO, the Organization for Security and Co-operation in Europe (OSCE) and the Council of Europe, one only finds supporters of the specific international organization. For instance, parliamentarians in the NATO political assembly tend to serve in foreign affairs and defence committees in their own national parliaments. They are largely pro-NATO. Most often, national parliamentarians critical of NATO do not bother to go to the parliamentary assembly. This, in turn, seriously affects the legitimacy and seriousness of political assemblies.

INTEREST GROUPS

Interest groups, such as civil society actors and private businesses, are also a source of inputs in the form of both demands and support. They can use either formal or informal channels, depending on the institutional structure and the inclusiveness of the international organization (see Chapters 4). There is a mutual benefit. Non-governmental actors frequently have an interest in gaining access to policy-making processes. At the same time, international organizations also need access to the information, expertise and legitimacy of non-governmental actors (Brühl 2003). As already mentioned, the extent of, and the institutional channels for, non-governmental actors' inputs vary considerably. In inclusive organizations such as the Global Fund, non-governmental actors are allowed to participate in the decision-making process of the organization with a vote. This is also the case with the International Labour Organization (ILO), in whose tripartite decision-making organs state representatives vote alongside employer and trade union representatives.

More frequently, however, non-governmental actors do not have a (formal) right to vote but can, more or less effectively, take part in policy deliberations (Steffek et al. 2008). Two channels of input can be distinguished: first, non-governmental actors can act through an institutionalized procedure, which gives them the opportunity to raise their concerns. As mentioned, according to Article 71 of the UN Charter and ECOSOC Resolutions 1296 (XLIV) of 1968 and 1996/31, civil society actors can obtain consultative status in ECOSOC and consequently participate in its meetings or those of its committees as well as submit oral or written opinions and agenda proposals. Second, non-governmental actors can act through their own representative organs within the institutional structure of an international organization. The European Economic and Social Committee (EESC) of the EU is an example of such an organ, consisting of approximately 350 representatives ranging from employers to trade unions, as well as other interest groups such as consumer organizations.

Of course, the expression of preferences does not always take the shape of formal input channels. In many international organizations informal input channels are at least as important as, or complement, formal input channels. Thus in the EU a large number of non-governmental actors try to gain influence on policy-making through lobbying activities. Around 12,000 lobby organizations are currently registered in the EU's transparency register. Most of the powerful lobby organizations bring together full industries. For example, the Committee of Professional Agricultural Organisations and the General Committee for Agricultural Cooperation in the European Union (COPA-COGECA) represents European farmers. The Confederation of European Business (known as BusinessEurope) represents enterprises and employer organizations. The European Trade Union Confederation (ETUC) is the umbrella organization for trade unions. This reflects the fields that are most advanced, given the depth of EU integration in the areas of agriculture, industry and employee representation.

The demands of non-governmental actors and their support for policy-making – no matter whether through formal or informal channels – relies on various material and immaterial resources. These include providing information, expertise and legitimacy, which they offer and which are essential for international organizations' goal achievement. In addition, interest groups can gain influence by mobilizing public opinion in favour of their own concerns. For example, Greenpeace was quite successful in mobilizing global public opinion against whaling, thereby forcing the IWC to agree on an international moratorium on major whaling operations (1982). With respect to the humanitarian catastrophe caused by the civil war in Somalia in the early 1990s, various aid organizations were able to activate public opinion in the USA to support a humanitarian intervention authorized by the UN Security Council (Hasenclever 2001). More recently, many NGOs provide support to the international community in its efforts to reduce global warming (Keohane & Victor 2011).

Transnational advocacy networks and transnational social movements are particularly successful in mobilizing public opinion (Keck & Sikkink 1998;

Smith et al. 1997). Such advocacy networks and social movements do not represent particular material interests, but claim to act in the global interest in supporting international organizations in their policy-making efforts. However, there are also transnational advocacy networks and transnational social movements that criticize the policies of major international organizations. For example, ATTAC, a global network linking groups that criticize economic globalization for its negative social and ecological effects, was able to mobilize public opinion against the World Bank, the IMF and the WTO through media campaigns (Green & Griffith 2002; Waters 2004). At the height of the Eurozone crisis, the Spanish grassroots movement Los Indignados launched a major protest against EU austerity policies.

COMMUNITIES OF EXPERTS

Some inputs to the political system of international organizations come from outside experts giving advice on policy-making. As the policies of international organizations have to respond to increasingly complex problems, the knowledge resources and advice of (frequently non-state) experts have a growing importance for their policy-making. The UN makes frequent use of committees of outside experts or consultants that are often chosen according to the usual geographic distribution criteria and provide the expertise the UN administrative staff cannot provide. Therefore the administrative staff often has an interest in bringing outside experts into the policy-making processes, while the experts themselves have an interest in being incorporated because this gives them influence on policy-making within the organization. It is therefore not always easy to clearly distinguish between the administrative staff (members of which are often experts themselves) and outside experts brought in to provide expertise for policy-making.

Experts' influence depends, among other things, on whether they agree or disagree on the advice that should be given for policy-making within the organization (Haas 1989, 1992a, 1992b). If all or most relevant experts agree on the causes and consequences of a given problem and how to deal with it – and therefore form an 'epistemic community' – the likelihood that their advice will have an impact is quite high because the member states find it more difficult to ignore that advice. If, however, these experts disagree on how to cope with a specific problem their advice will be taken less seriously. Moreover, member states can point to the disagreement among experts in order to justify why their advice does not have to be taken up. And member states with conflicting interests can justify their positions by relying on those experts whose advice is most in line with their own interests, which then can easily lead to an impasse in the policy-making process.

To illustrate the influence which experts, and in particular epistemic communities, can exert, let us look at the policy-making activities of various international organizations in relation to protection of the environment. Some of these activities came about in part on the initiative of experts within international organizations' administrative staffs. Thus we owe the activities of the UNEP and the World Meteorological Organization (WMO) for the protection of the stratospheric ozone layer to the efforts of committed experts (Breitmeier 1996; Haas 1992b). Almost all experts on the IPCC, founded in 1988 under the patronage of UNEP and the WMO, agreed on the causes as well as the consequences of climate change. Thus the experts of the IPCC were able to play a prominent role in the preparation of the UN Framework Convention on Climate Change, which was ready for signature at the UN Conference on Environment and Development in 1992, as well as of the Kyoto Protocol agreed to by the Conference of the Parties (COP) in 1997. However, the difficulties in agreeing on a stricter successor agreement to the Kyoto Protocol, initially during the COP meeting in Copenhagen in 2009 and later in Paris in 2015, also show the limits of the influence of expert knowledge when this conflicts with major states' vital economic interests.

CONCLUSION

This chapter has focused on the political actors within international organizations. Based on the broader developments in the international environment, political actors provide the inputs to international organizations through their demands and support. For instance, if human rights violations take place in a particular country (international environment), different political actors (from governments of member states to human rights advocates) may bring their concerns (input) to the relevant forums in international organizations. The chapter has, in this respect, identified a set of relevant political actors. These include member state governments, the administrative staffs of permanent secretariats, parliamentarians meeting in the parliamentary assemblies, interest groups, and communities of experts. In this chapter, we have analysed each group's contribution to the policy-making process of international organizations. In Chapter 6 we turn to the conversion of inputs into outputs and in Chapter 7 to the outputs themselves.

In terms of inputs, it is worth thinking both about the preferences of actors and their 'buy in' (support) in international organizations. Actors typically have a relatively fixed set of interests and values. Once an international problem comes on the agenda, they develop their preferences on the basis of those interests and values. We have seen that such preferences differ significantly across political actors but also across policy areas. While most of the members of administrative staff of international organizations often have pro-cooperation preferences, it is difficult to determine a priori what, for instance, UN officials may want on any given policy area. Similarly, while many members of the European Parliament are pro-European integration, they also have political left–right positions to defend. The representatives of member states may not even have their mind set on their final objectives. As part of regular negotiations, they may develop a clearer sense of their priorities.

In this chapter, however, we have not only focused on the preferences of political actors and the channels they use to achieve them; we have also discussed the support that the political actors provide for the work of international organizations. Member states can provide financial resources for international organizations. In addition to the assessed resources, they often have the ability to make unilateral voluntary contributions to specific projects of international organizations they support. Members of administrative staff often provide expertise to international organizations, as well as continuity. They also facilitate the policy-making process and may be delegated implementation tasks. Parliamentary assemblies lend international organizations additional legitimacy, whereas the involvement of civil society, business and NGOs may provide international organizations with more information and societal support. External experts can also help to increase the knowledge base of international organizations. To conclude, international organizations are no longer neutral forums where major powers fight their battles. Rather, much goes into international organizations. In the next chapter, we focus on the conversion process.

Discussion Questions

1. How do powerful states differ in their demands and support for international organizations?
2. To what extent do the administrative staffs of international organizations have their own preferences and how do they go about making an autonomous impact on policy-making?
3. Through which channels can non-governmental actors formulate demands on, and lend support to, international organizations? Give a concrete example for each channel of input.

Further Reading

Eckhard, Steffen & Ege, Jörn, 2016. International bureaucracies and their influence on policy-making: A review of empirical evidence, in: *Journal of European Public Policy* 23: 7, 960–78.

Graham, Erin R. 2015. Money and multilateralism: How funding rules constitute IO governance, in: *International Theory* 7: 1, 162–94.

Haas, Peter M. 1992. Introduction: Epistemic communities and international policy coordination, in: *International Organization* 46: 1, 1–35.

Kahler, Miles 2013. Rising powers and global governance: Negotiating change in a resilient status quo, in: *International Affairs* 89: 3, 711–29.

Keck, Margaret E. & Sikkink, Kathryn 2014. *Activists Beyond Borders: Advocacy Networks in International Politics*. Ithaca, NY: Cornell University Press.

6 Conversion: Decision-making in International Organizations

International organizations convert inputs into outputs. In this book, we argue that the conversion process is vitally important: two different international organizations may convert similar inputs into different outputs. So what does this conversion process look like? And what is so special about it? In this chapter, we discuss how inputs are transformed into outputs in international organizations. It is important to differentiate, in this respect, between two types of decisions: programme decisions and operational decisions. *Programme decisions* are decisions about a set of norms and rules aimed at directing the behaviour of actors. The programme decisions of international organizations mostly set normative standards for the behaviour of their member states and are comparable to law-making at the state level. International organizations that mainly take programme decisions have been defined as programme international organizations (see Chapter 1). Operational international organizations, by contrast, mainly take *operational decisions*. These decisions relate to the implementation of the norms and rules of existing programmes. This includes activities such as monitoring member states' compliance with normative standards and enforcing those standards in case of non-compliance. Distinguishing between programme decisions and operational decisions is important, because the decision-making processes frequently differ.

For both programme decisions and operational decisions, we identify the prominent modes of decision-making (Figure 6.1). The 'big' programme decisions are often made in the intergovernmental conferences that establish or amend the constitutional structure of international organizations. In those conferences, the member states dominate and normally have vetoes. Programme decisions are

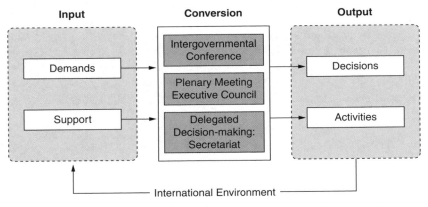

Figure 6.1   The political system of international organizations (conversion)

also made after international organizations have been established. The plenary organs and executive councils are, in this respect, the main bodies for programme decisions. In these bodies, government representatives from the member states take the lead, but the institutionalized nature of many plenary organs and executive councils also gives a role to officials from the permanent secretariats and occasionally access to non-state actors. Operational decisions, which implement programme decisions, are often of a less sensitive nature as they are taken within the confines set out by programme decisions. While in many international organizations operational decisions are also subject to input by the member states, a substantial number of international organizations work with delegated decision-making: the member states have delegated the authority to make operational decisions to the permanent secretariat or another implementing agency. To interpret programme decisions, they may also grant international courts the authority to make operational decisions. Subsequently, the member states control how the secretariat implements and the court interprets the programme decisions.

PROGRAMME DECISIONS

The programme decisions of international organizations directly affect the autonomy of member states, since they require the member states to submit to international norms and rules. As states are generally zealous to preserve their autonomy, they usually insist that they dominate and control the decision-making process for 'big' decisions leading to the making of such norms and rules. As such, programme decisions are normally taken at the intergovernmental conferences where treaties are negotiated or in the plenary organs and executive councils of international organizations. These are the organs where the member states dominate.

Intergovernmental decision-making: Conferences

Many of the 'big' programme decisions of international organizations are actually already included in the founding treaties. For instance, the United Nations (UN) Charter states that 'All Members shall refrain in their international relations from the threat or use of force against the territorial integrity or political independence of any state' (Article 2(4)). The North Atlantic Treaty, which established NATO, notes that 'The Parties agree that an armed attack against one or more of them in Europe or North America shall be considered an attack against them all' (Article 5). One of the purposes of the Treaty of Rome, which established the European Economic Community – the frontrunner of the European Union (EU) – was to ensure 'the elimination, as between Member States, of customs duties and of quantitative restrictions on the import and export of goods, and of all other measures having equivalent effect' (Article 3(a)). The founding treaties of the UN, NATO and EU therefore include ambitious policy programmes. The same goes for amending treaties. The Treaty of Maastricht (1993), for instance, introduced a common European currency: the euro.

The policy programmes included in the founding treaties often seriously impinge on the autonomy and sovereignty of the member states. For instance, the UN Charter limits a member state's sovereignty to use military force against other states (and also to pre-emptively protect itself). In the North Atlantic Treaty, member states commit to the collective defence of their allies. While Article 5 includes some qualifications, there normally is no 'opting out' in case of war. The Treaty of Rome not only meant that European states no longer could set their own tariffs, but it also meant a common customs tariff and a common commercial policy towards third countries (Article 3(b)) – in other words, it meant the end of unilateral trade policy. The adoption of the euro, furthermore, resulted in the end of national currencies (and monetary policy is set in Frankfurt by an independent European Central Bank, see Chapter 10). These treaties thus seriously reduced the autonomy of the member states in what they can do with their armed forces, their trade policy and their currency.

Given the important consequences for sovereignty, it is therefore not a surprise that the 'big' programme decisions at the level of founding or amending treaties tend to be taken by consensus during intergovernmental conferences which are dominated by the representatives from the governments of member states. It is, however, not a purely intergovernmental affair. For instance, during the various amending EU treaties, members of administrative staff from the European Commission and the General Secretariat of the Council of the EU made up the secretariat of the intergovernmental conferences and helped steer the member states towards pro-EU integration outcomes (Beach 2004, 2005). Furthermore, negotiations on the Treaty of Lisbon (2009) started with a European Convention (2001–03), which was composed of representatives from the member states, but also former politicians, national and European parliamentarians, and representatives from the accession countries. The final text of the Convention was then put to an intergovernmental conference of member states. Beyond the EU, we also see that many new international organizations build on established international organizations and that officials from the permanent secretariat are part of the intergovernmental conferences (Johnson 2014).

Because of the significance of 'big' programme decisions during the intergovernmental conferences, it is worth elaborating on this process. The EU programme decisions for the realization of the internal market and for the creation of a common currency, as determined in the European Single Act of 1987 and the Treaty of Maastricht in 1993, provide powerful examples. The decision-making processes were dominated by negotiations between the three most powerful EU member states at the time – France, Germany and the United Kingdom (Moravcsik 1998). Accordingly, the decision on the internal market project was only possible because in the mid-1980s the three major EU member states had – for the first time and simultaneously – a common interest in pursuing a neo-liberal economic policy and in the completion of the internal market, which had already been envisaged in the Rome Treaty of 1958. The positions of the three states came together when France, which had only just adopted a neo-liberal position favourable to the internal market project; the United Kingdom, which was in principle in favour of the internal market; and Germany, which was strongly in favour of the project, at last saw eye to eye. President Mitterrand, in his role as President of the European Council, met six times with Chancellor Kohl and Prime Minister Thatcher in order to coordinate their respective interests regarding the internal market project.

Similarly, the decision on the creation of a single European currency could only be achieved in the early 1990s because that was when the major EU member states actually developed a common interest in an economic and monetary union, even though this was already foreseen in the so-called Werner Plan of 1970 (Moravcsik 1998; Wolf & Zangl 1996). In this case, however, only Germany and France, which had been pursuing the same objectives in monetary policy as well as trade policy from 1988 onwards, took the initiative, while the United Kingdom remained more reserved. After German reunification the intergovernmental negotiations about monetary union were dominated by the Franco-German tandem led by President Mitterrand and Chancellor Kohl.

The role of the European Commission was, in both the negotiations for the Single European Act and those for the Maastricht Treaty, limited to the role of defining and facilitating the project for an internal market and that for a common currency in a way that reflected the common interests of the major European states (for a different view see Bornschier 2000). Moreover, the results of the two treaties are also typical of intergovernmental negotiations. On the one hand, both represent the 'lowest common denominator' of the interests of the most powerful member states. While the internal market and the common currency could be established, steps towards further integration favoured by France and Germany were blocked by the United Kingdom. Furthermore, there was a need to get the 'smaller' member states on board. This was largely done through financial 'side-payments' with the broadening of the Structural Funds and the creation of Cohesion Funds. These two funds, which give financial support to poorer regions and member states, can be interpreted as concessions by powerful member states intended to safeguard the support of less powerful states such as Greece, Ireland, Portugal and Spain (Moravcsik 1991, 1998).

The negotiations on the Treaty of Lisbon started off as a more inclusive attempt with the European Convention and an intergovernmental conference resulting in a Constitutional Treaty for Europe in 2004 (see above). Yet this 'European Constitution' failed due to its rejection in Dutch and French referendums in 2005. Based on the leftover broken pieces, the member states engaged in very difficult intergovernmental negotiations that ultimately led to the Treaty of Lisbon. The proposed European Constitution was no longer acceptable for European voters and therefore had to be amended. Yet the proposed European Constitution was a carefully crafted compromise between the member states. Opening up this compromise to do justice to the wishes of the European voters, while at the same time keeping all member states on board, proved difficult. In an enlarged EU it is even more difficult to find a viable compromise through intergovernmental bargaining than it was in the 1980s or 1990s when France, Germany and at times the United Kingdom led the way. Thus the Treaty of Lisbon has (albeit cautiously) increased the space for majority voting on EU programme decisions to guarantee the Union's capacity for effective decision-making (Carbone 2010; Hosli 2010).

The mode of intergovernmental decision-making is also relevant in the UN system. The UN regularly initiates international conferences that are intended to give rise to decisions binding on all participating states (e.g. international treaties). Since UN conferences can only make binding decisions when all states agree, it is primarily the states and their interests which dominate the decision-making process. Yet non-state actors are now regularly involved in major UN treaty conferences, and transgovernmental networks channel and substantively shape final decision-making through crucial preparatory work on treaties.

The relevance of intergovernmental state-centred decision-making was very evident at the Third UN Law of the Sea Conference from 1973 until 1982. In the course of a lengthy and at times complicated negotiating process to reformulate the law of the sea, it was a question of harmonizing the differing interests in maritime issues of over 150 states. The result, a colossal achievement, is a negotiating package which mainly reflects the interests of states with long coastlines as well as the interests of the great military powers. The extension of coastal waters, exclusive economic zones and the continental shelf met the interests of states with long coastlines, while the unimpeded transit of shipping through these zones corresponded to the commercial and military interests of the great powers. The agreement of states with short coastlines and of landlocked states, as well as of producers of certain minerals, was assured through various concessions. The states with short coastlines and landlocked states were to benefit from internationalization of the exploitation of the seabed through an International Seabed Authority, because this was expected to give them a share in the revenue from this exploitation. States which feared that exploitation by the Seabed Authority might lead to a decline in prices for the minerals they extracted on land were to benefit from agreed limits to the exploitation of the seabed. This comprehensive package illustrates how, in intergovernmental negotiations, the interests of all states have to be respected. But it also shows that states which have issue-specific power resources at their disposal – maritime powers and states with long coastlines – can influence the final decision to a larger extent than states that do not have equally effective resources (Talmon 2000; Wolf 1981: 76–273).

Programme decisions made at intergovernmental conferences are often subject to domestic ratification procedures. This means that while representatives of state governments negotiate and sign treaties establishing or amending international organizations, each state subsequently needs to ratify the agreement and the programme decisions following its own domestic constitutional procedures. Ratification is all but guaranteed. For instance, the US Constitution stipulates that the US Senate needs to approve international treaties with a two-thirds majority vote. Such a high threshold implies, in practice, that both parties need to support a treaty. While the Senate has approved many more treaties than it has rejected, the US president frequently decides not to forward a treaty to the Senate when unsure about the vote. For instance, the USA is the only state in the world that has signed but not ratified the UN Convention on the Rights of the Child. Ratification is, however, not only a challenge in the USA. The ratification of EU treaties has regularly involved referendums in several of the member states. When a decision precisely enters into force is mentioned in the decision itself. For instance, the Paris Agreement on Climate Change entered into force when 55 countries that produce at least 55 per cent of the world's greenhouse gas emissions ratified the agreement.

Institutionalized decision-making: Plenary organs and executive councils

While 'big' programme decisions are made at the level of founding and amending treaties normally in the context of intergovernmental conferences, most programme decisions are actually taken within the international organizations themselves. The plenary organs and executive councils (and their committees) are, in this respect, the principal venues where the majority of programme decisions are taken. All member states have a seat in the plenary organs. For the executive councils and the committees, member states representation varies. In the UN Security Council, only a fraction of the member states are present. In the committees of the UN General Assembly, all member states have a seat. The Board of Governors of the International Monetary Fund (IMF) and the World Bank include all members, whereas only a limited number of member states are on the IMF Executive Board and World Bank Board of Directors. In the EU, all member states are present in the Council of Ministers, the Committee of Permanent Representatives, and the large number of working groups. Participation in the executive councils and committees therefore varies across international organizations.

While the plenary organs and executive councils are often referred to as the 'intergovernmental organs' of international organizations (as opposed to the permanent secretariat which is the 'supranational organ'), the reality is more nuanced. The term 'intergovernmental' refers to relations solely between governments – normally at the ministerial level or higher – taking place on a largely ad hoc, non-institutionalized, basis. The intergovernmental conferences described above are normally ad hoc and dominated by states. International organizations, in contrast, are by definition permanent and have some degree of institutionalization (see Chapters 1 and 4). Therefore, the decision-making in the plenary organs, executive councils and committees is never truly intergovernmental. It always takes place within a constitutional and institutional structure, so the venue is determined and some fundamental rules are set. We therefore use the concept of institutionalized decision-making to describe the mode of decision-making within the plenary organs and executive councils.

Particularly in the EU, scholars have questioned the intergovernmental nature of decision-making in the Council of the EU, the Committee of Permanent Representatives (COREPER) and the working groups. Some suggest that EU decision-making processes are better understood as 'intensive transgovernmentalism' (Wallace 2010: 100–02) or 'new intergovernmentalism' (Puetter 2014; Bickerton et al. 2015). The concepts are, however, not only applicable to the EU. They are relevant for many of the prominent international organizations. Interactions between member states in the plenary organs, executive councils and committees of international organizations take place on a daily basis and are no longer irregular events. Discussions are also no longer solely at the political level between ministers, but civil servants from different member states also contact each other directly. Furthermore, member states are no longer the only ones present in the plenary organs and executive councils; indeed, significant input comes from permanent secretariats and even non-governmental organizations (NGOs) and experts. Meetings are run in a business-like fashion according to clear rules of procedure and established practices.

Apart from the very significant degree of institutionalization in international organizations, such as the EU, IMF and UN, we can also witness a process of 'elite socialization' (Checkel 2005; Lewis 1998, 2005). Contrary to, for instance, the one-off meeting of Roosevelt, Stalin and Churchill at Yalta in 1945, where they decided on the future of the world, ambassadors and diplomats may meet each other every single day in international organizations. This creates a social dynamic which affects actual negotiating behaviour. It is not just that diplomats need to be friendly with one another because they meet each other again the next day or because they get invited to the same receptions and barbecues. Socialization goes deeper. As a result of the intensive interactions, they learn to appreciate the interests of the other parties and the difficulties that other member states may have with certain decisions. Regularly, diplomats also need to convince their own ministries about the need to compromise with international organizations. Indeed, a long-standing risk in diplomacy is that diplomats 'go native': they may show more appreciation for the demands from their international organizations than their instructions from their own ministries.

Actors in plenary organs and executive councils

While member states are clearly the key actors in the plenary organs, executive councils and the committees, they are not the only ones. These meetings are run by a chairperson or presidency. They also include representatives from the permanent secretariat. Various NGOs and other actors may participate as well, either as observers or occasionally as full members themselves. The constitutional and institutional structures of international organizations often determine which actors can participate and contribute to the work of the plenary organs, executive councils and committees (see Chapters 4 and 5). The founding treaties provide, in this respect, the fundamental rules. Yet these are then often complemented by more detailed rules of procedure.

It is difficult to run any meeting without a *chairperson*. The same goes for the meetings of the plenary organs, executive councils and their committees. There are three different ways to appoint a chairperson (Tallberg 2010). First, these organs can have a permanent chairperson. The typical case is NATO, where the Secretary-General chairs the North Atlantic Council. Second, these organs can have an elected chairperson. An example is the UN General Assembly, which elects its President each year. Still, custom dictates that the UN General Assembly member states elect a president each year from a different region, that all countries should ultimately have the chance to hold the Presidency once, and that the five permanent members of the Security Council do not also take the Presidency of the General Assembly. Third, the chairperson rotates among the member states. The key example is the six-monthly rotating Presidency of the EU. Another example is the monthly rotating Presidency of the Security Council. While in international organizations with a relatively small membership there is often a rotating chairperson, this option is suboptimal for international organizations with a larger membership.

Being the chairperson of plenary organs, executive councils or committees is of significant symbolic value and brings prestige. In most international organizations, however, the chairpersons also have a substantive role and can exert influence on decisions: it matters who chairs the meetings and negotiations in international organizations. The starting point for discussing chairpersons is, however, their formal impartiality. Chairpersons are not supposed to promote the national interests from their home country. Instead they should act as an 'honest broker' trying to find compromise between the member states and, where necessary, defend the interest of the organ they represent against other organs and the outside world. For instance, the rotating Presidency of the Council of the EU defends the collective interests of the member states in their negotiations with the European Parliament. If chairpersons appear biased towards the national interests from their home countries, they may lose the confidence of the other member states.

While impartiality is critical, and many chairpersons take it seriously, being at the helm of decision-making offers significant opportunities to shape the actual decisions (Tallberg 2006). First, the chairperson often has a role in managing the agenda. He/she may prioritize or exclude certain topics on the agenda. The chairperson also typically decides on the order of the agenda and the time allocated to certain issues. Furthermore, in some international organizations, the chairperson may decide on the timing of meetings. For instance, the NATO Secretary-General has the procedural power to call for an emergency meeting of the North Atlantic Council. Second, the chairperson is often closely involved in brokering deals. Through informal bilateral negotiations with the relevant member states, the chairperson may get insider knowledge of bottom lines and therefore the 'zone of possible agreement' (ZOPA). Within the ZOPA, the chairperson can propose compromises that benefit their home country most. Finally, as noted above, the chairperson may represent their organ to the outside world and sometimes even negotiate on behalf of their organ. Such an external context allows the chairperson some discretion as well.

In addition to the chairperson, the administrative staff from the *permanent secretariat* is almost always present during decision-making. Members of staff from the secretariat take on different functions. A key function is to provide conference services, such as booking rooms, distributing documents, providing translation and security and ordering coffee. In addition, in many international organizations, the secretariat contains legal experts or even a legal service to advise the member states on legal and institutional questions. Yet another function is support for the chairperson. Especially when the chairperson is elected or rotating, it is important to have a set of more permanent assistants that can help the chair to run the meetings. They may take minutes, keep an eye on the speaking order, administer the votes and even provide the chairperson with procedural and political advice on negotiations. Because the members of staff of the permanent secretariat are also supposed to be impartial, they too may act as the honest brokers seeking compromise for the member states. An important part of the role of secretariats is thus to 'oil the wheel of compromise' (Beach 2004) in plenary organs and executive councils.

Particularly in the larger international organizations, the permanent secretariats have also been delegated a function as expert bureaucracy. Across many dossiers, for instance, the European Commission has the exclusive right of initiative. This means that the Commission sets the agenda in the EU and that the Commission presents and defends its proposals in the Council and the underlying (ambassadorial) committees. In the EU working groups, several Commission experts sit around the table and answer questions from the member states. At the level of ambassadors, the Commission is represented by the relevant Director-General. In the Council, the Commissioner is present. While the European Commission is an exceptionally strong permanent secretariat, we see the same practice in other international organizations. In the UN General Assembly and the Security Council, negotiations often start off by the Secretary-General (or the Under-Secretary-Generals) presenting a formal report with their views.

The rules of procedure often dictate how *the representatives of the member states* can participate in the formal meetings. For instance, the rules of procedure of the UN General Assembly note that the chairperson shall give the floor to speakers 'in the order in which they signify their desire to speak' (Rule 68). It is therefore 'first come, first served' and representatives from larger states are not privileged in line with the emphasis on sovereign equality in the General Assembly. The same rules stipulate that for formal meetings interpretation will be provided for the six working languages of the General Assembly (Rule 51). Speakers are allowed to speak in their own language, but then they need to provide interpretation in one of the six working languages themselves (Rule 52). So when the German Chancellor wants to address the General Debate in German – not one of the working languages – the German delegation has to provide and pay for interpretation. Based on the rules of procedure, the chairperson may also put time limits on interventions or cut national representatives off. Furthermore, in the EU it used to be custom to start discussions with a *tour de table*, in which every minister got a say. Following the 2004 enlargement round, it was decided to stop with this practice: if the representatives of all the member states got two minutes each, the *tour de table* would take a full hour.

Also important is the seating order (see Alger 2014). In the UN General Assembly, the Secretary-General each year randomly selects a member state to sit in the first seat. The rest of the member states then follow in English alphabetic order. This is significant, because it means that like-minded countries or regional groups do not sit together. In the EU, seats are allocated in the order that member states have the rotating Presidency. So if the rotating Presidency is coming up soon for a member state, it sits at the beginning. If a member state has just concluded the Presidency, it sits at the end. The order of the presidencies is also strategically determined so that there is a good mix between large and small member states as well as member states from the North, South, East and West. For instance, Germany normally sits between Croatia and Portugal. The other institutional actors are typically strategically located: the UN Secretary-General sits next to the President of the General Assembly and the President of the Security Council, whereas the European Commission has a prominent position with multiple seats at the table of the Council of the EU.

Non-member states, other international organizations and NGOs – including civil society actors and business representatives – often have access to plenary organs and executive councils. In some international organizations they are formal members (with voting rights) and sit at the same table. In many international organizations, they are observers of associate members and typically sit in the back or have to be invited to the table. In the UN General Assembly, the Holy See and the State of Palestine are non-member state observers. They have far-reaching participation rights, but cannot vote. The EU as an international organization has also been granted exceptional rights to participate in the UN General Assembly. A whole range of other international organizations participate in the General Assembly as well. NGOs have less access, but can instead provide their input to the UN Economic and Social Council (ECOSOC).

Negotiations in plenary organs and executive councils

The plenary organs, executive councils and committees provide a formal setting for negotiations and decision-making among member states. It is the place where member states present their views and provide official statements. This formal setting has a number of advantages. It guarantees access and equal participation for all member states and other actors. It ensures that minutes are made and an official record of discussions is kept. Many plenary organs and executive councils are currently open to the public and interested parties or are streamed online. This creates considerable openness and transparency. At the same time, these formalized meetings are not necessarily the most effective way of coming to decisions. Ministers or ambassadors may not make concessions when they are in public. Furthermore, having a negotiation where one needs to go back and forward via the chair is not necessarily a speedy process. Therefore, informal negotiations are often organized and complement formal negotiations.

The UN, in particular, has set up an elaborate network of informal meetings. First of all, the work of the General Assembly is divided over six sub-committees, in which all member states have a seat. The committees organize informal consultations ('formal informals') which still have a strong formal nature: each committee has a chairperson and all member states sit in the same order as the UN General Assembly proper. Therefore work on UN resolutions is mostly done in the so-called informal informal consultations ('informal informals'). These meetings are still published in the daily UN journal, so all interested member states can attend, but normally they only involve the main negotiating parties. The constellation of the main negotiating parties varies from issue to issue. In the Second Committee dealing with economic and development cooperation, the main negotiating parties could include the USA, the EU, Russia, Japan and the G77 representing 130+ developing countries. There is one further level of informality: ironing out a deal over a coffee in the Café Austria ('Vienna Café') or a drink in the Delegates Lounge Bar.

The situation is slightly different with the UN Security Council. It can meet formally in open and closed sessions. Closed meetings are obviously not open to the public (nor accessible for the rest of the UN membership), there is no live streaming and no verbatim record of statements is kept, but these are formal meetings. The Security Council also regularly holds informal consultations and also informal meetings that only include the five permanent members. These working methods of the Security Council are a matter of regular criticism; so much so that the Security Council has so far failed to adopt rules of procedure (it still operates under 'provisional rules of procedure'). On the one hand, the secretive nature of Security Council dealings provide the great powers with an opportunity to 'blow off steam', provide concessions and craft deals without the risk that these get undermined by external exposure. At the same time, this secretive, informal process allows for very little accountability of the permanent members.

While the UN members have formalized 'the informal' into the working methods, in the EU there is a stronger emphasis on formal meetings. If deadlocks appear during formal meetings, the chairman can call for a break and address the issue informally with the relevant parties. For instance, during high-level EU summits, national leaders can be summoned to the office of the President of the European Council for informal consultations. Within the EU, deals are also often 'pre-cooked' prior to formal meetings. Leaders of Germany and France may be directly in contact in advance of a meeting to discuss their differences and then present a common front to the other member states. What is clear, both in the EU and UN, is that informal negotiations benefit the powerful member states. They have the administrative capacity to attend all informal meetings and they are no longer constrained by the rules of formal negotiations.

It is not only important whether the mode of negotiations is formal or informal. It is also important to pay attention to negotiation styles. It is conventional to distinguish, in this respect, hard bargaining from problem-solving (Hopmann 1995; Elgström & Jönsson 2000; Odell 2010). The logic of hard bargaining resembles a zero-sum game: if one party wins something, the other parties lose. Despite the generally cooperative atmosphere in international organizations, and the polite language used by diplomats, one should not be mistaken. There is a lot of hard bargaining going on in international organizations: from the redistributive negotiations over the EU budget to whether the UN Security Council authorizes the use of force. At the same time, many observers note that the dominant negotiation style resembles problem-solving. Generally, member states establish international organizations to address problems (see Chapters 2 and 3), so it is logical that many of the negotiations on the programme decisions within international organizations also concentrate on solving problems. For instance, in the UN Security Council, diplomats may work hard on finding 'language' for resolutions that is acceptable to all permanent members.

Voting procedures in plenary organs and executive councils

The negotiation process ends with the adoption (or not) of a decision. Depending on the constitutional and institutional structure of a particular international organization, decisions in the plenary organs and executive councils can be taken by consensus or majority voting (see Chapter 4). The consensus rule applies in many international organizations. This means that member states need to negotiate as long as it takes to get everyone on board. While most smaller member states may not want to 'block the consensus' all the time, they will ensure that they get heard on topics they care deeply about. While a consensus rule potentially makes negotiations more difficult, it does not mean that international organizations are weak or permanently gridlocked. NATO, for instance, famously has a consensus rule, but most observers would still rank it among the strongest international organizations.

As a rule of thumb, the more a programme decision of an international organization impinges on member states' autonomy, the more decision-making can be expected to require the consensus of all member states. States show little readiness to submit to a majority vote if their fundamental autonomy is at stake. But the more a programme decision leaves member states' autonomy untouched, the more likely the decision-making mode is majority voting. Therefore, legally binding programme decisions of international organizations are usually (though not exclusively) made through intergovernmental negotiations, while legally non-binding programme decisions can be taken through majority voting. However, this distinction reflects a rule of thumb rather than an empirical law. There are legally binding programme decisions that are taken by majority vote, and they seem to be on the rise (Hooghe et al. 2017; Zürn et al. 2012). Examples are UN Security Council resolutions in the issue area of anti-terrorism policies that impose legislative and administrative obligations on all UN member states or the expansion of (qualified) majority voting in the Council of the EU (Johnstone 2008; Hix & Høyland 2011).

Because programme decisions are so important, member states often have a veto. Yet at the same time, such decisions can hardly be said to satisfy strict criteria of fairness: the more powerful states have greater influence on the decisions made than less powerful states (Krasner 1991; Steinberg 2002). Nevertheless, making decisions in an international organizational framework can be fairer than making decisions outside such a framework where the more powerful states can, to a large extent, make their own decisions while simply ignoring the interests of less powerful states. The decision-making procedures of international organizations help less powerful states (or non-state actors) to get their interests heard (the so-called 'voice' function of international organizations) and give them the opportunity to demand compensation from more powerful states in return for their support of decisions favoured by major powers. This holds especially true where less powerful actors form coalitions among themselves or join a coalition led by a powerful state which then has to take their interests into consideration (Peterson 2007; Voeten 2000).

Also, when the number of member states increases, reaching consensus becomes more difficult (all other things being equal). It is thus not a surprise that, particularly in international organizations with a large membership, states have adopted majority-voting rules (Hooghe & Marks 2015). Voting in plenary organs and executive councils should be seen as separate from negotiations. Essentially, when a plenary organ or executive council puts a decision to a (majority) vote, it means that negotiations have failed to reach a consensus. It is useful to think of voting as 'negotiation failure', because for the implementation of decisions, international organizations are often dependent on the goodwill of the member states. There thus exists a strong risk that states may 'win' the vote, but that it ultimately results in little as the outvoted states fail to comply. As a result, there is a strong commitment in most international organizations to continue negotiations – even on dossiers where voting is an option – until a consensus is finally reached. In the EU, the estimate is that about 80 per cent of decisions are taken by consensus even though majority voting would be possible (Häge 2013).

It is important to note that voting is not always for the purpose of adopting decisions. In the UN Security Council and General Assembly, for instance, votes are also occasionally orchestrated for symbolic reasons. Because of intensive informal negotiations in the UN Security Council, the use of vetoes normally does not come as a surprise. Indeed, when it becomes clear that one of the five permanent members will veto a resolution, the resolution is often not put to a vote. The five permanent members, particularly since the end of the Cold War, normally do not want to put each other on the spot and prefer a cooperative working relationship. For instance, between 1990 and 2014, only 35 vetoes were cast in total (Wallensteen & Johansson 2016: Table 2.1). This comes down to about half a veto per permanent member per year. The situation does seem to be changing. For symbolic reasons, the Western powers now regularly put resolutions to a vote on the use of chemical weapons in Syria. Between 2015 and 2017, Russia vetoed such resolutions and others about a dozen times. In the UN General Assembly, it has been a long practice to vote on symbolic resolutions, such as on Israeli aggression. When voting takes place, in many international organizations, member states are often able to give an explanation of their vote – before and/or after the actual vote. These statements become a formal part of the record.

Because voting over programme decisions is increasing, it is important to provide several examples. Since the coming into force of the Single European Act in 1987, programme decisions within the EU can be made by majority vote. In contrast to most other international organizations, majority voting in the EU applies to both non-binding decisions and to legally binding ones. By first introducing and then successively expanding qualified majority voting in the Council of Ministers, EU decision-making has not only become speedier, but the role of the European Commission in decision-making has changed as well. Rather than acting as a broker who has to introduce proposals that are in the common interests of all member states, it can now come up with proposals that reflect the interests of a majority of the member states and engage in active coalition-building for its proposals. For example, in the late 1980s the Commission proposed moderate EU-wide emission standards for small cars, which initially met with resistance from both environmental laggards and leaders among the member states. The Commission then engaged in coalition-building with those member states, advocating for even stricter regulations and managed to persuade two resisting countries, namely Italy and Spain, of the necessity of the measures. Thus a revised Commission proposal, which included more demanding obligations than the original one, was passed by the (qualified) majority of the Council members. In the absence of qualified majority voting both the role of the Commission and the substance of the regulation would have looked quite different (Engel & Borrmann 1991: 205–09).

Legally non-binding resolutions of the UN General Assembly can be passed by a qualified majority. The deliberations about a new international economic order in the 1970s are a case in point. In the course of these lengthy and complex deliberations the developing countries tried to use the weight of their great number of votes in the General Assembly to force the developed countries to correct the structures within the global economy. The majority tried (and failed) to concentrate the costs on a small group of developed states while distributing the benefits to a large group, that is the majority of developing countries (Wilson & DiIulio 1997). Although this majority managed to pass various resolutions, their non-binding character allowed the developed countries generally to ignore them. Conversely, recent resolutions of the UN Security Council on anti-terrorism measures and the non-proliferation of weapons of mass destruction (for example, Resolution 1373 (2001) and Resolution 1540 (2004)) are legally binding programme decisions in that they impose generalized rather than case-specific standards of behaviour on all UN member states. In these cases of 'legislation' by the Security Council, binding programme decisions can be taken by a qualified majority. This has led observers to the conclusion that the principle of consensus in international law-making no longer holds without exceptions (Talmon 2005).

OPERATIONAL DECISIONS

Operational decisions are about the implementation of the norms and rules of programme decisions. Because the programme decisions often infringe on the sovereignty of states, states have to give up some of their autonomy. Operational decisions of international organizations, on the other hand, do not affect member states' autonomy to the same degree as programme decisions do. While they may be important, operational decisions normally take place in the framework set by programme decisions. As a result, states are less eager to dominate the decision-making process for operational decisions and it is easier for the permanent secretariats of international organizations to act in a relatively independent manner. States may also allow international courts to interpret the programme decisions. Operational decisions are therefore also not necessarily made in the plenary organs and executive councils. Even though in many international organizations states also remain in charge of operational decisions, in some international organizations states may instead opt for a system of delegated decision-making where they grant decision-making authority to a permanent secretariat, an international court or another implementing agency.

Delegated decision-making: Secretariats and agencies

Under the model of delegated decision-making, the secretariat has the discretion to make decisions in the scope of its competencies. This can include simple, everyday decisions, such as making travel arrangements for the Secretary-General to visit one of the member states or ordering catering for the annual plenary meeting. Yet in various international organizations, delegated decision-making goes much further. In the EU, the European Commission, for instance, has the power to adopt 'delegated acts' and 'implementing acts'. These often deal with technical issues, such as food safety standards, agriculture or the customs union and its tariffs, but with significant consequences. For instance, the energy labels put on electrical appliances in Europe are designed by Commission experts. The Commission also made decisions with regard to body scanners at airports across Europe. In the UN system, decision-making is also often delegated. The formal command of peacekeeping operations has been delegated to the Special Representative of the Secretary-General. He/she decides – and not the Security Council – whether blue helmets go out on mission patrol and can intervene in conflicts (within the overall mandate set by the Security Council).

Delegated decision-making is nothing exceptional. In the national context, we are used to the fact that most decisions are taken by the executive rather than the legislative branch of government. The advantages of delegated decision-making is that decisions can be made more swiftly and that the executive branch has much more expertise and administrative capacity. Indeed, we do not expect parliamentarians making laws in the national parliaments to also be involved in the implementation of those laws. They do not have the expertise, time or interest to make, for instance, decisions in individual asylum cases, about whether tax forms have been filled out properly, or which garbage collecting company needs to be hired. At the same time, national parliamentarians do make sure that they set up a range of control mechanisms to ensure that the executive does its work properly: the delegation of tasks can be precise, leaving little scope for interpretation; the executive can be given incentives to do its job properly; parliamentarians can do some random checks or can rely on citizens to notify them in case of bad behaviour on the side of the executive (e.g. McCubbins & Schwartz 1984; McCubbins et al. 1987). While the comparison with the national context is fitting, delegated decision-making in international organizations tends to be more limited, because it is more difficult to control international organizations (Dijkstra 2016).

It is difficult to say which operational decisions in which international organizations fall under a mode of delegated decision-making. A large number of factors (both on the side of the permanent secretariats and on the side of member states) affect the competencies of the permanent secretariats, so that it is hard to make tenable and generalizable predictions. Nevertheless, one can claim that, all other things being equal, the more the programmes of international organizations affect member states' autonomy, the less states are prepared to transfer control over operational decisions – through which these programmes are implemented – to an international bureaucracy. And conversely, the less the programmes impinge on their autonomy, the more the states are willing to transfer authority over operational decisions to the bureaucracy. At the same time, the stronger the competencies of the permanent secretariats, the more control we can also expect from the side of the member states (Hawkins et al. 2006; Dijkstra 2016). In the EU, for instance, the member states have set up a rather elaborate system of 'comitology', consisting of around 250 member states committees where the Commission officials need to explain the contents of delegated implementing acts (Brandsma & Blom-Hansen 2017).

Also the fact that the member states may delegate their decisions to a permanent secretariat does not mean they leave the secretariat alone. States tend to continuously meddle in the affairs of the permanent secretariat (Urpelainen 2012). Powerful member states generally exert a large influence on appointments of the heads of international organizations' secretariats. For instance, the permanent five members of the Security Council have a veto right over who gets to be the UN Secretary-General. Yet the interference goes further. High-level positions within permanent secretariats (for instance, the UN Under-Secretaries-General or Directorate-Generals in the European Commission) are often informally given to the major powers which then use these positions to affect decisions (Kleine 2013). Yet even at the level of regular staff, we can witness the prominence of the major powers and donor countries, which are overrepresented (Parízek 2017). Still, empirical research on international bureaucracies has shown that the capacities of even the most powerful states to control, rein in and reform bureaucracies are frequently limited (Barnett & Finnemore 2004; Nielson et al. 2006; Weaver 2008).

How operational decision-making works in practice can be illustrated by looking at the EU as well as the UN. Important operational decisions that are entirely outsourced to implementing agents without much control by the member states tend to be rare. The decisions the European Central Bank (ECB) takes regarding European monetary policy are an important exception. Since economic and monetary union was completed, the ECB has been solely responsible for the monetary policy of the current 19 EU member states in the Eurozone. Decisions are made by the Governing Council, which consists of the six members of the Executive Board and the governors of the national central banks from the 19 euro countries. The Governing Council is independent in its monetary policy decisions from governments. Thus it can make decisions on interest rates entirely according to the requirement, given to it by statute, to safeguard currency stability in the Eurozone. The Governing Council analyses the prevalent economic situation in the Eurozone, especially with regard to possible inflationary risks. Having weighed up the costs and benefits of the different options it will take the decision which it thinks most likely to ensure currency stability.

Another example of delegated decision-making in the EU is the regulation of agricultural markets and subsidization of European farmers. This is characterized by a series of standardized and strictly programmed decision-making processes. While the broader agricultural policy programme of the EU is set by intergovernmental negotiations and majority-voting procedures, the implementation of European agricultural policies is reached through standard operating procedures of the competent department of the European Commission (see Von Urff 2000). Historically, guaranteed minimum prices for European farmers were fixed through standard operating procedures. To avoid external products undercutting the guaranteed prices on the EU market, levies were imposed on agricultural imports. These were payments similar to customs duties levied on products from states outside the EU to maintain the competitiveness of more expensive EU agricultural products. Given the price fluctuation of some of these products, the value of these import levies had to be set anew on an almost daily basis. It was therefore simpler to follow a standard operating procedure for this exercise, whereby the competent department in the European Commission set the levies in such a way as to level out the difference between world market prices and the internally guaranteed price (Von Urff 2000). While the European Common Agricultural Policy (CAP) has gradually moved away from this kind of routinized price stabilization, more recent means of support to farmers (such as direct payments) are also allocated through standard operating procedures. For example, the competent directorate of the Commission routinely checks whether farmers applying for direct payments meet certain standards concerning public, animal and plant health, the environment and animal welfare.

An important development in the EU is furthermore the establishment of more than 40 agencies located throughout Europe (Majone 1997; Keleman 2002; Wonka & Rittberger 2010). Many of these agencies have important implementing functions. For instance, the newly established European Border and Coast Guard Agency (previously Frontex) can deploy border guards to EU and non-EU countries to strengthen national capacities. It is also deployed in the Mediterranean Sea to guard against irregular migration. The 1000 staff members of the EU Agency for Law Enforcement Cooperation (Europol), meanwhile, support the police services of member states in preventing and combating serious cross-border crime. The European Medicines Agency approves new drugs for the European market, whereas the European Food Safety Authority provides expertise concerning food safety risks. Many of these EU agencies formally report to the European Commission, and are thus indirectly being held accountable, but have developed considerable de facto authority of their own (Busuioc 2013). The case of the EU agencies not only shows the extent of delegated decision-making in international organizations, but also how important operational decisions can actually be.

In the UN we can also find operational decisions made according to delegated decision-making. The decisions of the UN Special Commissions that had to verify the dismantling of weapons of mass destruction in Iraq after the Gulf War of 1991 are an example. These Special Commissions were established by the Security Council as a result of Resolution 687 (1991). In order to track down and eliminate all the components of the weapons of mass destruction programme, the Special Commissions – first the United Nations Special Commission (UNSCOM) (1991–97) and later the United Nations Monitoring, Verification and Inspection Commission (UNMOVIC) (1999–2007) – had to take many decisions. For example, they had to determine how to inspect Iraqi installations suspected of storing weapons of mass destruction, how to react to Iraq's refusal to allow the inspection commission access to certain installations and how to guarantee that Iraq would be permanently unable to manufacture or acquire new weapons of mass destruction. The necessary operational decisions were taken by the Special Commissions in close cooperation with the UN Secretary-General. Furthermore, the chairpersons of the Special Commissions were obliged to report regularly to the Security Council through the Secretary-General on the implementation of their mandate. Thus the Special Commissions were not entirely free in their decisions yet, were not totally constrained in reaching decisions either by the Security Council or by the Secretary-General. Rather, decisions occurred by means of bureaucratic politics between the Special Commissions and especially its chairpersons, the Secretary-General, the Security Council and, in particular, the representatives of the latter's permanent members.

Delegated decision-making: Courts

Delegated decision-making also takes place through international courts. In various international organizations states have delegated the authority to interpret programme decisions to courts. As such, the judgments of international courts are also operational decisions. After all, through their judgments courts help to implement the norms and rules of programme decisions (see Chapter 7). There are different sorts of international courts. The most frequent are arbitration tribunals that aim to settle conflicts between member states by providing relatively neutral third-party interpretation of the norms and rules that member states have set themselves. The EU provides a clear example. In the original treaties, for instance, the EU member states adopted a policy programme on the freedom of movement of workers. Yet an important question was how to define a 'worker'. Would freedom of movement also extent to part-time workers, interns or even unemployed job seekers? It was also up to the European Court of Justice (ECJ) to make operational decisions. It eventually came up with a rather expansive interpretation of the freedom of movement. Other types of courts are the international criminal courts and war crimes tribunals. They too make operational decisions through their judgments, for instance by deciding whether individuals are guilty of war crimes.

One of the key debates among academics is the politics of international courts. Precisely because arbitration courts need to settle conflicts between the member states, they need to maintain some distance and stand above the parties. Similarly, the main reason to have war crimes tribunals is their moral authority to interpret the law. The control of member states over delegated decision-making by international courts is therefore more limited than their control over secretariats (Tallberg 2000). This raises the question of whether international courts may use their considerable authority to pursue a political agenda. For instance, the ECJ is often said to push for more European integration (Alter 2001). The member states nevertheless exert still some control over courts. For instance, they often nominate the judges to be appointed to international courts (Elsig & Pollack 2014). International courts are also aware that they cannot make member states comply with their judgments, so they will have to take political sensitivities into account (see Chapter 7). Member states may also change the law if they feel that judgments are unsatisfactory.

CONCLUSION

International organizations produce many decisions every day. And how international organizations convert inputs into outputs matters. International organizations are more than the simple sum of their member states. Based on an elaborate constitutional and institutional structure, member states and other actors have to follow a set of rules and procedures in order to arrive at a final decision. How international organizations convert inputs into outputs depends on the institutional particularities of the individual international organizations: the UN Security Council votes over questions of war and peace, whereas the North Atlantic Council takes decisions by consensus. To explain such an important difference, we need to know the historical context and understand how political power is situated in both international organizations. That said, this chapter has outlined two general models of decision-making, based on whether the relevant decision concerns a programme or operational decision.

Programme decisions involve the generation of norms and rules that apply to the member states (and occasionally even non-member states and other actors). Member states are therefore reluctant to grant permanent secretariats substantial decision-making authority over programme decisions. Indeed the 'big' programme decisions are often made at intergovernmental conferences with limited input by the permanent secretariats. More day-to-day programme decisions within the context of international organizations often require consensus of the member states. Operational decisions, on the other hand, relate to the implementation of these norms and rules. This allows for delegated decision-making by the secretariat or other implementing agencies. It does not imply that operational decisions do not matter. Indeed, operational decisions may have actual concrete consequences. While secretariats can have considerable decision-making authority over operational decisions, their authority is not absolute. Normally, delegated decision-making comes with fine-grained control by the member states. The important point is to distinguish different types of decisions taken in international organizations and to offer a heuristic device to analytically simplify the ever-growing complexity of international organizations' decision-making.

Discussion Questions

1. What are the main differences between programme decisions and operational decisions? Illustrate your answer with specific examples of decision-making in international organizations.
2. If you compare programme decisions with operational decisions, which have the greatest potential to infringe on the autonomy of member states? How is this reflected in the decision-making processes?
3. What is potentially more significant: the provision in the UN Charter that states shall refrain from the use of force, or the delegation of decision-making authority to a UN peacekeeping commander in Mali who has to make life/death decisions? Provide arguments for both.

Further Reading

Dimitrov, Rado S. 2016. The Paris agreement on climate change: Behind closed doors, in: *Global Environmental Politics* 16: 3, 1–11.

Hawkins, Darren, Lake, David A., Nielson, Daniel L., & Tierney, Michael J. (eds) 2006. *Delegation and Agency in International Organizations*, Cambridge: Cambridge University Press.

Lewis, Jeffrey 2005. The Janus face of Brussels: Socialization and everyday decision making in the European Union, in: *International Organization* 59: 4, 937–71.

Reinalda, Bob & Verbeek, Bertjan (eds) 2004. *Decision Making Within International Organisations*, London: Routledge.

7 Output: What International Organizations Produce

International organizations convert inputs into outputs. In the preceding chapters, we have focused on the inputs as well as the structures, actors and processes that shape decision-making in international organizations. But arguably, what matters most is what comes out of international organizations: the policies that international organizations produce. In this chapter we take a systematic look at the main outputs of international organizations. We differentiate between *policy programmes* and *operational activities* (see Figure 7.1).

Policy programmes are the result of policy decisions and set norms and rules for the member states of international organizations and occasionally also non-member states and private actors. We can distinguish between regulatory policy programmes that aim at directing the behaviour of social actors and redistributive policy programmes that aim at redistributing rights and duties among the member states of international organizations. Apart from the objectives of policy programmes, it is also important to distinguish between binding and non-binding policy programmes. Through operational activities, international organizations implement policy programmes. While in many international organizations implementation is done by the member states themselves, various international organizations do perform a number of operational tasks. They can, for instance, further specify the policy programme or implement a policy programme. In addition, operational activities may include the monitoring of implementation by the member states, adjudicating between the member states in case of conflicts, or imposing sanctions for non-compliance. As part of the operational activities, international organizations take operational decisions, often through delegated decision-making procedures (see Chapter 6).

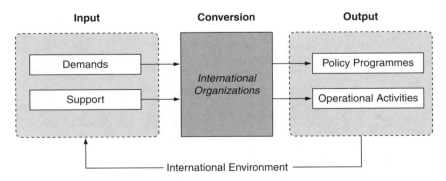

Figure 7.1   The political system of international organizations (output)

After discussing different kinds of outputs, this chapter addresses the effectiveness of outputs produced by international organizations. While international organizations can adopt a variety of outputs, such as policies, laws, statements and declarations, and launch all kinds of operational activities, such as development programmes or peacekeeping missions, this still tells us little about the outcomes of such outputs. The fact that the United Nations (UN) Security Council puts something in a resolution does not mean that it will ultimately happen on the ground in a peacekeeping mission in Africa. Furthermore, even if the outcomes are broadly in line with the intended goals of an international organization, it is not yet guaranteed that the intended outcomes also have the intended impact. Peacekeeping missions, for instance, can be very effective in bringing security and safety on the ground, but it does not mean that they provide a durable solution to an ongoing conflict.

POLICY PROGRAMMES

Policy programmes are sets of norms and rules aimed at directing the behaviour of social actors. While they usually set normative standards for the behaviour of their members, they can also touch upon the interaction between the members and the international organization itself. Sometimes international organizations also formulate norms and rules that directly address non-state actors that are not members of the international organization. Policy programmes are the result of programme decisions of international organizations. Policy programmes can be differentiated, first, according to the objectives their norms and rules are intended to reach and, secondly, according to the degree to which their norms and rules are legally binding.

Objectives

Policy programmes in general, and not just in international organizations, are intended to have diverse effects, depending on whether they are regulatory programmes, distributive programmes or redistributive programmes (Lowi 1964). For international organizations, the distinction between regulatory and redistributive programmes is particularly relevant. Few international organizations engage in distributive programmes.

Regulatory programmes aim to direct the behaviour of social actors in order to achieve desirable interactions. To this end, norms and rules of behaviour are set that prescribe or proscribe certain behaviour in specified circumstances. They act as guidelines for actors (Lowi 1964: 694). National examples of regulatory programmes whose norms and rules regulate interactions are criminal law, environmental law, human rights law and consumer protection law. At the international level, regulatory policy programmes help states to avoid undesirable interactions such as wars, or to achieve desirable interactions such as peace. Hence the UN Charter's ban on the threat or use of force is an example of a regulatory programme. Other examples are the Nuclear Non-Proliferation Treaty (NPT), proscribing the acquisition of nuclear weapons for all states apart from China, France, Russia, the United Kingdom and USA; the General Agreement on Tariffs and Trade (GATT), prescribing that all World Trade Organization (WTO) member states have to grant most-favoured nation treatment to all other member states; or the Montreal Protocol on Substances that Deplete the Ozone Layer to the Vienna Convention for the Protection of the Ozone Layer, prescribing that all states have to ban the use of chemicals such as chlorofluorocarbons (CFCs) which contribute to the depletion of the ozone layer.

The European Union (EU) is perhaps the international organization with the most elaborate regulatory programmes. It has been compared to a regulatory state (Majone 1994). In support of its internal market, the EU has vigorously tried to take away all possible obstacles to the freedom of people, goods and services. It has done so partially through 'negative integration' – that is to try to establish the principle that goods (but also people and services), which are legally brought to the market in one member state, should be allowed automatic market access in all member states. For instance, if a bottle of alcohol is considered safe in one member state (and does not cause a health risk), it should be considered safe in all the member states (and cannot be excluded from the market on health grounds). While this simple rule is attractive and has resulted in considerable market integration in the EU, the process of negative integration has also been criticized: it results, almost by default, in deregulation, social dumping and a 'race to the bottom'. After all, companies may move production to member states with business-friendly rules. This negative integration approach has therefore been complemented by additional regulatory programmes that focus on the harmonization of rules across the EU. For instance, the EU has adopted a rule on the maximum energy that vacuum cleaners can use. Rather than having separate rules in every member state and a potential race to the bottom, the EU considers that such harmonization results in a stronger internal market.

Redistributive programmes are directed towards social actors' behaviour in order to change the distribution of goods and services among them. They benefit some actors while others are burdened with additional costs (Lowi 1964: 711). The best-known examples of redistributive programmes at the national level are welfare state policies of providing housing, education, unemployment benefits or health care. Many of these programmes are subsidized by the state, which collects taxes through a progressive income tax scheme in which those with a higher income pay a proportionately higher level of income tax than those with a lower one. Hence costs are concentrated on certain social groups to reallocate them as benefits to other groups. At the international level, within international organizations, there are also examples of redistributive programmes. For instance, much of the UN system is concerned with development assistance and the EU has its Structural and Cohesion Funds which redistribute money to the poorer member states and regions. At the same time, member states of international organizations are not necessarily keen to redistribute a lot of funding. International solidarity tends to be lower than national solidarity. While taxpayers may be willing to make money available for citizens in a different country struck by humanitarian disaster, they may not be willing to hand out unemployment benefits or pay for social housing in other countries. Donor countries have only committed to spend 0.7 per cent of their gross domestic product (GDP) on development assistance (yet most donor countries do not meet this target).

We find a large number of redistributive programmes run by international organizations such as the UN Development Programme (UNDP), World Food Programme (WFP) or the UN Industrial Development Organization (UNIDO). Their principal concern is the transfer of resources from developed to developing countries (Marshall 2008; Murphy 2006). The Bretton Woods institutions, such as the World Bank and International Monetary Fund (IMF), can also be said to engage in redistributive programmes. That said, the World Bank provides loans and thus eventually wants its money back. It does not provide a blank cheque. The same goes for the IMF, which provides bridging loans for member states unable to get money from the financial markets. It is also important to note that in the case of both international organizations, the 'donor' countries benefit as well. As a result of the support of the IMF, borrowing member states may not have to default on their loans.

Within the EU, programmes such as those of the Structural and Cohesion Funds redistribute material resources between member states (Hix 2005: 289–95). While the costs of these programmes are carried by all member states, the benefits are concentrated on less advanced member states or poor regions within member states. More recently, the EU has also established the European Globalisation Adjustment Fund, the European Social Fund, and the Youth Employment Initiative. These are all smaller-scale redistributive initiatives that target some of the economic and social discrepancies within the European internal market. It is also worth underlining that the Common Agricultural Policy (CAP) and the Research and Innovation Framework have significant redistributive effects. While the CAP supports all farmers, some member states have more farmers than others and thus benefit more. The Research and Innovation Framework is interesting, because it goes in the other direction: member states from north-west Europe mainly benefit at the expense of some of the poorer countries.

Binding nature

In addition to the differentiation based on the objectives that norms and rules of policy programmes may have, one can also distinguish them according to whether their norms and rules are legally binding (Abbott et al. 2000; Abbott & Snidal 2000). The degree of legal obligation does not necessarily correlate with the level of member states' compliance. Nonetheless, it certainly remains an important characteristic of the programmes, whether they contain legally binding obligations or are simply political recommendations. It is not unusual to find within one and the same international organization the coexistence of both legally binding and non-binding programmes.

The EU is one of the few international organizations that have the authority to make programmes directly binding not only on member states but also on private actors within member states. In particular, in matters pertaining to the internal market the EU has long used regulations and directives as part of its policy programme. Regulations are legally binding and applicable from the moment they have been enacted by the EU, without the need for national authorities to implement them through domestic law. Directives, although binding, give member states' authorities some discretion in how to make them applicable by implementation through domestic law. In addition, there are also EU programmes which are not legally binding, embodying recommendations or opinions which express political objectives rather than legal obligations. Since the coming into force of the Treaty of Lisbon (2009) the EU's competencies to pass legally binding policy programmes (directives and regulations) are no longer limited to internal market policies but also include issues dealing with police and judicial cooperation.

In the UN, many policy programmes have no legally binding effect. With the exception of decisions on budgetary questions or the UN's internal organization, resolutions and declarations of the UN General Assembly merely have the character of recommendations. If repeated frequently the programmes contained in such resolutions may become legally binding as international customary law, but only if most UN member states agree (in their practice and their legal opinions) to that effect. By contrast, resolutions of the UN Security Council under Chapter VII of the UN Charter are immediately binding. Conventions, agreements or treaties negotiated within the framework of the UN or its Specialized Agencies can also become legally binding on member states. But this usually requires their ratification by the states who are party to the relevant treaty, agreement or convention (see Chapter 6). In the case of many treaties, agreements and conventions the UN General Assembly avails itself of the possibility of recommending an early signature and ratification in a resolution to the member states.

OPERATIONAL ACTIVITIES

In addition to policy programmes, a large part of the output of the work of international organizations takes an operational form. Operational activities of international organizations are the result of operational decisions which relate to the implementation of policy programmes (Mayntz 1977). We can differentiate five types of operations:

1. specification of the norms and rules of policy programmes;
2. implementation of (specified) norms and rules;
3. monitoring of the implementation of policy programmes;
4. adjudication in cases of alleged non-compliance;
5. imposition of sanctions in cases of non-compliance.

Specification

The norms and rules of policy programmes generally require further specification in order to implement them. This specification is often done by member states' authorities. Member states' parliaments, governments or bureaucracies select the means and measures to fulfil the commitments laid down in international organizations' policy programmes. Yet in numerous international organizations such as the EU, the IMF, the World Bank and also the UN, the specification of programmes has become the responsibility of the organizations themselves. For example, as noted above, the EU internal market programme requires the harmonization of technical and legal standards. But rather than defining these standards in the member states, the programme provides that the specification of the actual standards be made by the organs of the EU themselves. Similarly the World Bank draws up detailed conditions for projects in developing countries. And several measures taken by the UN Security Council should be interpreted as operational decisions specifying its programme of maintaining international peace and security. For instance, the Security Council referred the situation in Sudan/Darfur in 2005 to the International Criminal Court for a war crimes investigation.

Sometimes, international organizations do not conduct the specification of general policy programmes themselves, but either explicitly transfer this task to transnational expert bodies or endorse the activities of private bodies for that purpose. For example, the EU only defines broad minimum requirements in technical product standards and mandates private standard-setting bodies to specify which conditions must be met for these broad requirements to be fulfilled (Abbott et al. 2000). In a similar way, the EU decided that stock market-listed European companies should use uniform international accounting standards. Rather than defining these standards itself, the EU endorsed the standards developed by the private International Accounting Standards Board. Another example is the WTO's practice of referring to decisions of the Codex Alimentarius Commission in regulations on food safety.

Implementation

Through the specification of programmes international organizations not only help states to implement norms and rules, but sometimes provide a starting point for international organizations to implement the norms and rules directly themselves. In general, however, this possibility is limited and the implementation of internationally agreed programmes remains the prerogative of member states' authorities, their parliaments, governments and bureaucracies. Thus the standards for the quality of drinking water, for instance, are set for all member states by the EU, but the measures necessary for their implementation, such as the construction of water-purification plants, are taken by the relevant authorities within EU member states.

The direct implementation of policy programmes through international organizations occurs whenever those organizations, on the basis of their informational, financial and personnel resources, can provide support for the activities desired by member states. The EU, for instance, directly administered the fixed-price system for European agricultural markets while the UN, along with many of its Specialized Agencies, is heavily engaged in providing humanitarian aid for war-torn countries, managing technical assistance for developing countries, administering funds for development, and keeping up research institutions. Examples of direct implementation by the UN can also be found with respect to its many peacekeeping missions. In 2018, it nearly had 100,000 blue helmets under its command spread over 16 missions on different continents. Through its peacekeeping activities the UN even assumed full administrative responsibilities in Kosovo and East Timor for a limited period of time under the Security Council Resolutions 1244 (Kosovo) and 1272 (East Timor) (both 1999) (Schmitt 2009).

International organizations may also transfer the implementation of policy programmes to non-state actors who then act on behalf of the international organization. For example, the UN and several of its Specialized Agencies have for a long time relied on humanitarian non-governmental organizations (NGOs) in the implementation of development assistance, humanitarian relief and disaster response programmes. The Basel Committee on Banking Supervision (BCBS) heavily relies on private actors (banks and credit rating agencies) in the implementation of international capital reserve standards. The BCBS requires banks to fulfil certain minimum capital reserve requirements. These capital reserve requirements are based on banks' credit risk exposure: the more risky banks' investments are, the higher their capital reserve requirements will be. But the BCBS does not measure banks' credit risk itself. Instead, it relies, among others, on banks' and private credit rating agencies' risk assessments (see Kruck 2011). These examples illustrate that international organizations do not necessarily implement their policy programmes themselves, even if they have the authority to do so. They increasingly opt for transferring or outsourcing the implementation of policy programmes to non-state actors whom they endorse, support, coordinate and/or monitor (see Abbott et al. 2015). This is particularly likely when the international organization lacks time, knowledge and/or material resources to implement the programmes itself.

Monitoring

Since implementation of norms and rules is still mostly undertaken by member states rather than by the international organization itself or its agents, monitoring is required. Without monitoring, member states might feel tempted to disregard the policy programmes of international organizations, because they would expect this would go unnoticed or that other states could disregard these programmes without being caught. In order to mitigate this temptation, many international organizations are given the task of monitoring member states' compliance with agreed policy programmes (Chayes & Chayes 1995; Moravcsik 1998; Underdal 1998).

A good example is the International Atomic Energy Agency (IAEA), which monitors member states' compliance with the NPT of 1968. Its safeguard system allows the IAEA to request reports about civilian nuclear activities from the signatory states. More remarkably, it also has the right to undertake on-site inspections of civilian nuclear facilities. Through these inspections the IAEA is able to sustain the expectation among most signatory states that none of them could divert nuclear material from civilian to military uses. This expectation – undermined, for instance, by Iraq's undetected nuclear weapons programme of the 1980s – was not only the precondition for signatory states to comply with the NPT, but was also for many states a precondition for renouncing nuclear weapons by signing the treaty in the first place.

The far-reaching monitoring activities by the IAEA are certainly an exception. Even the European Commission's abilities to monitor member states' compliance with EU norms and rules are more limited. This is illustrated, for example, by the Commission's inability to get a clear picture of Greece's fiscal policies that ultimately led to a severe debt crisis and a massive EU/IMF bailout package in 2010. Greece had actually broken EU debt ceilings for years before its financial collapse. As a result, the EU has introduced a stronger monitoring mechanism within the context of the so-called European Semester. Nonetheless, many international organizations responsible for the implementation of international environmental agreements have noteworthy monitoring options. For instance, if the International Whaling Commission (IWC) allows the resumption of commercial whaling, it will have the right to place international observers on whaling vessels in order to monitor whalers' compliance with IWC regulations. Moreover, many of today's arms control treaties provide for far-reaching 'verification' activities.

Again, international organizations do not only pursue monitoring on their own. They also lend support to, and draw on, the contributions of non-state actors to the monitoring of compliance with international norms and rules. This is particularly salient in the issue area of human rights protection. On the one hand, international organizations provide human rights NGOs with information, an organizational platform for action and internationally agreed human rights instruments that serve as authoritative standards and benchmarks against which states' human rights records can be measured. On the other hand, due to time, resource and political constraints, international organizations such as the UN Office of the High Commissioner for Human Rights (OHCHR) are heavily dependent on human rights NGOs such as Amnesty International or Human Rights Watch for monitoring and information provision. Therefore, organizations such as OHCHR have created institutionalized channels of access through which NGOs can pass on information on human rights abuses (Sweeney & Saito 2009). International organizations thus coordinate, actively support and make use of NGOs' monitoring activities.

Adjudication

Monitoring alone cannot reliably guarantee the compliance of member states. A serious source of non-compliance is that, in doubtful cases, the member states concerned can often claim that they are in compliance while other member states may accuse them of violating the organization's programmes. If no third party is allowed to adjudicate such disputes and provide authoritative interpretations of the relevant policy programmes, the door is wide open to violations of the organization's policy programme. Member states' compliance can only reasonably be expected if they cannot effectively ignore programme requirements through arbitrary interpretation. For this reason many international organizations are given the task of adjudicating disputes about member states' compliance. They can thereby contribute to a relatively unbiased interpretation of their policy programmes. This is particularly the case for those organizations which do not only sustain member states' efforts to settle disputes by diplomatic means but also have their own courts or court-like bodies able to adjudicate disputes about legal claims and obligations independently of member states (Keohane et al. 2000; Zangl 2008).

In the UN, the International Court of Justice (ICJ) is generally responsible for the adjudication of disputes about member states' compliance. Its competencies are, however, very limited since it can only become involved if the disputing states accept its jurisdiction. In fact, the Security Council and the Human Rights Council are more important with respect to the adjudication of disputes about member states' non-compliance with UN programmes. Under Article 39 of the UN Charter the Security Council can ascertain breaches of the ban on the use of force and condemn such violations of the UN Charter (Mondré 2009). Likewise, one of the Human Rights Council's tasks is to decide in disputes about member states' alleged violations of human rights obligations. That is to say, both the Security Council and the Human Rights Council are authorized to condemn member states that are violating fundamental legal obligations (Cronin 2008).

In the EU, the European Court of Justice (ECJ) is generally responsible for the adjudication of disputes about member states' compliance (Alter 2001). The ECJ, unlike the Security Council and the Commission on Human Rights but similarly to the ICJ, is politically independent. Unlike the ICJ, and similarly in this regard to the Security Council and the Human Rights Council, it can examine breaches of binding policy programmes without being dependent on special authorization by the parties in dispute. The ECJ provides access not only for states but also for both supranational and private actors. Thus the European Commission can charge member states before the ECJ if it deems that they have violated community laws. What is more, even private actors can, under certain conditions, appeal to the ECJ if member states do not comply with EU laws (Alter 2001; Oppermann et al. 2009: 267–90).

Sanctions

Adjudication by international organizations may help to bring about member states' compliance with the norms and rules of their policy programmes. If, however, a member state is not prepared to abide by the ruling handed down by a court or a court-like body, sanctions may be needed. In fact, international organizations can sometimes help efforts to employ sanctions against states that continuously disregard their international commitments. Nevertheless, international organizations should in most cases not be regarded as central authorities entrusted with the capacities to employ sanctions against states violating their policy programmes. Rather, they serve as agents that help to coordinate member states' efforts to impose sanctions against cheats.

In many international organizations sanctions are limited to the publication – and possible condemnation – of a member state's violation of international commitments. Nevertheless, these sanctions, albeit moderate, expose the relevant state to moral pressure, internationally by other states and domestically by concerned groups (Risse-Kappen 1995). In addition, this might damage the state's reputation as a trustworthy partner that respects the principle of *pacta sunt servanda* (agreements must be kept), grounded in international law. Losing this reputation can create marked negotiating disadvantages within and outside international organizations (Guzman 2008). It might, for instance, have the effect that other states make reliable monitoring activities of international organizations henceforth a precondition for negotiated agreements with the disreputable state (Keohane 1984; Young 1979: 19). Overall, it might make striking a deal that benefits the disreputable state more costly for this state.

Some international organizations can go beyond mere moral sanctions. They can exclude member states that continuously violate their obligations. This option is enshrined in the foundation treaties of many international organizations. In the UN the General Assembly can, on the recommendation of the Security Council, exclude members who have persistently acted against the Charter. The Statute of the Council of Europe provides for states violating the principles of the organization to be asked to resign. In inclusive organizations such as the Global Compact, non-state members that persistently and severely neglect standards of behaviour defined by the organization can be 'de-listed', that is their membership can be temporarily suspended or even completely terminated. However, the exclusion of members from international organizations has proved to be a double-edged sword. On the one hand, the organization can punish violators through their exclusion, but, on the other hand, it thereby loses the possibility of further influencing these states. This was the experience of the Council of Europe with human rights violations in Greece after the Colonels' Coup of 1967 (List 1991). The Council of Europe, on the other hand, stopped short of expelling Russia from the organization at the end of the 1990s despite its human rights violations in Chechnya.

A further possibility for some international organizations lies in suspending certain rights enjoyed by the state concerned through its membership of the organization. Thus the UN General Assembly, on the recommendation of the Security Council, can suspend member states' right to vote in the General Assembly if the Security Council has imposed enforcement measures against them (Article 6 UN Charter). Only since the Treaty of Amsterdam (1999) does the EU have the possibility of limiting member states' rights deriving from their membership. However, this is not possible for a simple infringement of the organization's policy programmes but rather presupposes a serious and persistent violation of the principles of democracy, human rights and basic freedoms, and the rule of law. This violation must be unanimously established by the Council (meeting in the composition of the heads of state or government with the defaulting member state being excluded) with the agreement of the Parliament.

The EU also has the possibility of imposing fines on states that persistently infringe an EU directive or regulation. If a member state, after having been condemned by the ECJ for infringing an EU directive or regulation, is unwilling to correct its infringement the Commission can ask the ECJ to decide upon fines. However, the EU depends on the cooperation of the member state concerned to collect the fine. If the respective member state refuses to pay, the EU can hardly do anything about it (Oppermann et al. 2009: 259–62).

In the UN, the Security Council can impose non-military sanctions on states to counter a breach of, or threat to, the peace or an act of aggression. However, to be able to effectively impose sanctions such as an arms, air or trade embargo, it has to rely on the support of other member states to implement the sanctions decided by the Council. Yet even in cases where member states actually impose sanctions the effectiveness of such measures cannot be taken for granted. For example, the 1977 arms embargo against South Africa did not lead to a behavioural adjustment by the castigated state. The poor effectiveness of sanctions has led some authors to question whether they can be an effective instrument to secure member states' compliance with international obligations (Chayes & Chayes 1995). Other authors support 'smart sanctions' like financial sanctions, boycotts on specific commodities (diamonds, oil, timber products), travel sanctions and arms embargoes targeting specific persons and areas of an economy (Drezner 2011).

If the UN Security Council deems it necessary it can go beyond embargoes and impose military enforcement measures. To do so, however, it again depends in fact, if not strictly speaking in law, on member states being ready to supply troops and to deploy them under UN tactical and operational command. In authorizing military enforcement measures the Security Council is thus in practice limited by states' willingness to engage in enforcement actions. In the 1990s the Security Council authorized some member states to intervene with force in the humanitarian catastrophes in Somalia (1992), Bosnia (1992), Rwanda (1994) and Haiti (1994) which it determined to be threats to peace (Abiew 1999; Pape 1997). Finally, in September 2001, for the first time, the Security Council authorized military measures to combat international terrorism particularly (though not exclusively) in Afghanistan. It agreed that the USA had been attacked and therefore had the right to defend itself. As a next step, in December 2001, the Security Council (Resolution 1386) approved of the creation of a peace-enforcing International Security Assistance Force (ISAF) for Afghanistan led by NATO (2003–14) which officially focused on the political and economic reconstruction of Afghanistan but also tried to prevent international terrorism.

POLICY EFFECTIVENESS

International organizations convert inputs into outputs. Some international organizations are good at performing this function and produce a lot of outputs. Other international organizations are less successful in turning input into output (Tallberg et al. 2016). Member states may veto decisions, insufficient expertise may be available in the permanent secretariat, or mechanisms for monitoring, adjudication or sanctions may be absent. Yet even when an international organization produces output, it is not guaranteed that the output will ultimately have the intended effect. It is therefore important to take one additional step: to evaluate the effectiveness of the output.

Scholars usually discuss the effectiveness of policy in terms of (1) output, (2) outcome and (3) impact (Easton 1965; Underdal 1992, 2004; Young 2001, 2004; Gutner & Thompson 2010; Tallberg et al. 2016). Much of this chapter has already discussed output. When the permanent members of the UN Security Council reacted to member states' concerns about the aggression of the Gaddafi regime against the Libyan people in 2011 (input) by adopting within days a resolution (output), the Security Council showed a remarkable *output* effectiveness: the resolution was adopted quickly, had substance, and was legally binding. The adoption of this resolution, in turn, resulted in the NATO military intervention establishing a no-fly zone and taking out convoys of Gaddafi forces (outcome). In this sense, *outcome* effectiveness was also high: the outcome was broadly in line with the objectives set by the Security Council. The immediate effect of the NATO military intervention was the security and protection of the Libyan population (impact). This impact was in line with the logic of the resolution and the Security Council's general mandate in peace and security: therefore *impact* effectiveness was also high. At the same time, when looking back at this episode in 2011, we can also conclude that the death of Gaddafi (which was an outcome) has resulted in enduring civil unrest in Libya and ultimately led to the death of thousands of civilians (impact). The longer-term impact was therefore perhaps not very effective.

The effectiveness of an international organization therefore depends on whether the international organization 'solves the problem that motivated its establishment' (Underdal 2002: 11; cf. Young 1999: jacket). The UN Framework Convention on Climate Change (UNFCCC) is therefore effective to the extent that it reduces climate change. The WTO is effective when it reduces trade barriers and increases trade volumes among the membership. And since the goal of a UN peacekeeping mission is to 'keep the peace', it makes sense to measure whether the peace was kept after a (civil) war (Doyle & Sambanis 2000; Fortna 2004a, 2008). While international policy can thus be measured against the status quo and the optimal policy outcome (Underdal 1992; Sprinz & Helm 1999; Helm & Sprinz 2000), optimal policy outcomes are not necessarily realistic. The optimal policy outcome in global warming may be to bring the average global temperature back to pre-industrial levels, but this will not be possible. Therefore the Paris Agreement negotiated under the framework of the UNFCCC set the benchmark to keep the global temperature rise below 2 degrees Celsius above pre-industrial levels. Its effectiveness should therefore be judged against this 2 degrees target.

While such a conceptual approach seems straightforward, there are several complications in evaluating effectiveness. International organizations, for instance, may set themselves modest goals: in the UN it has become established doctrine not to send blue helmets to places that are too dangerous where there is 'no peace to keep' (see Panel on United Nations Peace Operations 2000). While there is good reason for this choice – following the disasters of UN peacekeeping in Bosnia, Rwanda and Somalia in the mid-1990s – it does create a selection bias which affects our understanding of effectiveness. As Page Fortna and Lise Howard (2008: 290) note, a critical question is 'whether peacekeepers tend to undertake easier cases or harder ones'. It is also often quite difficult to establish a causal relationship between the intervention of the international organizations and the final outcome. For instance, if advances in technology help us to further develop renewable energy sources that lead to less global warming, is it then fair to conclude that the UNFCCC has been effective? Perhaps member states and private industry have been inspired by the various climate change agreements to invest in research and development, but establishing a direct causal link is difficult.

CONCLUSION

The output of international organizations is a crucial component of contemporary global governance. International organizations are involved both in the establishment of norms and rules and in their implementation. They perform actions which, in the absence of a central authority such as a global state, might make it easier for states and non-state actors to regulate their social relations in a predictable manner.

In this chapter and the preceding chapters, we have analysed international organizations as political systems that convert inputs into outputs. We have discussed inputs, outputs and the conversion process. In doing so, we have provided examples from different relevant international organizations. However, so far we have not investigated whether their policy programmes and their operational activities do actually support global governance in various issue areas. In Part III we shall therefore examine whether the outputs of international organizations really enhance cooperative outcomes between states (and non-state actors). We shall also consider the extent to which these programmes and operational activities of different international organizations contribute to global governance particularly in the fields of security, development and economic relations, the environment and human rights.

Discussion Questions

1. How are policy programmes different from operational activities?
2. To what extent do international organizations have to rely on, and partner with, non-state actors to effectively fulfil crucial operational tasks?
3. Why is it so difficult to evaluate the effectiveness of international organizations?

Further Reading

Abbott, Kenneth W. & Snidal, Duncan 2000. Hard and soft law in international governance, in: *International Organization* 54: 3, 421–56.
Gutner, Tamar & Thompson, Alexander 2010. The politics of IO performance: A framework, in: *The Review of International Organizations* 5: 3, 227–48.
Tallberg, Jonas 2002. Paths to compliance: Enforcement, management, and the European Union, in: *International Organization* 56: 3, 609–43.

Part III Activities of International Organizations

8 Peace and Security

International cooperation in the area of security has traditionally been difficult to achieve. Because today's allies can turn into tomorrow's enemies, states try to avoid relying on others for their own security and survival. Furthermore, the efforts of states to enhance security by enlarging power (through increasing military capabilities and the formation of alliances) are frequently perceived by other states as threatening. This results in a vicious circle of mutual distrust, security competition and strife for power. Pervasive distrust lies at the heart of this security dilemma (Herz 1950; Jervis 1983). Such mistrust is regarded, in the realist school, as the most fundamental obstacle to international cooperation in the field of security. In addition, states caught in the security dilemma tend to focus not on the absolute gains from cooperation but mostly on their gains relative to others. Even when a state gains from security cooperation in absolute terms, a relative loss compared to others equals a relative decrease in power. This often makes security cooperation a zero-sum game: it is not possible for all states to gain in relative terms.

Yet against these odds, states have tried time and again to establish cooperation in the area of security. Perhaps because the potential benefits of cooperation are so large, and the prospects of war so frightening, they have created a wide range of security institutions from the Concert of Europe to the League of Nations and the United Nations (UN) (see Chapter 3). Indeed, according to the institutionalist and constructivist schools, international organizations can help to facilitate cooperation, also in the field of security. While they may not be able to overcome the security dilemma or international anarchy, they can at least provide some norms, a forum for diplomacy, and some transparency among the member states. This, in turn, can foster a degree of trust. In this first chapter on the policies of international organizations, we focus on the policy programmes and operational activities of the UN and the International Atomic Energy Agency (IAEA). UN policy programmes have been developed to deal with the use of force as well as arms control. In terms of operational activities, the UN itself implements much of the policy programme on peace and security, whereas the IAEA plays a key role in arms control.

BANNING FORCE AND KEEPING PEACE

Inherent in the security dilemma is the danger of the threat or use of force by states, independently of their good or bad intentions. Even states that prefer mutual non-aggressive behaviour can be tempted to threaten or use force to guarantee their own security. The fundamental security problem is therefore about stabilizing states' expectations about the non-violent behaviour of others to make it possible for them to reciprocate and refrain from the threat or use of force as well.

International organizations can contribute to stabilizing such expectations through their policy programmes as well as operational activities. We focus, in this chapter, on the UN as the most significant international security organization. It has a policy programme that puts restrictions on the use of force and operational activities aimed at keeping the peace.

Policy programme of the UN

The principal aim of the UN is 'to maintain international peace and security' (Article 1 of UN Charter). To achieve this end, the UN Charter already contains a policy programme. This has since been complemented by detailed acts such as resolutions of the General Assembly and the Security Council, and also agreements reached by international conferences organized by the UN. The result is a regulative programme which attempts to curb the threat and use of force. In fact, the Charter lays down, for the first time in history, a general ban on the threat or use of force between states. Article 2(4) states that 'all Members shall refrain in their international relations from the threat or use of force against the territorial integrity or political independence of any state, or in any other manner inconsistent with the purposes of the United Nations'. This general ban on the threat or use of force is complemented by Article 2(3) according to which 'all Members shall settle their international disputes by peaceful means in such a manner that international peace and security, and justice, are not endangered'.

The UN Charter provides only for two exceptions from the general ban on the use of force. First, Article 51 confirms the right of states to individual and collective self-defence in case of aggression by others. Second, Chapter VII of the UN Charter gives the Security Council the right to authorize military enforcement to maintain peace and security. Since the UN Charter recognizes the 'inherent right of individual or collective self-defence' (Article 51), the use of military force by states is justified if it is an act of self-defence. Yet the right to self-defence could also provide a potential cover for states that want to engage in aggressive warfare. To reduce the risk of such an abuse of the right to self-defence, the UN General Assembly was tasked to define the concept of aggression. This proved difficult: the General Assembly only decided on a definition in 1974 after lengthy and tough negotiations (Resolution 3314 (XXIX)). On a basic level, one could say that an act of aggression is committed when a state uses military force first. But as states may engage in pre-emptive actions (to get a 'first-mover advantage' and to strategically use the element of surprise) when an act of aggression by another state is imminent, things are more complicated.

The Resolution 3314 (XXIX) defines a whole range of state actions which can be considered as acts of aggression. These include an invasion or an attack, a blockade of ports and coasts, and the deployment of armed groups, irregulars or mercenaries by a state (Article 3). This Resolution has thus contributed to specifying which actions amount to an act of aggression, even though international legal discussions on the precise definition of aggression continue to the present day. For instance, the USA and its coalition partners have used Article 51 to justify their intervention in Syria (since 2014) against the terrorist organization the Islamic State. Israel also uses Article 51 to attack targets in neighbouring states, much to the dismay of those states. Russia and Georgia still quarrel over which side started their war in 2008. In other words, while it is now well-accepted that unilateral interventions are unlawful, Article 51 on self-defence still leaves some room for manoeuvre.

Military enforcement measures are also legitimate when they are authorized by the Security Council under Chapter VII as a response to acts of aggression, threats and breaches to the peace. The definition of what constitutes a threat to peace has expanded significantly over time. Originally only threats of *interstate* warfare were considered as threats to peace. Nowadays *internal* wars and internal massive human suffering are also regarded as threats to peace (Pape 1997). The first time that the Security Council declared an internal conflict as a threat to peace was in 1991 (Resolution 688). In the aftermath of the Gulf War, Iraqi military forces took action against the Kurdish and Shiite populations within Iraq. Even though it was an internal conflict, these actions resulted in a massive outflow of refugees, which created cross-border problems. In 1993, the Security Council went a step further. It determined the civil war in Angola as a threat to peace without mentioning any interstate problems (Resolution 864). It based its conclusion entirely on the situation inside the country (Chesterman 2003: 137–38). The Security Council has since considered the internal wars in, for instance, Somalia, Bosnia, Kosovo, East Timor, the Democratic Republic of the Congo, Sudan, Libya and Syria as threats to peace.

Apart from internal violent conflict between government and rebel forces, the Security Council increasingly views serious human rights violations within states as a threat to international peace and security (for more details see Chapter 12). This may also result in military intervention. For instance, since the late 1990s, the norm of the Responsibility to Protect (R2P) has emerged (International Commission on Intervention and State Sovereignty 2001). This norm states that while the primary responsibility for the protection of civilians lies with the state, the international community needs to step in if the responsible state fails to fulfil its duty. The Security Council has, nonetheless, been keen to point out that only the Security Council can determine whether a state has failed in its duty. Therefore, only the Security Council can authorize intervention on the basis of R2P (UN General Assembly 2005: Paragraph 139). It has done so on one occasion: by adopting Resolution 1973, it authorized military enforcement measures against the Libyan regime of Muammar Gaddafi in 2011. The impact of this Resolution is, however, contested. China and Russia underline that Resolution 1973 authorized the international community to protect civilians, but that it did not include a mandate for regime change or the killing of Gaddafi. On the basis of this specific outcome, China and Russia have therefore reconsidered their stance on R2P (Morris 2013). They are currently much more sceptical and put again strong emphasis on non-interference.

Beyond the two above-named exceptions – self-defence and Security Council decisions to enforce the peace – the Charter does not foresee any further exceptions from the general ban on the threat or use of force. However, the Charter does not explicitly ban the intervention by one state at the request of the government of another state. This provides a loophole to circumvent the general ban on the threat or use of force. For instance, the Iraqi government has invited the USA and the other members of the coalition to fight the Islamic State on Iraqi territory since 2014. The Malian government invited France in 2012 to take on rebel Islamist forces approaching the capital. The Somali government has invited the EU to attack pirates within Somali territorial waters. While such invitations are justified, in principle, in purely legal terms it is often not clear in many internal conflicts which political group has legitimate state power and is therefore entitled to request intervention by another state.

Operations of the UN

The operational activities of the UN can be analysed on the basis of the different elements of the political system of international organizations (see Chapters 4–7). The sequence is often as follows. First, a dispute between states or within states breaks out. This is brought to the attention of the Security Council either by the Secretary-General or an interested member state (input). Second, consultations are normally held within the Security Council (conversion). This may include the conflicting parties. Furthermore, the Secretary-General and his/her officials in the UN Secretariat may be asked for advice or a formal report. Third, following the decision-making process, the UN Security Council can adopt a resolution (output) launching operational activities such as (a) the peaceful settlement of disputes, (b) peace enforcement or (c) peacekeeping. Some of these operations are carried out by the UN itself. For other operations, the UN can rely on its member states or a regional organization, such as the North Atlantic Treaty Organization (NATO) or the African Union (AU). Fourth, if the UN output does not have the satisfactory outcome or impact – such as ending the dispute – the process starts again: negative outcomes/impact may provoke new input. The UN Security Council may then, for instance, decide to scale up its decisions.

Peaceful settlement of disputes

The first operational activity of the UN, as defined by Chapter VI of the Charter, concerns the peaceful settlement of disputes. This is about 'consensual security': measures undertaken always require a consensus of all the parties involved. While the peaceful settlement of disputes is, first and foremost, a question for the conflicting parties themselves (Article 33 of UN Charter), the UN supports peaceful settlement. Its most obvious institution is the Security Council (and the General Assembly). The Security Council provides a forum for diplomacy and is the principal venue where matters of peace and security are discussed. The UN Charter indeed makes clear, under Chapter VI, that any UN member state 'may bring any dispute ... to the attention of the Security Council or of the General Assembly' (Article 35(1)). The Security Council also has a task to 'call upon the parties to settle their dispute by [peaceful] means' (Article 33(2)). The Charter thus makes clear to conflicting parties that they have to try to settle disputes through peaceful means and that the UN organs provide the principal forums to turn to.

The UN's role, however, goes further. It also has a set of formal and informal instruments at its disposal. One formal instrument of peaceful dispute settlement is the conduct of investigations by the UN Security Council. If the UN uses investigations as a means of peaceful dispute settlement it sets up a commission which is given the task of clarifying the facts behind a dispute. This provides the disputing parties with reliable information through a neutral third party. Although the disputing parties are not bound by these findings, such information can be helpful in reaching a settlement. Article 34 of the Charter specifically authorizes the Security Council to establish commissions of inquiry. It has used this possibility in two situations (1946 in relation to Greece and 1948 in relation to Kashmir) with explicit reference to Article 34. In various other cases, the Security Council has ordered investigations but has not made explicit reference to Article 34. For instance, in 2014, it stressed the need for an international investigation into the downing of Malaysia Airlines flight MH17 above Ukraine (Tanaka 2018: 79–80).

In addition to the Security Council, the UN Secretary-General (or an appointed envoy) can play a key role in peaceful settlement through 'good offices'. When engaging in good offices, the Secretary-General offers indirect communication channels to the disputing parties that are unwilling to directly communicate with each other (Whitfield 2007). The parties concerned, for instance, can make use of the good offices of the Secretary-General to agree on conditions for starting negotiations. They can communicate in this way without officially entering into negotiations, that is without recognizing the other side as a negotiating partner. The good offices of the Secretary-General may contribute to the initiation of negotiations which may then lead to the peaceful settlement of the dispute. And, when tensions between parties run high, the good offices of the Secretary-General can keep an (indirect) dialogue going. The Secretary-General has repeatedly offered his good offices (and the prestige of his office) to conflicting parties.

Related to good offices is the role of the UN as a mediator. Mediation goes beyond good offices and investigation since it is concerned with procedures, factual information and the specific content of a peaceful settlement (Bercovitch 2007; Wallensteen & Svensson 2014). As a mediator, the UN plays an active role in the negotiations and can contribute to a negotiated settlement by suggesting solutions. The Secretary-General has repeatedly been appointed by the Security Council to mediate in conflicts between states or asked to name a UN envoy as mediator. UN mediation activities currently spread out over all continents. For instance, the former Secretary-General Kofi Annan was appointed to mediate in the civil war in Syria in 2012. After his attempt at a peace plan failed, he was replaced by other high-level UN officials. Within the UN Secretariat, a Mediation Support Unit was set up in 2006. This Mediation Support Unit has acquired considerable mediation expertise. Its experts can also deploy within 72 hours, allowing for immediate mediation if tensions between different parties suddenly emerge. The Mediation Support Unit does not only support the operational activities of the UN. It also provides support for other regional organizations and member states through capacity-building and sharing best practices. Mediation has therefore become a critical function of the UN.

Going yet one step further, the UN has established a whole range of special political missions and peacebuilding missions in conflict countries and regions. These missions are civilian in nature, but perform a wide variety of functions: from electoral observation to political support for a peace process to civilian capacity-building. Many of them are relatively small missions and consist of several dozen officials. Some are, however, larger in scale. The UN Assistance Mission in Afghanistan (UNAMA), for instance, was established by the Security Council through Resolution 1401 (2002). It employed more than 1300 officials (of which 350 were international officials) in 2018. Its mandate includes good offices, working with the local authorities, supporting peace and reconciliation, monitoring human rights and other functions. Such special political missions and peacebuilding missions are often difficult to distinguish from peacekeeping missions (see below). For instance, the UN Mission in Kosovo (UNMIK), which is the only civilian peacekeeping mission, could have well been a special political mission. A big difference is that special political missions and peacebuilding are funded under the biennial UN Regular Budget. Peacekeeping missions are funded separately through an extraordinary annual peacekeeping budget.

A final way for conflicting parties to peacefully settle their disputes is through adjudication. They can bring their conflicts to international courts, of which the International Court of Justice (ICJ) is the most prominent (Kolb 2013; Hernández 2014). Going to the Court, whose Statute is part of the UN Charter, can be an effective means of peaceful settlement of a dispute, since its judgments are binding on all parties. The problem with the ICJ is that it is not automatically competent to take on a dispute. The ICJ becomes competent in one of three cases: first, if both conflicting parties enter into a special agreement to put their dispute in front of the ICJ; second, if both parties are bound by a treaty which stipulates that disputes need to be brought to the ICJ; third, if parties have unilaterally declared that the ICJ has compulsory jurisdiction – that is, if they accept going to the ICJ in all possible disputes. In 2017, a total of 73 UN member states had declared their general submission to the jurisdiction of the Court. The remaining states have to declare their acceptance for each specific case where the Court is asked for a judgment. For this reason, many disputes do not reach the ICJ. Between 1946 and 2018, the ICJ has taken on about 160 cases.

Peace enforcement

The UN has also devoted parts of its operations to peace enforcement. This falls under the rubric of collective security. The UN Charter allocates far-reaching competencies to the Security Council to implement collective security (Thompson 2006; Voeten 2005). The Security Council can authorize collective enforcement measures in the event of a breach of, or acute threat to, international peace. Only the Security Council can determine whether an infringement of the ban on the threat or use of force has occurred. Threatened or attacked states may themselves inform the Security Council of any aggression against their territorial integrity or political independence. In addition, other states or the UN Secretary-General may bring to the attention of the Security Council any matter which in their opinion may threaten international peace and security (Article 99). The Security Council has to determine 'the existence of any threat to the peace, breach of the peace or act of aggression' (Article 39). Only such a conclusion by the Security Council allows for further measures of collective enforcement within the framework of the UN system of collective security.

The number of breaches of the peace or acts of aggression determined by the Security Council has been modest. During the Cold War, the Security Council was hamstrung by a veto of one or the other of the main contenders in the East–West conflict. As a result, it only repeatedly determined that there was a breach of, or threat to, the peace or an act of aggression in the case of pariahs like South Africa and the former Rhodesia. The Security Council also exceptionally took action against North Korea for its attack on South Korea in 1950. Another example was Resolution 502 (1982) which allowed the United Kingdom to claim self-defence in its military action against Argentina following the occupation of the Falkland Islands. Another explanation for the limited number of breaches of the peace or acts of aggression is the fact that during the Cold War period, the Security Council focused largely on international wars and not on civil wars. Yet the number of international wars in comparison with civil wars has also been modest (Harbom & Wallensteen 2010): the majority of wars are within countries rather than between them.

Since 1990, however, the number of condemnations by the Security Council acting under Chapter VII has increased considerably (Human Security Report 2010: Chapter 4). The end of bipolarity after the Cold War accounts for much of this development. It also facilitated the above-mentioned broadening of the concept of a threat to peace. In the cases of Somalia (Resolution 746 (1992)) and Rwanda (Resolution 918 (1994)), for instance, the Security Council saw the threat to peace in humanitarian crises resulting from internal armed struggles. Over time, the Security Council has increasingly condemned internal conflicts as threats to peace (see, for instance, Resolution 1272 (East Timor, 1999); Resolution 1925 (DR Congo, 2010); Resolution 1973 (Libya, 2011)). Moreover, the Security Council no longer reserves condemnations of threats or breaches of peace exclusively to states' actions. The Security Council has also determined activities of non-state actors such as the Taliban, al-Qaeda and pirates to be threats to peace. The Security Council has even determined that the destruction of cultural heritage can constitute a war crime (Resolution 2347 (2017)). By 2014, the Security Council adopted some 40 Resolutions under Chapter VII, compared to on average one resolution every two years during the Cold War (Wallensteen & Johansson 2016: 29–31).

Once the Security Council has determined the existence of a breach, it can impose legally binding obligations onto states. Thus the Security Council condemned Iraq's invasion of Kuwait in 1990 and demanded the immediate and unconditional withdrawal of its armed forces (Resolution 660 (1990)). It simultaneously called on Iraq and Kuwait to settle their differences through negotiations. In the Kosovo crisis in 1998–99, the Security Council condemned the acts of aggression by the Serb police forces in Kosovo as well as acts of terror by the Kosovo Liberation Army (Resolution 1160 (1998)). It demanded a political dialogue and to link such dialogue with concrete proposals such as the reestablishment of the Kosovo region's autonomous status, which later proved to have paved the way for Kosovo's controversial declaration of independence from Serbia (2008). The Security Council can demand cessation of military action and human rights violations, withdrawal from occupied territories, respect for the sovereignty and territorial integrity of a state or the destruction of chemical and nuclear weapons. In short, the Security Council imposes clear limits to the freedom of action of the parties concerned and prescribes specific behavioural guidelines aimed at maintaining or restoring international peace and security.

If actors ignore the demands of the Security Council, the Security Council can decide what measures of collective enforcement 'are to be employed to give effect to its decisions' (Article 41). This includes a range of both non-military and military enforcement measures. The first step is usually non-military enforcement. During the Cold War, the Security Council only twice used Article 41 of the Charter to enforce its resolutions through non-military means. In the first case, it imposed economic sanctions on the former Rhodesia in 1966 (Resolution 232) after having determined that the declaration of independence by the white minority regime constituted a threat to peace (in accordance with Article 39). Subsequently the Security Council intensified its enforcement measures through a series of additional resolutions. These economic sanctions were lifted following Rhodesia's independence (as Zimbabwe) in 1979 under a black majority government. In the second case, that of the apartheid regime in South Africa, the Security Council imposed an arms embargo (Resolution 418 (1977)) following the bloody unrest in the black townships in 1976. Legally binding economic sanctions were not imposed and the Security Council chose instead to recommend to member states a voluntary imposition of comprehensive economic sanctions against South Africa. These were lifted in 1994 after the end of the apartheid regime.

Since 1990, the Security Council has imposed sanctions in numerous instances: Afghanistan, Angola, the Democratic Republic of the Congo, Ethiopia and Eritrea, Haiti, Iran, Iraq, Ivory Coast, Liberia, Libya, Rwanda, Sierra Leone, Somalia, Sudan and the former Yugoslavia. For example, only four days after the invasion of Kuwait by Iraq in 1990 a comprehensive trade embargo was imposed (Resolution 661). To stem the fighting in the former Yugoslavia, the Security Council decided on a total arms embargo (Resolution 713 (1991)). To stop the violence against civilians in Libya in 2011, the Security Council decided 'that all Member States shall immediately take the necessary measures to prevent the direct or indirect supply, sale or transfer [of weapons to Libya]' (Resolution 1970 (2011)).

In addition, the Security Council has increasingly relied on so-called 'smart sanctions'. These are not directed at states, but rather at individuals, who are seen as being a threat to peace. Such sanctions often include a travel ban and the freezing of assets. The listing of terror suspects whose bank accounts states are required to freeze are the most obvious example for this trend (Cortright & Lopez 2002; Drezner 2011). Sanctions may also be imposed against governmental leaders or military officers accused of war crimes. In conjunction with this development, the Security Council has established a number of sanctions committees such as the Ivory Coast Committee or the al-Qaeda and Taliban Sanctions Committee (1267 (1999)).

These administer the application of sanctions, for example by compiling and revising lists of targeted individuals and entities. The trend to directly target individuals through non-military enforcement actions goes, however, further. For instance, the Security Council decided in its Resolution 1593 (2005) and Resolution 1970 (2011) to refer 'the situation' in, respectively, Darfur and Libya to the International Criminal Court. This has resulted in indictments for key individuals, such as the Sudanese President Omar al-Bashir as well as members of the Gaddafi family.

Compliance with sanctions and other non-military enforcement actions against states and individuals can be a challenge. While the USA and EU member states will normally automatically enforce travel bans on their territory and instruct their banks to freeze assets, compliance elsewhere in the world is not guaranteed. To increase compliance, the Security Council can ask its member states to help with the implementation of enforcement. This can also happen through military means. For instance, the United Kingdom led military enforcement of the sanctions against Rhodesia by blocking oil tankers. Warships of NATO and the Western European Union have enforced arms embargoes against the former Yugoslavia in the 1990s and Libya in 2011. This included inspecting and verifying the cargo of maritime vessels sailing into the territorial waters of those countries. Furthermore, even if compliance is not watertight, it may put severe restrictions on the behaviour of those targeted by the non-military enforcement actions. The Sudanese President Omar al-Bashir, for instance, can no longer travel around the world freely. Any time he steps on a plane to a different country, he runs the risk that he gets arrested. For instance, he narrowly escaped an arrest warrant by South Africa's High Court when he attended an AU summit in Pretoria in 2015.

When the effect of non-military enforcement measures is inadequate, the Security Council can resort to measures of military enforcement. According to the Charter it can take 'such action by air, sea, or land forces as may be necessary to maintain or restore international peace and security' (Article 42). During the Cold War, the Security Council never agreed on measures of military enforcement. The measures decided in relation to the Korean War in 1950 came close to enforcement as stipulated by the UN Charter. This was only possible because of the exceptional situation that the former Soviet Union at the time was boycotting Security Council meetings and thereby losing the possibility of using its veto (it objected to the fact that the 'China seat' was held by Taiwan and not the People's Republic of China). Therefore, in accordance with Article 48, the Security Council recommended UN members to provide assistance to the Republic of Korea. The USA was asked to lead this effort (as 'framework nation'). The military deployment therefore had the character of an authorized US-led operation rather than that of a UN deployment.

After the Cold War, measures of military enforcement by the Security Council have become (slightly) more common. The Security Council has authorized peace-enforcement missions in Iraq in 1991, Somalia in 1992, Bosnia in 1992–93, Haiti and Rwanda in 1994, Afghanistan in 2001 and Libya in 2011. In all of these cases member states and regional international organizations, rather than the UN itself, implemented the military actions. The Gulf War of 1991 is a case in point. In the aftermath of Iraq's invasion of Kuwait the Security Council did not take military action itself (in accordance with Article 42), nor did it call upon its members to take military enforcement measures (in accordance with Article 48). It only gave its consent 'to use all means necessary', thereby in effect authorizing member states collaborating with Kuwait to employ military force against the Iraqi occupation. Thus the liberation of Kuwait can be seen as an act 'of individual or collective self-defence' (Article 51), albeit explicitly supported by the Security Council.

By contrast, the Security Council really called for military enforcement measures when it asked member states 'acting nationally or through regional organizations' (that is: NATO) to implement the no-fly zone over Bosnia-Herzegovina (Resolution 816 (1993)). Moreover, in the cases of Somalia (Resolution 746 (1992)) and Haiti (Resolution 940 (1994)), the Security Council considered humanitarian crises as threats to peace and security under Chapter VII. It authorized so-called humanitarian interventions: military intervention in states that aims to stop violations of human rights rather than sanctioning acts of aggression committed against another state. Similarly, Resolution 1973 (2011) authorized UN member states 'to take all necessary measures ... to protect civilians and civilian populated areas under threat of attack' from the Libyan regime of Muammar Gaddafi. Whereas a foreign occupation force on Libyan territory was excluded, Resolution 1973 served as authorization for air strikes against positions of Muammar Gaddafi's troops by NATO allies.

In addition to the UN-authorized peace-enforcement operations, there are two notable cases where intervention took place in the absence of a UN Security Council mandate. The NATO mission 'Allied Force' in the Kosovo conflict in the spring of 1999 was carried out without the approval of the Security Council. Despite Resolution 1244 (1999), passed by the Security Council *after* the cessation of military hostilities, NATO strikes against the former Federal Republic of Yugoslavia were not authorized according to the UN Charter. Neither did the Security Council authorize the invasion of Iraq in 2003 by a US-led multinational 'coalition of the willing'. The USA and the United Kingdom had argued that the possibility of Iraq possessing and employing weapons of mass destruction posed a threat to international peace and security. However, the UN Monitoring, Verification and Inspection Commission (UNMOVIC), which conducted on-site inspections of suspect facilities in Iraq, found no conclusive evidence of weapons of mass destruction. The USA and the United Kingdom nevertheless took Iraq's failure to unconditionally cooperate with UN weapons inspectors as justification for military enforcement actions against Iraq.

Peacekeeping

Peacekeeping is not mentioned in the UN Charter but it has become the major UN operational activity in the field of security (Koops et al. 2015). The repeated recourse to peacekeeping and its recognition by the community of states have become part of customary international law. Peacekeeping activities were first developed at the time of the Cold War and required the consensus of all the parties involved. Since the classic form of peacekeeping is based on the agreement of the parties to the dispute to deploy UN observers or a UN force ('blue helmets'), it mostly falls under the peaceful settlement of dispute (Chapter VI) rather than peace enforcement (Chapter VII). However, peacekeeping missions normally involve the deployment of military personnel. This is why peacekeeping has also been called 'Chapter Six and a Half' (Dag Hammarskjöld, cited in Weiss et al. 2007: 39). Moreover, more recent 'robust' peacekeeping missions have been mandated under Chapter VII to restore a 'secure environment', if necessary by force, and are no longer contingent upon the consent of all parties.

The Security Council authorizes all peacekeeping operations through its Resolutions. These Resolutions are normally quite precise in terms of specifying the mandate, the area of operations, and the material conditions for deployment. The Security Council is, however, not the only relevant actor. Peacekeeping missions are planned by the UN Secretariat. Based on this planning, the Secretary-General advises a mandate and implementation plan to the Security Council. The Security Council is free to ignore the planning of the UN Secretariat – and does so occasionally (Dijkstra 2015) – but it also ultimately relies on the Secretary-General and the UN Secretariat to implement the mission. After the adoption of a Security Council resolution, the Secretary-General appoints a Special Representative of the Secretary-General (SRSG) who commands the operation on the ground. The UN Secretariat also liaises with Troop Contributing Countries, which provide the actual soldiers. In other words, there are multiple actors involved in peacekeeping operations.

Peacekeeping operations have had a variety of functions. These have expanded progressively over time. Traditionally, such operations dealt with the monitoring of ceasefire agreements. The UN would send observers or a relatively small peacekeeping force to a border region with the aim of observing and supervising adherence to a ceasefire. The 400-strong UN Iran–Iraq Military Observer Group (UNIIMOG) was charged with supervising the ceasefire between Iraq and Iran (1988–91). It was a classic example of an observer mission. The observer group or peacekeeping force also keeps the Secretary-General, who writes regular reports to the Security Council, informed. In case of a breach of a ceasefire, the peacekeeping mission normally determines which party to the conflict is responsible. Thus the party violating a ceasefire agreement is subjected to international pressure. Traditional peacekeeping was therefore not about forcefully separating conflicting parties, but rather about helping to create a minimum level of trust in a ceasefire situation (Fortna 2004a). UN military observers have also been deployed preventively to deter the outbreak of hostilities.

In recent years, more encompassing, 'multidimensional' peacekeeping operations have been established. The basic idea is that ensuring a ceasefire is not sufficient to establish a durable peace. Peacekeeping (and peacebuilding) should therefore also be concerned with continued political mediation, providing rule of law and humanitarian assistance, ensuring human rights, democratization, good governance, gender equality, and other things. As such, the scope of the peacekeeping mandates has increased dramatically and is occasionally likened to a 'Christmas tree': just as Christmas trees are full of ornaments, the mandates of peacekeeping missions get overloaded as well. While it is undoubtedly true that a durable peace does not materialize if blue helmets only monitor border regions, 'multidimensional' peacekeeping has put tremendous demands on the UN as an international organization. Such new tasks not only require funding and manpower, but also expertise. The UN, furthermore, had to learn how to do all these new tasks and this has taken considerable time (Benner et al. 2011).

However, multidimensional peacekeeping mandates are not the only challenge. Compared to traditional peacekeeping, the UN has had to face another challenge. Traditional peacekeeping normally involved the monitoring of peace agreements between two states. Current-day peacekeeping operations are deployed, however, in areas of civil war. The fact that the government of the host country gives consent to such peacekeeping operations does not necessarily mean that all the rebel groups do as well. Peacekeeping missions are now often authorized under Chapter VII of the UN Charter and involve a task to create a secure environment – if necessary by force – to enable them to fulfil their mandate. While there was already some 'robust peacekeeping' in the 1990s, the current ongoing missions in Congo and Mali entirely fit the profile. For instance, the UN peacekeeping mission in Congo now includes a Force Intervention Brigade with a mandate to 'take all necessary measures' to 'neutralize' and 'disarm' groups that pose a threat to 'state authority and civilian security' (Karlsrud 2015: 40). The UN peacekeeping mission in Mali is supposed to 'stabilize' the insecure territories in the North. In doing so, more than 300 blue helmets lost their lives in Mali between 2013 and 2018.

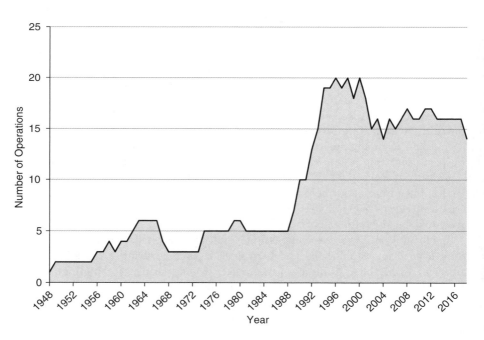

Figure 8.1   Number of UN Peacekeeping Operations, 1948–2018

Source: Based on data from the UN Department of Peacekeeping Operations.

Evaluation of the organization's effectiveness

One of the most important questions in the study of international organizations relates to the issue of whether international organizations are effective. Do their outputs (policy programmes and operational activities) have the desired outcomes in line with organizations' self-set objectives and do they help to resolve international problems individual states are unable to tackle (effectiveness on the impact level) (see Underdal 2002, 2004; Young 2004)? In this section, we draw on empirical studies to assess the UN's effectiveness in preventing, mitigating and ending violent conflict. We look at both the outcomes (in terms of modifying the behaviour of actors) and the impacts (in terms of resolving the political problem of violent self-help) that the UN's activities generate. We will offer parallel assessments of international organizations' effectiveness in all the issue areas we cover in Chapters 8–12.

Does the UN make a relevant contribution to overcoming the threat or use of force in international relations and to stabilizing the peace? Simply by prohibiting the use or threat of force between member states, the UN already makes an important contribution to international peace. Since 1945, we have witnessed a decreasing number of interstate armed conflicts. While this is not definite proof of the UN's effectiveness, as this may have causes unrelated to the UN ban on the use of force, it may be seen as one indication of this effect (see Figure 8.2).

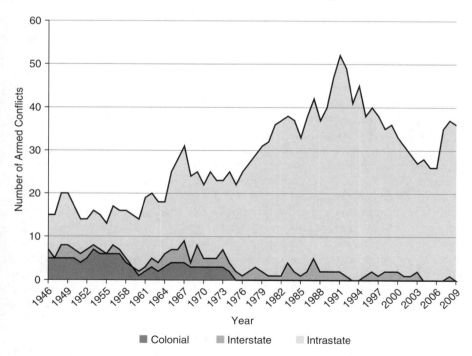

Figure 8.2   Number of global armed conflicts, 1946–2009
Sources: Based on data from Harbom and Wallensteen (2010).

With regard to the UN's operational activities, peacekeeping has attracted most scholarly attention. Measuring the effectiveness of UN peacekeeping is, however, not straightforward. For instance, peacekeepers are not sent to every conflict: Because they are a scarce resource, one can expect that they are only sent to the more difficult cases, rather than to ones in which peace will likely last in any case (Fortna 2004b: 491, 499). When one takes this into account, Fortna (2004b: 517) finds that 'peace lasts substantially longer when international personnel deploy than when states are left to maintain peace on their own'. Peacekeepers enhance the stability of peace by raising the cost of aggression, they make surprise attacks more difficult and they serve to reassure belligerents about each other's intentions through continuous monitoring. Moreover, peacekeepers serve to minimize the risk of accidents or skirmishes from escalating to full-scale fighting (Fortna 2004b: 516; see also Fortna 2008). Therefore, when peacekeepers are deployed after a war, the risk of another international war drops by more than 85 per cent relative to cases in which belligerents are left to their own devices.

The bulk of empirical studies on the effectiveness of peacekeeping focus on civil wars, however. There is a strong inverse correlation between the number of UN peacekeeping operations and the prevalence of civil armed conflict. The number of peacekeeping operations has increased substantially since the end of the Cold War; in the same period of time the number of civil armed conflicts has considerably declined (see Figures 8.1 and 8.2). Correlation is certainly not the same as causation; nonetheless, quantitative studies have meanwhile produced the robust result that peacekeeping makes civil war much less likely to resume once a cease-fire is in place (Doyle & Sambanis 2000, 2006; Fortna 2004a, 2008; Hartzell et al. 2001; Walter 2002). As is the case with interstate wars, peacekeepers tend to be sent to more difficult cases of civil conflict (Ruggeri et al. 2016). If this is taken into account, peacekeeping has a large and statistically significant effect on the duration of peace after civil wars (Fortna 2004a; Fortna & Howard 2008: 290). The deployment of peacekeeping missions also results in fewer battle deaths in civil wars (Hultman et al. 2014).

It is less clear which types of missions are most effective. Some studies show that peacekeeping missions are better at keeping the peace than establishing it (Greig & Diehl 2005). Doyle and Sambanis (2000) argue that the success of peace-building depends, among other factors, on the type of mission. Multidimensional peacekeeping missions significantly improve the chances of success (defined as absence of violent conflict two years after the end of a war). There is weaker evidence in their study that robust peace-enforcement missions improve the prospects for peace. Whereas Doyle and Sambanis (2000) are more sceptical about the effects of traditional peacekeeping on the chances for (modestly) stable peace, Fortna (2008) finds that relatively small and militarily weak consent-based peacekeeping operations are often just as effective as larger, more robust enforcement missions. Yet she finds no strong difference between the effects of Chapter VI and Chapter VII missions. Thus, the literature remains inconclusive about the conditions under which force may be effective in the context of peace operations (Fortna & Howard 2008: 292). A recent thorough qualitative analysis of all peacekeeping operations also shows that the overall score is positive (Koops et al. 2015).

That said, UN peacekeeping missions have also included major failures, particularly in the 1990s in Bosnia, Rwanda and Somalia, where peacekeepers were unable to prevent genocide from taking place (Barnett & Finnemore 2004: 121–55). Regular human rights abuses, including sexual abuses, by peacekeepers against the most vulnerable continue to occur, and the UN leadership has been insufficiently capable of addressing this major problem. Furthermore, in 2010, UN peacekeepers unintentionally brought cholera to Haiti. This caused an epidemic resulting in nearly a million sick local people and 8,500 deaths (Pillinger et al. 2016). Importantly, the UN often takes a critical approach to itself. It has launched frank and transparent investigations into its own role in the Rwanda and Srebrenica genocides. Furthermore, it has established several high-level panels to evaluate the practice of peacekeeping. The United Nations Panel on Peace Operations ('Brahimi Report') (2000) and the report by the High-Level Independent Panel on Peace Operations (HIPPO) (2015) are landmark documents that have helped the UN to further establish a peacekeeping doctrine, develop its own organization and address some of its shortcomings.

ARMS CONTROL AND DISARMAMENT

The security dilemma can sometimes cause an arms race even among states which would prefer friendly relations with each other. Because states have to look after their own survival, they may feel they have to increase and modernize their military capabilities. Such behaviour may be perceived by other states as threatening, resulting in a situation where all states focus on increasing their power and capabilities. Matters are exacerbated by the problem of limited transparency about armaments: because of their strategic value, states typically do not tell other states where they hide their assets. So how can states keep control over the pressures to engage in an arms race? How can international organizations facilitate security cooperation in this domain and therefore contribute to the stabilization of arms control? While the need for arms control applies equally to conventional weapons, this chapter focuses on the non-proliferation of nuclear weapons.

Policy programme of the UN

The UN Charter is rather vague on how to address the problem of arms races. Precise instructions about the size of arsenals, the legality of specific types of arms or even the implementation of possible arms limitations are not mentioned in the Charter. In Article 26 it states that 'the Security Council shall be responsible for formulating ... plans to be submitted to the Members of the UN for the establishment of a system for the regulation of armaments'. Policy-making in the Security Council was, however, blocked during much of the Cold War. Therefore the General Assembly, in accordance with Article 11 of the Charter, assumed this task in its place. It discussed the principles for disarmament and the regulation of armaments and made recommendations.

The first specific initiative to create norms and rules to prevent the proliferation of nuclear weapons was taken to the General Assembly in 1958 by neutral Ireland. It was met with no support. Following a further Irish initiative in 1961, the General Assembly unanimously endorsed the goal of the non-proliferation of nuclear weapons in Resolution 1665 (XVI). Four years later, the General Assembly demanded that the Eighteen-Nation Committee on Disarmament, which had been founded in 1961 and which met in Geneva, should concentrate on negotiating a nuclear weapons non-proliferation treaty. The Committee, consisting of five states each from the Western and Eastern blocs as well as eight representatives of the non-aligned states, entered into an intergovernmental negotiating process that is typical for reaching policy programme decisions (see Chapter 6).

The negotiations were dominated by the most powerful states, especially the USA and the Soviet Union. These nuclear weapons states insisted on keeping their nuclear weapons (for the time being). They also insisted that non-nuclear weapons states should not be allowed to develop nuclear weapons: in other words, non-nuclear weapons states would need to give up their right of acquiring nuclear weapons. At the same time, the powerful nuclear weapons states made two concessions. First, non-nuclear weapons states would be allowed to develop nuclear energy for civilian use (this was considered an 'inalienable right'). Second, nuclear weapons states made a promise of (future) nuclear disarmament. In 1968, members of the Committee were able to agree on a text which was accepted by the General Assembly in that same year (Resolution 2373 (XXII)). It was recommended that the member states should sign and ratify it speedily (Müller et al. 1994).

This regulatory policy programme, known as the Treaty on the Non-Proliferation of Nuclear Weapons (NPT), largely mirrors the material power inequality of states in its distribution of rights and duties. While it constrains the behaviour of non-nuclear weapons states in very significant ways by prohibiting them from getting nuclear weapons, the Treaty constrained those states with nuclear weapons (such as the USA, the Soviet Union, France, the United Kingdom and China) to a far lesser degree. The only restriction on nuclear weapons states is 'not to transfer to any recipient whatsoever nuclear weapons or other nuclear explosive devices or control over such weapons or explosive devices directly, or indirectly' (Article I). In terms of the promise of future disarmament, the treaty instructed nuclear weapons states 'to pursue negotiations in good faith on effective measures relating to cessation of the nuclear arms race at an early date and to nuclear disarmament' (Article VI). This linkage of the ban on horizontal proliferation (the spread of nuclear weapons to states that have not previously possessed them) with the limit on vertical proliferation of nuclear weapons (further nuclear build-up of the superpowers), however, remained very tenuous (Krause 2007).

Besides the promise to disarm, nuclear weapons states were able to tie non-nuclear weapons states to the NPT with the promise to drop the policy of refusing to transfer nuclear technology as a weapons non-proliferation strategy. They guaranteed the nuclear 'have-nots' participation in the international civilian nuclear trade on the basis of equal opportunity (Article IV). However, the NPT requires safeguards for the civilian nuclear trade 'with a view to preventing diversion of nuclear energy from peaceful uses to nuclear weapons or other nuclear explosive devices'

(Article III, paragraph 1). For their part, the nuclear weapons states committed themselves only to trade in nuclear matters with those non-nuclear weapons states which had accepted the safeguards (Article III, paragraph 2). In other words, nuclear weapons states agreed to help non-nuclear weapons states to develop nuclear energy, but only if non-nuclear weapons states can prove that it is for civilian purposes only.

When looking at the NPT with the benefit of hindsight, it is actually quite extraordinary that the international community managed to come to a treaty at all in the midst of the Cold War. The NPT has certainly also helped to strengthen the non-proliferation norm. Non-nuclear weapons states that have tried to obtain nuclear weapons, such as North Korea and Iran, have been branded as the pariahs of the international community and have met with significant economic sanctions. At the same time, the NPT also suffers from non-membership. India, Israel and Pakistan have not signed the NPT and North Korea has withdrawn from the NPT. These countries are all believed to have acquired nuclear weapons. Furthermore, many of the non-nuclear weapons states have had enough of the empty promises of nuclear disarmament. In 2017, no less than 122 states took the radical step to adopt the Treaty on the Prohibition of Nuclear Weapons (Ban Treaty). While this effort was ignored by all nuclear weapons states, it may present a challenge to the NPT in the longer term.

Operations of the IAEA

The IAEA was established in 1957 and therefore predates the NPT. The current 190 parties to the NPT are furthermore also not all member states of the IAEA. Nevertheless, with the NPT, these parties delegated important functions to the IAEA to ensure the proper implementation of Article III. The IAEA was tasked to establish a system of safeguards to prevent non-nuclear weapons states diverting 'nuclear energy from peaceful uses to nuclear weapons or other nuclear explosive devices' (Article III).

Under Article III paragraph 2, countries can only provide fissile material and equipment to non-nuclear weapons states if such material and equipment is subject to the appropriate safeguards. Yet the definition of fissile material and equipment in the NPT was not precise and therefore needed to be specified. To harmonize their export practices, the states that actually possessed fissile material and equipment (originally only 15 states) formed the NPT Exporters Committee (known as the Zangger Committee). In this Committee they negotiated which materials and equipment were suitable for export (with safeguards). This took a long time. It was not until 1974 that the nuclear supplier states reached the first, still rather general and limited, agreement about their nuclear export policy (the 'trigger' list, INFCIRC/209).

The first real crisis for the NPT came when India tested its first nuclear device (also in 1974). India had not signed the NPT, because it principally objected to the discrimination of the non-nuclear weapons states under the treaty. In response to the Indian nuclear test, the nuclear supplier states stepped up their cooperation, but this time outside the framework of the IAEA. They set up the Nuclear Supplier Group, originally meeting in London (Spector 2002: 127–28). Their strategy was to refuse technology transfer to potential nuclear states among the developing countries of the South. This created further discrimination between the countries importing nuclear technologies. At the same time, adherence to these agreements was left to the discretion of the supplying countries. Due to this lack of control, the nuclear supplier states could keep exporting nuclear technologies without running the risk of discovery. This practice of non-compliance became evident in the early 1990s following the disclosure of the clandestine nuclear weapons programme of Iraq (Spector 2002: 128–29). The discovery of Iraq's nuclear weapons programme led members of the Nuclear Suppliers Group to renegotiate the obsolete export guidelines.

It has therefore been difficult for the nuclear supplier states to specify and implement export control norms. The IAEA itself, on the other hand, has been rather successful in specifying, implementing and monitoring safeguard norms. The specification of the safeguards proceeded relatively quickly (Chellaney 1999: 380–82). Even before the coming into force of the NPT, the IAEA had safeguards at its disposal in the form of the model safeguards agreements INFCIRC/26 and INFCIRC/66, adopted by its Board of Governors in 1961 and 1966, respectively. A new model safeguards agreement INFCIRC/153 was worked out only one year after the signing of the NPT in 1968. Coming into force in 1970, the treaty retained its validity until the decision was taken to proceed to a fundamental reform of the safeguards regime in the mid-1990s.

According to INFCIRC/153 every non-nuclear weapons state which concluded a safeguards agreement with the IAEA was obliged to notify the IAEA of all facilities and materials deployed in the peaceful use of nuclear energy. Furthermore, it had to keep a record of nuclear materials for the declared facilities, which enabled verification of whether nuclear material for peaceful uses had been diverted to military purposes. This system of accounting for and control of all nuclear materials was supervised by the IAEA. IAEA inspectors had the right to check the declared facilities on site and install surveillance equipment, such as cameras, at key measurement points (Den Dekker 2001: 274–97). Despite these far-reaching control mechanisms, the safeguards system of the IAEA did not provide complete protection against diversion of nuclear material suitable for weapons. The loopholes in the safeguards system of the IAEA became obvious in 1991 when a UN Special Commission encountered signs of a substantial nuclear weapons programme in Iraq. The country had made false declarations to the IAEA concerning both its facilities and the available nuclear source material (Chayes & Chayes 1995: 181).

In 1991 the Director-General of the IAEA formulated a reform programme with three goals. First, the organization was to gain unhindered access to all suspicious facilities. Second, its inspectors should be able to share their knowledge with the secret services. Third, the UN Security Council was to cooperate with the IAEA to strengthen the sanctions process. In 1997 the Board of Governors adopted a new model safeguards agreement INFCIRC/540. Although the Director-General's wish for unhindered access was not granted, the new model safeguards agreement contains a substantial extension of member states' duty to report, as well as of the IAEA's inspection rights (Colijn 1998: 95–97; Den Dekker 2001: 297–305; Loosch 2000). In 2005, the IAEA Board of Governors agreed on further modifications to what is known as the Small Quantities Protocol (SQP), designed for states that have little or no nuclear material. The previous SQP standard text allowed states to possess small amounts of nuclear material without having to report those holdings to the IAEA.

The IAEA safeguards system can be seen as an important contribution to the non-proliferation of nuclear weapons. Supervision by the IAEA provides some guarantee that non-nuclear weapons states will not gain an advantage in arms technology and procurement by diverting nuclear energy from peaceful uses. Of course, the limits to these trust-building activities are quite obvious when we look at the nuclear programmes of North Korea, Pakistan and Iran, as well as the alleged Iraqi nuclear programme before the 2003 Iraq War. Even though IAEA and UN weapons inspectors found no evidence of a renewed nuclear programme in Iraq, the USA and the UK, as well as some supporters, invaded Iraq nonetheless. The case of North Korea, which left the NPT in 2003, sent IAEA inspectors out of the country and conducted a nuclear arms test only three years later, points to the problematic feature of the NPT that it is not possible to prevent a state from leaving the treaty in order to elude IAEA controls. The case of Iran, which is still a member of the NPT, is also illustrative of the difficulties with the NPT. Despite the Iran deal of 2015, in which Iran promised to give up its civilian nuclear programme and agreed to be subjected to a stringent monitoring system, the Trump administration decided to withdraw from this agreement in 2018. Part of the argument was that the Iran deal only addressed the civilian nuclear programme and not its broader hostile foreign and military activities in the Middle East region.

The IAEA can pass resolutions condemning a lack of cooperation and breaches of the NPT, as it did in 2006 with the Iranian nuclear programme, but it cannot impose legally binding sanctions. For that matter, it is dependent on the Security Council. Thus in the case of a breach of the NPT the imposition of sanctions is not automatic: the Board of Governors of the IAEA can only pass this information. The Security Council has the right to impose collective enforcement measures against the respective state (Müller et al. 1994), if it sees the breach of contract as a threat to international peace and security. But even if the Security Council agrees to impose sanctions, as it did with repeated sanctions against Iran prior to 2015, this does not automatically bring violators back into compliance with the treaty. Indeed, while extensive economic sanctions, which included its complete financial sector and its oil exports, brought Iran back to the negotiations table, the equally extensive sanctions regime has not prevented North Korea from acquiring nuclear weapons.

Evaluation of the organizations' effectiveness

In an evaluation of the effectiveness of UN and IAEA activities, first of all, the contribution of these organizations to the non-use of nuclear weapons must be acknowledged (Tannenwald 1999, 2007). A normative prohibition on nuclear weapons use has developed in the global system, which has stigmatized nuclear weapons as unacceptable weapons of mass destruction (see also Daase 2003). According to Tannenwald (1999: 434), the normative prohibition against nuclear weapons is essential to explaining why nuclear weapons have remained unused after the Second World War and to accounting for their special status as 'taboo' weapons. The USA, which had used nuclear weapons at the end of the Second World War in 1945 and which had still considered using them during the Korean War of 1950, hardly considered their use during the Vietnam War of the 1970s. In the 1990s, during the Iraq War, the non-use of nuclear weapons was already taken for granted (Tannenwald 1999). The decreasing legitimacy of nuclear weapons is institutionalized in an array of international arms control agreements and regimes, including the NPT and the Ban Treaty. These circumscribe the realm of legitimate nuclear weapons use and restrict freedom of action with respect to nuclear weapons. The UN constituted a permanent institutional forum for the stigmatization of nuclear weapons playing a central role in the creation and dissemination of norms against the use of nuclear weapons (Tannenwald 2005: 18–19).

Apart from this positive effect on the non-use of nuclear weapons, the UN and the IAEA make an important contribution to regulating arms procurement, especially with the view to preventing the proliferation of nuclear weapons between states (horizontal proliferation). Although India, Israel, Pakistan and North Korea have acquired a nuclear weapons capability, it is widely acknowledged among scholars of nuclear (non-)proliferation that, without the UN's and the IAEA's policy programmes and their operational activities, we would likely face a far greater number of nuclear weapons states (Beckman et al. 2000: 222–25). Not only has the number of nuclear weapons states remained relatively low, but it has also grown more slowly after the coming into force of the NPT in 1970 (see Figure 8.3).

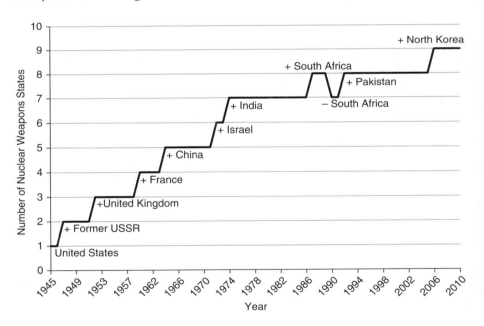

Figure 8.3   Number of states possessing nuclear weapons

Note: The Soviet Union turned into the Russian Federation in 1991, and the former Soviet republics of Belarus, Kazakhstan and Ukraine abandoned nuclear weapons.

Sources: Beisheim et al. (1999: 180–82); Norris & Kristensen (2010).

Therefore, Müller (2010) argues that the nuclear non-proliferation regime, despite being frequently criticized for an alleged lack of effectiveness, is in fact a success story as far as horizontal proliferation is concerned. The number of states which had conducted nuclear weapons activities in various stages but which have terminated them surpasses the number of nuclear weapons states by far (see also Levite 2002/2003; Müller & Schmidt 2010). No fewer than 26 states which once seriously explored the idea of moving towards nuclear weapons have renounced these activities or have been forced to do so (Müller 2010: 189), with the NPT marking an important waterline beyond which nuclear weapons aspirations lost their legitimacy. However, it cannot be overlooked that international organizations have not been effective in preventing a small number of determined states, which have broken the NPT rules or have left the treaty regime, from pursuing nuclear weapons programmes.

Notwithstanding the partial success non-proliferation policy may have had regarding horizontal proliferation, the NPT has contributed little to halt or at least slow down the nuclear arms race of the superpowers (vertical proliferation). The USA had actually already started to reduce its nuclear arsenal prior to the NPT which entered into force in 1970 (see Figure 8.4). The sharp reduction in the nuclear arsenal of the Soviet Union, starting in the mid-1980s, was the result of a direct rapprochement between US President Reagan and Premier Gorbachev (not the result of the NPT). Even today, the world's two largest nuclear powers, the USA and Russia, show no sign of entirely giving up nuclear weapons. Despite the initial ambition of US President Obama to aim for 'Global Zero', he immediately cautioned that it might not happen in his lifetime. Indeed, Russia has made great efforts to 'modernize' its nuclear force. Neither has US President Trump

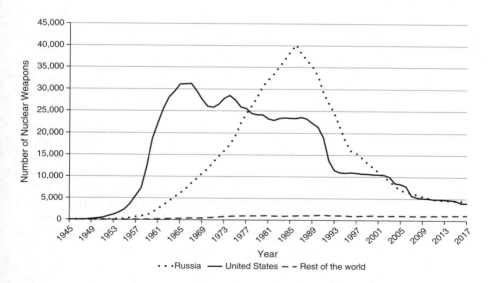

Figure 8.4   Vertical proliferation: nuclear weapons inventories, 1945–2017

Source: Based on data from Kristensen & Norris (n.d.).

been championing the reduction of nuclear weapons. The disarmament promise made by the nuclear weapons states in the NPT is therefore still far away. This also explains why 122 non-nuclear weapons states adopted the Ban Treaty. This new treaty, once it enters into force, presents a direct challenge to the NPT. Even if the nuclear weapons states ignore this treaty, it is nevertheless a clear signal that the non-nuclear weapons states are dissatisfied with the status quo.

CONCLUSION

Following the horrors of the Second World War, the UN member states have set up an elaborate policy programme which bans the use of force. While this policy programme is not entirely complete, leaving exceptions for cases of self-defence, it provides an important set of norms and rules that constrain states in questions of peace and security. This UN policy programme is complemented by a plethora of operational activities. The UN is at the forefront of providing a peaceful settlement of disputes, it has launched many peacekeeping missions and the Security Council occasionally authorizes peace enforcement. The chapter has also discussed questions of (nuclear) arms control. It has analysed the development of the NPT, which strikes a grand bargain between powerful nuclear states and weaker non-nuclear states. An important aspect of the NPT has been the specification of how fissile material and equipment can be shared for peaceful energy purposes. The operational activities of the IAEA play a key role here. It monitors, including through inspections of nuclear facilities in countries across the globe, whether fissile material and equipment is indeed used for peaceful purposes and not diverted for military aims.

It is important to recognize that the need for cooperation resulted from pressures from the international environment. While the UN policy programme initially focused on interstate wars, the changing nature of war over the last three decades has resulted in a situation where the UN also gets involved in civil wars. Something similar can be said about the NPT, which was a response to the increasing number of states gaining access to nuclear weapons in the decades after the Second World War. As a result of such developments in the international environment, states and other political actors have formulated their preferences and demands for international cooperation (input). For instance, the USA and other Western states have become supportive of UN-authorized action to protect human rights, whereas China and Russia have insisted on non-interference. In the context of the NPT, it hardly needs to be said that nuclear weapons states have very different preferences than non-nuclear weapons states. How all these inputs are channelled through the decision-making processes of the UN and IAEA (conversion) is also critically important. The UN Security Council has continuously insisted over the decades on remaining the only venue for questions of peace and security. This obviously privileges the permanent members.

The UN and IAEA provide a wide range of outputs in the area of peace and security. The UN Security Council has, for instance, almost adopted 2500 resolutions (per 2018). These Security Council resolutions are legally binding and can be used to authorize the use of force, establish a peacekeeping mission or put in place economic sanctions. These are significant outcomes. For instance, in 2018, the UN had nearly 100,000 blue helmets under its command based on those Security Council resolutions. When it comes to arms control, we similarly see important outputs. The IAEA has been tasked with nuclear inspections to ensure that fissile material and equipment is only used for peaceful purposes. In this context, IAEA inspectors made nearly 3,000 in-field verifications of almost 1,300 nuclear facilities in 2017. The IAEA is also monitoring 130 facilities remotely with the use of cameras. On the basis of its inspections, the IAEA issues reports and provides verification seals. While the UN and IAEA thus provide considerable output and often achieve the intended outcomes (such as the instalment of economic sanctions), both organizations are still often criticized over their impact. UN peacekeeping has not been entirely successful and the IAEA has been unable to prevent instances of nuclear proliferation. Overall, however, we can conclude that even in the area of peace and security, international organizations play a key role.

Discussion Questions

1. Has the UN Security Council succeeded in establishing itself as the prime guardian of international peace and security after the Cold War? Justify your position with the appropriate empirical evidence.
2. How have UN peacekeeping operations evolved in the past few decades? To what extent do UN peacekeeping operations succeed in creating and/ or keeping the peace?
3. Why are the operational activities of the IAEA so important in preventing the horizontal proliferation of nuclear weapons?

Further Reading

Fortna, Virginia Page 2008. *Does Peacekeeping Work? Shaping Belligerents' Choices after Civil War*, Princeton, NJ: Princeton University Press.

Koops, Joachim, MacQueen, Norrie, Tardy, Thierry & Williams, Paul D. (eds) 2015. *The Oxford Handbook of United Nations Peacekeeping Operations*, Oxford: Oxford University Press.

Tannenwald, Nina 2007. *The Nuclear Taboo: The United States and the Non-Use of Nuclear Weapons Since 1945*, Cambridge: Cambridge University Press.

Voeten, Erik 2005. The political origins of the UN security council's ability to legitimize the use of force, in *International Organization* 59: 3, 527–57.

9   Trade and Development

In the area of trade – as in security – there is a dilemma which sets the parameters for international cooperation. The starting point is that free trade tends to be good for economic growth and development. It allows countries to specialize in industries where they have a comparative advantage and larger international markets allow for economies of scale (Ohlin 1933; Krugman 1979; Dixit & Norman 1980). Yet without a central authority, each state can decide its own trade policies. Thus each state may be tempted to raise tariffs, impose import restrictions or provide state aid. This is known as mercantilism: the policy of maximizing trade and accumulating wealth *at the expense of other states*. It may result in short-term economic gain or provide a lifeline for struggling domestic industries. If, however, all states engage in such opportunistic behaviour, it comes at the expense of overall growth. The economic dilemma thus describes a trap in which trade policies aimed at increasing wealth for individual states place the community of states, and ultimately also each state individually, in a worse situation than would have been the case with effective cooperation. This economic dilemma therefore resembles the Prisoner's Dilemma (see Chapter 2). An open international economy may furthermore result in greater economic disparities between richer and poorer countries. For instance, if poorer countries specialize in labour-intensive industries (as they have the comparative advantage of lower wages), it will be difficult for them to 'upgrade' their economy (Lin & Chang 2009). There is thus a need to provide assistance to developing countries to allow them to compete in the international economy.

The creation of strong international treaties and organizations is the classic solution to this economic dilemma. They allow states to credibly commit to free trade. States can, for instance, rely on international organizations to monitor the implementation of trade agreements and to adjudicate in case of trade disputes. This significantly increases the chance of compliance and reduces the risk of cheating. Given the obvious direct benefits, economic cooperation is often more extensive than security cooperation (Lipson 1984). Furthermore, international organizations have become central players when it comes to development assistance and providing loans to poorer countries. Through international organizations, the donor countries can pool their development assistance and as such provide more effective support than through bilateral development channels. While there are many international organizations dealing with economic relations, we shall limit our discussion to a few. In this chapter, we take a detailed look at the policy programmes and operational activities of the World Trade Organization (WTO) and the European Union (EU) relating to trade. We also focus on the World Bank Group and its extensive loans to developing countries.

GLOBAL TRADE RELATIONS

The economic dilemma can lead to undesirable results in international trade relations if states try to increase their own share of global trade at the expense of others through tariffs and non-tariff barriers. To counter such mercantilist trade policies, states can benefit from economic cooperation and international organizations. States need to, in this respect, first agree on policy programmes. At least as important, however, is that states agree to a variety of operational activities by international organizations: policy programmes need to be specified and it is critical that they get uniformly interpreted and implemented. The activities of the WTO serve as examples of institutionalized attempts to overcome barriers to cooperation in global trade relations.

Policy programme of the WTO

The General Agreement on Tariffs and Trade (GATT) of 1947 was provisionally established, as a substitute for the failed International Trade Organization (ITO), in the form of a governmental agreement regulating international trade relations (see Chapter 3). Since 1995, the revised GATT has formed the programmatic core of the newly created WTO (Cohn 2002: 216–18; Wilkinson 2000: 11–30). Thus, the WTO sets norms and rules aimed at the realization of liberal trade relations. Yet neither the GATT nor the WTO have established a world trade order based entirely on free trade (or 'pure liberalism'). They are committed to 'embedded liberalism' (Ruggie 1982). They strive for liberal trade relations while at the same time allowing states to shield their national markets from the global market to the extent necessary for the pursuit of domestic economic steering and social policy measures. However, the creation of the WTO also brought along a softening of the principle of 'embedded liberalism' in favour of 'pure liberalism' (Ruggie 1994; see Chapter 3).

The regulatory programme of the WTO, complemented by some redistributive elements, is only to a small extent the result of programme decisions of the international organization itself. The original GATT (and later extensions and alterations) already contained the constitutive norms and rules which still govern international trade relations today under the WTO (Matsushita et al. 2004; Senti 2000). At the heart of the WTO programme is the norm of non-discrimination. This consists of two elements. First, this norm prohibits the 164 member states (as of July 2016) to discriminate between the other WTO member states (Wilkinson 2000: 80–84). The so-called 'most-favoured-nation' principle requires that:

> any advantage, favour, privilege or immunity granted by any contracting party to any product originating in or destined for any other country shall be accorded immediately and unconditionally to the like product originating in or destined for the territories of all other contracting parties. (Article 1, GATT 1947)

In other words, the USA cannot treat China and Germany differently, as both are WTO members. If the USA reduces its tariffs for German products, it also needs to reduce its tariffs for Chinese products. There is an important exception. If several members of the WTO establish among themselves a customs union or free-trade zone, they are allowed to give preferential treatment to their trade partners (Article 24, GATT 1947). To give an example, member states of the EU (a customs union) can make better trade deals within their own internal market than with the other WTO members. The assumption is that, on the whole, the effect of customs unions and free-trade zones is to create trade rather than merely to divert it (Wilkinson 2000: 93–95).

The second part of the non-discrimination norm obliges WTO member states to treat products of foreign origin – once they have cleared customs – the same as domestic products. More precisely, national treatment is defined as follows:

> The products of the territory of any contracting party imported into the territory of any other contracting party shall be accorded treatment no less favourable than that accorded to like products of national origin in respect of all laws, regulations and requirements affecting their internal sale, offering for sale, purchase, transportation, distribution or use. (Article 3, paragraph 4, GATT 1947)

For instance, a member state is not allowed to impose a sales tax of 15 per cent on domestic products and a sales tax of 20 per cent on similar foreign products. It is also not allowed to have different health or safety standards or labelling requirements for foreign products. National treatment only applies after the products have been imported and does not affect what happens at the border: member states are still allowed to impose tariffs on foreign goods. Also member states remain perfectly in their right to impose taxes or to stipulate product requirements, as long as they do not discriminate between domestic and foreign products. So member states can still insist on product labelling in their local language, because such a law applies to both domestic and foreign products equally.

In addition to these norms, the GATT and WTO have a progressive policy programme: they oblige member states to go beyond mere non-discrimination by limiting tariff and non-tariff trade barriers. In particular, restrictions in the form of import quotas are prohibited (Article 11, GATT 1947). Other non-tariff barriers as well as tariff barriers in the form of duties are tolerated in principle, but member states are obliged to strive for their reduction in recurring rounds of trade negotiations, convened by the Ministerial Conference of the WTO (formerly the GATT Council), on the principle of reciprocity (Wilkinson 2000: 109–11). The Ministerial Conference, the highest decision-making organ of the WTO, meets at least every two years and all member states are represented. Although majority decisions are possible, decisions are normally reached by consensus.

The WTO has substantially widened the scope of its policy programmes when compared with the original GATT (Cohn 2002: 235). This expansion has gradually evolved through several GATT negotiating rounds. The scope has also considerably increased with the transition from GATT to the WTO: in the Uruguay Round (1986–94), for example, agriculture, textiles and trade in services were integrated into the WTO framework. This was a significant first step towards liberalization of trade in products other than manufactured goods. This is important because agricultural goods and textiles are especially significant for developing countries, whereas trade in services is more advantageous for industrialized countries where the services sector contributes up to 50 per cent or more to the economy. However, after the programmatic expansion at the inception of the WTO, attempts to increase the scope further through intergovernmental negotiations in the Doha Development Round (launched in 2001) have largely stalled since the late 2000s. Growing conflicts of interest between developed countries, led by the EU and the USA, and emerging economies, such as Brazil, China and India, have blocked further programmatic progress on vital issues like agricultural trade or trade in services (Jones 2009; Hopewell 2015).

The WTO policy programme allows for waivers to WTO rules. The impact of such waivers should not be underestimated. One such waiver refers to the grave distortion of domestic markets as a result of superior foreign competition (the norm of market security). It allows states temporarily to protect one of their industrial sectors if they find themselves exposed to a considerable increase in imports from a specific foreign industrial sector (Article 19, GATT 1947). It enables member states to reduce social hardships resulting from the liberalization of trade. Another exception concerns preferential treatment for developing, and in particular least-developed, countries (the development norm). The norm allows developing countries to suspend or at least reduce the obligation of reciprocity. This should help to improve export opportunities for developing countries without forcing them to immediately open their own markets to imports from industrialized states. Indeed, the ban on discrimination and the requirement of most-favoured-nation status is partially lifted for trade between industrialized countries and developing countries.

Operations of the WTO

Making sure that the policy programme gets properly implemented can be very difficult, as states have incentives to cheat in the area of trade. The operational activities, for which international organizations are responsible, are therefore critically important. Specifying the norms and rules set in the WTO's policy programmes is an important operational activity. The WTO programmes determine which trade barriers have to be removed and in which sector, but do not provide concrete prescriptions by which states must abide. The specification of existing programmes and the development of new ones within the WTO is the task of the recurring negotiating rounds (Cohn 2002: 231–75). The decision-making process in these negotiating rounds remains largely dominated by the member states, but officials from the WTO staff provide input. Particularly, the high-level negotiating rounds aimed at furthering the trade programme of the WTO are clearly dominated by the interests of the large trading countries or blocs such as the USA and the EU. More recently, emerging economies, such as Brazil, China and India, increasingly take the lead in the formation of developing countries' coalitions. These emerging economies take a hard bargaining stance towards developed states. The preferences of the member states indeed vary (input): while the USA and EU are keen on liberalization in the area of services, the emerging countries focus on liberalization in the area of agricultural and industrial products.

Three high-level negotiation rounds in the GATT are viewed as particularly successful: the Kennedy Round (1964–67), the Tokyo Round (1973–79) and the Uruguay Round (1986–94) brought about a reduction of tariffs for manufactured goods of one-third each time. In other words, average tariffs, which in 1947 made up over 40 per cent of the import value of goods, were reduced by the year 2000 to approximately 3 per cent. Thus tariffs as trade barriers were largely eliminated from international trade in industrial goods, after decades of multilateral negotiations (Hauser & Schanz 1995: 63–70).

Furthermore, in the Tokyo Round and especially in the Uruguay Round, the member states reached agreements to push back non-tariff trade barriers, by adopting anti-subsidy and anti-dumping rules (Kahler 1995: 29–47). Thus it is no longer in the purview of states to simply determine dumping, subsidies or market distortions (Hauser & Schanz 1995: 72–110; Senti 2000). The Tokyo and Uruguay Rounds also reduced considerably the trade barriers set up through national regulations to protect public health, consumers and the environment. The original GATT had stipulated that such regulations must not be applied in a discriminatory fashion (Article 20, GATT 1947). However, this agreement was so vague that the definition of these regulations was left to individual states, which were able to exploit them as trade barriers. The new and much more precise rules of the current WTO largely limit this abuse by prescribing that technical regulations must not be more restrictive than necessary to satisfy public health, consumer and environmental concerns. Moreover, the national regulations of other member states must be recognized as valid if these are equally suitable to protect public health, consumers and the environment (Beise 2001: 47–50).

While the global trade order based on the WTO still retains some loopholes, the more recent negotiating rounds have contributed to increasing the scope and specificity of the norms and rules governing global trade relations. However, the stalemate of the Doha Round since the late 2000s also points to the limits to cooperation. Negotiations in the Doha Round between developed economies and developing, as well as emerging, economies have stalled over divisions on a number of substantive issues, including agricultural trade liberalization, liberalization of trade in services and manufactured products. Within the WTO context, states have not been able to reconcile their conflicting inputs. Indeed, the preferences of the membership have diverged. Emerging economies are pursuing their interests more assertively as their economic and political weight has grown. Developed countries, on the other hand, no longer allow emerging economies to free ride on trade liberalization. This conflict makes progress on substantive issues and thus further specification of the WTO's policy programme difficult to achieve. The WTO is ultimately a member states-driven organization whose capacity for programme development and specification largely depends on member states' willingness and ability to strike mutually beneficial deals (Steinberg 2002).

The decisions taken in high-level negotiating rounds are often further specified within the member states' bureaucracies and the WTO's executive councils and committees. For this purpose a multitude of thematic councils, committees and working parties exist within the framework of the WTO. There are three thematic councils: the Council for Trade in Goods; the Council for Trade in Services; and the Council for Trade-Related Aspects of Intellectual Property Rights. These councils consist of all WTO members and are responsible for the more specific workings of the WTO agreements dealing with their respective areas of trade. These councils have subsidiary bodies where trade diplomats from the member states discuss the specification and the 'nitty-gritty' application of the still rather abstract trade rules that are agreed upon in the negotiating rounds. For example the Goods Council has ten committees dealing with specific subjects (such as agriculture, market access, subsidies, anti-dumping measures and so on).

Agreeing on international trade rules is one thing; adhering to them is another. States may often be tempted to ignore or contravene agreed rules in order to obtain additional advantages for themselves. Thus monitoring, adjudication and (to a lesser extent) sanctioning are important operational activities undertaken by the WTO. While the GATT limited itself mainly to obliging its member states to report regularly upon the implementation of norms and rules, the WTO has more far-reaching powers of supervision at its disposal. In particular, the large trading states and blocs must submit to regular supervision of their trade policies. On these occasions each member state, as well as the secretariat of the WTO, has to present a report on the implementation of existing norms and rules. Both reports are then submitted to a body specifically charged with supervising trade policies, the Trade Policy Review Body (TPRB), where the two reports are compared (Van den Bossche 2008: 121–24). States practices are therefore monitored. It renders the supervision of practices by states within the WTO much more reliable than was the case for GATT.

Nevertheless, the norms and rules of the WTO still leave scope for interpretation. Disputes about the interpretation of norms and rules as well as alleged non-compliance with agreed rules can seriously hamper cooperation. The WTO provides an answer to this cooperation problem with its Dispute Settlement Understanding (DSU) (Jackson 2004; Merrills 2017). The DSU represents an agreement to adjudicate cases of a dispute through a judicialized, court-like, dispute-settlement procedure. The procedure can be activated by any member state being affected by another state's breach of norms and rules laid down in the WTO agreements. The complaining state can request scrutiny by a panel consisting of three to five neutral trade experts. The panel investigates the case and hears complainants and defendants. It examines the norms and rules which apply to the case and assesses whether these have been violated. It thus establishes what speaks in favour of and what against the complaint. The panel finally draws up a report in which it describes and assesses the dispute from its point of view and gives its verdict. Panel reports become automatically binding unless they are rejected by consensus by the Dispute Settlement Body (DSB).

Yet, before panel reports are accepted by the DSB both defendants and complainants may file an appeal with the Appellate Body. The Appellate Body consists of seven independent experts in trade law who are elected for four years. Appellate Body reports cannot be blocked by individual member states. They also become binding unless all members of the DSB reject them. Consequently, disputes about the interpretation of WTO norms and rules are subject to judicialized procedures which produce much more reliable decisions than was the case with the largely diplomatic dispute-settlement procedures of GATT (Wilkinson 2000: 115–36; Zangl 2008). Meanwhile, the WTO has made it possible for parties other than member states, such as non-governmental organizations (NGOs), to participate in a dispute-settlement procedure. Although they cannot be a party to a dispute, they can nevertheless forward information to the panel in the form of an '*amicus curiae* brief' which provides information and thereby exerts influence on the dispute-settlement outcome. However, the dispute-settlement bodies are free to decide what use they will make of the information obtained (Ohloff 1999).

If a state fails to implement a panel or Appellate Body report, it ultimately faces trade sanctions. These sanctions are implemented by the complainant state ('countermeasures') rather than the WTO itself. However, complainant states cannot resort to any sanctions. They must wait for the DSB to approve specific sanctions (formally: the suspension of trade concessions that had previously been granted to the losing defendant). These sanctions are approved unless they are opposed by all DSB member states, making it considerably easier to act in the event of norm and rule infringements in the WTO than used to be the case under GATT (Bown & Pauwelyn 2010: 2). Thus, while sanctioning still occurs in a decentralized manner, the fact that sanctions must be authorized gives the WTO an operational role in sanctioning which aims at preventing escalation to 'trade wars'. Whether the improved possibility of imposing sanctions has increased the observance of norms and rules remains uncertain. However, there is evidence that the improved scrutiny of trade policies and practices and the dispute-settlement procedure of the WTO have improved compliance with WTO law (Jackson 2004: 114–19; Zangl 2008; Davey 2014).

Evaluation of the organization's effectiveness

Since the 1960s the volume of world trade has grown faster than the global production of goods and services. The trade ratios of major economies, that is the ratio of their exports and imports to their gross domestic product (GDP), have increased substantially (see Figure 9.1). For the EU member states (both intra-EU and extra-EU trade, see below), the USA and China, the trade ratios have more than doubled. We have, however, witnessed a new development since the mid-2000s. In addition to the interruption in 2008–09 of the economic crisis, trade ratios in the case of China have further declined. This is the result of the deliberate stimulation of the domestic economy after the major trade gains in the early 2000s following China's entry into the WTO. To put it differently, China benefited dramatically from the WTO in terms of trade, but has been trying to absorb this (positive) shock. For the EU member states and the USA, where trade ratios seem to have stabilized since the economic crisis, it is still too early to draw conclusions. Overall, the conclusion remains that world trade has significantly increased since the 1960s.

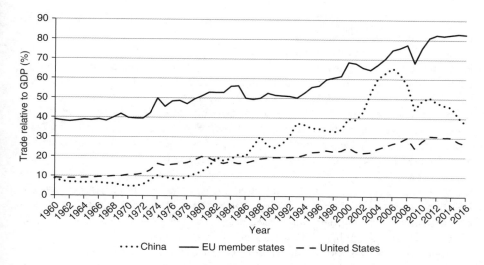

Figure 9.1   Trade ratios of major economies, 1960–2016

Source: Ratio of imports plus exports of goods and services to GDP, %, based on data from the World Bank.

There is a growing scientific consensus that the GATT/WTO can be cred-ited with this rise of world trade. In fact, the GATT/WTO has long been cited as one of the most successful international institutions. Membership of the GATT/WTO has expanded dramatically since 1947, and international trade has grown in tandem. Many observers have assumed that these trends are linked (Goldstein et al. 2007: 38; see Bagwell & Staiger 2002; Irwin 1995; Jackson 1999; Kahler 1995). Goldstein et al. (2007) demonstrate that, over the decades, the GATT/WTO has indeed substantially increased trade among its member states. The benefits of the GATT/WTO in terms of increased trade have not been limited to developed economies, but have extended also to developing countries (Goldstein et al. 2007: 63–64). These positive results refute Rose's (2004) earlier, much-debated analysis which found no evidence that the GATT/WTO increased trade among members, after controlling for national income, geography, and other factors that affect the flow of goods between countries. A positive assess-ment of the GATT/WTO's effectiveness in enhancing trade is supported by a number of further studies. For example, Mansfield and Reinhardt (2008) find that the GATT/WTO has served to reduce volatility in trade policy and trade flows. In so doing, these institutions have increased long-term global trade levels (see also Ingram et al. 2005).

Empirical evidence also suggests that flexibility clauses in the WTO's policy pro-gramme have done more good than harm. Opportunities to temporarily suspend or circumvent trade-liberalizing provisions increase states' readiness to both conclude trade agreements in the framework of the WTO and make deeper concessions when doing so. States able to take advantage of these flexibility provisions are significantly more likely to agree to more ambitious tariff-reduction commitments and to implement lower applied tariffs as well (Kucik & Reinhardt 2008; see also Rosendorf & Milner 2001: 832).

Apart from promoting progressive trade liberalization, GATT and the WTO have furthermore contributed to avoiding a protectionist spiral, despite numerous trade conflicts between, for example, the USA and the EU. While the WTO cannot prevent powerful trading states like the USA and China or trading blocs like the EU from occasionally breaching rules, existing regulations have, by and large, been observed satisfactorily (see Jackson 1999). Even though the GATT and WTO have escape clauses for countries to temporarily suspend trade rules when an economic crisis hits, scholars have shown that the institutionalized context of the GATT/WTO prevents abuse of those escape clauses (Pelc 2009). Analysing among others the economic crisis of the late 2000s, Davis and Pelc (2017) show that the WTO has promoted a strong norm: when all member states face hard times (e.g. a global economic crisis), they exercise self-restraint in using escape clauses 'to avoid beggar-thy-neighbor policies' (Davis & Pelc 2017: abstract).

There are, however, points of friction within the WTO which compromise its effectiveness, in particular with a view to the further development of its policy programme. Intergovernmental negotiations over new norms and rules in the various negotiating rounds can easily get stuck in deadlock due to national protectionist pressures or conflicts over the distribution of gains from international trade. This is evidenced by the negotiations in the Doha Round, which have made little progress since their inception in 2001. Restrictions to market access are still a main impediment to trade in agriculture, and there is still a shortage of multilateral rules on trade in services. The industrialized states frequently insist on trade liberalization while protecting or subsidizing sectors of their own economies in which developing countries have a comparative advantage, as in the agricultural and textile sectors. Moreover, the economic rise and growing political assertiveness of states such as Brazil, China and India (besides the traditional trading powers, the EU, USA and Japan) has hardly facilitated progress on further trade liberalization.

Indeed, as a result of the stalled Doha Round in the WTO, states are moving away from the negotiation of multilateral trade agreements in favour of comprehensive bilateral trade agreements. The EU has been at the forefront of negotiating bilateral free-trade agreements with South Korea (2011), Canada (2016) and Japan (2018) as well as a range of neighbouring countries. It has started negotiations with Australia and New Zealand and is modernizing a series of existing agreements. Perhaps most relevant of all, the EU and USA started negotiations, in 2013, on a Transatlantic Trade and Investment Partnership (TTIP), thereby signalling that the Doha Round had failed. The negotiations on TTIP have, however, been slow amidst a lot of domestic opposition and criticism. With the election of US President Trump, the TTIP negotiations have also been stalled. President Trump furthermore withdrew the US signature from the not-yet-ratified Trans-Pacific Partnership (TPP), a major trade deal between the USA and various Pacific countries, such as Australia, Canada, Chile, Japan, Singapore and Vietnam. While we have thus seen a strong move towards new bilateral free-trade agreements, rather than further WTO negotiations, the record of bilateral free-trade negotiations is also mixed.

These deficits in policy programme development of the WTO can be contrasted with a high degree of effectiveness in the adjudication of trade disputes (Davey 2014). Not only has there been a remarkable increase in disputes that were brought before the DSB, there is empirical evidence that the establishment of the WTO has contributed to further enhancing states' readiness to settle trade disputes according to multilateral rules and procedures. States demonstrably act more in accordance with the judicialized WTO dispute-settlement *procedures* than with the previous diplomatic GATT procedures: in the case of trade disputes states tend to follow, rather than avoid, manipulate or openly disregard WTO dispute-settlement procedures (Zangl 2008; see also Jackson 1999). The dispute-settlement system has also improved compliance with the substantive outcomes, that is the *decisions* of the DSB (Iida 2004; Leitner & Lester 2005). However, critics still argue that WTO dispute-settlement proceedings which work for powerful, developed countries are not equally helpful for the less powerful, developing countries that sometimes cannot even afford to invoke them (Busch & Reinhardt 2003; Guzman & Simmons 2005). Notwithstanding this limitation, one can claim that in the WTO context an international rule of law is gradually emerging, at least among equally powerful actors (Zangl 2008: 848). Whether this continues, with the Trump administration unilaterally imposing new tariffs on steel and other products, remains to be seen.

EUROPEAN TRADE RELATIONS

The global trade norms and rules under the WTO framework, including the most-favoured-nation principle, allow for further (regional) trade relations in the context of free-trade agreements or customs unions. This is not only to pave the way for further trade liberalization at the regional and bilateral level, but it is also a reflection of the wide range of already pre-existing regional trade agreements. Indeed, trade relations at the regional level can be deeper and more institutionalized than global trade relations. The states involved in regional trade regimes such as the EU, the North American Free Trade Agreement (NAFTA) or the Association of Southeast Asian Nations (ASEAN), for instance, are more homogeneous and should therefore have a broader basis for consensus. This kind of regional integration of trade policies is by far most advanced in the EU. The EU aimed from the very beginning at establishing a common market going far beyond a traditional free-trade area.

Policy programme of the EU

The policy programme of the EU on issues pertaining to trade among its members is much more ambitious than that of the WTO. From the Treaty of Rome setting up the European Economic Community (EEC) in 1958 to the Treaty on European Union (TEU) in 1993 and beyond, the aim has been to establish a common market (Moravcsik 1998: 86–158). This common market was to be established by

1969 through the complete elimination of barriers to free trade in goods, services, capital and labour. Initially, a detailed programme was developed only for trade in goods. This programme foresaw the elimination of 'customs duties and quantitative restrictions on the import and export of goods' between member states to unite them within a free-trade area (Treaty of Rome, Article 3, paragraph 1). Importantly, the member states also decided to establish a joint external tariff and trade policy (Treaty of Rome, Article 3, paragraph 2), thus forming a customs union from the very beginning (Nugent 2006: 43–47).

By 1969, internal customs duties had been abolished and an external tariff set up. Yet a true common market did not exist since – despite the harmonization of nearly 400 regulations by 1982 – non-tariff obstacles, such as different product standards, continued to persist (Moravcsik 1998: 159–237). In addition, different tax rates distorted competition. Furthermore, apart from the trade in goods, not much progress had been made in the free trade in services, capital and labour. Only in 1986, 16 years after the deadline for establishing an internal market had passed, did the Community take up the challenge. It established a programme for a 'single market by 1992'. After nearly two years of intergovernmental negotiations the member states proceeded to a thorough renewal and extension of the Treaty of Rome (Moravcsik 1991, 1998: 314–78). Of fundamental importance for the single market programme was the fact that the Single European Act of 1987 set 31 December 1992 as the new date for completion of the single market and created a new decision-making framework, since amended by the Treaties of Maastricht (1993), Amsterdam (1999), Nice (2003) and Lisbon (2009). For decisions in the Council of the EU the unanimity principle was abandoned in favour of majority decisions in order to facilitate those elements essential for the establishment of a single market, such as harmonization or mutual recognition of legal, technical and fiscal standards. Moreover, the European Parliament's role in the decision-making process has gradually been strengthened (see Chapter 4; Rittberger 2005).

The EU has come a long way since the 1992 Single Market Programme. Yet it is important to note that the internal market is not yet entirely complete. For instance, to further promote trade in services, the European Commission proposed, in 2004, to adopt a Services Directive. It suggested the companies should be able to offer their services across the EU in line with the laws of their home country. This mirrored the liberalization of trade in goods, for which the laws of the country of production apply. The Services Directive was, however, criticized for its potential to encourage social dumping. Particularly in France, the prospect of cheap 'Polish plumbers' providing unfair competition resulted in domestic opposition and also contributed to the French 'non' in the 2005 referendum on the Constitutional Treaty. As a result, the Services Directive was significantly watered down, which means that the EU still does not have a truly internal market for services.

The EU as a political system has also been slow to catch up with the inputs resulting from the revolution in communication and digital technology. For instance, the telecom market developed, during the 1990s and 2000s, entirely in the domestic context of the member states. Notwithstanding the pan-European consolidation of telecom companies, like Deutsche Telekom, Orange and Vodafone, calling and texting still remains a domestic affair. This is slightly bizarre given the prominence of the mobile phone. The EU has strongly reduced roaming rates and formally abolished them in 2017, but this has taken a long time. Furthermore, regular phone calls to numbers abroad still cost considerably more than domestic calls. Similar problems occur with digital streaming across borders ('geo-blocking'). For many years, content providers were capable of discriminating between member states in terms of where they were offering their services. While the EU has banned unjustified geo-blocking since 2018, it is yet another example of the unfinished internal market.

Operations of the EU

The agreement to establish a single market programme by member states in 1987 was not enough to guarantee its implementation. This ambitious policy programme set out which obstacles were to be removed. But it did not specify how. Operational activities by the EU were required to further specify the norms and rules. In addition, compliance with the policy programme by the member states was not guaranteed. Therefore the EU was tasked to monitor implementation, adjudicate in case of disputes, and to sanction member states when necessary.

To implement the single market programme, the Council of Ministers has adopted a wide range of detailed regulations or directives. Most of the decisions by the Council are taken by a qualified majority, along with the European Parliament, in an institutionalized decision-making process (see Chapters 4 & 6 on conversion). The European Commission has to monitor and ensure equal application of decisions in all member states. For that purpose, the Commission issues thousands of so-called implementation instructions each year. To fulfil this task the Commission has to rely on cooperation from member states through various committees, a procedure generally referred to as 'comitology' (Wallace 2010: 75). Instructions are worked out by the Commission in agreement with a multitude of committees made up of top civil servants and experts from the relevant ministries of member states (Joerges & Falke 2000; Nugent 2006: Chapter 9). The Commission must consult the competent committees. If the Commission and the committees fail to reach an agreement the committees can ask the Council to intervene, although this is rarely the case.

The committees allow member states to keep an eye on the Commission. However, the latter can call on civil servants and specialist members of these committees to use their expertise in the preparation and implementation of decisions (Joerges & Neyer 1997a, 1997b). This is essential, given the relatively small administrative apparatus of the Commission consisting of around 30,000 officials. Since the national civil servants who generally sit on these committees are the same people who are entrusted with implementation of the EU's regulations and directives, their implementation is almost guaranteed. Any problems with implementation would have been raised in the relevant committee.

The EU is an unusual international organization in that it grants supranational bodies exceptionally broad operational competencies. While much implementation is still left to the member states, since 1970, for example, the EU is solely responsible for external trade relations. This transfer of competencies had become necessary after the setting up of the customs union. In trade negotiations within the WTO, for instance, EU member states are represented by the European Commission. However, the Commission does not act fully autonomously. It is limited in its competencies by a negotiating mandate from the Council. The Trade Policy Committee, which consists of member states' civil servants, ensures that the Commission stays within its mandate. In addition, negotiated outcomes achieved under GATT or in the WTO had or have to be approved by the Council by a qualified majority. The Commission is therefore in charge of external trade policy, but is still carefully controlled by the member states (Vanhoonacker & Pomorska 2017: 101–04; Woolcock 2010).

While the EU is authorized to implement its norms and rules directly in only a few areas, the Commission has the competency in supervision. It can request reports about implementation of the EU's regulations and directives from member states and is also entitled to carry out on-site inspections in member states with a small team of inspectors. However, its capabilities are far too small to supervise reliably adherence to norms and rules, and it has to limit itself to ad hoc inspections. To ensure reliability the Commission has to make use of other means of supervision, especially information provided by private actors such as enterprises. Private actors can therefore be important in supplying information about a member state's non-compliance with European law.

If there is doubt about the proper implementation of European law in a member state the Commission will contact the relevant member state by letting it know informally that it may have contravened existing norms and rules. In this way the member state may agree to obey the norms voluntarily or else the Commission will send a 'letter of formal notice' in which it expresses the view that the state may be in breach of the law. This is usually sufficient to rectify the situation. However, if the member state concerned refuses to observe the norms and rules as required, the Commission will issue a 'reasoned opinion' outlining why it considers the member state to be in violation of the relevant treaty. If there is still no satisfactory response the Commission can take the member state to the European Court of Justice (ECJ). However, this only happens in a very small fraction of cases. The ECJ issues binding judgments which are accepted by the member states practically without exception (Hix 2005; Jönsson & Tallberg 1998; Tallberg 2002b).

Not only the Commission, but also citizens and corporations can ask the ECJ to ascertain breaches of EU norms and rules (Alter 2001: 16–27; Stone Sweet & Brunell 1998). However, they must first go through the courts in their own member states, which then must ask the ECJ for authoritative guidance in the form of a 'preliminary ruling'. The findings of the ECJ are passed back to the member state's court, which must base its judgment on the preliminary finding. In this way the courts of member states, under the guidance of the ECJ, ensure that the interpretation of EU law is not left to individual member states' governments.

The far-reaching monitoring and adjudication procedures within the EU are, however, complemented by a rather limited sanctions mechanism. Individual member states are formally forbidden to impose sanctions against other member states in breach of EU law. Even when a member state refuses to abide by a judgment of the ECJ the other member states may not respond with sanctions. Not even the European Commission could impose sanctions against a member state in breach of European law until the Treaty of Maastricht in 1993. If a member state does not rectify its breach, the Commission can request the ECJ to impose a fine (Oppermann et al. 2009: 259–61). Stronger sanctions seem unnecessary, given the very high observance of ECJ judgments, whose authority seems sufficient to make member states comply (Tallberg 2002b; Wallace 2010: 84–86). Furthermore, the EU may suspend certain rights deriving from membership, including voting rights, in case of 'a serious and persistent breach by a Member State' (Article 7(2) TEU). This possibility is, however, politically difficult: it requires unanimity among the other member states and it challenges the consensus-oriented nature of the EU. While the EU disposes of weak possibilities for imposing sanctions on member states, it has comparatively strong possibilities of using sanctions to force citizens or corporations to comply with existing EU law. For instance, in the area of competition, the Commission is partly entitled to impose sanctions, for instance substantial fines, on enterprises in breach of European competition rules (McGowan 2000: 118–38).

Evaluation of the organization's effectiveness

On a general level, the EU has achieved one of the main goals it was created for: securing economic prosperity for its people. Trade is the EU's oldest, and most successfully integrated, common policy (Meunier 2003: 69; Moravcsik 2002: 606–08). We have already seen in Figure 9.1 that EU member states have a significantly higher trade ratio than other major powers, such as the USA and China. The trade ratios for France and Germany were respectively 60 per cent and 84 per cent in 2016 (World Bank n.d.).

What is more, between the completion of the Single Market (1993) and the start of the global financial and economic crisis in 2007–08 the intra-EU trade ratio, that is the ratio of exports and imports among EU members to EU-wide GDP, has increased considerably (see Figure 9.2). Within the decade from the mid-1990s to the mid-2000s, the intra-EU trade ratio increased from around 30 per cent to almost 45 per cent. Despite a drop as a result of the economic crisis, the intra-EU trade ratio has again stabilized. Moreover, there is a large gap between the intra-EU and the extra-EU trade ratios. This means that trade among EU members is much more pronounced than trade of EU members with non-EU members. For instance, 58.5 per cent of German exports in 2017 went to other EU member states (European Commission 2018: 62). While this may in part be due to geographic proximity, it is likely that the Single Market has also contributed to this gap between intra-EU and external EU trade (see Figure 9.2).

Scharpf (1999) has shown that the European Commission and the ECJ have helped in freeing trade and capital movements ('negative integration') in Europe – though not fully in services, as shown above. Negative integration, that is activities that lead to the removal of barriers to trade or of obstacles to undistorted competition in Europe, has been developed by the Commission and the ECJ into a powerful tool aimed at removing national measures that distort the free movement of goods, services, capital and labour (Kohler-Koch & Rittberger 2006: 40–41; see Stone Sweet 2004). This is corroborated by econometric findings which suggest

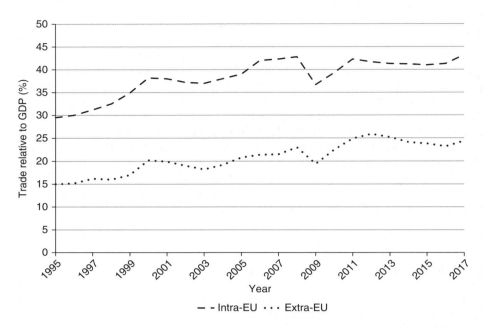

Figure 9.2   Intra-EU and extra-EU trade in comparison, 1995–2017

Sources: Ratios of exports and imports of goods to EU GDP, %, based on data from Eurostat; Ilzkovitz et al. (2007: 30).

that overall the Single Market is a powerful instrument to promote economic integration within the EU. It has also been the source of large macroeconomic benefits in terms of both economic growth and job creation, even though cross-border barriers remain, due to slow and sometimes incomplete implementation of EU directives and the persistence of (non-tariff) barriers to cross-border trade and investment, particularly in the realm of services (Ilzkovitz et al. 2007). In fact, the EU's model of economic integration is now being explored by countries around the world (Meunier & McNamara 2007).

In contrast to the success in bringing about negative integration, the EU has been far less successful in terms of 'positive integration', that is the adoption of common policies especially in social policy and taxation (Scharpf 1999). This is not to say that instances of regulation that succeed in resolving or mitigating European problems in the areas of economic policy, social policy and regional development do not exist (see Eichener 1997; Genschel & Jachtenfuchs 2014). However, the potential for the EU's supranational actors to bring about measures of positive integration is much more limited because such measures generally require explicit approval by the Council of Ministers and the European Parliament, and thus a consensus among a wide range of divergent national and group interests (Kohler-Koch & Rittberger 2006: 41; Scharpf 1999: 71). Decision-making procedures that, depending on the scope and depth of Europeanization of (redistributive) economic policies, require unanimity or at least large majorities in both organs have thus limited the EU's effectiveness in the realm of positive integration.

The transfer of sovereignty to the EU institutions has not only produced a single market and policy integration in trade and other economic policies but has also led to the current complaint of a 'democratic deficit'. The move from unanimity to qualified majority decisions in the Council has far-reaching consequences for member states' democracies. National parliaments cannot hold their governments accountable for decisions for which they did not vote in the EU Council of Ministers but which are nevertheless binding on all member states. This means that member states' parliaments have been deprived of the authority to take decisions in a wide area of public policy as well as of the possibility to effectively hold their governments to account. To accommodate such concerns, the Treaty of Lisbon (2009) has introduced a procedure by which national parliaments can express their objection to Commission proposals for EU action which, in their view, violate the principle of subsidiarity. However, national parliaments can only delay rather than ultimately block such initiatives. The problem of democratic accountability is somewhat mitigated, however, by the fact that the European Parliament has continually been given greater co-decision power (Rittberger 2005). The Lisbon Treaty extended the 'ordinary legislative procedure' to several new fields, including trade and agricultural policies. Nonetheless, as more and more Council decisions follow the qualified majority rule the EU will continue to suffer from a democratic deficit as long as the European Parliament does not obtain in full (and in all areas of binding decision-making) those competencies which until now have usually been vested in member states' parliaments (see Chapters 4 and 5).

To this we must add the challenges related to the EU enlargement, which raises questions of both efficiency and democratic legitimacy of decision-making. The more member states there are, the more difficult it becomes to ensure reasonably smooth and at the same time democratic decision-making. Unanimity turns out to be ever-more difficult to achieve for the decisions required to further nurture integration in the trade policy of the Union. If the EU wants to function effectively, it will need to rely to an even greater extent on qualified majority decisions in the Council. This is reflected in the Treaty of Lisbon's provisions on the scope of qualified majority voting and the calculation of the necessary double majority (55 per cent of the member states representing at least 65 per cent of the Union's population; see Chapters 4 and 6). Despite these reforms in decision-making and the strengthened (but still limited) role for the European Parliament, the enlarged EU continues to face the challenge of finding a way of increasingly consolidating the integration process which allows effective decision-making without simultaneously weakening its feedback to the democratic representative bodies.

DISPARITIES IN DEVELOPMENT

International organizations in the field of trade, such as the WTO and EU, facilitate mutually beneficial solutions of the economic dilemma: to avoid countries engaging in mercantilism at the expense of overall growth. However, simultaneously, they may give rise to or exacerbate disparities in development. Market forces in a liberal economic order only distribute benefits equally to all participating states if they dispose of roughly similar conditions for market participation. If this premise is not fulfilled, an eventuality which is the rule rather than the exception, there is a strong risk that markets exacerbate existing development disparities. Enterprises in developing countries may not withstand global competition, or in these countries free trade may result in further emphasis on labour-intensive industries. To mitigate such risks, the WTO programme allows for exceptions, for instance giving preferential trading opportunities to least-developed countries. The EU has furthermore established a range of cohesion and regional funds. In this final section of the chapter, we focus on development assistance and loans by the World Bank Group.

Almost all developing countries are interested in an international economic order that can provide for a more equitable distribution of benefits. But developed countries, too, have a long-term stake in a fairer distribution of the benefits of liberal international trade and financial relations: the unequal distribution of benefits contains a real danger of undermining the legitimacy of the liberal global economic order. Most developed countries thus find themselves caught between long-term and short-term interests. While in the long term they favour a fairer distribution of wealth, in the short term the existing distribution is more attractive. Developed countries' tendency of preserving existing disparities may even increase as serious economic contenders emerge from the ranks of developing countries. What is more, even if all developed countries were to favour a fairer distribution, for each one there would still remain the temptation to take a free ride by avoiding the costs, for instance, of development assistance. Ultimately, this development dilemma can only be overcome through international cooperation. We take the World Bank Group as an example.

Policy programme of the World Bank Group

The policy programme of the World Bank Group is mainly redistributive, which sets it apart from the regulatory programmes of the international organizations discussed so far. It is the mandate of the World Bank Group to support the development of its less-developed member states in 'the South', and also, following the end of the Cold War, the countries in transition in 'the East'. Its main task is to provide these countries with loans, some at the usual market rates and some under preferential conditions, as well as offering technical assistance. The loans and technical assistance are allocated for specific projects for which private finance is not available or which could not be implemented independently without technical assistance from outside (Gilbert & Vines 2000; Metzger 2002).

The World Bank Group consists of the International Bank for Reconstruction and Development (IBRD), usually known as the World Bank, which was conceived at Bretton Woods in 1944 (Gilbert & Vines 2000: 12–17). The World Bank's affiliate organizations, the International Finance Corporation (IFC), the International Development Association (IDA) and the Multilateral Investment Guarantee Agency (MIGA) were established in 1956, 1960 and 1988, respectively. Although the IBRD, IDA, IFC and MIGA are formally independent organizations with different sources of finance and loan conditions, they are de facto so much intertwined organizationally that they can be seen as a single organization, the World Bank Group (Gilbert & Vines 2000: 12–21).

Originally the World Bank concentrated almost exclusively on rebuilding the war-ravaged areas of Europe. This changed following the process of decolonization in the 1960s and 1970s. The growing number of developing countries turned developmental disparities into a problem for developed countries; in particular their greater voting power in the UN compelled the developed countries to take into account the developing countries' request for a more equitable distribution of welfare (Krasner 1985: 141–51). They had to react to protect the stability of the liberal world economic order against the challenge of a 'new international economic order' (NIEO) demanded not only by the 'Third World' but also by public opinion in their own societies. Developments in the international environment thus resulted in clear input for the World Bank and its member states. To prevent an NIEO, the developed world accepted the expansion of the multilateral financing of development through, inter alia, the institutions of the World Bank Group (Marshall 2008; Spero & Hart 2003).

The financial basis of the World Bank itself is its share capital, subscribed by member states, which the Bank uses to sell bonds on international financial markets. The subscriptions are based on a state's relative weight in the world economy, which also determines its voting share in the Board of Governors and the Board of Directors. However, the World Bank only has a small amount of this share capital directly at its disposal. Member states must only pay 20 per cent of their quotas in a freely convertible currency, the Bank being able to call on the remaining 80 per cent at any time. This makes the World Bank creditworthy on private capital markets and thus it can borrow to make capital available to its loan recipients (Gilbert & Vines 2000: 10–21; Marshall 2008: 59–92).

The Board of Governors of the World Bank, on which member states are represented by their finance and development aid ministers, had raised the share capital of the World Bank step by step to approximately US$270 billion by 2017. The IBRD uses this capital to sell (top-rated) bonds on international financial markets, which in turn finance lending to developing countries. Its capacity for making loans has broadened substantially, mainly by borrowing on the international capital markets and through repayments of earlier loans. Since 1964 net gains from financial transactions are no longer used to provide loans from the IBRD, but are mostly passed to the IDA. IBRD loans are almost exclusively granted to states. Loans to private investors are exceptional and must be backed by a repayment guarantee from a sovereign government (of the investor or of the country where the investment is to take place). Loans are normally granted for 15 to 20 years (with a three-to-five-year grace period before repayment of principal begins) and at a somewhat more favourable rate of interest than commercial market rates.

IDA loans are 'soft loans'. They run for 20, 35 or 40 years and are de facto interest free with a merely administrative fee of 0.75 per cent. Repayments are made after a grace period of ten years. Because of these very favourable terms, only the poorer member states of the World Bank which lack the financial ability to borrow from IBRD can request these loans. In 2018, some 75 states had the right to such loans. Unlike the IBRD, which operates almost like a conventional bank, the IDA is more of a fund administration. To be able to provide such favourable loan conditions it requires regular restocking of its financial means and relies on repayments of IDA loans from recipient countries and interest-free contributions from member states, as well as allocation of IBRD resources. The financially strong members of the World Bank Group meet every three years to determine the extent of replenishment. The IDA makes US$13 billion-worth of loans a year.

The financial sources of the IFC are practically identical to those of the IBRD, but states must pay their contributions to the share capital in full. Just as with the IBRD, the IFC's share capital has been raised repeatedly by decisions of the Board of Governors. Repayable external means are only sought from the IBRD and not on the private capital markets. The decisive difference between this organization and the IBRD and the IDA lies in the fact that loans can be allocated to private investors in developing countries without a sovereign government's repayment guarantee. Furthermore, the IFC can become an equity partner in a business for a limited period.

The MIGA aims at promoting foreign direct investment in developing countries through investor insurances. The MIGA insures investors against political risks such as currency transfer restrictions, expropriation, internal violent conflict, or breach of investment contracts by governments. Corporations or financial institutions are eligible for coverage if they are either incorporated in, or have their principal place of business in, a member country. The MIGA prices its guarantee premiums based on a calculation of both country and project risk, with annual premiums ranging between 0.45 per cent and 1.75 per cent of the insured amount of investment per year. Since its inception, MIGA has issued hundreds of guarantees for projects in more than 100 developing countries. The MIGA also advises governments on attracting investment and mediates disputes between investors and governments.

Operations of the World Bank Group

Since redistributive programmes like those of the World Bank Group are particularly difficult to implement, its operational activities are of considerable significance. These programmes, within which resources are transferred to specific projects, require specification, formulated in two stages. In the first stage, the Group presents a global development strategy, giving first clues to the nature of the project or the countries deemed worthy of support. In the second stage, it selects specific development projects and countries which are then to receive financial and technical assistance.

Formally, it is the responsibility of the Board of Directors of the Bank to determine the basic features of project financing. In reality, the President and the bureaucratic apparatus determine the development strategy and the guidelines for the allocation of loans, though, of course, they cannot ignore donor states' interests in loan allocations. On the whole, the Board of Directors merely approves or rejects the development strategies and guidelines worked out by the bureaucratic apparatus. Thus, while both NGOs and large donor states are trying to influence decisions and Bank staff is building coalitions with these actors, the World Bank Group, through its President and administration, is still enjoying a relatively high degree of autonomy in designing development projects (Woods 2000: 137–47).

The development strategy, as specified by the World Bank Group, has gone through four phases. The changes from phase to phase mainly reflect new research findings, some by the Group itself, as well as a reaction to the dynamics of the world economy (Kanbur & Vines 2000). In the first phase of 'modernization without worry' (Tetzlaff 1996: 73), it mainly supported large infrastructure projects in transport, energy, telecommunications and the like. The development strategy of the 1970s saw a significant shift in emphasis. Robert McNamara, as President (1968–81), promoted financing of projects of various sizes in agriculture and rural development. The new key concepts were basic-needs orientation, investment in the poor and redistribution with growth.

The sobering effect of the growing debt crisis of many developing countries from the start of the 1980s, and the change in paradigm to a neo-liberal monetary economic policy in the USA and the United Kingdom (Higgott 2001), forced the World Bank Group to respecify its programme for the gradual removal of developmental disparities. In this third phase, in conjunction with the International Monetary Fund (IMF), the strategy of structural adjustment was developed. With the help of Structural Adjustment Programmes (SAPs) the creditworthiness of developing countries was to be re-established as quickly as possible in order to focus once again on the fight against poverty. The Group and the IMF linked the allocation of loans initially to macroeconomic conditions and later even to political conditions (Barnett & Finnemore 2004). While the later political conditions were inspired by Western liberal thought on democracy and good governance, the macroeconomic conditions were influenced by neoclassical economics (Chwieroth 2009; Ferreira & Keely 2000: 159–74). The application of neoclassical economics to the area of development assistance led to a ten-point catalogue of measures which the Group and the IMF made the benchmark for their policies in relation to countries receiving loans. This became known informally as the 'Washington Consensus' (see Box 9.1; Higgott 2001; Williamson 1990).

Box 9.1 The ten-point catalogue of the Washington Consensus

1. fiscal discipline
2. redirection of public expenditures (from subsidies to investment in education and infrastructure)
3. tax reform (combining a broad tax base with moderate marginal tax rates)
4. liberalization of interest rates (market-determined interest rates)
5. competitive exchange rates
6. trade liberalization
7. liberalization of inward foreign direct investment
8. privatization (of state enterprises)
9. deregulation (of business activities)
10. guarantee of effective property rights

Source: Williamson (1990).

At the beginning of the 1990s, the World Bank Group had to deal with criticism from both without and within. A report it had commissioned to look into the failures of the structural adjustment programmes strategy, the Wapenhans Report of 1992, started a lengthy learning process which had also been called for by several large NGOs such as Oxfam and World Vision. In early 1999, the then President, James D. Wolfensohn, submitted a plan for a new, fourth development strategy, that of a Comprehensive Development Framework (CDF) which, in many points, is also reflected in the UN Millennium Development Goals. For the first time, the Group set itself concrete targets. Thus, in conjunction with the Organisation for Economic Co-operation and Development (OECD), the IMF and the UN, six key targets were to be met by 2015. Among these were halving the number of people living in absolute poverty, the reduction of child mortality by two-thirds, and the achievement of primary education for all. Discarding the emphasis on macroeconomic reforms, the CDF focused attention on the other side of the coin – the structural, social and human aspects of development. The integration of economic policy (the IMF) and social policy (the World Bank Group) represents the cornerstone of the new strategy which has since been dubbed the 'Post-Washington Consensus' (Higgott 2001).

In 2013, the Board of Governors of the World Bank Group adopted a new strategy that entirely focuses on ending extreme poverty and promoting shared prosperity. Its first target is to decrease the percentage of people living with less than $1.90 a day from 18 per cent in 2010 to no more than 3 per cent by 2030. Its second target is to promote income growth of the bottom 40 per cent of the population in each developing country. These two targets correspond with Sustainable Development Goals (SDGs) 1 and 10 agreed in the framework of the UN. As such the World Bank Group makes a concrete contribution to the global development agenda. At the same time, with only the two key targets, the World Bank Group's development strategy is much more focused than the overall SDGs agenda of the UN. While not formal targets, the World Bank Group furthermore stresses the need for sustainable development that will secure 'the future of the planet and its resources, promote social inclusion, and limit the economic burdens that future generations inherit' (World Bank Group 2014: 1).

On the basis of the relevant development strategy, with its specific selection criteria, the World Bank Group chooses definite projects for its loans. To identify projects worthy of support the Group draws up a *country report* for each possible beneficiary in which the general economic situation of the country is analysed. On the basis of such a report the Group's development experts proceed to a *sector analysis*. This is a detailed analysis of the economic, financial, technical, infrastructural and social contexts of the country deemed worthy of support. The country report and sector analysis provide the basis for the five-year *development plan* drawn up by the Group for the relevant country. It lists projects that could be supported and thus represents a catalogue from which to select projects. The final selection occurs in an *expert report* drawn up after a World Bank Group delegation has inspected conditions locally. After further scrutiny by its Loans Committee the Group starts negotiations with the recipient country in which a *loan agreement* is drawn up describing the project in detail and determining the loan conditions.

The agreement is then submitted to the Executive Directors for approval (Marshall 2008: 66–70; Mosley et al. 1995).

Even then the World Bank Group does not entirely relax control over the projects it supports. It often participates directly in the form of technical assistance. But the largest share of technical assistance by the Group is provided before project selection, since the country reports, sector analyses and development plans give indications to the states as to how they could organize their development strategy more effectively. Another important form of technical assistance are the *missions* to assess development projects. Through direct contact with the local institutions and civil society actors involved in the implementation of projects, important changes of direction can be undertaken during the preparatory phase. Although formally states are supposed to submit project proposals to the Group in order to obtain a loan, in reality they are often drawn up by Group experts and discussed locally during a delegation's assessment visit.

Despite this close involvement from the start, the World Bank Group undertakes further inspections to ensure adherence to the agreed loan conditions. It can request either interim reports from the recipient country or send a delegation to inspect whether the project is following agreed procedures. If a country repeatedly disregards the loan agreement, the Group has sanction options at its disposal. It can interrupt or suspend loan disbursement until a state fulfils the agreed conditions (Marshall 2008: 112–35; World Bank 2007: 76–81).

Evaluation of the organization's effectiveness

An assessment of the World Bank's effectiveness can be made at several levels. In general, there can be little doubt that the World Bank Group is relatively effective in achieving the transfer of sizeable resources to developing countries through projects (Einhorn 2001). However, the real question is whether World Bank grants and loans contribute to improving the socioeconomic conditions of living in developing countries. Thus a look at global trends in the prevalence of absolute poverty provides a first, albeit very broad, clue as to whether the World Bank's activities have had a positive impact (see Figure 9.3). Within the period from 1981 to 2013 the share of people living in absolute poverty (i.e. on less than US$1.90 a day) has decreased on the global scale. However, a closer examination of regional trends casts some doubts on the proposition that the World Bank has played a major role in this positive development. The largest decrease of poverty has occurred in Eastern Asia, first of all in China, where World Bank lending has been limited. On the other hand, in Latin America and especially in sub-Saharan Africa, where the World Bank has been much more involved in funding development projects, the reduction of absolute poverty is much smaller – though by no means negligible (see Figure 9.3). Whereas these broad macro-indicators certainly do not prove the uselessness of World Bank development assistance, they do suggest that the World Bank's impact is limited: large-scale multilateral lending seems to be neither a necessary nor a sufficient condition for lifting countries and people out of poverty.

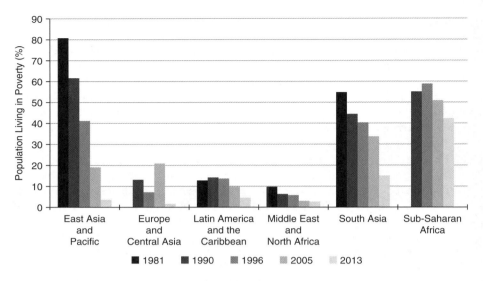

Figure 9.3   Decrease of absolute poverty: population living on less than US$1.90 per day, 1981–2013 (%)

Sources: Based on data from the World Bank.

On a somewhat more specific level, scholars have investigated whether World Bank lending promotes (sustainable) economic growth in developing countries. In this regard, the empirical record is inconclusive. On the negative side, Easterly (2005), confirming an earlier study by Harrigan and Mosley (1991), finds that none of the top 20 recipients of repeated adjustment lending from the World Bank over the period 1980–99 were able to achieve reasonable economic growth. Harrigan and Mosley (1991) also identify a negative correlation between Structural Adjustment Loans to a country and foreign investment in this country. Moreover, there is empirical evidence that aid conditionality has often been ineffective, in part because conditions and policy reforms have not been implemented (Kilby 2009). However, on the positive side, there are also studies citing evidence that World Bank lending stimulates growth in some cases, primarily by increasing public investment (Butkiewicz & Yanikkaya 2005). Crisp & Kelly (1999) also show for 16 Latin American cases that structural adjustment was weakly associated with economic growth. Moreover, they found that, surprisingly, structural adjustment programmes were statistically associated with declining socioeconomic inequality (Crisp & Kelly 1999: 548). So we must state that the scholarly literature is split on whether World Bank programmes promote growth and that we know very little for sure about the World Bank's impact on economic growth in developing countries.

What the 1990s did show, though, is the extent to which the success or failure of World Bank development programmes is linked to the development strategy. The shock of the Asian financial crisis of 1997, just like that experienced during the debt crises of Mexico in 1982 and Brazil in 1987, led to another rethink by encouraging an (albeit hesitant) move away from the development model of neoclassical economics. After the scope of the Bank's activities had dramatically increased with the rise of structural adjustment and conditionality in the 1980s and the collapse of communism in the 1990s, criticism increased at the turn of the twenty-first century, challenging the effectiveness, legitimacy and reach of the Bank. Additions to the neo-liberal agenda were made throughout the 1990s as concerns by various interest groups came to the fore, including poverty alleviation, debt relief, gender equality and environmental safeguards, among others (Park & Vetterlein 2010: 7). As a result, the World Bank set new targets for its programmes at the end of the 1990s on the basis of a 'Post-Washington Consensus' (Higgott 2001). A key element of this new strategy is the Poverty Reduction Strategy Papers (PRSPs). However, preliminary evidence on the impact of PRSPs in Latin America has not been encouraging so far (Dijkstra & Komives 2011; Guimarães & Avendaño 2010).

Apart from these inconclusive, if not disappointing, results concerning the impact of World Bank programmes on growth and poverty alleviation, the World Bank's effectiveness in addressing global disparities in development is hampered by the prevalence of organized hypocrisy in and around the Bank (Weaver 2008). The World Bank faces ever-increasing and at least in part conflicting demands from donor countries, recipients, NGOs and private investors, which are very hard to satisfy at the same time, especially in an organization with an entrenched bureaucratic culture that makes fundamental reform difficult.

CONCLUSION

International organizations make a significant contribution to cooperation in economic relations. Within the context of the WTO, the member states have established an ambitious policy programme on global trade. The EU member states have set up an internal market policy programme and many have even adopted a common currency and monetary policy. These policy programmes are not only ambitious; they have been complemented with extensive operational activities by the WTO and EU institutions. Through the operational activities, these international organizations operate quite autonomously from direct member state interference, though are by no means devoid of deficiencies in effectiveness. At the same time, it is also clear that even in the area of economic cooperation, the member states still play a key role. It is the conflict between the member states that prevents progress in the WTO development round. It was equally the major EU member states that only allowed for the internal market programme once their preferences converged.

When thinking about international organizations as political systems, it is worth pointing out some of the key developments in the international environment that led to further cooperation. For both the EU and WTO, it is clear that the stalemates of the 1970s and 1980s and the increasing prominence of non-tariff barriers made member states reconsider their inputs. At the same time, the emergence of new 'problems' (from intellectual property rights to new communication and digital technology) also resulted in further input for cooperation. What should also not be underestimated is the momentum of both organizations. Successful previous negotiation rounds in the GATT gave impetus for the WTO. Similarly, the successful Treaty reforms in the EU during the 1990s gave, in turn, momentum for the next rounds of cooperation. At the same time, we have also seen how more difficult crises have affected the WTO and EU differently. Whereas the failure of the Doha Round has resulted in a move from multilateral trade to bilateral trade, the Eurozone crisis has effectively led to further EU integration. In conclusion, such developments in the international environment are vital for how member states and other political actors formulate their inputs.

In terms of the conversion process, both in the WTO and EU much of the policy programme has come about through high-level intergovernmental conferences. In the GATT/WTO these were repeated negotiation rounds, whereas in the EU these were formal intergovernmental conferences resulting in treaty change. Despite the member states' dominance in these conferences, it also needs to be said that these were not one-off ad hoc events. High-level negotiations also took place in an institutionalized context. When focusing on the operational activities of both organizations, we see the prominence of the plenary organs and executive councils as well as delegated decision-making. The plenary organs and executive councils in the WTO and EU have been critical in terms of specifying the norms and rules. Through delegated decision-making, the WTO members settle their trade disputes through the DSU. In the EU, the Commission and ECJ have been instrumental in monitoring member states, providing adjudication over trade disputes.

As a result of these policy programmes and operational activities (output), we have seen a significant reduction in trade barriers (outcome) and a subsequent increase in trade (impact). This is impressive both in the WTO and EU. However, it also needs to be said that both organizations have been particularly effective in addressing trade in goods. They are less successful in dealing with trade relations in other areas such as services: the Doha Round has not delivered a result in this respect and EU rules also remain underdeveloped.

This chapter has also identified a need to address economic disparities between richer and poorer countries. As a result of trade liberalization, inequalities can increase, which poses a development dilemma. While there are many international organizations dealing with development, this chapter has focused on the World Bank Group. It has highlighted the different policy programmes available, but also stressed how the World Bank Group has (slowly) addressed its objectives over time as a result of negative feedback from previous outcomes. For instance, the World Bank Group now pays central attention to human development, including eradicating poverty, rather than the macro-level development of countries. Furthermore the World Bank Group now prioritizes sustainable development, which does not come at the expense of the environment, rather than economic development per se.

Discussion Questions

1. What are the main obstacles for the further formulation and specification of trade policy programmes within the WTO?
2. What are the strengths of the EU's internal market? Why are trade relations in the EU more advanced than in the WTO?
3. To what extent have World Bank's objectives changed over time and why?

Further Reading

Matsushita, Mitsuo, Schoenbaum, Thomas J., Mavroidis, Petros C. & Hahn, Michael 2015. *The World Trade Organization: Law, Practice, and Policy*, 3rd edn, Oxford: Oxford University Press.

Moravcsik, Andrew 1998. *The Choice for Europe. Social Purpose and State Power from Messina to Maastricht*, Ithaca, NY: Cornell University Press.

Weaver, Catherine 2008. *Hypocrisy Trap. The World Bank and the Poverty of Reform*, Ithaca, NY: Cornell University Press.

10 Finance and Monetary Relations

In the previous chapter, we outlined the economic dilemma. Through tariffs and non-tariff barriers, states can pursue economic advantages at the expense of other states. Such mercantilist policies ultimately result in a situation where all states are worse off. International organizations can provide an answer to this dilemma by monitoring the implementation of trade agreements and providing adjudication in case of trade disputes. Yet by having open economics and engaging in international trade, states face another range of potential problems. First, there is a financing problem: for international trade, states need some stability in the exchange rates. They also need guarantees that they – and the companies in their countries – get their investment and loans back and that other states do not simply default on their debts. If states do not have such guarantees, they will less likely engage in international trade. Second, there is a monetary problem: states can try to get a competitive advantage for their domestic industries through the devaluation of their national currencies. If states put on the 'money press', their currencies may lose value, resulting in more beneficial exchange rates, which benefits exporting industries. This may, once again, result in a negative 'race to the bottom' in which countries compete by reducing the values of their currencies.

International organizations play a key role in addressing these international finance and monetary problems. In this chapter we focus on the role of the International Monetary Fund (IMF) and the European Union (EU). The IMF has been critical, in its early years, to guaranteeing a fixed exchange rate and has thereby stabilized international monetary policy. The IMF has also become the leading international organization for bailing out indebted countries. By making loans available with clear conditions attached, the IMF has helped countries out of bankruptcy, which has had positive effects for global financial stability. This chapter also focuses on monetary policy in the case of the EU. Many EU member states have adopted the euro as their common currency. We focus, in this chapter, on the policy programme of the EU in monetary affairs as well as the operational activities of the European Central Bank (ECB) in this area.

GLOBAL FINANCIAL RELATIONS

The limitation of convertibility and the devaluation of currencies are instruments that states can use to achieve similar effects to the setting of tariffs. If several states make use of these options for their own short-term gain, international exchange relations suffer lasting damage, to the detriment of all in the long term.

In the long term all states are worse off, both collectively and individually, if they do not cooperate to eliminate such financial practices. The IMF serves as an example of how international organizations can contribute to international cooperation in finance. The IMF has, furthermore, become the lender of last resort for heavily indebted countries. As such, it is a crisis manager that can safeguard global financial stability.

Policy programme of the IMF

After the Second World War, the IMF's policy programme (see Chapter 3) created a limited liberal financial order corresponding to the world trade order of the time. The 1944 intergovernmental negotiating process at Bretton Woods, dominated by the USA and the United Kingdom, established norms and rules for the IMF which were intended to strengthen the envisaged liberal trade relations eventually agreed under GATT (1947) while simultaneously leaving states some leeway for national economic steering and welfare state policies (Gilpin 2000: 57–68; Helleiner 1994: 25–72). The norms and rules obliging states to establish the free convertibility of their currencies were particularly aimed at promoting liberal trade relations. The logic was that the smooth payment transactions necessary for international trade can only take place if the free exchange of one currency for another is guaranteed (in the absence of a world currency).

The original norms and rules of the IMF committed the member states to fixed, but adaptable, exchange rates for their currencies (Kahler 1995: 48–64; Spero & Hart 2003). This solution tried to combine the advantages of a system of fixed exchange rates with those of flexible rates without burdening member states with the disadvantages of either. In the case of both fixed and flexible exchange rates, supply and demand on international financial markets determine the value of a currency because of its free convertibility. While with flexible exchange rates demand and supply are not influenced by states (allowing for relatively free fluctuation), in the case of fixed exchange rates national central banks influence supply and demand on international financial markets so that the exchange rate remains stable at the agreed level. This means that international business can take place without the constant fear of fluctuations in the currencies in which the value of services or goods is calculated. However, in order to keep the value of their currencies constant, states must orientate their entire economic and financial policy towards maintenance of international equilibrium. Unlike in the case of flexible exchange rates, they largely lose the scope for using domestic measures in areas which affect competitiveness, like social and environmental policies.

Within the IMF's system of fixed but adaptable exchange rates, all currencies were linked to the US dollar acting as a currency anchor. The dollar was itself protected through its gold parity of US$35 to one ounce of gold (the 'gold standard'). The various currencies were allowed to deviate from the rate fixed in relation to the US dollar by up to 1 per cent up or down, which means that in relation to other currencies there could be deviations of up to 2 per cent. Furthermore, it was possible to adapt the exchange rate of a national currency in cases of severe balance-of-payments imbalances, which continuously threatened the agreed fixed exchange rates. This possibility gave states the leeway to take, for instance, social policy measures or measures of economic steering that otherwise would have accentuated balance-of-payments imbalances (Helleiner 1994: 25–50; Spero & Hart 2003).

To enhance the domestic leeway for economic steering and social policy measures independently of potential exchange rate adaptations, each member state transferred currency reserves, called 'quotas', to the IMF which were then available as temporary foreign currency loans to be drawn on by individual states in times of balance-of-payments deficits. This was to enable states to finance interventions on financial markets in favour of their currencies. The amount of the loan, called 'drawing rights', was calculated in relation to the amount of currency reserves which the state concerned had put at the IMF's disposal. Thus states with high quotas disposed of a higher amount of credit than states with lower quotas. In case of balance-of-payments problems, states were allowed to borrow up to 100 per cent of their quotas without having to fulfil certain conditions. If they wanted to borrow up to 125 per cent of their quotas certain conditions were set. This loan facility created a currency buffer which enabled states to maintain liberal trade relations despite a system of fixed exchange rates, even when they got into balance-of-payments difficulties (Gilpin 2000: 59–62; Helleiner 1994: 25–50).

In the spirit of a limited liberal financial order the norms and rules of the IMF did not oblige member states to renounce controls over capital movements. States were able to use controls over capital movements to finance domestic measures through their taxation system or debt policy without fear of a flight of capital (Gilpin 2000: 139–40). In addition, it was hoped that a restricted movement of capital would strengthen the system of fixed exchange rates because it limited the possibility of speculative foreign exchange movements and the resulting attacks on one or the other currency (Helleiner 1994: 25–72; Pauly 1997: 79–97).

The Bretton Woods system embedded in the IMF became operative in the 1950s and 1960s but was only effective as long as the movement of capital could really be limited. Yet this became less and less feasible with the creation of the 'eurodollar markets' that arose in the late 1950s and early 1960s: British and US banks in London attempted to circumvent existing controls on the movement of capital for their international financial business. While British banks began to conduct their international financial affairs in US dollars, American banks transferred their international financial affairs to London. Since British controls on the movement of capital only applied to deals in pounds sterling and American controls applied only to deals in the USA, this created a financial centre in London allowing for a largely unregulated movement of capital (Eichengreen 1996: 93–152; Helleiner 1994: 81–122).

The rapidly growing eurodollar market put pressure on the Bretton Woods system because the freer movement of capital enabled speculative attacks on individual currencies, making it more and more difficult to maintain the fixed exchange rate parities. The IMF's loans were insufficient to counter these attacks effectively, especially as speculation was directed at the dollar as well. The USA faced a dilemma and could do little about it. If it reduced its balance-of-payments deficits, which began to show up in the 1950s, international trade relations would have suffered lasting damage since international trade would have lost the liquidity the deficits provided. But by continuing its policy of balance-of-payments deficits the US dollar lost its gold standard parity credibility. It was impossible to maintain the dollar–gold parity in the long term since the policy resulted in a loss of gold reserves (Helleiner 1994: 81–122). To defuse this dilemma the IMF created Special Drawing Rights (SDRs) in 1969 as an additional means of payment which were to supply the liquidity necessary for international trade. But since this did not provide a way out of the dilemma the USA finally gave up gold parity with the dollar in 1971 and the fixed rates became untenable. After a futile attempt to revive the fixed rates in the Smithsonian Agreement of 1971, with revised exchange rates and revised fluctuation bands of up to 4.5 per cent, exchange rates were finally set free in 1973 (Gilpin 2000: 124–25; Spero & Hart 2003).

The passage from fixed to flexible exchange rates fundamentally altered the function of the IMF's loans allocation. In the 1970s, the IMF had become superfluous as a currency buffer and, since the 1980s, it has been operating as a lender of last resort in the framework of a liberal financial and currency order largely without controls on capital movements. Through its allocation of loans, the IMF is supposed to ensure that national or regional financial crises, such as those in Asia and Russia in 1997 or debt crises like the Mexican one of 1982 and the Brazilian one of 1987, do not spread or possibly threaten the entire global financial and currency system (Helleiner 1994: 169–91). Nevertheless, the IMF (with 189 member states in 2018) could not prevent the US financial (mortgage) crisis of 2007 from escalating to the most severe global financial and economic crisis after the Second World War.

In the case of debt and/or financial crises, the IMF's mandate is to help the states concerned, which would otherwise be unable to pay for imports or service their debts. However, recipients must agree to certain structural adaptations. These should ensure that the recipient will be able to service its debts. In other words, these loans come with conditions: the IMF requires the state concerned to alter its domestic and foreign economic policies if it wants to avail itself of the loan. To be able to respond to the demand for loans and fulfil its role as lender of last resort, the IMF has had to restock its quotas several times, with the largest increase in quotas being agreed upon in late 2010 when the Executive Board decided to double quotas to about US$750 billion.

Operations of the IMF

The granting of loans forms the major part of the IMF's operations. Specification of the norms and rules for the allocation of loans is of special significance. The IMF determines the size and conditions of the loan to be granted to a state with balance-of-payments problems. Although each state is immediately entitled to draw a temporary loan of 25 per cent of its quota in case of balance-of-payments problems, if it wants a loan up to a (normal) maximum of 300 per cent of its quota it must submit a proposal to the IMF giving details of how it intends to solve its problems. A state can submit such a proposal in the form of a 'letter of intent' whose implementation should help to overcome its balance-of-payments problems and guarantee repayment of the loan to the IMF. The IMF lays down conditions for budgetary, financial, market and labour policies, often with far-reaching consequences for the society of the state requesting the loan (Barnett & Finnemore 2004; Martin 2006). The state's policies must be approved by the Executive Board of the IMF before the loan requested can be granted. The loan is usually released in instalments, with later instalments dependent upon the state adhering to its commitments (Driscoll 1998: 19–24).

The IMF disposes of a number of loan instruments, or 'facilities', tailored to different types of countries and the specific nature of the most common problems (see IMF 2011). The three main non-concessional facilities, which are subject to the IMF's market-related interest rate, are the Stand-By Arrangements (SBA), the Extended Fund Facility (EFF) and the Flexible Credit Line (FCL). Under the SBA the IMF gives loans to help states deal with short-term balance-of-payments problems. The loan will be paid in instalments over normally one to two years provided that the state keeps to its promised reforms. Repayments are expected within three to five years. The EFF is generally used for structural difficulties in the balance of payments, which is why instalments are phased over a period of three to four years with repayment within four to ten years. The FCL, introduced in 2009, is intended as an instrument for countries with strong economic fundamentals facing current balance-of-payment pressures. It is meant to serve crisis-prevention and crisis-mitigation purposes. The length of the FCL is one or two years and the repayment period the same as for the SBA.

In addition, low-income countries may borrow on concessional terms through a number of short-term and long-term facilities. In 1996, the IMF launched the Heavily Indebted Poor Countries (HIPC) initiative to provide rapid debt relief for such countries. In 1999, the HIPC initiative was modified to improve debt relief and to strengthen the links between debt relief, poverty reduction and social policies. The enhanced HIPC initiative foresaw macroeconomic adjustment and structural and social policy reforms including higher spending on basic health and education. In 2010, during the economic crisis, the IMF again reformed its system of support to low-income countries and established three new concessional facilities: the Extended Credit Facility (ECF), the Standby Credit Facility (SCF) and the Rapid Credit Facility (RCF). Financing under the ECF carries a zero interest rate, with a grace period of five and a half years and a final maturity of ten years. The SCF provides financial assistance to low-income countries with short-term balance-of-payments needs. It can be used in a wide range of circumstances, including on a precautionary basis. It comes with a zero interest rate, with a grace period of four years, and a final maturity of eight years. The RCF provides rapid financial assistance with limited conditionality to low-income countries facing an urgent balance-of-payments shortfall. With a zero interest rate, it has a grace period of five and a half years and a final maturity of ten years.

The IMF's operational activities refer not only to the provision of loans but also to their financing. The main sources of finance are the quotas which member states pay on joining the organization, based broadly on each country's relative weight in the world economy. Up to a quarter is paid in a widely accepted foreign currency and three-quarters in the state's own currency. This represents the maximum financial contribution which a state must put at the IMF's disposal. However, given constant change in the overall world economy and in that of individual states resulting in a growing need for loans, the quotas need to be regularly adapted to new circumstances. Accordingly, the Executive Board reviews the quotas at least every five years to recommend a possible increase, which requires the approval of at least 85 per cent of member states' votes in the Board of Governors. For example, in December 2010 the IMF's Board of Governors approved to conclude a review of quotas that foresees an unprecedented 100 per cent increase in total quotas (up to more than US$730 billion) and a realignment of quota shares (to the benefit, particularly, of Brazil, China, India and Russia) to better reflect the changing relative weights of the IMF's member states in the global economy.

Since the IMF quotas might not suffice to provide the loans needed, the organization has the possibility of itself borrowing from its members based on the General Arrangements to Borrow (GAB) of 1962 and the New Arrangements to Borrow (NAB) of 1997, which have been renewed and slightly reformed several times. Both arrangements were negotiated on several levels between the IMF and some of its member states. 40 participating states (as of 2018) have agreed to make available loans of up to US$264 billion to the IMF when large sums are necessary to secure the stability of the international financial and monetary system. This amount, however, is flexible and can be renegotiated over time. For instance, as a result of the economic and financial crisis of 2007–09, the NAB was expanded significantly to about US$550 billion. This was to ensure that the IMF had enough financial means at its disposal in the event of a renewed crisis to prevent this crisis from spreading to and jeopardizing the international financial system as a whole. In 2016, however, when the crisis was clearly over, the NAB was reduced again to US$264 billion.

The IMF not only specifies norms and rules; it also implements them directly. This holds in particular for the disbursement – and repayment – of loans. After agreeing to such a loan the IMF disburses it itself by making available, to the state concerned, funds in widely accepted foreign currencies obtained from other states either as quotas or as a loan. The borrowing state 'purchases' these foreign currencies with its own currency. For example, Russia may draw its loan in dollars, yen or euros by depositing roubles with the IMF. When repaying, the state in question will repurchase its own currency with the foreign currency.

Loans are provided under an arrangement which stipulates in advance the performance criteria for success or failure of the recipient's agreed reform plan. This reduces the need to supervise how the plan is implemented and concentrates on verifying whether the agreed targets have been reached. Measures for success are mostly macroeconomic indicators such as the inflation rate, national savings or the external debt of a country, usually checked quarterly or semi-annually, in the framework of a standard operating procedure. If, in the light of these criteria, a reform plan is deemed not to have been implemented successfully, the IMF can withhold further instalments or tie their continuation to new reform efforts to be negotiated.

The IMF does not limit its monitoring to reform plans agreed as part of a loan, but extends this to the entire economic, currency, financial and monetary policies of its member states. In essence, this is done through annual consultations with each member state, when four or five members of the IMF staff visit a country for about two weeks to collect and sift through data about growth, foreign trade, unemployment, inflation, interest rates, salaries, money supply, investments and public expenditure. Furthermore, they hold intensive discussions with government representatives to establish whether the economic policy being pursued is successful or whether, and if so how, it should be changed. Thereafter, the IMF representatives write a detailed report which is submitted to the Executive Board. Since 1997 these reports have been published along with the Executive Board's assessment. With this monitoring system the IMF aims at recognizing potential financial crises in advance and at being able to prevent them (Schirm 2007: 267–73). In the wake of the economic crisis of 2007–09, the IMF has reasserted its roles not only as lender of last resort, but also as monitoring guardian of global financial stability through strengthened surveillance of financial markets at the national, regional and global level.

Evaluation of the organization's effectiveness

The record of the IMF in contributing to a stable global financial and monetary order is mixed. It was unable to prevent the debt crises of developing countries in Latin America in the 1980s as well as the financial crises in Asia or Russia in the 1990s. Nonetheless, until the most recent economic crisis, it did manage to prevent national or regional financial crises from escalating into global ones. This crisis has unveiled the serious limits to the IMF's capacity in crisis prevention. In that sense, the IMF, just like many other national and international financial supervisors, has failed seriously. Serious deficiencies in the IMF's capacity to predict and prevent financial crises have even been pointed out by the Independent Evaluation Office (IEO) of the IMF. In the run-up to the recent crisis a high degree of organizational groupthink within the IMF's staff, intellectual capture by the transnational financial industry as well as supervisory authorities in the most advanced economies, and inadequate analytical approaches, undermined the IMF's ability to detect important risks and to alert the membership to these risks (IEO 2011: v). Moreover, the IMF's effectiveness in monitoring member states' financial policies and consulting with them is limited in that multilateral surveillance fails to be organized in a way that promotes institutional learning. Multilateral surveillance is further constrained by the fact that a greater delegation of authority by member states to the organization is missing (Lombardi & Woods 2008).

Paradoxically, the recent crisis has reinvigorated the IMF, for its function as international public lender of last resort has been underlined in the rescue of Greece, Hungary, Iceland, Romania, Ukraine and other economies after a decade in which states had increasingly turned to private capital markets for borrowing (Moschella 2010: 148–51; Underhill et al. 2010: 4). However, the empirical record of IMF lending in terms of promoting financial stability and economic growth is subject to controversial scientific debate. A number of studies find no significant effect of IMF lending on economic growth, and some even argue that IMF programmes have had a negative effect on growth (Steinwand & Stone 2008: 124, 141–43; Vreeland 2007: 89–90). In fact, very little is known with certainty about the effects of IMF lending on economic growth. However, it does seem that IMF programmes can indeed contribute to containing budget deficits, lowering inflation levels and improving the balance of payments in recipient states (Steinwand & Stone 2008: 141–43; Vreeland 2007: 89–90). The success of these kinds of financial stabilization policies can be undermined by the politicization of loan decisions and conditions along the economic and political interests of the most powerful shareholder states (as well as of IMF bureaucrats), which can be at odds with the objective of promoting country-level and, even more so, global systemic stability (Copelovitch 2010: 6; Momani 2004).

One further criticism directed at the IMF is that it has been preoccupied mainly with the developed countries' interest in financial stability while neglecting the specific interests of developing countries and countries in transition (Stiglitz 2002). Thus it has not dealt with the crises of developing countries unless they threatened to unleash chain reactions liable to affect developed countries as well. The IMF has equally been criticized because loan conditions imposed on developing countries have made it more difficult for them to combat poverty effectively. The IMF has reacted to this criticism by altering its loans programmes in such a way as to focus more on the fight against poverty and to assist developing countries in escaping from the debt trap, though preliminary empirical evidence does not look too promising (see the discussion on the World Bank, Chapter 9). The new facilities introduced in 2010 offer loans at more concessional rates and explicitly stress the importance of poverty reduction programmes.

EUROPEAN MONETARY RELATIONS

In addition to establishing extensive trade relations, the EU member states have integrated their national monetary policies in the context of the Eurozone. Following the end of the gold standard, and the reintroduction of a system of flexible exchange rates, several international organizations attempted to keep fixed exchange rates, at least at the regional level. Here again, as in the area of trade, the EU can be seen as a precursor in internationally harmonized monetary (and fiscal) policy. By having a common currency (the euro) and a central bank (European Central Bank), the EU is clearly an exceptional international organization when it comes to monetary relations.

Policy programme of the EU

Originally, the EU policy programme did not envisage common monetary policies. Nevertheless, when the existing global fixed exchange rates began to change to a system of flexible rates, efforts to base currency relationships within the European

Community on a regime of fixed exchange rates emerged quite rapidly. However, neither the Werner Plan of 1970, which already foresaw the establishment of an economic and monetary union, nor the 'monetary snake' of 1972, which aimed at transferring the IMF's monetary order to Europe, were put into practice (Eichengreen & Frieden 2001: 2–6).

It was not until the joint initiative of French President Valéry Giscard d'Estaing and German Chancellor Helmut Schmidt in 1978 that the European Monetary System (EMS), aimed at stabilizing the exchange rates of member states' currencies, was successfully launched. The regulative programme of the EMS, developed in an intergovernmental negotiating process, became effective in 1979 and defined a system of largely stable exchange rates using the European Currency Unit (ECU) as a point of reference. Accordingly, a fixed exchange rate was set for all the European national currencies. Base rates could only be changed if it became impossible to hold the exchange rate relationships of the currencies. The ECU was not an independent currency like the euro as we know it today. It can be better compared to the SDR of the IMF, a 'currency basket' composed of member states' currencies on the basis of their economic weight (Levitt & Lord 2000: 32).

At the heart of the EMS (which most but not all EU member states joined) was the commitment of each member state to intervene in international financial markets to maintain exchange rates within the range of 4.5 per cent (although in exceptional cases 6 per cent was permissible) in the grid of bilateral base rates. There was a duty of direct intervention if the currencies of two or more member states simultaneously reached the upper (+2.25 per cent) or lower (-2.25 per cent) limit of the range. If, for example, the German mark was at the upper limit and the Italian lira at the lower one the German federal bank and the Italian national bank were obliged to buy lira and sell German marks on the international financial markets. This created an additional supply of German marks and an additional demand for the lira, allowing the two currencies to converge towards the base rate. To ease such interventions the EMS provided for different credit mechanisms of which the central banks of the countries concerned could avail themselves to finance their interventions, in addition to their own currency reserves (Eichengreen & Frieden 2001: 2–4).

In the late 1980s and early 1990s, exchange rate stability of the participating states was largely maintained with the help of the EMS. This success provided input for further integration. In the context of the single market project, the economic and monetary union already envisaged in the Werner Plan of 1970 was taken up again (Moravcsik 1998: 379–471). In 1989 a committee headed by the then President of the European Commission, Jacques Delors, submitted a report (the 'Delors Report') proposing the establishment of a European Economic and Monetary Union (EMU) in which the individual European currencies would be replaced by a European currency under the supervision of a European Central Bank (ECB). The EMU was to be created in three stages (Wolf 1999: 77–105). In the first stage greater coordination of economic and monetary policies was envisaged, to be followed by the creation of a European system of central banks and the establishment of an independent ECB. Finally, in the last stage, the different member states' currencies were to be replaced by a common European currency.

After lively discussions between those in favour of monetary union, especially France and Germany, and those who viewed this project rather sceptically, especially the UK, the breakthrough came in the intergovernmental negotiations, leading to the consensus anchored in the Treaty of Maastricht (Cameron 1995: 57–73; Moravcsik 1998: 379, 471; Wolf & Zangl 1996). As a result, on 1 June 1998 the ECB was established, with its monetary policy committed exclusively to the stability of the euro. The ECB would be completely independent in its monetary policy and free from political interference following the model of the German Bundesbank. Thus neither the governments of the participating states, nor any other organ of the EU, can direct European monetary policy. This is strictly a matter for the ECB (Nugent 2006: 326–27).

The policy programme on monetary integration was complemented with a policy programme on fiscal coordination. Prior to the euro, the member states had to observe fiscal prudence, because running large deficits would negatively affect the national currency. With the euro, there was a risk that some member states would start to excessively spend money and therefore put the common currency under threat. Therefore the future Eurozone members introduced convergence criteria into the Treaty of Maastricht: only states that met these criteria could become members of the EMU. The annual budget deficit of a member state was not to exceed 3 per cent of its gross domestic product (GDP) and its total debt no more than 60 per cent of GDP. In addition, its inflation rate was not to exceed the average of the three best-performing states by more than 1.5 percentage points, while its interest rates were not to exceed the three best by more than 2 percentage points. These criteria are part of the formal Stability and Growth Pact between the member states.

The coordination of fiscal policy, in effect, has presented the biggest challenge to monetary relations in the EU. In 2003, shortly after the introduction of the euro, Germany and France breached the 3 per cent budget deficit rule. This resulted in a serious dispute among the Eurozone members and significantly weakened the reputation of the common currency. The outcome was more relaxed rules that take into consideration the exceptional economic situation within the member states. The situation got worse when in 2007–08 the economic crisis broke out, followed by the Eurozone crisis. Few Eurozone states were capable of keeping their budget deficits within the agreed 3 per cent margins. This time it was mostly Germany insisting on the other member states meeting their commitments. To address this fiscal problem, the Eurozone member states adopted far-reaching coordination mechanisms for fiscal policy. These included the European Semester in 2011, which requires member states to submit their draft budgets to the European Commission, as well as the Fiscal Compact of 2013, which is an intergovernmental treaty that puts serious budgetary constraints on most EU member states. The development of a monetary policy programme for a common currency has therefore also resulted in a policy programme focusing on fiscal coordination.

Operations of the ECB and the Commission

The states participating in the EMU have transferred to the ECB important operational activities relating to the stability of the euro. This follows a delegated decision-making model where the ECB has the authority to make decisions independent from the political preferences of the member states. The highest organ of the ECB, the Governing Council, consisting of the 19 governors of the participating central banks and the six members of the Executive Board of the ECB, sets the base (interest) rate. The Executive Board comprises the President and Vice-President of the ECB and four other members nominated by the governments of the participating states on a basis of consensus. Both the supranational Executive Board and the presidents of the central banks of the participating member states have to coordinate monetary policy within the framework of the ECB.

Base (interest) rates are the central instrument of the ECB since they determine the conditions under which commercial banks can borrow money from the central banks. In this way the ECB controls monetary stability because commercial banks will borrow less from the central banks when the base rate is high than when it is low. Stability of the currency is influenced because commercial banks will themselves raise their interest rates when the base rate is high, thus reducing the risk of inflation. During the Eurozone crisis, the ECB adopted a policy of 'forward guidance' to stabilize the markets. It stated explicitly that interest rates would remain low for the foreseeable future. This gave confidence to European businesses that low rates would remain available. In addition to setting the interest rate, the ECB can decide to intervene in the international financial markets. If the exchange rate is weak it can decide to use its reserves to buy euros, thus strengthening the euro vis-à-vis other currencies such as the US dollar. If the exchange rate is too high, it will use euros to purchase other currencies such as the US dollar to lower the euro exchange rate. If the ECB needs the assistance of members' central banks for the implementation of decisions taken by the ECB Governing Council, the ECB Executive Board is authorized to issue directives to them.

As a result of the Eurozone crisis, the ECB has also adopted the controversial policy of so-called 'quantitative easing', which effectively comes down to printing extra money by buying up government debt. The problem was as follows. During the Eurozone crisis, the ECB had already repeatedly reduced the interest rate to almost zero. This had resulted, however, in very little extra investment, loans and spending by companies and consumers. After all, in the middle of the Eurozone crisis, few companies saw worthwhile investment opportunities and even fewer banks were willing to provide loans for such investments. Indeed, this resulted in a situation of negative interest rates where companies and banks were actually willing to pay the ECB for safeguarding their deposits. In order to kick-start the economy and also to bring inflation closer to the 2 per cent target, the ECB therefore followed the quantitative easing policy pioneered by other central banks across the world. This policy aimed at bringing more money into the real economy and reducing the risk of deflation. While the effectiveness of this policy can be debated, it resulted in strong political disputes. In particular, Germany and the governor of the German Central Bank have been very critical of this policy, fearing that it results in overall inflation and, for instance, inflated real-estate prices.

In fiscal policy the situation is more complicated, and overall less compelling. The debt situation of states must be monitored and, particularly since the

Eurozone crisis, the EU has put in place a dedicated monitoring system (the 'European Semester') (European Commission 2017). Based on preparatory work by the European Commission, such as estimating annual economic growth, and overall policy guidance provided by the different EU institutions, all Eurozone member states have to submit each spring their budgetary plans for the following year. These are then scrutinized by the experts of the European Commission who make country-specific recommendations for each of the member states. After these recommendations are approved by the Council of Ministers, member states are expected to implement them. Such implementation is subject to monitoring by the European Commission. The purpose of this 'preventive arm' of the Stability and Growth Pact is to avoid that countries run excessive budget deficit, surpassing more than 3 per cent of GDP, in the first place. In addition to focusing on the budget for the following year, the European Semester is also concerned with the medium-term objective of the Stability and Growth Pact to have balanced budgets.

If Eurozone member states fail to achieve the budgetary objectives, they become subject to the 'corrective arm' of the Stability and Growth Pact: the excessive budgetary procedure (European Commission 2017). Whenever there is the risk of a budgetary deficit (planned or actual) exceeding 3 per cent of GDP, the European Commission automatically writes a report. The same goes if member states do not make sufficient progress towards an overall government debt of maximum 60 per cent of GDP. On the basis of this report the Council of Ministers decides whether to formally open the excessive budgetary procedure. The relevant member state gets three to six months to implement the recommendations of the Commission. On this basis, the Commission assesses whether effective action has been taken by a member state and informs the Council. If no effective action is taken, the Council can issue new guidelines and also sanction the member states with a fine of up to 0.5 per cent of GDP. Fines are, however, problematic because they put countries in even further debt. In 2016, the Council therefore agreed not to impose fines on Portugal and Spain despite their failure to take effective action to correct their excessive deficits.

As a result of the Eurozone crisis, the EU member states have therefore significantly stepped up the fiscal monitoring and compliance mechanisms. There is now considerable attention to avoid countries amassing excessive deficits in the first place, as happened with Greece, Ireland and Portugal. Their debts threatened the financial stability of the whole euro area. Apart from these fiscal measures, further crisis mechanisms, such as the European Stability Mechanism (ESM), European Financial Stability Facility (EFSF) and the European Financial Stabilization Mechanism (EFSM), have been established to help bail out member states. The member states furthermore established a banking union. Discussions on the future reform of the Eurozone area are, however, continuing with proposals on the table for a 'Eurozone budget' and a 'European Monetary Fund'. These remain subject to high-level political negotiations and resistance, but there is a strong incentive for the EU to put the relevant mechanisms in place to prevent future Eurozone crises.

Evaluation of the organization's effectiveness

Making a judgement about the effectiveness of Eurozone governance and the ECB is difficult. After the Eurozone crisis, it appears that almost everywhere in Europe people are critical of the ECB and the euro. In the various indebted countries, including Greece, Portugal, Ireland, Spain and Italy, the public opinion is that the ECB is too strict and that the intervention by the EU has resulted in a signifi-cant reduction of economic growth. In the various Northern countries, including Germany, Austria and The Netherlands, the public opinion is completely the oppo-site: the ECB has gone beyond its mandate by keeping the interest rate artificially low through quantitative easing. Perhaps, exactly because the ECB is under fire from both sides, we can actually conclude that it has been doing its job properly. It is, in this respect, important to recall the criteria for effectiveness (Chapter 7). We should, first and foremost, judge the ECB on the basis of the main task given to it by the member states: keeping inflation below, but close to, 2 per cent. As the ECB's mission reads: 'Our main aim is to maintain price stability ... Price stability is essen-tial for economic growth and job creation ... and it represents the most important contribution monetary policy can make in that area.' (European Central Bank, n.d.)

Looking at the inflation data, we can only conclude that the ECB has been remarkably successful in keeping inflation close to the target (see Figure 10.1). During the last two decades, the inflation in the eurozone has been more stable than the inflation in the USA or the United Kingdom (a non-Eurozone EU member state). A recent 'problem' has actually been that there is not enough inflation in

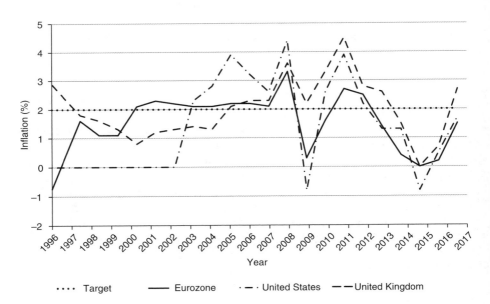

Figure 10.1   Inflation in the Eurozone (varying composition), the United Kingdom and the USA, 1996–2017

Source: Based on data from Eurostat.

the Eurozone. Worries that the euro would result in hyperinflation, which particularly in Germany remains a historical trauma, are therefore so far completely unfounded. What is more, there has not been much variation in the inflation rate within the Eurozone and across countries. In 2017, the inflation in Estonia and Lithuania was 3.7 per cent while it was 0.3 per cent in Ireland. This shows that there has not been a full convergence, yet the difference is not a cause for worry. In fact, this current gap is higher than it has been during the Eurozone crisis.

Clearly, the Achilles heel of European monetary relations is the EU's weak capacity to ensure fiscal soundness within the Eurozone and to coordinate and adjust national macroeconomic policies (De Grauwe 2006; Von Hagen & Wyplosz 2010). The obvious problems the Commission encounters in monitoring fiscal policies and cautioning states when they are in danger of failing to meet the stability criteria show the precarious state of cooperation between member states in the fiscal area. Despite all the mechanisms in place, the impact is sobering (see Figure 10.2). It is, in this respect, important to consider two key objectives that the Eurozone members have set themselves. First, in the medium-term, they are aiming for a balanced budget. It is clear that this objective is difficult to achieve. Only Germany, and some of the other Northern states, can realistically be said to have reached this goal. While the Eurozone as a whole is currently moving in the direction of a balanced budget, it has actually never achieved this goal during the existence of the euro. Indeed, countries such as France and Italy keep running budget deficits even during the best of times.

The second target is to have a budget deficit of maximum 3 per cent during periods of economic recession. A quick look at the data (Figure 10.2) shows that

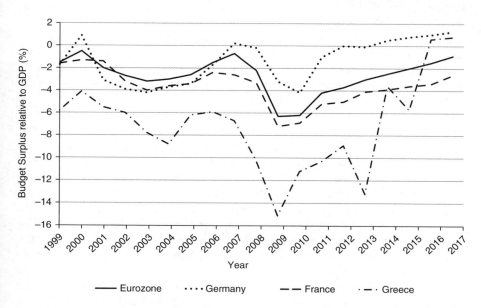

Figure 10.2   Government deficit in the Eurozone, France, Germany and Greece, 1999–2017
Source: Net borrowing, % of GDP, based on data from Eurostat.

during the most recent economic crisis, only Germany came close to achieving this goal. Greece has run deficits up to 15 per cent of GDP (and was already violating the rule on a permanent basis prior to the economic crisis), whereas even major countries such as France have run budget deficits larger than 3 per cent from 2008 until 2016. Given these enormous budget deficits, it is not surprising that overall government debt has also sky-rocketed during the economic crisis. While the Eurozone target is maximum 60 per cent of debt in comparison to GDP, the Greek public debt was nearly 180 per cent in 2017. Italy followed with 132 per cent and France had a debt amounting to 97 per cent of GDP. Even Germany, despite its prudence, had a public debt of 64 per cent and thus was above the target. These high public debts leave the eurozone countries in a weak position when the next recession hits.

CONCLUSION

International trade and open economies raise a series of financial and monetary dilemmas. States want to benefit from stable exchange rates and guarantees concerning loans and investments in order to optimally benefit from trade. If currencies are not fully convertible or if countries manipulate their own currencies through devaluation, this creates indirect barriers to free trade and ultimately results in less economic cooperation between countries. However, to fully address these problems requires significant intervention by international organizations. This in turn can pose considerable constraints on member states. In the most extreme cases of the Eurozone, where countries have given up their national currencies, devaluation is no longer a policy option during downturns. In addition, Eurozone countries are now under strict budgetary scrutiny through the preventive and the corrective arms of the Stability and Growth Pact. The situation is no different in the case of the IMF. As a lender of last resort, it makes loans available to countries on the verge of bankruptcy. But such loans normally come with strict conditionality and monitoring requirements.

The political system perspective of this book is also helpful in understanding how policy is made in the area of finance and monetary affairs. Once it appears that a country can no longer pay its bills, it can request support from the IMF (input). Further input comes from borrowing countries and the IMF staff which assesses the situation and makes recommendations. The next step is political decision-making by the IMF executive directors (conversion) resulting in programme and operational decisions concerning the loans supplied to the indebted country and the conditions attached (output). The outcome will be the loan given to the country, whereas the impact of such a loan may be that the economic situation in the country stabilizes and that the country can ultimately return to the capital markets on its own.

It is worth comparing this to the dynamics of the political system in the EU. When it comes to monetary policy, through its operational activities the ECB has long been successful in setting the interest rate to ensure price stability in the Eurozone area. When it realized, however, that its near-zero interest rates did not have the desired effects, it was under considerable pressure to adopt a policy of quantitative easing (input). Following debate in the Governing Council (conversion), it eventually established such a policy (output), which resulting in the ECB buying up government debt (outcome) leading to better capital supply (impact). The EU, and particularly the European Commission, however, has been much less successful in keeping budget deficits in the Eurozone under control. The new institutional procedures surrounding the Stability and Growth Pact do neatly show how the political system works in practice. Member states' reports on the forthcoming budgets together with Commission recommendations provide a starting point (input). The Council makes decisions, for instance, on whether to launch an excessive deficit procedure or impose a fine (conversion). This results in guidelines for member states to implement (output). If the outcome or impact at the member states level is not satisfactory, the whole process starts again.

Discussion Questions

1. What are the International Monetary Fund's contributions to preventing and managing financial crises? To what extent have its main functions and instruments changed?
2. Do you think that the adoption of the euro has been a success or a failure? Please provide arguments for both.

Further Reading

Copelovitch, Mark 2010. *The International Monetary Fund in the Global Economy: Banks, Bonds, and Bailouts*, Cambridge: Cambridge University Press.

Howarth, David & Quaglia, Lucia 2016. *The Political Economy of European Banking Union*, Oxford: Oxford University Press.

Reinhart, Carmen M. & Trebesch, Christoph 2016. The international monetary fund: 70 years of reinvention, in: *Journal of Economic Perspectives* 30: 1, 3–28.

Schimmelfennig, Frank 2014. European integration in the euro crisis: the limits of postfunctionalism, in: *Journal of European Integration* 36: 3, 321–37.

11 The Environment

When it comes to environmental protection, states face similar dilemmas to those in security and the economy. While states may protect the environment within their own territories, for instance by designating national parks or fining polluters (Hardin 1968), they may be less concerned about environmental protection beyond their borders. The trouble is that many environmental problems have a cross-border or even global dimension. The effects of river pollution – whether in the Rhine, the Danube or the Nile – will be felt downstream. Increased greenhouse gas emission in one state may result in further global warming. In an anarchical international system, this may lead to a situation where states have an incentive to free ride on the efforts of other states. After all, if other states already reduce greenhouse gases, why bother to join them? If, however, all follow this strategy of free riding, not a single state would benefit economically and the environmental situation would worsen for all. Thus the environmental dilemma describes a social trap in which behaviour aimed at gains for individual states places both the community of states collectively and also each state individually in a worse situation than would have been the case with effective international cooperation.

As with security policy and economic relations, international organizations offer states the opportunity to mitigate this environmental dilemma and achieve international cooperation (Ostrom 1990; Dietz et al. 2003). Through international organizations, states can make binding agreements. International organizations can furthermore help to specify and monitor those agreements as well as adjudicate in disputes. Also, given the (scientific) complexity of many environmental problems, international organizations can play a key role in providing states with reliable information based on expert assessment. Unsurprisingly, a whole range of international organizations and regimes have been established, particularly since the 1970s, to address problems in the area of environmental protection. In this chapter, we analyse in detail the protection of the stratospheric ozone layer and the treatment of climate change as examples to evaluate the activities of the United Nations (UN) – including the UN Environment Programme (UNEP) and the World Meteorological Organization (WMO) – in the environmental field.

PROTECTION OF THE OZONE LAYER

In 1974 two American scientists, Mario Molina and Sherwood Rowland, first drew attention to the depletion of the stratospheric ozone layer as a potential consequence of the emission of chlorofluorocarbons (CFCs). A lively scientific discussion followed about the validity of this observation, which had a lasting influence on policy programmes for the protection of the stratospheric ozone layer (Chasek et al. 2010: Chapter 4; Haas 1992b; Wettestad 2002: 155). These scientific findings provided input for the international community, and international organizations such as UNEP, to address this problem. Once all the member states were convinced about the scientific evidence, and the USA insisted on cooperation, the international community adopted policy programmes and operational activities. The outcome of these policy programmes and operational activities was a phasing-out of CFCs, which ultimately had a positive impact on the ozone layer.

Policy programme of UNEP

Based on input from scientists, UNEP, with the support of environmental non-governmental organizations (NGOs), pushed for rapid generation of a programme for the protection of the ozone layer (Andersen & Sharma 2002; Breitmeier 1996: 108–24). It did this initially by convening and preparing international conferences, in which state representatives were for the first time able to discuss the risks of the then-only-assumed depletion of the ozone layer and consider possible action. The international conference in Washington, DC of 1977 issued the World Plan of Action for the Ozone Layer, requesting an international agreement for the protection of the stratospheric ozone layer (Wettestad 1999: 125–26). However, it was not until 1982 that concrete steps were taken, pushed globally by environmental groups. The UNEP Governing Council set up an ad hoc working party charged with drafting a framework convention for the protection of the ozone layer (Andersen & Sharma 2002; Parson 2003).

The working party, consisting of government experts from 22 countries, met seven times up to 1985 in order to work out a draft convention. In lengthy intergovernmental negotiations the USA, Canada and the Scandinavian countries – the Toronto Group – demanded the rapid phasing-out of the use of chlorofluorocarbons (CFCs). The European Union (EU), with 45 per cent of the global production capacity of CFCs (ahead of the USA with 30 per cent), together with Japan and the Soviet Union, however, had different preferences. They were only prepared to accept freezing of production on the basis of existing capacity. They argued that the link between the use of CFCs and the depletion of the ozone layer had not yet been definitely proven (Breitmeier 1996: 108–16). In other words, the inputs from the different (groups of) states conflicted significantly. It made agreement on specific measures for the reduction in CFC production and consumption impossible at the time. The Vienna Convention for the Protection of the Ozone Layer was signed by 22 states on 22 March 1985, but it amounted to little more than a general statement. Furthermore, these states agreed to cooperate more closely in research and to exchange information (Parson 2003).

On the basis of new scientific information, and in particular the discovery of the hole in the ozone layer above the Antarctic (further input), the UNEP secretariat and the Toronto Group insisted on continuing negotiations for the internationally coordinated phasing-out of CFC use (Canan & Reichman 2002; Haas 1992b: 189–213). In the search for a compromise with the EU, a negotiating marathon followed. However, the convergence of positions was a very slow process. The USA, the leader of the Toronto Group, was under pressure from the American public. Its initial demand was for a reduction of CFC production by 95 per cent. The EU, on the other hand, was only prepared to accept a reduction of 20 per cent. Eventually, in 1987, the main negotiating parties agreed on the Montreal Protocol on Substances that Deplete the Ozone Layer – a regulative programme which foresaw a step-by-step phasing-out aimed at reducing the global consumption of CFCs by 1999 to 50 per cent of the 1986 level (Andersen & Sharma 2002; Parson 2003).

The change in the EU's position, on the Montreal Protocol of 1987, came about partly due to pressure exerted by Germany on its European partners for more far-reaching concessions. The main driving force, however, was the USA which had threatened to impose an import ban on products containing or produced with the use of CFCs. This threat clearly shows the importance of a state's (market) power in intergovernmental negotiations. Equally typical for intergovernmental negotiations, whose success depends on the consent of all (or most) negotiating parties, was the agreement of weaker states to the regulative programme following concessions granted by richer and more powerful countries. Developing countries, whose part in the worldwide consumption of CFCs amounted to 14 per cent, gained the concession of increasing their annual consumption of CFCs, independently of their then situation, to 300g per capita. In addition, they were promised technical aid to give them access to environmentally friendly alternatives and technologies (Andersen & Sharma 2002).

Yet the Montreal Protocol was only a beginning. Shortly after the signing of the original Montreal Protocol, scientific research not only proved clearly and beyond doubt the existence of a connection between CFC emissions and depletion of the ozone layer but also laid bare the insufficiency of the agreed limits to production and consumption (Canan & Reichman 2002). Based on such scientific input, in 1989 stricter measures were negotiated in Helsinki, as demanded by environmental protection groups and the expert community of atmospheric scientists. The EU, previously a reluctant participant in the negotiations, now became a driving force for a more rapid phasing-out of the production and consumption of CFCs. In a non-binding declaration with 81 other states it affirmed its readiness to accept a total ban on the production and consumption of CFCs by the year 2000. Furthermore, the developing countries were promised financial assistance in implementing the decisions (Breitmeier 1996: 127–29; Parson 2003).

In London the following year the non-binding decisions reached in Helsinki were taken into account by strengthening the Montreal Protocol through an amendment. The time allowed for the phase-out was reduced so that it was envisaged that production and consumption of CFCs would cease completely by the year 2000. It was also agreed to set up the Multilateral Fund for the Implementation of the Montreal Protocol, aimed at subsidizing developing countries for the additional costs they were going to incur by complying with the ozone regulations. The Fund has since been replenished ten times between 1991 and 2020, providing assistance in the range of US$3.6 billion to developing countries. Interestingly, the London negotiations were based on changing positions by the member states. The USA, which had previously welcomed the phasing-out of production and consumption of CFCs, was now trying to slow things down, whereas the EU had joined the group of states that were pushing for a total end to production and consumption (Breitmeier 1996: 129–38). Nevertheless, it was possible to reduce the time allowed for compliance through negotiations leading to Protocol amendments at several subsequent conferences (Parson 2003; Wettestad 1999: 138–40). As efforts to end the production and use of CFCs proved very successful, the parties to the Montreal Protocol have started negotiations at their annual conferences to expand the ozone treaty into the much more contested area of climate change. For instance, during the summit in Rwanda in 2016, parties to the Montreal Protocol also agreed on phasing down hydrofluorocarbons (HFCs), emissions which have a significant impact on global warming. This envisaged broadening of the Montreal Protocol underlines both the Protocol's success and its weaknesses in the current climate regime (see below).

In global efforts to stop the depletion of the ozone layer, UNEP has offered a forum for intergovernmental negotiations and pushed the negotiating process along through the organization of conferences and the preparation of draft programmes (Wettestad 1999: 140–41). Like the many environmental groups and the expert community of atmospheric scientists that focused on the ozone problem, it acted as a catalyst for programme generation by putting the states permanently under pressure to act until they finally not only agreed on basic norms and rules to protect the ozone layer but subsequently continued to strengthen them (Andersen & Sharma 2002; Parson 2003). By June 2015, all UN member states and the EU had ratified the Montreal Protocol, committing themselves to phase out provisions not only for CFCs but also for other ozone-depleting substances.

Operations of UNEP

The implementation of the policy programmes concerned with environmental pollution is generally in the hands of the states themselves (Breitmeier 1997; Chasek et al. 2010). The competencies of international organizations in the implementation of the Vienna Convention of 1985, the Montreal Protocol of 1987 and the various revisions of the Montreal Protocol are limited to administering financial support for environmental protection efforts by developing countries and granting them technical assistance. Crucial support comes through the World Bank, UNEP, the UN Development Programme (UNDP) and the UN Industrial Development Organization (UNIDO) which serve as implementing agencies for programmes financed by the Multilateral Fund for the Implementation of the Montreal Protocol. The Multilateral Fund is managed by an Executive Committee, which comprises seven members from developed countries and seven members from developing countries and meets three times a year. The Executive Committee's main tasks include specifying criteria for project eligibility and monitoring their implementation, allocating resources among the four implementing agencies, and approving country programmes and projects. In the fulfilment of these tasks the Executive Committee is assisted by the Fund Secretariat.

Additional operational activities, such as supervising compliance and sanctioning states for non-compliance, are not well defined. The only commitment imposed on states by the Montreal Protocol is the submission to the secretariat of an annual report on the production and consumption of CFCs. The secretariat then examines whether states have fulfilled their obligations (Bauer 2009; Greene 1998: 92–95; Victor 1998). The relatively high level of transparency inherent in the production and consumption of CFCs makes supervision of compliance by an international organization appear less urgent, since it is difficult for states clandestinely to withdraw from their agreed commitments. This holds all the more because of the existence, in most industrialized states, of environmental NGOs and green parties which keep a watchful eye on the implementation of international environmental agreements and are prepared to make public any breach of norms and rules (Greene 1998: 109–10). Domestic protest against such breaches can be seen as the functional equivalent of sanctioning by an international organization (Gemmill & Bamidele-Izu 2002; Zangl 1999: 98–99, 248–50).

A substantial part of the operational activities of international environmental organizations concern information, expertise and scientific research. When analysing the policy programme on the protection of the ozone layer, much of the input came from scientific experts (see above). This was not a one-time input. It took time before states, including the EU, recognized the adverse effect of CFCs on the environment. So it was about the repeated input of experts. The ozone layer regime is, in this respect, not exceptional. In many environment areas, international organizations rely heavily on such outside expertise. And, importantly, they actively stimulate the acquisition of new information on policy problems as part of their operational activities. Both UNEP and the WMO made an important contribution to generating information about the depletion of the ozone layer and were especially successful in coordinating and disseminating international ozone research (Andersen & Sharma 2002; Canan & Reichman 2002). In particular, UNEP was instrumental in the formation of a transnational epistemic community of atmospheric scientists and, consequently, a scientific consensus on the ozone problem (Haas 1992b). The starting point was the creation in 1977 of the Coordinating Committee on the Ozone Layer (CCOL) following a meeting of experts in Washington, DC. The UNEP Governing Council had set up CCOL to promote scientific understanding of the ozone problem and to collect and publish scientific findings. The Committee, essentially composed of experts from state and non-state organizations dealing with the problem of ozone depletion, met eight times between 1977 and 1986. Its results were regularly published by UNEP in the *Ozone Layer Bulletin*.

Coordination of international ozone research by UNEP considerably hastened the establishment of a scientific consensus about the causes and effects of depletion of the ozone layer (Haas 1992b). UNEP, in collaboration with the WMO and a series of national research institutes, was able, during the 1990s, to publish a large number of important studies of the effects of greenhouse gases on the ozone layer and the world climate. To sum up the knowledge and state of the art concerning the ozone layer in 1985, UNEP and the WMO, jointly with other national and international environmental organizations, presented a three-volume stocktaking report, *Atmospheric Ozone*. This was seen at the time as the best and most comprehensive treatise on the state of the ozone layer (Canan & Reichman 2002).

These international information activities made it increasingly difficult for CFC-producing and hitherto hesitant states to justify their wait-and-see attitude towards ozone depletion, since there was no longer any uncertainty about the causal nexus between CFC emission and depletion of the ozone layer (Canan & Reichman 2002). A final and decisive impetus for an international regulatory intervention in economic activities damaging the ozone layer came from a conference of experts in Würzburg, convened by UNEP in 1987. By comparing the research results of different scientists the last scientific doubts about the urgency of worldwide abandonment of CFC production and consumption were removed. Comparison of the scientific assumptions and models showed that even a reduction of CFC emissions by 50 per cent would only slow down, but not halt, the damage to the ozone layer. Furthermore, the experts were able to reach a consensus as to which individual substances in particular threatened the ozone layer. As a result of this activity, with the help of UNEP and the WMO, a transnational epistemic community of scientific experts was formed. The consensual knowledge of the experts put pressure on the state representatives to meet a few months later in Montreal (Andersen & Sharma 2002). This epistemic community definitively undermined the foundations of the argument to reject CFC reduction on the grounds of scientific uncertainty (Canan & Reichman 2002; Haas 1992b: 211–12).

Thanks to the continuing information activities of UNEP and the WMO, which acted as generators, disseminators and coordinators of epistemic knowledge, it soon became clear that the framework agreement reached in Montreal was insufficient. A report by the Ozone Trends Panel, a multinational group of researchers set up in 1986 by UNEP, the WMO and the US National Aeronautics and Space Administration (NASA) to examine and evaluate the many years of ozone measurement data, confirmed the causal nexus between CFC emissions and the depletion of the ozone layer. This report also showed the existence of a global depletion of the ozone layer in addition to the hole over the Antarctic. These new findings gave UNEP the scientific basis and the effective support of public opinion to move the states to adopt more far-reaching measures, culminating in a strengthening of the Montreal Protocol with the amendments noted above.

Evaluation of the organizations' effectiveness

The global ozone regime supported by UNEP, the WMO, a transnational expert community of atmospheric scientists and environmental NGOs is widely considered a success story and one of the most effective international environmental regimes (Greene 1998; Haas 1992c; Victor 1998; Wettestad 2002). In the late 1980s and early 1990s, global consumption and production of CFCs stopped expanding and began to decrease substantially (see Figure 11.1). By the mid-1990s, almost all developed countries had, by and large, phased out production and consumption of CFCs. Assisted by resources from the Montreal Protocol's Multilateral Fund, most developing countries devised programmes to do the same. This global decrease in the production and consumption of CFCs has continued to a point where production has virtually ceased and consumption has become marginal. Meanwhile, controls

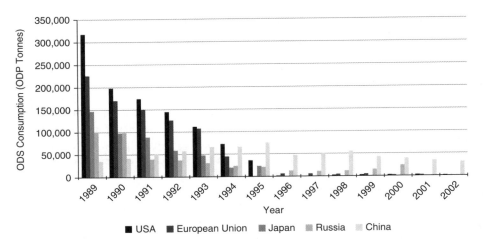

Figure 11.1   Total chlorofluorocarbon (CFC) production major states, 1986–2003 (ODP Tonnes)*

Note: *ODP Tonnes are metric tonnes of CFCs weighted by their Ozone Depletion Potential (ODP).

Source: Based on data from UNEP.

have been extended to hydrochlorofluorocarbons (HCFCs) and have proved success-ful in this area as well. Negotiations about the phasing-out of hydrofluorocarbons (HFCs), which have even greater global warming potential than carbon dioxide, have also been successful, with the Rwanda summit in 2016 pointing to a further poten-tial expansion of the ozone treaty into the issue area of climate change.

There is little doubt that the ozone regime, as well as the collaboration of UNEP and the WMO with the transnational expert community, have made these achievements possible (Greene 1998: 89–90). To be sure, the phasing-out of the consumption of CFCs was relatively easy to achieve when compared to the reduc-tion of greenhouse gas emissions (see below) because the gradual ban of CFCs 'only' affected particular, delimited industrial sectors, and alternative chemicals and technologies were available at a reasonable cost (Rittberger et al. 2010: 579). Nonetheless, it is fair to conclude that, without the presence of UNEP and the WMO and their cooperation with the transnational expert community:

> it is likely that there would have been less cooperation, that its form would have been less comprehensive (that is fewer pollutants covered and less sensitivity to related issues), that its enforcement would have been slower and less aggressive, and that the variation among national regulatory efforts would have been much broader. (Haas 1992c: 51)

Despite the success of UNEP and the WMO in establishing an international regime for the protection of the stratospheric ozone layer, the question remains whether the period of time between discovery of the ozone problem and implementation of measures to phase out CFCs was short enough from an ecological point of view. We know that depletion of the ozone layer due to a delayed reaction to CFC emissions will continue unabated for a while. It thus seems obvious that, in general, reaction

time to environmental problems is too slow. This is at least in part related to prevalent intergovernmental decision-making procedures in programme generation and
specification which slow down policy programme development and constrain the
effectiveness of international environmental governance.

CLIMATE CHANGE

For states, climate change poses a dilemma similar to the one encountered in combating ozone depletion. Although states share the ecological interest in reducing
global greenhouse gas emissions in order to prevent or slow down climate change
and particularly global warming, each state has an economic interest in not having to reduce household or industrial greenhouse gas emissions on its territory
or at least to keep associated costs as low as possible. If all states therefore suc-
cumb to their short-term economic interest they will forego their long-term ecological interest in slowing down or halting climate change, which has meanwhile
progressed substantially (see Figure 11.2). Whereas the basic dilemmas are quite

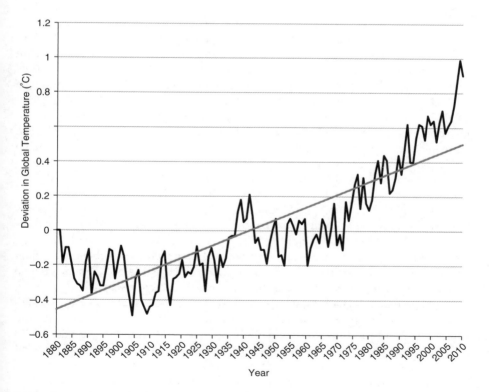

Figure 11.2 Global rise of temperature, 1880–present

Sources: Yearly deviation from the average temperature in the period 1951–80, °C, based on data from
NASA's Goddard Institute for Space Studies (GISS).

similar in both environmental issue areas, international organizations have not been nearly as successful in climate protection as they have been in dealing with the ozone problem.

Policy programme of UNEP and the WMO

The question of human-induced (anthropogenic) climate change was discussed by meteorologists as early as the 1960s and 1970s. At that time, the previously held belief that humankind could not endanger the global climate through environmental pollution, and in particular through carbon dioxide emissions, was challenged for the first time. Initially, both the scenario of the earth warming and that of its cooling seemed equally plausible. As the academic thesis of global warming through the greenhouse effect was gaining in strength, political efforts intensified to achieve a significant reduction in greenhouse gas emissions, particularly those of carbon dioxide. The intergovernmental negotiating process dealing with this issue was not only spurred by the advocacy activities of international NGOs such as Greenpeace and the Worldwatch Institute, but was also influenced by international organizations, especially UNEP and the WMO (Chasek 2001: 124–33; Luterbacher & Sprinz 2001; Rowlands 1995: 65–98).

UNEP and the WMO together made the first moves towards negotiations on collective regulatory efforts to halt climate change by convening a world climate conference in Geneva in 1979. But it was not until the 1988 Toronto Conference on the Changing Atmosphere, bringing together governments, environmental NGOs and scientists, that the demand for an international framework convention for the protection of the world's climate was raised for the first time (Breitmeier 1996: 188). This framework convention was to be complemented by subsequent protocols prescribing the compulsory curbing of carbon dioxide emissions. According to the demands voiced at the Toronto conference, carbon dioxide emissions were to be reduced by 20 per cent by 2005 compared with their 1988 levels.

After the UN General Assembly had also expressed its approval for global environmental protection in Resolution 43/53 (1988), UNEP convened another conference on global warming in Washington, DC in 1990. Climate change became a central international environmental concern, as had been demanded by many environmental NGOs. At the Washington conference many EU states insisted on an initial freezing of carbon dioxide emissions before gradually reducing them. According to them the causal nexus between carbon dioxide emissions and climate change had been sufficiently substantiated by scientific research, necessitating a rapid binding agreement on curbing such emissions. But the USA opposed such an agreement, arguing the opposite case. It did not want to accept any reduction until the causal link had been proven beyond doubt, at least to its mind (Breitmeier 1996: 187–93). This shows, once more, that 'problems' need to be broadly recognized before states can take action in the framework of international organizations.

This fundamental conflict between the USA and most EU members also dominated the second formal world climate conference in 1990 in Geneva which followed the 'working' conferences in Toronto and Washington. As a result, the closing declaration of the second world climate conference merely endorsed the general necessity to stabilize greenhouse gas emissions, but did not impose any concrete reductions requirements (Brenton 1994: 183–85). Greater impetus for international climate protection manifested itself in the autumn of 1990 when the UN General Assembly set up an Intergovernmental Negotiating Committee (INC) which, supported by UNEP and the WMO, was given the task of presenting a plan for a framework convention on climate change in time for the 1992 Rio de Janeiro UN Conference on Environment and Development (the 'Earth Summit').

However, these intergovernmental negotiations were hindered by the continuing conflict between the EU, supported by the Alliance of Small Island States (AOSIS) and the USA, seconded by members of the Organization of Petroleum Exporting Countries (OPEC) (Ott 1997: 205–08). Nevertheless, under the influence of a growing participation by environmental NGOs, a compromise was reached for a framework convention acceptable to all in time for the 1992 Earth Summit in Rio. The Framework Convention on Climate Change, signed by 150 states in Rio, does not oblige states explicitly to freeze or reduce their carbon dioxide emissions, but commits them to 'the aim of returning ... to their 1990 levels these anthropogenic emissions of carbon dioxide and other greenhouse gases not controlled by the Montreal Protocol' (Article 4 IIb, UNFCCC). In addition, the Convention provides for a regular reconvening of a Conference of the Parties (COP), with the aim of negotiating concrete agreements for the reduction of greenhouse gas emissions. The Climate Secretariat, established as an institutional follow-up to the Rio Conference, is tasked to support intergovernmental negotiations by organizing meetings and by analysing and reviewing climate change information and data reported by Parties (Wettestad 1999: 205–06).

The Conference of the Parties in Berlin (COP 1) in 1995 and in Geneva (COP 2) in 1996, which had come under massive pressure from environmental NGOs, did not yet succeed in agreeing on concrete commitments (Wettestad 1999: 206–07). In Berlin, however, consensus was reached to start negotiations for a protocol to the Framework Convention, setting out specific commitments to reduce emissions. These negotiations, in a specially established ad hoc group, eventually allowed a breakthrough. For the first time, the USA relaxed its resistance to EU demands for compulsory reductions in greenhouse gas emissions, enabling agreement on a protocol for the third Conference of the Parties in 1997 in Kyoto (COP 3). In the Kyoto Protocol, the developed countries committed themselves to reductions in emissions of the six most important greenhouse gases by 2012 by an average of 5 per cent of their 1990 levels. The USA and EU, as the two biggest polluters at that time, were supposed to reduce their emissions by 7 and 8 per cent, respectively (Aldy & Stavins 2007; Sprinz 1998; Wettestad 1999: 208–10). However, in order to enter into force the Protocol needed to be ratified by developed nations accounting for at least 55 per cent of global greenhouse gas emissions.

International climate policy was still a long way from a breakthrough, since two unresolved fundamental conflicts prevented the Kyoto Protocol from coming into effect quickly. First, the modality of the planned emissions trading needed to be agreed. This allowed polluting states to buy unused emission rights from other states and thereby to free themselves from the obligation of reducing their own emissions. Whereas the EU wanted to allow only limited trading in emissions, the USA and also Russia insisted on an unlimited system. The other remaining issue was how to count so-called greenhouse gas stores or sinks, the creation of which opened up the possibility of freeing oneself, through reafforestation, from the obligation to reduce emissions. Here again the EU was pushing for a limited system, while the USA and Japan favoured a far broader one (Betsill & Hoffmann 2011; Skjærseth & Wettestad 2008).

It was impossible to resolve either conflict during the Conference of the Parties in Buenos Aires in 1998 (COP 4), Bonn in 1999 (COP 5) or The Hague in 2000 (COP6), leaving the coming into effect of the Kyoto Protocol doubtful. The final breakthrough on these issues did not occur until the conference in Bonn in 2001 (a continuation of the failed COP 6 in The Hague) and the Conference of Parties in Marrakesh, also in 2001 (COP 7). But meanwhile the USA, responsible for about 20 per cent of the world's carbon dioxide emissions, had withdrawn from the Kyoto Protocol, with the US Senate signalling its unwillingness to consent to the treaty after President Clinton had signed it. The Senate found it unacceptable that developing countries and emerging economies should initially be exempt from the obligation to reduce emissions. Thus neither President Clinton nor his successor George W. Bush presented the Kyoto Protocol to the Senate for approval (Holtrup 2001: 31–36; Victor 2001), and the Protocol came into force on 16 February 2005 without US participation. Attainment of the threshold of 55 per cent of global emissions required for the Protocol to enter into force was finally made possible by Russia's ratification of the Protocol in November 2004 (Aldy & Stavins 2007).

The Kyoto Protocol set targets for 2012, but since it took until 2005 to enter into force the key question was not whether targets would be met, but rather what successor agreement should be negotiated for after the commitment period. In other words, states were forced to start working on a successor agreement to the Kyoto Protocol. The 2007 conference in Bali (COP 13/CMP 3) adopted the Bali Roadmap, which outlined a schedule for new intergovernmental negotiations. Negotiating a successor agreement, however, would be much more complicated. At the time of the Kyoto Protocol, the USA and EU were by far the largest polluters. Therefore, they were the ones to make commitments in addressing climate change. Yet with the rise of China and the other emerging economies, it became quickly clear that those countries should be included in a successor agreement as well. For instance, as a result of economic growth, China overtook the EU in the early 2000s and the USA in the late 2000s in terms of its carbon dioxide emissions (Olivier et al. 2012: Figure 2.2). Making an agreement between exclusively the EU and the USA would therefore not make sense, because it would exclude the world's largest polluter.

Including China and the other emerging economies into a new agreement proved difficult. Even though China was now the largest polluter, its carbon footprint per capita was still much lower than those of the EU and USA. It would therefore be difficult to insist that China and the other emerging countries would need to reduce their emissions at the same rate. The EU, which had been the self-declared leader of the climate change negotiations during the difficult era of President George W. Bush, saw an opportunity to push for an ambitious legally binding new agreement at the Copenhagen summit (2009, COP 15/CMP5). The EU was, however, sidelined during the summit by the USA and China making a deal among themselves. It was now clear that the international community would not be able to produce a new agreement that would take effect after the expiration date of the Kyoto Protocol in 2012. It was indeed not until 2015, during the Paris summit (COP 21/CMP11), that states adopted the new Paris Agreement. The emphasis in this agreement is on nationally determined commitments without an enforcement mechanism for states that fail to meet their targets. The Paris Agreement did give a significant boost to the Green Climate Fund (GCF), which helps developing countries in addressing climate change challenges. In 2018, the Trump administration announced that it would withdraw from the Paris Agreement at the earliest possible moment at the end of 2020.

Operations of UNEP, the WMO and the Climate Secretariat

The Framework Convention on Climate Change, the Kyoto Protocol and the Paris Agreement assign a significant role to international organizations such as UNEP, the WMO or the United Nations Climate Change Secretariat for their implementation (Oberthür 2004; Yamin & Depledge 2004). As with protection of the ozone layer, they are involved in the direct financing of environmental efforts by developing countries. Here, the Global Environmental Facility (GEF) established by the World Bank, UNEP and UNDP enables developing countries to obtain financial assistance for the additional costs incurred in replacing old energy-sapping technologies that are harmful to the climate with modern energy-efficient ones. This is complemented by the GCF, which provides funding specifically for the area of climate change.

In the area of climate protection, international organizations also develop important operational activities. The UN Climate Change Secretariat, based in Bonn, for instance, maintains the registry for Nationally Determined Contributions (NDCs) established under the Paris Agreement. According to the Paris Agreement, countries make national commitments, but should communicate these NDCs publicly to the secretariat. As such it is possible to verify when countries are indeed living up to their own commitments. The secretariat also provides the technical expertise necessary to analyse and review all these national commitments. The secretariat does not have a monitoring, let alone a sanctioning, mechanism, but the public sharing of the NDCs provides some incentive for the different countries to comply.

The Climate Secretariat, like the Secretariat for the Protection of the Ozone Layer, also collects the annual reports which states are obliged to submit concerning their progress in curbing greenhouse gas emissions. But unlike the reports on CFC emissions, these reports are scrutinized by a Compliance Committee composed of 20 independent experts nominated by the COP. This independent scrutiny is important, given the lower level of transparency in climate protection due to the many sources of greenhouse gas emissions. Those states which observe the rules therefore do not have to fear that other states will gain an unfair advantage through unnoticed non-compliance (Oberthür & Marr 2002; Oberthür & Ott 1999). In cases where the scrutiny reveals non-compliance by a state, sanctions can be imposed. If during the first reduction period a state's emissions reduction is insufficient, it will be obliged to reduce its emissions additionally in the second phase. This is seen as a deterrent to ensure compliance with states' obligations (Busch 2009; Yamin & Depledge 2004).

As with the ozone layer regime, the information activities of international organizations have had a lasting influence on protecting the world's climate. The intergovernmental negotiating processes which led to the Framework Convention on Climate Change and the Kyoto Protocol were shaped by the results of research into anthropogenic climate change supported by UNEP and the WMO (Rowlands 1995). Both organizations ensured that climate change was taken seriously as a global environmental problem and put on the political agenda in a timely fashion. The Intergovernmental Panel on Climate Change (IPCC), jointly established by UNEP and the WMO in 1988, proved especially important (Bolin 2007; Wettestad 1999: 221–24). Composed of researchers from the countries participating in the negotiations, the IPCC was tasked by UNEP and the WMO to conduct an audit of research into climate change and update it periodically. The IPCC's First Assessment Report in 1990 provided a detailed analysis of risks to the world's climate that resulted from growing greenhouse gas emissions. The report predicted that unchecked greenhouse gas emissions would lead to an increase in world temperatures of between 1.5 and 4.5 °C on average by 2025. This assessment report was submitted to the second world climate conference (Geneva 1990), which then asked the participating states to initiate negotiations immediately on an international framework convention on climate change (Breitmeier 1996: 164–66).

Even after the 1992 Rio Framework Convention was signed, the IPCC's contribution to the ensuing negotiations in the COPs remained decisive in helping to form a consensus, which was reinforced through its Second Assessment Report in 1995. An epistemic community of some 3,000 researchers assembled for this Report observed almost unanimously that climate change was due to accrued greenhouse gas emissions. They added that, if the existing emission trends were to continue, an average rise in temperature of about 2 °C could be expected in the twenty-first century. The report also warned that sea levels would rise by about 50 cm (Rowlands 1995).

This second IPCC assessment report had its full impact on the first COP 1 in 1995 in Berlin. Supporters of specific reduction commitments could point to the report in arguing for urgent action to counteract climate change, while opponents were finding it harder to dismiss the idea that greenhouse gas emissions are responsible for climate change. This helped to shift the balance of power between supporters and opponents, and it became possible to begin specific negotiations on a climate protocol to reduce emissions. The Third Assessment Report in 2001 confirmed that anthropogenic climate change would continue. It helped to underline yet again the vital need for global climate protection by curbing emissions. The Fourth Assessment Report of 2007 contained numerous, quite specific findings and prognoses on trends in global warming and on the ecological consequences of climate change, for example for sea levels, vegetation zones and biodiversity. The 2007 IPCC report found unprecedented resonance not only among policy-makers but also with the larger public. At the end of 2007, the IPCC (jointly with the former US Vice-President Al Gore) was even awarded the Nobel Peace Prize for its 'efforts to build up and disseminate greater knowledge about man-made climate change, and to lay the foundations for the measures that are needed to counteract such change' (The Norwegian Nobel Committee 2007).

Thus the information activities of UNEP and the WMO helped considerably to reduce the uncertainties about the causal link between greenhouse gas emissions and climate change, put global climate change on the political agenda and push states to enter into negotiations leading to binding, though still modest, commitments to cutting their greenhouse gas emissions.

Evaluation of the organizations' effectiveness

UNEP and the WMO, in conjunction with environmental international NGOs, promoted a relatively early scientific recognition of the climate change problem and contributed to the rapid formation of a consensus among scholars and experts upon which international climate policy could be based. They have also furthered reaching an agreement on reducing greenhouse gas emissions in the Kyoto Protocol. The establishment of internationally binding emission reductions under the Kyoto Protocol was certainly no small achievement (see Aldy & Stavins 2007). The scale and the complexity of the problem – its truly global nature, the great incentives to free ride on the efforts of others, and the need to regulate domestic level behaviour – have brought forth one of the most ambitious projects in the history of international law (Thompson 2010: 270).

Nonetheless, even taking into account the formidable challenge and exceptional difficulty of reducing global carbon dioxide emissions, the overall record of international organizations' effectiveness in addressing the global problem of climate change is sobering (Breitmeier 2009; Rittberger et al. 2010: 594–95). Global greenhouse gas emissions continue to increase. Emerging economies, such as Brazil, China and India were not bound to any reduction commitments under the Kyoto Protocol. The very basis of the Paris Agreement was furthermore the NDCs rather than international legally binding commitments. It is now widely acknowledged among scientists (and many policy-makers) that previous and current reduction commitments – under the Kyoto Protocol and the Paris Agreement – are insufficient to stop or significantly slow down global climate change (Aldy & Stavins 2007). Few states met their Kyoto Protocol emission reduction commitments, and it remains a big question whether countries can achieve their NDCs. On top of this, the decision of President Trump in 2018 to withdraw from the Paris Agreement hardly helps. Thus, not only on the impact level (mitigating climate change) but also on the outcome level (changing states' emission policies), international organizations are relatively ineffective. This is evidenced by a cross-country comparison of reduction commitments under the Kyoto Protocol and actual developments of carbon dioxide emissions. Figure 11.3 shows that many states have not lived up to their (overall modest) reduction commitments under the Kyoto Protocol when we compare the actual development of their emissions between 1990 and 2005 with the emission cuts prescribed by the Protocol.

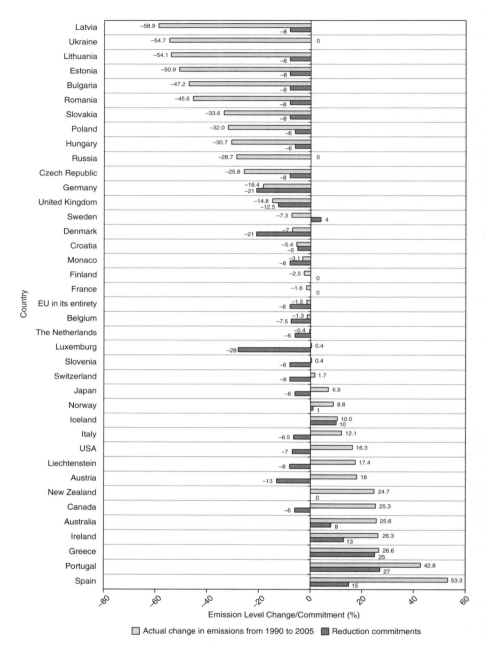

Figure 11.3   Global reduction commitments (% of emission cuts compared to 1990 levels) under the Kyoto Protocol and actual emission trends

Source: Based on data from Rittberger et al. 2010: 595.

CONCLUSION

In the area of environmental protection – both regarding the ozone layer and climate change – we can identify some clear dynamics by approaching international organizations as political systems. As a starting point, it is important to point out the input provided by scientists and the extensive lobbying of international NGOs and other transnational expert networks. It is also significant to pay attention to the input provided by states themselves. Here, we have identified changing constellations of states as well as changing preferences. While the EU was initially sceptical of international cooperation to address problems with the ozone layer, it has come out as one of the strongest supporters of global environmental cooperation, including in the area of climate change. The USA, at the same time, has also shifted its position. Particularly important these days is whether the US President is a Democrat or a Republican. Furthermore, China and the other emerging economies have become powerful actors in the field of environmental protection. Their input is also increasingly relevant.

The mode of decision-making is rather particular to the area of the environment. There is not a single traditional international organization where decisions are being made on a continuous basis. Rather, most of the decision-making takes place through COPs on an annual, or at least regular, basis. While intergovernmental bargaining between the states dominates, many of these COPs have also become major events (gatherings) where thousands of representatives from NGOs and the scientific community meet. Just organizing these events is already a major job for the relevant secretariats, such as the United Nations Climate Change Secretariat in Bonn. The fact that these conferences have become such big gatherings also puts tremendous pressure on states. Leaving the COPs without an agreement creates a significant disappointment. In this sense, even though the prominent mode is intergovernmental negotiations, the process is rather institutionalized.

The output of international organizations in the area of environmental protection includes both policy programmes and operational activities. The policy programmes in both the area of the protection of the ozone layer and climate change provide ambitious targets and roadmaps how to address environmental problems. The big question is implementation, which has been delegated to the member states themselves. While member states make clear commitments and communicate about them publicly, they ultimately remain responsible for achieving them. The monitoring and sanctioning mechanisms remain weak. This is one of the reasons why, particularly in the area of climate change, both the outcome (lower emissions) and impact (less global warming) are not fully achieved. With respect to the ozone layer, the international community has been more successful. It was, however, easier to phase out CFCs than greenhouse gases altogether. What the policy area of the environment also neatly shows is that the impacts of international organizations feed again into international organizations as input. If it becomes clear that the impact is insufficient, this creates feedback and returns to the agenda as a problem to be addressed.

Discussion Questions

1. What explains the difference between international organizations' effectiveness in the issue areas of protection of the stratospheric ozone layer and containment of climate change?
2. What effects did the information activities of international organizations have in the field of environmental policy-making and why are they particularly relevant in this issue area?

Further Reading

Falkner, Robert 2016. The Paris Agreement and the new logic of international climate politics, in: *International Affairs* 92: 5, 1107–25.

Haas, Peter M. 1992. Obtaining environmental protection through epistemic communities, in: Rowlands, Ian H. & Greene, Malory (eds) *Global Environmental Change and International Relations*, Basingstoke: Palgrave Macmillan, 38–59.

Keohane, Robert O. & Victor, David G. 2011. The regime complex for climate change, in: *Perspectives on Politics* 9: 1, 7–23.

12 Human Rights

Human rights pose a different dilemma for international cooperation from security, the economy and the environment (Donnelly 2006; Simmons 2009). The human rights dilemma is not based on material interdependencies between states. Human rights violations in one country do not automatically affect the human rights situation in another country. The human rights dilemma derives 'only' from moral interdependencies across state borders: human rights violations in one state can give rise to moral outrage in other states resulting in an active international human rights policy (Risse & Sikkink 1999: 22–24). The existence of such international moral interdependencies crucially depends on the activities of transnational networks of human rights organizations, which construct local human rights violations as global problems requiring governance beyond the state. Even more than in other issue areas, global human rights problems are socially constructed rather than naturally given issues of international governance. Indeed, until rather recently, human rights were mostly considered domestic rather than international matters.

Despite increasingly strong global concern, individual states may still be reluctant to 'lecture' other states on human rights, let alone to unilaterally pursue sanctions in the case of human rights violations. For instance, Western states have been rather cautious to confront China over its human rights record, afraid that this may affect economic relations. Therefore collective international cooperation, including through international organizations, is needed in order to bring about active human rights policies aimed at those states that violate such rights. Furthermore, delegating monitoring and compliance tasks to international organizations avoids individual states needing to point to each other.

Whereas cooperation is comparatively easy to organize among democratic states that have a good human rights record, it is particularly difficult to achieve cooperation with authoritarian states that regularly violate human rights (Moravcsik 2000). Nonetheless, international organizations working jointly with civil society actors can contribute to achieving international cooperation in the issue area of human rights. Through generating reliable information about human rights violations and by mobilizing civil society, transnational networks of human rights organizations can exert pressure on governments to act against offending states (Finnemore & Sikkink 1998: 896–901; Risse & Sikkink 1999: 22–25). International organizations can support these efforts through their policy programmes and operational activities. To understand the contributions of international organizations to international cooperation in the human rights we concentrate on the activities of the United Nations (UN) at the global level and the Council of Europe at the regional level.

GLOBAL HUMAN RIGHTS PROTECTION

During the late nineteenth century and early twentieth century, the international community adopted a number of international human rights treaties, including the Geneva Convention of 1864 and the Brussels Act against slavery of 1890. A major input for securing human rights internationally, however, was the reaction of states and civil society to the crimes against humanity committed by Nazi Germany during the Second World War (Krasner 1999: 106–10). This resulted in the adoption of the Universal Declaration of Human Rights by the UN General Assembly in 1948. During the last few decades, the human rights violations by General Pinochet in Chile, the politics of apartheid in South Africa, the massacre in Tiananmen Square in Beijing, the Rwandan genocide and the atrocities committed in the civil war in the Darfur region of Sudan – to name but a few – have kept human rights issues on the international political agenda. In all these cases, it was apparent that pressure by international civil society actors, rather than states, was the trigger for an active human rights policy. Nevertheless, it was only with the support of powerful states that a policy of international human rights protection became possible (Donnelly 2006: Chapter 1; Krasner 1999).

Policy programme of the UN

The reactions of the international community to the atrocities committed by Nazi Germany during the Second World War provided significant input for the UN human rights regime developed after 1945. The Preamble to the UN Charter reaffirms 'faith in fundamental human rights, the dignity and worth of the human person, in the equal rights of men and women and of nations large and small'. However, the Charter does not mention the specific human rights which states have to guarantee beyond Article 55, which urges the promotion of 'universal respect for, and observance of, human rights and fundamental freedoms for all without distinction as to race, sex, language, or religion'. Thus, initially, human rights protection by the UN remained limited.

The UN Economic and Social Council (ECOSOC) was charged with translating this general declaration into a human rights policy programme. To this end, as early as 1946, ECOSOC set up a Commission on Human Rights as a subsidiary body to develop programmes for international human rights protection. Until it was replaced by the UN Human Rights Council in 2006, the Commission on Human Rights – with the support of the Sub-Commission on the Promotion and Protection of Human Rights – represented the central forum for the intergovernmental negotiations in the UN on policy programmes for the protection of human rights. Initially, the decision-making process was dominated by the Western coalition of liberal democracies under the leadership of the USA. It was thus possible to reach an international consensus based on liberal ideas about what rights should henceforth be recognized and guaranteed as human rights. As a result, in 1948 the UN General Assembly adopted the Universal Declaration of Human Rights (GA Resolution 217A (III)). The General Assembly decision was taken by majority vote and the Declaration remained legally non-binding. The Declaration was significant nonetheless: it meant that human rights were now issues for the agenda of the principal organs of the UN. In other words, states' exercise of authority over their citizens was removed from their exclusive jurisdiction and the principle of non-interference in domestic affairs began to lose some of its validity insofar as human rights were concerned.

The Universal Declaration of Human Rights established a normative frame of reference. It was to be followed by the legally binding codification of human rights. Immediately after the adoption of the Declaration, the Commission on Human Rights proceeded with lengthy intergovernmental negotiations about the International Covenant on Civil and Political Rights and the International Covenant on Economic, Social and Cultural Rights. Both covenants had largely been negotiated by 1954, but it took the General Assembly until 1966 to formally adopt them and to recommend them to states for signature. Another ten years passed before a sufficient number of states had ratified them. They came into force in 1976. The number of parties to the covenants grew steadily throughout the 2000s and by 2018 stood at 170 (Civil Pact) and 167 (Social Pact), respectively.

The Universal Declaration of Human Rights and the two Covenants form the core of the UN's policy programme on human rights. They contain a large number of human rights norms. Each individual norm has a prescriptive status and together the human rights standards form an international normative structure (Donnelly 2006: 15; Ramcharan 2007; Risse & Ropp 1999; Tomuschat 2008: Chapter 3). The UN programme on human rights, starting with the dignity and equality of all people (Articles 1 and 2, Universal Declaration of Human Rights), formulates a canon of liberal rights for the protection of individuals against a state's arbitrary and excessive exercise of power (Articles 3 to 21, Universal Declaration of Human Rights; Articles 6 to 27, International Covenant on Civil and Political Rights). They include the right to life, liberty and personal security; protection against discrimination; prohibition of torture and slavery or servitude; protection of the private sphere; the right to freedom of thought, conscience and religion; the right to freedom of expression, assembly, association and movement; protection of the family; the right to marry; the right to equal access to public service and the right to take part in the government of one's country; the right to participate in elections; entitlement to equality before the law and to a fair and public hearing in courts of law; the right to legal assistance and to be presumed innocent until proved guilty; and the right of being convicted only on the basis of laws in existence at the time the offence was committed.

In addition, the UN programme mentions basic economic, social and cultural rights (Articles 22 to 27, Universal Declaration of Human Rights; International Covenant on Economic, Social and Cultural Rights). These include, among others, the right to sufficient food and an adequate standard of living as well as the right to physical and mental health; the right to work and to just and favourable conditions of work; the right to strike; the right to leisure, holidays and social security; and the right to education and to participation in the cultural and scientific life of one's country.

To these rights, which are subject to a multitude of reservations, others have been added in a series of conventions for the protection of human rights. The most important ones include the 1948 Convention on the Prevention and Punishment of the Crime of Genocide, the 1965 Convention on the Elimination of all Forms of Racial Discrimination, the 1979 Convention on the Elimination of all Forms of Discrimination against Women, the 1984 Convention against Torture and Other Cruel, Inhuman or Degrading Treatment or Punishment, the 1989 Convention on the Rights of the Child, the 2006 Convention on the Rights of Persons with Disabilities and the 2006 Convention for the Protection of All Persons from Enforced Disappearance (see Table 12.1).

The activities of the UN regarding human rights violations have benefited from significant support through the activities of non-governmental organizations (NGOs). This involvement became apparent in the 1970s when the number of internationally active NGOs in the issue area of human rights multiplied (Boli & Thomas 1999: Chapter 2). But in fact the NGO involvement dates back even to the negotiations over the Universal Declaration of 1948 (Korey 1998: Chapter 1). Since the end of the Cold War, human rights organizations have made abundant use of the platforms available to them in the UN system, both through human rights conferences (such as the 1993 Second World Conference on Human Rights in Vienna or the 2001 World Conference against Racism in Durban) and access to standing bodies (such as the Human Rights Council), to give an impetus to new programmes and insist on reliable implementation of existing norms.

The special value of the UN policy programme for human rights protection is its function as a system of reference for criticism of violations. Thus societies affected by human rights violations can use the UN programme to exert pressure on their governments by pointing out their disregard of internationally recognized norms. The activities of transnational supporters of human rights contribute to the creation of a 'boomerang effect': when members of national civil society do not address their human-rights-violating government directly, since access to it is frequently blocked or suppressed, but seek international and transnational allies. Frequently, they establish links to transnationally networked NGOs able to mobilize international organizations, civil society and governments in liberal democracies. These external actors can translate the information obtained from the affected societies into pressure on the offending state (Keck & Sikkink 1998: 12–14; Risse & Sikkink 1999: 18–20).

A good example for the interplay between national and transnational human rights actors is provided by developments in Eastern Europe and the former Soviet Union after the 1975 CSCE Final Act of Helsinki (see Chapter 3). The Conference on Security and Co-operation (CSCE) was established in the early 1970s as a multilateral forum for dialogue and negotiation between members of the Warsaw Pact and the North Atlantic Treaty Organization (NATO). After two years of negotiations in Helsinki and Geneva, the 35 CSCE member states reached agreement on the Helsinki Final Act in 1975. Apart from provisions aimed at a détente in the political relations between states of the East and the West, the Final Act also included human rights provisions that became central to the so-called Helsinki process. So one of the ten fundamental principles (the 'Decalogue') of the Helsinki Final Act referred to respect for human rights and fundamental freedoms, including the freedom of thought, conscience, religion or belief. The inclusion and even

Table 12.1 The main global human rights conventions

Convention	Treaty body	Year opened for signature	Year entered into force	Number of ratifications (2018)
Convention on the Prevention and Punishment of the Crime of Genocide	None	1948	1951	149
Convention on the Elimination of all Forms of Racial Discrimination	Committee on the Elimination of Racial Discrimination	1965	1969	179
International Covenant on Civil and Political Rights	Human Rights Committee	1966	1976	170
International Covenant on Economic, Social and Cultural Rights	Committee on Economic, Social and Cultural Rights	1966	1976	167
Convention on the Elimination of all Forms of Discrimination against Women	Committee on the Elimination of Discrimination against Women	1979	1981	189
Convention against Torture and Other Cruel, Inhuman or Degrading Treatment or Punishment	Committee against Torture	1984	1987	163
Convention on the Rights of the Child	Committee on the Rights of the Child	1989	1990	196
Convention on the Protection of the Rights of All Migrant Workers and Members of their Families	Committee on Migrant Workers	1990	2003	51
Convention on the Rights of Persons with Disabilities	Committee on the Rights of Persons with Disabilities	2006	2008	177
Convention for the Protection of All Persons from Enforced Disappearance	Committee on Enforced Disappearances	2006	2010	58

Source: Based on data from OHCHR.

more the implementation of these human rights provisions were supported by NGOs in the East and the West. Numerous groups of dissidents were formed, such as Charter 77 in the former Czechoslovakia, while in the Western democracies the NGO Human Rights Watch (initially named Helsinki Watch) was established as a reaction to the dissidents' activities. The 'Helsinki effect' on domestic political change in the former Eastern bloc resulting from dissidents' as well as Human Rights Watch's efforts, and strengthened by subsequent CSCE meetings, has been well documented (Thomas 2001) and would not have been possible without reference to the existence of a UN human rights programme.

Operations of the UN

After concentrating until the mid-1960s almost exclusively on the generation of human rights policy programmes, the UN has since increasingly striven for their implementation. However, the great progress on the programme side is not matched by the UN's operational activities (Forsythe 2006: 57–59; Ramcharan 2007: 453). In analysing the UN's operations we must differentiate between supervisory organs or procedures existing by virtue of the UN Charter or emanating from it, and those organs and procedures created as part of particular international human rights treaties. The latter only supervise the activities of parties to those treaties and not those of all UN member states. ECOSOC and the Human Rights Council belong to the former group.

Throughout the post-Second World War period until the creation of the Human Rights Council in 2006, the Commission on Human Rights was the main human rights-monitoring body of the UN. It relied on two supervisory procedures, procedure 1235 and procedure 1503, named after ECOSOC resolutions. Procedure 1503 allowed individuals and groups of individuals to submit reports to the Commission on Human Rights alleging gross and systematic human rights violations. The Commission then confidentially examined whether such violations had taken place. If the allegation was upheld the Commission could recommend measures against the offending state in its annual report to ECOSOC. Under procedure 1235 the Commission on Human Rights handled information about gross and systematic human rights violations, this time publicly. During its annual session, in which government representatives and representatives of NGOs could refer in public meetings to human rights violations, the Commission could decide on thorough investigations on country-specific human rights conditions or major instances of specific gross human rights violations in more than one country.

In 2006, after lengthy intergovernmental negotiations, the Commission on Human Rights was replaced by the Human Rights Council through General Assembly Resolution 60/251. The Council replaced the Commission on Human Rights, whose reputation had increasingly suffered from a stand-off between Western states and a group of frequently criticized states trying to prevent country resolutions and the appointment of special rapporteurs (Heinz 2006: 131–32; Rittberger et al. 2010: 643–46). The Human Rights Council, which is a standing body, consists of 47 member states elected by the General Assembly.

The membership rights of states with gross and systematic human rights violations can be suspended by a two-thirds majority vote of the General Assembly. Nonetheless, some states with a bad human rights record are still represented in the Human Rights Council (Heinz 2006: 137–39).

The supervisory procedures of the Human Rights Council resemble those at the disposal of the Commission on Human Rights (see Table 12.2; Rittberger et al. 2010: 644–45). In the Universal Periodic Review (UPR) the compliance of all UN member states with their human rights obligations is assessed once every four years. For that purpose, a working group, consisting of the members of the Council, is set up. It takes into account reports and comments from the state under review, the Office of the UN High Commissioner for Human Rights (OHCHR), and other UN and treaty organs, as well as civil society organizations. However, it mainly asks states to declare what actions they have taken to improve the human rights situations in their countries. Its main output is a final report ('outcome report') which documents the questions, comments and recommendations directed at the country under review, as well as the responses by the reviewed state. In the review that follows, the state must provide information on how it implemented the recommendations from the preceding review.

Special Procedures are mechanisms established by the Human Rights Council to address country-specific situations or global thematic issues. As of August 2017 there are 44 thematic and 12 country mandates. The mandate holders ('special rapporteurs' or 'independent experts') ask for information from governments on their human rights policies, carry out country visits and prepare reports as well as draft resolutions and provide technical assistance and capacity-building measures. These procedures were largely taken over from the Commission on Human Rights. The Special Procedures do not provide for hard sanctions in the case of

Table 12.2   Monitoring procedures of the Human Rights Council

Procedure	Object of investigation	Providers of relevant information	Investigating actors
Universal periodic review	Compliance with human rights obligations of all states	States under review, OHCHR, human rights treaty organs, NGOs	Working group of the Human Rights Council
Special procedures	Situation in specific countries; global thematic issues of human rights protection	Special rapporteurs, working groups of the Human Rights Council, states, NGOs	Special rapporteur, independent experts, or working group of the Human Rights Council
Complaints procedure	Massive and systematic human rights violations by one state	Individuals, (state and non-state) organizations	Working Group on Communications, Working Group on Situations

Source: Based on data from Rittberger et al. (2010: 645).

states' non-compliance with their human rights obligations. Finally, the Human Rights Council uses complaints procedures which are open to individuals as well as organizations and generally correspond to the 1503 procedure of the Commission on Human Rights. Incoming complaints ('communications') are first examined by a Working Group on Communications, which consists of five independent experts and assesses the admissibility of a communication. If the communication is admissible, it is transferred to the Working Group on Situations, which finally presents the Council with a report on proven human rights violations and policy recommendations for the respective country. Again, apart from suspension of membership in the Council, there are no sanctions beyond 'naming and shaming' available to the Human Rights Council, even in cases of reliably attested gross and systematic human rights violations (Heinz 2006: 133–35).

The powers to examine human rights practices by way of the second group of supervisory organs or procedures, those based on human rights treaties, are limited to the signatory states. All major human rights treaty systems share the relatively weak instrument of accepting and examining reports. In these reports, which have to be completed every four to five years or at the request of the competent treaty organ, signatory states give an account of their implementation of the respective human rights treaty. However, these reports are frequently lacking in detail, and often merely contain a general assurance that the binding human rights obligations are being observed, or a list of the national laws meant to guarantee national observance of the internationally negotiated rights (Liese 2006b). Many states fail to comply with their reporting obligation (Steiner & Alston 2000: 774). The competent treaty organ simply examines the reports in the light of the information available to it, which it may have gained through the media or human rights NGOs. In the case of inconsistencies the organ can publicly request further information from the country under examination. The results of this state-by-state scrutiny are contained in reports published by the treaty organ, which are circulated to all parties to the treaty and to ECOSOC (Liese 2006b).

In some treaty systems for the protection of human rights the possibilities for supervision go beyond the duty to report. With the exception of the procedures for states within the framework of the Convention on Racial Discrimination, these additional supervisory procedures can only be used by the treaty organs once the parties to the treaty have either ratified an additional protocol or declared their willingness to submit to these far-reaching procedures. The best known of such protocols, the first Optional Protocol to the 1966 International Covenant on Civil and Political Rights, establishes the right of individuals, or their families, who claim to have been the victims of human rights violations to submit a complaint to the Human Rights Committee (Simmons 2009: Chapter 5). The Human Rights Committee was founded on the basis of the Covenant and not only receives complaints from individuals as well as states, but is also the competent treaty organ to examine the periodic reports submitted by member states. This committee of 18 experts, which meets three times a year for four-week sessions in Geneva and strictly speaking is not a UN organ, analyses the complaints submitted by individuals or states.

The human rights violations treated under the Optional Protocol do not have to be gross and systematic. Individual human rights violations can be examined by the Committee. Between its start in 1977 and 2016, more than 2,700 complaints (by individuals and states) had been registered and more than half of them were deemed admissible. If the Committee decides that human rights have been violated it will communicate its findings to the state concerned and the individuals who have complained. In its annual report, which reaches the General Assembly through ECOSOC, the committee lists the states that have been investigated, thus putting violations by a state into the public domain. These investigations, although relatively well conducted, are limited by the fact that the Optional Protocol needs to be ratified. By 2018, 116 states, that is approximately two-thirds of all signatories, had ratified it and were therefore subject to its procedures.

The four other human rights treaty systems – the Convention against Torture and Other Cruel, Inhuman or Degrading Treatment or Punishment, the Convention on the Elimination of All Forms of Discrimination against Women, the Convention on the Elimination of all Forms of Racial Discrimination, and the Convention on the Rights of Persons with Disabilities – which foresee the possibility of complaints by individuals after agreement by the state parties (in the form of ratification of an optional protocol or a formal declaration) – are in a similar situation (Simmons 2009: Chapters 6–8). In all these cases cooperation restraining the arbitrary or excessive exercise of state authority is easiest to achieve where it is least required; those states which have ratified the protocols or have made additional declarations generally do not belong to the group of 'black sheep' in the international human rights field (O'Flaherty 2002; Ramcharan 2007: 451–52).

The plethora of organs dealing with human rights violations raises the question of coordination of the preparatory work of all the committees. The response, in 1993, was the establishment of the OHCHR by the General Assembly (Resolution 48/141). Following restructuring in 1997, operational activities now form the core of the High Commissioner's role. The OHCHR endeavours to promote worldwide respect for the human rights enshrined in international law by supporting the bodies created by human rights treaties and the Human Rights Council as well as through technical assistance programmes in many countries. However, its work is severely hampered by financial constraints and lack of personnel (De Zayas 2002).

Despite these serious efforts, an effective supervisory system is still a long way off. However, there is sufficient transparency to make human rights violations more susceptible to discovery. This has been substantially facilitated through information supplied by NGOs such as Amnesty International and Human Rights Watch (Baehr 2009; Keck & Sikkink 1998). The NGOs also make it their business to scrutinize the operational activities of the UN and the various treaty bodies (Liese 1998: 40). Effective supervision of human rights practices through international organizations presupposes the employment of sanctions against states committing violations. Despite significant advances during the 1990s, such sanctions are still in their infancy. The most frequent although not the only form of sanction remains the publication and denunciation of violations by individual states, that is 'naming and shaming' (Franklin 2008; Hafner-Burton 2008; Lebovic & Voeten 2006).

Far-reaching collective sanctions against a state are only possible in cases where the UN Security Council declares the human rights violations of that state to be endangering international peace and security. This allows the Security Council to take all the measures listed in Chapter VII of the Charter (see Chapter 8). With the end of the Cold War the Security Council redefined its role in implementing the human rights codified in the framework of the UN. Whereas before 1990 the Security Council did not take collective enforcement measures against perpetrators of human rights violations – with the exception of economic sanctions against the former Rhodesia and the arms embargo against South Africa (see Chapter 3) – the behaviour of the Security Council has changed somewhat (Forsythe 2006: 59–61). Since the early 1990s the Security Council has agreed to enforcement measures in a substantial number of humanitarian crises such as those in Bosnia, Kosovo, Haiti, Somalia, East Timor, the Democratic Republic of Congo and Libya.

If, however, one compares the number of resolutions in which the Security Council declares itself 'worried' about human rights violations or humanitarian crises with the frequency of enforcement measures – that is, sanctions – a substantial gap comes to the fore (Kühne 2000: 299; Petersohn 2009). For example, the civil war in the Darfur region of Sudan (2003–10), in which gross and systematic human rights violations took place and several hundred thousand people were killed, was condemned by the Security Council in several resolutions. At the same time, resembling its previous hesitancy and ineptitude in the Rwandan Genocide (1994), the Security Council was unable to reach agreement on substantial enforcement measures to stop these gross human rights violations. Moreover, there have been many humanitarian crises on which the Security Council did not agree in time or did not agree at all. For example, gross human rights violations in Darfur during the 2000s and Syria during the 2010s have been widely ignored by the Security Council. In addition, in some humanitarian crises the enforcement measures decided by the Security Council have failed; this is the common perception of the humanitarian intervention in Somalia (1992–95; see Chapter 8). These failed interventions and non-interventions overshadow the successes of the UN, such as the intervention in East Timor.

However, at least in part driven by motives to avoid costly military sanctions (Forsythe 2006: 98, 103; Rudolph 2001), the Security Council has revitalized another instrument of adjudication and sanctioning, that of international courts for the legal pursuit of individuals – rather than states – who are accused of being responsible for gross infringement of international humanitarian law. Acting under Article 29 of the UN Charter, the Security Council set up two international (ad hoc) tribunals for the former Yugoslavia and for Rwanda. With its Resolution 827 (1993) the Security Council, starting from the procedures adopted by the Allied Powers after the Second World War in Nuremberg and Tokyo, created the International Criminal Tribunal for the Former Yugoslavia (ICTY) in The Hague for the prosecution of persons accused of being responsible for serious violations of international humanitarian law. Later Security Council Resolutions 955 (1994) and 977 (1995) established the International Criminal Tribunal for Rwanda (ICTR). The offences prosecuted are genocide, crimes against humanity and war crimes. Both tribunals have led to the arrest, handover and sentencing of a number of prominent war criminals. The ICTY has indicted 161 high-profile persons and has sentenced 90 persons for war crimes. This includes, among others, Bosnian Serb leader Radovan Karadžić and General Ratko Mladic, both convicted of genocide. The ICTR has had a lower exposure, but sentenced the former Prime Minister of Rwanda, Jean Kambanda, to life imprisonment for genocide in 2000 (Gareis & Varwick 2005: 230).

Whereas the ICTY and the ICTR were clearly subsidiary organs of the UN, there have also been so-called hybrid tribunals with a mixed composition of national and international personnel. These hybrid tribunals, such as the Special Court for Sierra Leone (SCSL, 2002) or the Extraordinary Chambers in the Courts of Cambodia ('Khmer Rouge Tribunal', 2004), rest on a contractual agreement between the UN and the national government to address past international crimes in post-conflict societies (Goldstone 2007; Hoffmann-Van de Poll 2011).

The symbolic significance of these tribunals and their precursor role in relation to the Statute for an International Criminal Court, signed in Rome in 1998 by representatives of 120 states, is widely recognized (Boekle 1998: 14–16; Schabas 2011: 11–15). Equally important was the advocacy work by a transnational Coalition for the International Criminal Court (CICC) which supported a substantial number of small and middle powers (the Like-Minded Group) in calling for a strong, independent court (Deitelhoff 2009: 37; see Fehl 2004). In contrast to the ICTY and the ICTR, the authority of the International Criminal Court (ICC) is not limited to prosecuting and sentencing gross violations of international humanitarian law on the territory of two countries, namely the former Yugoslavia and Rwanda. It can sentence crimes against humanity, war crimes, crimes of aggression and genocide either committed on the territory of a country that has ratified its statute or committed by a citizen of such a country (Rudolph 2001). While the ICC is an independent international organization located in The Hague and is not part of the UN system, it maintains in general cooperative relations with the UN, in particular with the Security Council. The ICC prosecutor can initiate investigations on the basis of a referral from any state party or from the Security Council, but also by his or her own initiative on the basis of information received from individuals or (civil society) organizations. State parties must cooperate with the Court, which also includes surrendering suspects upon request of the Court. As of 2018, 123 states have ratified the Rome Statute, with powerful states such as China, India, Russia and the USA still not being party to the ICC. The ICC has begun its work in 2002, conducting investigations, issuing arrest orders and hearing cases concerning situations in the Democratic Republic of Congo, Uganda, the Central African Republic and Sudan (Deitelhoff 2009: 34).

Evaluation of the organization's effectiveness

The effectiveness of the UN's response to human rights violations must be assessed against the background of particularly challenging conditions for international cooperation in this field. International human rights protection affects the core of states' domestic sovereignty since it proscribes particular practices of rule within states. Authoritarian states, in particular, tend to reject their domestic practices of rule being subject to international scrutiny. Moreover, it is still debated in how far human rights constitute truly universal or culturally specific (above all Western liberal) values, which further complicates consensus on international human rights norms and their implementation (Jetschke 2006; Renteln 1990).

A first indication that UN activities in the human rights field can nonetheless have a positive impact on the human rights situation within member states might be that the global human rights situation has improved since the 1980s. This finding is underlined by a comparison of country ratings by the American NGO Freedom House. Freedom House rates all countries in the world based on criteria of political participatory rights and civil liberties. Figure 12.1 shows that between 1972 and 2017 the share of 'free' countries has increased whereas the proportion of 'not free' countries has become smaller, even though there has been a stagnation since 2000. This improvement in the global human rights situation correlates with UN human rights activities being no longer limited to policy programme activities, but increasingly including operational activities as well. However, this improvement of the global human rights situation (particularly in the field of political rights and civil liberties) might have many reasons, some of which are unrelated to the UN human rights regime. A closer look at the effectiveness of specific UN activities is warranted.

Some, mainly qualitative, studies suggest that international human rights norms have a positive impact on states' human rights policies. Keck and Sikkink (1998) show that, especially in Latin America, transnational networks of human rights NGOs relied on international organizations' programme and operational

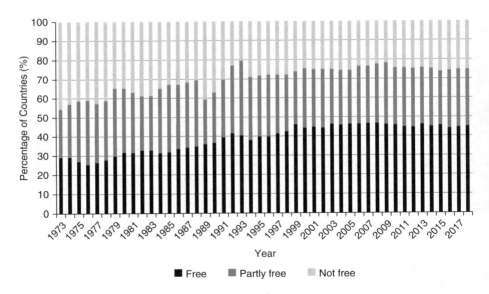

Figure 12.1   Proportion of 'free', 'partly free' and 'not free' countries, 1972–2017
Source: In % of overall number of states, based on ratings and data from Freedom House.

activities in bringing about significant change in the human rights policies of particular states. In a similar vein, Risse et al. (1999) find evidence that cooperative efforts by transnationally operating networks of human rights NGOs, international organizations, Western states and domestic opposition groups have indeed brought about improvements in domestic human rights practices in 11 countries representing five different world regions – Northern Africa, sub-Saharan Africa, South East Asia, Latin America and Eastern Europe. They show that UN human rights norms provide transnational human rights networks with an important reference system, allowing them to put pressure on states to improve their record of human rights protection (Risse et al. 2002). Furthermore, UN human rights norms offer transnational human rights networks important arguments with which to convince democratic states to engage in more active human rights policies, which then lead to improved human rights policies in, or even a democratic transition of, non-democratic countries (Klotz 1995; Risse et al. 1999). Klotz (1995) was, for instance, able to demonstrate that international human rights norms helped advocacy groups to force the US government to impose sanctions on South Africa which, in the late 1980s, clearly contributed to the collapse of the apartheid regime.

In a large-scale, statistical study, Simmons (2009) finds that, at state level, international human rights law has made a positive contribution to the respect for human rights, in particular in the fields of civil rights, equality for women, prevention of torture, and the rights of the child. States' ratifications of treaties do lead over time to improved human rights practices by influencing legislative agendas, altering intrastate political coalitions, and defining the terms of acceptable state action. However, other scholars are more sceptical. In a quantitative analysis encompassing 166 states over a period of almost 40 years in five areas of human rights law, Hathaway (2002) examines whether countries comply with the requirements of human rights treaties that they have joined. Hathaway finds that, although the practices of countries that have ratified human rights treaties are generally better than those of countries that have not, non-compliance with treaty obligations is still common. Hathaway explicitly blames weak monitoring and enforcement of human rights treaties for these incidences of non-compliance which give rise to a gap between formal acceptance and actual implementation of human rights norms. Institutional weaknesses in monitoring and sanctioning allow states to reap the reputational benefits of treaty membership, while the risks of detection or even hard sanctions in the case of non-compliance are relatively low.

As outlined above, for most human rights treaty regimes mandatory state reporting is the most important monitoring mechanism. Against this background, Liese (2006b) analyses the impact of the Civil Pact's mandatory system of state reporting on national human rights policies. She finds that, despite the restricted competencies and limited resources of the Human Rights Committee, the reporting procedure contributes to a certain extent to compliance *de jure*, i.e. states usually comply with their reporting obligations. However, it is much more difficult to establish whether the reporting procedure contributes to the de facto improvement of national human rights performance, i.e. whether it has a positive impact on the human rights situation in reporting states (Liese 2006b). There seems to be a clear gap between compliance with reporting on human rights practices and their actual improvement.

Naming and shaming of human rights violations is still the most common instrument of (promoting) international and transnational human rights enforcement. Thus it is encouraging that states' practices of naming and shaming in UN organs is indeed based less on partisan ties among political allies and power politics, and more on countries' actual human rights records and treaty commitments. This holds especially for the time after the end of the Cold War (Lebovic & Voeten 2006). Moreover, naming and shaming by NGOs, organs of the UN human rights regime, and the Council of Europe (see below) can contribute to some change in intrastate human rights policies, especially as far as the adaptation of formal-legal and institutional provisions is concerned (Liese 2006a). It is also noteworthy that international organizations that do not belong to the core of the international human rights regime may give bite to multilateral naming and shaming in UN and human rights treaty bodies. The World Bank and other multilateral aid institutions have sanctioned human rights violators based on shaming in the (then) UN Commission on Human Rights (Lebovic & Voeten 2009). The adoption of a resolution condemning a country's human rights record regularly produces a sizeable reduction in multilateral, and especially World Bank, aid – whereas it has no significant effect on the country's aggregate bilateral aid receipts (Lebovic & Voeten 2009).

However, naming and shaming by no means guarantees sustained norm compliance in political practice; its impact on the actual day-to-day human rights situation within countries is often limited. Hafner-Burton (2008) quantitatively analyses the effect of naming and shaming on states' human rights policies in 145 countries from 1975 to 2000. Her statistics show that governments put in the spotlight for abuses continue or even exacerbate some violations afterwards, while reducing others. Governments may make improvements in response to international pressure to stop violations of particular rights for which they are publicly named and shamed; however, at the same time they frequently continue with other less exposed (and less criticized) violations (Hafner-Burton 2008). Moreover, human rights improvements are often not sustained once international criticism ebbs away (Franklin 2008).

One way to make sense of these mixed results of the UN's programme and operational activities in terms of improving human rights policies within states is to contextualize their impact (Neumayer 2005). International commitments and activities of UN and treaty bodies are more likely to improve the human rights situation the more democratic the country is or the more international NGOs its citizens participate in. By contrast, there is empirical evidence that in autocratic regimes with weak civil society, ratification can be expected to have little or no positive effect (Neumayer 2005). While this contextualization seems highly plausible in the light of the mechanisms that are commonly associated with domestic change of human rights policies, it also suggests a conclusion that is sobering from a normative point of view: the more improvement of domestic human rights policies is needed, the harder it is to achieve.

For cases of gross and systematic human rights atrocities, international criminal tribunals provide relatively hard adjudication and sanctioning mechanisms – and they do so in increasing scale and normative scope (Sikkink & Walling 2007). Despite their proliferation, international criminal tribunals such as the ICTY and the ICTR have often been regarded as relatively ineffective or at least inconsistent in the promotion of international justice (Barria & Roper 2005: 349; Hoffmann-van de Poll 2011). Sceptics of international criminal tribunals argue that these tribunals are irrelevant or even dangerous for achieving the goals of justice, deterrence of human rights violations and peace (see Snyder & Vinjamuri 2004). Ku and Nzelibe (2006) doubt that international criminal tribunals can deter crimes because perpetrators' calculations are much more influenced by harsh local sanctions than uncertain and usually lighter international ones. Thus pessimists are largely unconvinced of international criminal tribunals' transformative potential (Simmons & Danner 2010: 225–26; see Bloxham 2006; Goldsmith 2003). All-too bleak assessments of international criminal tribunals do not seem justified, though. It can be shown that international criminal tribunals have important influences on domestic values and cultural orientations towards violence (Kiss 2000; see also Sikkink & Walling 2007). Moreover, while there are certainly deficits in the reliability with which perpetrators of gross human rights violations have actually been brought before the tribunals, sweeping claims that international criminal tribunals are unable to deter any atrocities are questionable on both methodological and empirical grounds (Akhavan 2001; Gilligan 2006; Scheffer 2002).

At any rate, these ad hoc international criminal tribunals were important precursors for the establishment of the ICC, which enjoys considerably broader authority. As the ICC has been operating for only about 15 years, it is too early to make definite assessments of its effectiveness in combating impunity, deterring human rights violations and reducing intrastate violence. In an early study of the ICC's effects on member states' human rights policies in violent conflict, Simmons and Danner (2010) come to the conclusion that ratification of the Rome Statute is associated with tentative steps towards violence reduction and peace, at least in some countries, and that the ICC is potentially helpful as a mechanism for governments to credibly commit to reducing violence and get on the road to peaceful negotiations (Simmons & Danner 2010). At the same time, the ICC has been criticized, particularly by African Union member states, as only addressing human rights violation in Africa. This resulted in 2017 in Burundi leaving the ICC and South Africa threatening to do so. The ICC is under further pressure with the Philippines also leaving in 2018.

Finally, the hardest sanction available to the UN in cases of gross and systematic human rights violations is military intervention authorized by the Security Council under Chapter VII. The Security Council needs to find that these human rights violations constitute a threat to international peace and security. However, as mentioned above, Security Council authorization of military intervention to stop massive atrocities within states is highly selective (Petersohn 2009), which hampers its effectiveness in stopping or even deterring gross human rights violations. Multilateral military interventions to protect citizens from their government are thus far from being a reliable bulwark against the worst human rights atrocities.

EUROPEAN HUMAN RIGHTS PROTECTION

In Western Europe, during the immediate post-Second World War period there were three conditions that made international cooperation in the field of human rights feasible (Moravcsik 1995, 2000): the common experience of Fascist and Nazi terror, the rejection of the Communist system, and a high degree of consensus on fundamental values. In the early 1990s, after the end of the Cold War, Eastern European societies were confronted with similar conditions. Here, too, the desire to prevent a return to the Communist system and a consensus on basic values helped cooperation in the field of human rights. These conditions were conducive to the adherence of the states from the former Eastern bloc to the human rights agreements of Western European states. We shall focus on how the Council of Europe contributed to sustaining international human rights cooperation in Europe.

Policy programme of the Council of Europe

Significantly, the first steps towards the protection of human rights came from members of Western European societies and not from their states. In 1948, at the Hague Congress, more than 700 participants from 16 European countries formed the European Movement. They demanded a European Human Rights Charter under the protection of European courts. The states reacted swiftly, and as early as 1949 the Council of Europe was formed. Its statute provides that 'every member of the Council must accept the principles of the rule of law and of the enjoyment by all persons within its jurisdiction of human rights and fundamental freedoms' (Article 3). The Council of Europe thus established an institutional framework for the protection of human rights in Western Europe (see Chapter 3).

In the same year, the European Movement submitted a plan for a European convention on human rights to the Committee of Ministers, the intergovernmental organ of the Council of Europe. The Consultative (now Parliamentary) Assembly, the parliamentary organ of the Council of Europe, actively supported the European Movement's proposal. It requested that the Committee of Ministers should agree immediately on a convention for the protection of human rights. The governments were therefore put under pressure. After a year of intense intergovernmental negotiations, repeatedly spurred on by the European Movement as a transnational civil society actor, the European Convention for the Protection of Human Rights and Fundamental Freedoms (ECHR) was signed in 1950. Since then it has been supplemented by 14 additional protocols, requiring ratification. A further improvement to the human rights policy programme was made in 1961 with the signing of the European Social Charter (revised in 1996), which guarantees citizens of signatory states social and economic rights dealing with housing, health, education, employment, social and legal protection, free movement of persons and non-discrimination. Like the earlier ECHR and its additional protocols this Charter, too, was negotiated within the framework of the Council of Europe (Janis et al. 2000: 16–23). With the end of the Cold War, the Western European human rights programme was extended to Eastern Europe. The states of the former

Eastern bloc changed from Communist regimes into democratic states and joined Western European states in the Council of Europe, thereby adopting the ECHR. Its membership nearly trebled from 16 in 1990 to the current 47 members, including most of the successor states of the former Soviet Union.

In its content the regulatory policy programme of human rights protection contains all the normative essentials of democratic states respecting the rule of law. To be sure, it does not go far beyond the human rights programme of the UN, but the human rights standards of the Council of Europe are formulated more precisely, making it more difficult for states to invoke a let-out clause due to special circumstances (Steiner & Alston 2000: 787–89).

Operations of the Council of Europe

In the field of human rights, the main difference between the UN and the Council of Europe is not the policy programme but rather operational activities. The procedures for supervision of human rights practice in Europe are without parallel elsewhere (Brummer 2005; Donnelly 2006: 68–72; Janis et al. 2000; Keller & Stone Sweet 2008). This supervision rests on three different procedures: a complaint by individuals, a complaint by states, and the duty to report (Klein & Brinkmeier 2001). The weakest form of supervision is the duty to report, just as in the UN system. It is part of the Convention for the Protection of Human Rights and Fundamental Freedoms and the European Social Charter. Under the latter it is the only possibility for supervising member states. Every two years member states are obliged to send a report to the Secretary-General of the Council of Europe on the implementation of their commitments. However, writing the reports is not just left to governments as they must be submitted to trade unions and employers' organizations for comment (Clements et al. 1999: 246–48). Their comments are sent to the nine-member Committee of Experts which examines and evaluates the reports (Harris 2000).

Within the framework of the ECHR the duty to report is given little prominence. Although the Secretary-General can request a report from a member state on its implementation of the Convention, this has only happened very rarely. This is due to the effectiveness of supervision through complaints from individuals and states within the ECHR and its protocols. Not only states, but also individuals have the right to file a complaint to the European Court of Human Rights about human rights violations by a member state of the Convention. Since the coming into force of the 11th Additional Protocol of 1998, which fundamentally reformed the court system, the competency of the Court to accept individual complaints and not just state complaints no longer requires a separate declaration of acceptance of its competency by the so-called High Contracting Parties. If the Court, made up of the same number of judges as there are state parties to the Convention (Article 20 ECHR), receives an individual or state complaint (individual or state application), it must first examine its admissibility. Each individual application is examined by a Court rapporteur who decides whether it should be dealt with by a single judge, a three-member committee or a seven-member chamber. The designated single judge or committee may decide to declare inadmissible or strike out an application, if the inadmissibility of the complaint is evident. An individual complaint is only admissible when all state procedures have been exhausted. Individual applications which are not declared inadmissible by a single judge or committee, or which are referred directly to a chamber by the rapporteur, and all state applications are examined by a chamber. Chambers determine both admissibility and merits of a case. If a case is admitted then the procedure is almost identical, whether for complaints by individuals or those by states. Yet, compared to individual complaints, state parties rarely take cases against other state parties to the Court.

In any case, after a case is admitted the Court first must establish the facts. A chamber of the Court proceeds to examine the facts in cooperation with the parties before the Court, by questioning witnesses and local inspection of state institutions, for example prisons. This is like a preliminary investigation aimed at eliminating clearly unfounded complaints. Even then no decision is taken about the alleged violation of the Convention. The chamber dealing with the complaint is available to facilitate a 'friendly settlement' of the dispute on the basis of the observation of human rights. Where no out-of-court settlement is reached the Court, represented by a chamber of seven judges, decides whether there has been a violation of the norms of the Convention. The judgment is final if there is no request to refer the case to the Grand Chamber, the third body of judges, consisting of 17 judges, or if the Grand Chamber rejects the request for referral. If the Court upholds the complaint, the accused state is requested to take measures to avoid future cases of the specified violation. In addition, the state can be obliged to pay compensation to the natural or juridical person having suffered a human rights violation. The Committee of Ministers supervises implementation of these measures, which has to be reported upon in detail by the state concerned (Brummer 2008: Chapter 5; Leach 2001).

The European Court of Human Rights' authority to receive and examine complaints from individuals or states and to make binding rulings is an unusually effective form of supervising the human rights practices of states (Keohane et al. 2000: 459–69). However, the sanctions available when states refuse to correct the behaviour deemed by the Court to be in violation of the Convention are not well developed. Thus supervision of human rights practices can only function as long as the states are constitutional democracies and willingly submit to the decisions of the Court or those of the Committee of Ministers (Moravcsik 2000). Where a state abandons its constitutional democratic system, the legally binding ruling of an international court is unlikely to move it to correct its human rights practices. In such situations the Council of Europe does not have many options to intervene beyond publicly charging the state as being in breach of human rights norms. Nonetheless, compliance with Court rulings is exceptionally high when compared with other international courts (see the evaluation below).

Evaluation of the organization's effectiveness

The European human rights system seems to be able to bring about real changes in states' human rights policies. Although naming and shaming by the Council of Europe is not always successful in changing governmental actors' human rights practices, the strong standing of the European Court of Human Rights gives European human rights norms considerable impact. The frequent use of the individual petition – over 60,000 new individual petitions are submitted every year – is a first indicator for the effectiveness of the European human rights regime. In comparison, the number of state petitions is far smaller (in fact there have been fewer than 20 interstate applications since the establishment of the Court). This is an indication that the right of individuals to submit petitions to the Court enhances the likelihood of human rights violations being discussed and prosecuted. It is difficult to give exact figures, since many petitions are inadmissible or joined in the proceedings, but the Court gave 1,068 judgments in 2017. The almost total compliance with the Court's verdicts provides further proof of the Council's effectiveness in protecting human rights.

According to data from the secretariat of the Committee of Ministers, the rate of compliance within the time allowed is 90 per cent (Klein & Brinkmeier 2001). Thus, compliance with the Court's judgments can be considered almost 'as effective as those of any domestic court' (Helfer & Slaughter 1997: 283; see also Janis et al. 2000). In fact, the European human rights regime is widely acknowledged as being the world's most advanced and effective international regime for promoting and enforcing human rights (Moravcsik 2000: 218; see Liddell 2002). At the same time, one also needs to note that most of the petitions come from Russia, Turkey, Ukraine and Romania. It shows that, particularly outside the EU member states, significant work still needs to be done in the area of human rights. Importantly, researchers also find that robust domestic institutions and capacity are required for the successful implementation of the Court's judgments (Anagnostou & Mungiu-Pippidi 2014; Hillebrecht 2014). Obviously, these are often lacking in the countries with most human rights violations.

Over time, the Court has substantially increased its autonomy from member states. The Court has not flinched from passing negative rulings even against powerful member states; it has increasingly exercised its authority vis-à-vis all member states in highly contested public policy issues (Hawkins & Jacoby 2006: 220–21). For example, the Court has required the United Kingdom to allow people who are gay in the military, to curtail wire-tapping and other police powers, and to ban corporal punishment in state schools (Hawkins & Jacoby 2006: 214). In a wide range of issues, governments have amended legislation, granted administrative remedies, reopened judicial proceedings, or paid monetary damages to individuals whose rights protected by the European human rights treaties had been found to be violated (Moravcsik 2000: 219; see Polakiewicz & Jacob-Foltzer 1991). Blackburn & Polakiewicz (2001) show in a survey of 32 member states that every single state had to change important domestic policies, practices or legislation in response to Court rulings (see also Hawkins & Jacoby 2006: 214; Shelton 2003: 147–49).

Shelton (2003: 147) reports that, for example, Belgium has amended its Penal Code, its laws on vagrancy, and its Civil Code; Germany has modified its Code of Criminal Procedure regarding pre-trial detention, given legal recognition to transsexual people, and taken action to expedite criminal and civil proceedings; The Netherlands has modified its Code of Military Justice and the law on detention of mental health patients; Sweden introduced rules on expropriation and legislation on building permits; and France has strengthened the protection for privacy of telephone communications. Despite its politically costly verdicts, states have displayed a constant high level of judicialization in their dispute-settlement behaviour vis-à-vis the Court. In most cases, states followed Court procedures when they were accused of violating the European Convention on Human Rights rather than disregarding or avoiding Court procedures (Zangl et al. 2012).

However, the overall effectiveness of the Court is constrained by the fact that the implementation of Court rulings within member states can be quite lengthy (Shelton 2003: 148). Moreover, the Court has, to an extent, become the victim of its own success (Blome & Kocks 2009: 264; Shelton 2003: 148–49). Its caseload has virtually exploded, with the Court receiving more than 60,000 petitions a year now, compared to a 'meager' 4,000 in 1988. This creates a huge load of pending cases before the Court. The continuous enlargement of the Council's membership from ten original members to 47 states has also put a strain on the Court's resources. The Court must often examine petitions submitted in an unfamiliar language in order to ensure that the right of petition for every citizen is guaranteed. To deal with these challenges, reforms of the Court's proceedings have been undertaken in recent years to speed up the screening and processing of petitions.

CONCLUSION

International organizations are playing a critical role in the area of human rights. While human rights were long considered domestic issues, particularly since the Second World War, human rights violations are seen as an international problem. Domestic publics, predominantly in the Western countries, have little sympathy for regimes that violate human rights and urge their national leaders to address these problems at the international level. Furthermore, gross human rights violations can also result in civil war, refugee flows and cross-border problems. At the same time, addressing problems of human rights can be costly for (Western) countries. Few countries are willing to take on China over its human rights record and risk trading relations as a result of it. Therefore, it is quite understandable that states have organized their human rights policies through international organizations and also support human rights NGOs. International organizations may also have more authority in monitoring and criticizing regimes that violate human rights than individual states. Thus, in the context of the UN and the Council of Europe, states have developed policy programmes and also operational activities targeted at improving human rights.

Much of the input for international organizations in the area of human rights comes from outside developments. Through the UPR, Special Procedures and the Complaints Procedure, instances of human rights violations are brought to the attention of the Human Rights Council by states, NGOs or even individuals. Through an investigation, the Human Rights Council subsequently converts this input into output, including the suspension of the offender from the Human Rights Council or 'naming and shaming'. In the case of the Council of Europe, there is a stronger degree of institutionalization. Individual citizens can bring their complaints to the European Court of Human Rights (input). It assesses the merits of the complaint and issues judgments (output). Whether the outcome is compliance with the actual judgment of the Court varies from case to case and member state to member state, but it is a clear example of how the political system of international organizations works.

Discussion Questions

1. To what extent do international governmental organizations and (local as well as transnational) NGOs depend on one another's activities in bringing about improvements of states' human rights policies?
2. Why has a more effective system of human rights protection developed in the regional European context than on the global level?

Further Reading

Forsythe, David 2006. *Human Rights in International Relations*, 2nd edn, Cambridge: Cambridge University Press, Chapters 3, 5 & 7.

Moravcsik, Andrew 2000. The origins of human rights regimes: Democratic delegation in postwar Europe, in: *International Organization* 54: 2, 217–52.

Simmons, Beth 2009. *Mobilizing for Human Rights. International Law in Domestic Politics*, Cambridge: Cambridge University Press, Chapters 2 & 5–8.

Part IV Conclusion

13 Between a World State and International Anarchy: Images of World Order

In this book we have shown that international organizations through their programme and operational activities contribute to the cooperative management of international problems. We have argued that the creation and implementation of international norms and rules depends on the existence and internal workings of international organizations. By considering international organizations as political systems, we can identify how they convert inputs into outputs and thus respond to developments in the international environment. This approach is important, because it allows us to analyse how different international organizations convert inputs into different outputs. While our evaluations of the effectiveness of international organizations have also shown that they are no panacea, international organizations are nonetheless key actors in global governance and the broader international environment.

When thinking more broadly about international relations and the international system, what do we make of all of this? In this concluding chapter, we put forward four 'images' of world order to consider more carefully what international organizations actually mean: international anarchy, world hegemony, world state or global governance. These four images of world order should not be compared to the clear-cut theories of international organization that we presented in Chapter 2. Instead, they are heuristic models, which provide a simplified reproduction of the real world that highlights some of its crucial aspects (King et al. 1994: 50; Schimmelfennig 1995: 20–22). A heuristic model describes empirical observations in more abstract conceptual terms but, unlike a theoretical model, it does not explain them by providing substantial explanatory hypotheses.

In our view, the image of global governance is most compatible with the findings in our book that international organizations are able to encourage and stabilize international cooperation. We put forward a model of what can be called 'heterarchical' global governance. It does not presuppose the establishment of a hierarchically superior international authority; it does embody a remarkable transformation of the social structures within which international relations are taking place. This transformation is characterized by the growing importance of internationally agreed norms and rules. International organizations are central pillars of global governance and will likely remain so in the future.

MODELS OF WORLD ORDER

For this final chapter, we differentiate between four images of world order. We distinguish, on the one hand, between models which emphasize the existence and effectiveness of *international norms and rules* and those which deny the existence and effectiveness of international norms and rules. On the other hand, we differentiate those models which assume the existence of *international hierarchy* from those which insist that there is no international hierarchy in world politics. Combining the two distinctions, we are presented with four images of world order (Table 13.1).

International anarchy

It is difficult to reconcile the image of competition under international anarchy with the conclusion that international organizations can promote sustained international cooperation (see Mearsheimer 2001; Waltz 1979). This model postulates the impossibility, or at least the long-term ineffectiveness, of universally valid norms and rules in international politics, due to the absence of an international authority capable of regulating the behaviour of states. Thus sovereign states remain the basic actors in international politics. States seek to protect and defend their existence and that of their citizens through self-help. They are involved in a permanent competition for guaranteeing and improving their security and welfare, often at the expense of others. International anarchy is not synonymous with chaos, since the resulting security and welfare dilemmas force states to conform to a certain regularity in their behaviour. Yet this order is not normatively anchored because behaviour, though regular, is not bound by norms but instead opportunistic. In this view, sustainable cooperation and governance on the basis of voluntary submission and adherence to norms and rules are virtually ruled out. Thus this model is essentially a model of international 'non-governance'.

And yet this picture emerging from the model of competition under international anarchy seems too bleak. Our analysis has shown that states can create norms and rules, with the help of the programme activities of international organizations, and more often than not they also comply with these norms and rules. In addition, the operational activities of international organizations can enable states to orient their behaviour towards agreed norms and rules rather than unilaterally seeking relative advantages in competition with other states. What is more, we have seen that international organizations may even have a transformative impact on states' interests. For example in the European Union (EU) – at least to some

Table 13.1   Four images of world order

	No international authority	International authority
No effective norms and rules	International anarchy	World hegemony
Effective norms and rules	Global governance	World state

extent – states identify with one another and define their own interests in the light of community values and interests.

Still, we cannot reject this model out of hand, since international politics is not characterized in all issue areas by sustained cooperative modes of behaviour. In some issue areas there is no effective system of rules. No meaningful international organizations may exist. Or, due to external constraints and/or internal pathologies, existing international organizations have failed to produce such rules. The security relations between rival states, for example between the Arab states and Israel, are deeply anarchical (Hinnebush & Ehteshami 2002; Walt 1987). Yet the model of international anarchy no longer corresponds adequately to the structures of international politics as a whole. It fails where, with the help of international organizations, sustainable cooperative behaviour based on collective norms and rules has emerged between states in various issue areas.

World hegemony

Neither do international organizations play a primary role in the image of world hegemony. At best, international organizations are vehicles of hegemonic power. A hegemonic power, which may be a single state, but also a transnational political-economic elite in a neo-liberal world order, can use its pre-eminent military, economic or ideological resources to set up a social order conforming to its own interests and maintain it through the use of carrots and sticks (Cox 1981, 1983; Gill 1989; Gilpin 1981; Keohane 1980; Mastanduno 1999). Here norms and rules do not have the same effect on all actors in the global system: non-hegemonic actors have only limited influence on the form and content of this world hegemonic order, but nonetheless shirk from trying to overthrow it. This may be due to the strongly asymmetrical distribution of power, the hegemonic provision of public goods, from which others may also benefit, or the successful ideological reproduction of the prevailing world order. While international organizations have some role to play in this model as the hegemonic power's instrument to promote its interests and values, to provide public goods or institutionally stabilize current material and immaterial power structures, their autonomous impact (independent from the hegemonic actors) remains marginal.

The world hegemony image is inconsistent with the fact that states and other political actors cooperate through international organizations in a sustained manner on the basis of voluntary compliance with agreed norms and rules. In a critical neo-Gramscian variant, the world hegemony image underplays the autonomous effects of international organizations on international cooperation by conceiving of them as mere instruments of transnational corporate and political elites. In a more conventional state-centric variant, the world hegemony image tends to overemphasize the centrality of US hegemony for international cooperation. For example, while the General Agreement on Tariffs and Trade (GATT) and the International Monetary Fund (IMF) were set up on the initiative of the USA, they continued to function regardless of the albeit temporary erosion of American dominance in the course of the 1970s, proving that cooperation after US hegemony was possible (Keohane 1984). Today, the hegemony of the USA is challenged if not already undermined by its relative economic decline, which accelerated after the recent economic crisis, and the rise of emerging economic and political powers in Asia and Latin America, most notably of China (Christensen 2006; Layne 2006; Zakaria 2008). Thus, in many issue areas such as climate change or trade policy, an active contribution of the USA to the provision of public goods is still necessary, but no longer sufficient for effective global cooperation. What is more, as US hegemony wanes, the empirical relevance of the world hegemony model decreases.

Nevertheless, the world hegemony image, like that of international anarchy, reflects at least in part the practice of world politics at the beginning of the twenty-first century. Power differentials between and among political actors continue to shape world order and the design, decision-making procedures and outputs of international organizations. Materially and immaterially less powerful actors risk being marginalized by hegemonic powers (and their ideas, values and interests) in international organizations. In a state-centric view, the USA still endeavours to initiate and participate in flexible and informal patterns of cooperation outside international organizations. For example, the USA takes part in clubs such as the G-7. Working through clubs helps the USA to circumvent the constitutional constraints of international organizations and to promote its conceptions of (sectoral) world order. However, even in such informal clubs, most notably in the G-20, the US capacity for hegemonic leadership is seriously contained by the rise of non-Western economic and political powers. In sum, the world hegemony image seems to reflect an ever-smaller part of today's international politics.

World state

The world state image (Wendt 2003) assumes that the greater interdependence between social actors resulting from intensified economic relations and the development of a monopoly of the legal use of force represent the basic elements of a process of civilization. Norbert Elias (2000), who has traced this process in the development of modern societies in the Western world, argues that this advancement of civilization did not end with the creation of sovereign states but will find its conclusion with the establishment of a world state characterized by its ability to set and implement binding norms and rules on the global level (see also Wendt 2003). Hierarchically, this is above states, and therefore presupposes an irrevocable transfer of the sovereignty of individual states, even though the world state may be organized as a subsidiary and federal world republic leaving considerable autonomy to today's nation-states (Höffe 2001). The world state's effectiveness in implementing programmes is guaranteed by its formal-legal superiority, with a monopoly of the legal use of force and a resource base of its own for the provision of public goods. The world state commands formal-legal and (potentially) democratic authority, but also disposes of means for coercion. International organizations are the precursors of a developing world state. This is particularly the case of the UN, with the Security Council's monopoly of legitimizing collective enforcement at its core (Höffe 2001: 199–202; Rittberger et al. 1997: 58–61).

However desirable such reliable international cooperation and government under the auspices of a world state may appear at first sight, on closer inspection it seems both problematic and unrealistic. It is difficult to imagine all states joining a world state voluntarily through a large founding treaty and submitting to it. We must thus assume that reluctant states would have to be constrained or coerced by the use of military force. Given the military potential widespread in the world of the twenty-first century, it is difficult to justify the putatively necessary use of force, even with the aim of civilizing international relations through a world state. This seems even more problematic as it is very doubtful that a world state could establish a pacified world. It seems more likely that it would be plagued by internal conflicts. Today, the numbers of internal violent conflicts, as well as of people killed in internal conflict, by far exceed the numbers for international wars (Human Security Report 2010; Slaughter 2004: 8). This sheds considerable doubt on the proposition that the establishment of a world state would be sufficient for ending armed conflicts.

The establishment of a world state also seems unrealistic since the creation of a world community, that is, of a *demos* of global citizens with a common identity spanning national borders, has not kept pace with the creation of a world society, reflected in ever denser economic interdependencies and webs of international institutions. This is demonstrated even at the relatively homogeneous European level, where economic and institutional integration have outstripped community building. Furthermore, there are no discernible indications that democratic states are willing to give up their sovereignty to a world state which is unable to guarantee the same democratic standards globally. As long as democracies feel threatened by dictatorships and authoritarian systems they will not surrender their sovereignty or allow transfer of the legal monopoly over use of physical force to a world state.

The fact that programme decisions in international organizations are made through intergovernmental negotiations, often by majority vote, shows that the absence of a world state does not prevent states from engaging in sustained collective action to deal with global problems. What is more, in a few organizations, such as the UN Security Council, the International Court of Justice (ICJ), the WTO's dispute-settlement procedure and more recently the International Criminal Court (ICC), there are instances of a supranational, hierarchical order that contains at least some world state features. In these cases, international organizations are placed hierarchically above member states. As the supranationalization of international organizations progresses (see Zürn et al. 2007), the empirical relevance of the world state image increases, since hierarchical modes of world order gain in importance. Nevertheless, as with the previous two images considered, at best the world state image can serve to illustrate a small proportion of current international relations.

Global governance

The starting point of the image of global governance is the possibility of sustained cooperation between states and non-state actors on the basis of international agreement on binding norms and rules. These norms and rules constitute a normative order beyond the nation-states which mitigates and partly supersedes the structural conditions of international anarchy. This is captured by the image of global governance to designate a world order which differs from both anarchic self-help systems and (formally or de facto) hierarchically structured systems such as a world state or hegemonic rule (Kruck & Rittberger 2010: 58; Rittberger et al. 2008: 42–45; see also Donnelly 2009; Neyer 2002, 2004; see Jessop 2002 for a critical view). Rather than relying on vertical top-down steering, it is based on horizontal, networked policy coordination and cooperation between states (and sub-state agencies), international organizations and non-state actors which together constitute a system of multi-level governance (see Bache & Flinders 2004; Benner et al. 2004; Hooghe & Marks 2001).

This means that the effectiveness of the agreed norms and rules is independent of a centralized, hierarchically superior authority with a monopoly on the legal use of force. Whereas there is no superior authority to generate, implement and, if necessary, enforce by sanctions such norms and rules (Reinicke 1998), rules-based cooperation among states but also between states and non-state actors is still expected. It occurs in and through the programme and operational activities of international organizations. International organizations thus constitute an organizational backbone and network hub for the policy coordination and cooperation among various state and non-state actors. However, not only do they provide forums for international cooperation, but, through their programme, operational and information activities, they actively contribute to global governance.

Like the other images, this model of global governance does not fully describe the present structures of world politics. Norms and rules which effectively regulate relations among states as well as between states and non-state actors do not exist in all issue areas, even where there are a marked interdependence and resource interdependencies, such as in international migration (Straubhaar 2002; Zolberg 1991). Despite these limitations it is noticeable that the structures of international politics seem to be getting closer to this model. In an increasing number of issue areas relatively stable patterns of policy cooperation among states and between states and non-state actors have emerged (see Chapters 8–12). This model of global governance captures both traditional forms of inter-state policy coordination in exclusive intergovernmental organizations and more recent forms of the public–private management of transnational, cross-border problems in open or inclusive organizations. This suggests an alternative to Elias's process of civilization (Elias 2000); that is, a process of civilization without a hierarchical world order at the end. States may prefer collective action among each other and in cooperation with non-state actors to self-help, thus reducing the possibility of the use of force in their relationships and fostering the mitigation of transnational, cross-border problems, at least in the long term. Thus, effective and legitimate global governance, as well as the abandonment of the self-help option in favour of forms of collective action and the diminished expectation of the use of force, are not dependent on the existence of a hierarchically superior authority.

CONCLUSION

All four images are ideal types which will never completely match empirical complexity. Obviously, different scholars hold different views on the usefulness of the models of world order we have introduced in this chapter. Nonetheless, in our view, the last model of global governance is most compatible with our finding that international organizations are able to encourage and stabilize international cooperation. In any case, it is more compatible with this finding than the images of competition under international anarchy, of world hegemony and of a world state. Whereas the model of global governance does not presuppose the establishment of a hierarchically superior international authority, it does embody a remarkable transformation of the social structures within which international relations are taking place. This transformation is characterized by the growing importance of internationally agreed norms and rules. As we have seen, these norms and rules are more often than not generated and implemented with the support of international organizations.

While we expect international organizations to remain the central pillars of global governance, it is important to point at some of the significant challenges that they currently face. For much of the period since the Second World War, contestation took place *within* the political system of international organizations: from the Cold War vetoes in the UN Security Council to the discussions over global human rights and the Washington Consensus in the area of development. While this has regularly resulted in 'gridlock' (Hale et al. 2013) – for instance during the many environmental conferences – international organizations have often been considered the primary forums for global discussions. In addition to political contestation within the political system, we have also seen much debate about the *constitutional and institutional structure* of the political system. For instance, the emerging powers, but also Germany and Japan, have long demanded the reform of the international institutions. Furthermore, questions have also been raised about whether rigid formal international organizations (the ones discussed in this book) provide the best answers to cooperation problems. For instance, more flexible informal international organizations (Vabulas & Snidal 2013) increasingly play a key role as well.

Some of the current challenges to international organizations are, however, not about the politics within the political system or the structure of the system. Rather they question the political system of international organizations in its entirety. The United Kingdom has voted for Brexit to distance itself from the premier international organization on the European continent. The United States, under the Trump administration, is rapidly withdrawing from all sorts of international organizations and treaties. In the preface of this book, we have talked of the crisis of the Western liberal order and the post-war international institutions. At the same time, the book has also made clear that a strong case remains for international organizations to address cooperation problems. Significant dilemmas underpin international cooperation in areas of security, trade, finance, the environment and human rights. These can only be met by equally formidable international organizations. Indeed, even if current events seem negative, over the last two centuries we have witnessed a progressive institutionalization of world politics and resilient international institutions. The fact that international organizations now make the news on a day-to-day basis only further underlines their importance.

Discussion Questions

1. What are the main differences between the four models of world order: competition under international anarchy, world hegemony, world state and global governance?
2. Which model is empirically most plausible?
3. What roles do international organizations play in these competing images of world order?

Further Reading

Karns, Margaret P. & Mingst, Karen A. 2010. *International Organizations. The Politics and Process of Global Governance*, 2nd edn, Boulder, CO: Lynne Rienner, Chapters 1 & 12.

Zürn, Michael 2018. *A Theory of Global Governance: Authority, Legitimacy, and Contestation*. Oxford: Oxford University Press.

References

Abbott, Kenneth W., Genschel, Philipp, Snidal, Duncan, Zangl, Bernhard (eds) 2015. *International Organizations as Orchestrators*, Cambridge: Cambridge University Press.

Abbott, Kenneth W., Keohane, Robert O., Moravcsik, Andrew, Slaughter, Anne-Marie & Snidal, Duncan 2000. The concept of legalization, in: *International Organization* 54: 3, 401–20.

Abbott, Kenneth W. & Snidal, Duncan 1998. Why states act through formal international organizations, in: *Journal of Conflict Resolution* 42: 1, 3–32.

Abbott, Kenneth W. & Snidal, Duncan 2000. Hard and soft law in international governance, in: *International Organization* 54: 3, 421–56.

Abiew, Francis Kofi 1999. *The Evolution of the Doctrine and Practice of Humanitarian Intervention*, The Hague: Kluwer Law International.

Adler, Emanuel & Barnett, Michael 1998. A framework for the study of security communities, in: Adler, Emanuel & Barnett, Michael (eds) *Security Communities*, Cambridge: Cambridge University Press, 29–65.

Adler, Emanuel & Haas, Peter M. 1992. Conclusion: Epistemic communities, world order, and the creation of a reflective research program, in: *International Organization* 46: 1, 367–90.

Adler, Emanuel & Pouliot, Vincent 2011. International practices, in: *International Theory* 3: 1, 1–36.

Adler-Nissen, Rebecca & Pouliot, Vincent 2014. Power in practice: Negotiating the international intervention in Libya, in: *European Journal of International Relations* 20: 4, 889–911.

Akhavan, Payam 2001. Beyond impunity: Can international criminal justice prevent future atrocities? in: *American Journal of International Law* 95: 1, 7–31.

Aldy, Joseph E. & Stavins, Robert N. 2007. Introduction: International policy architecture for global climate change, in: Aldy, Joseph E. & Stavins, Robert N (eds) *Architectures for Agreement. Addressing Global Climate Change in the Post-Kyoto World*, Cambridge: Cambridge University Press, 1–30.

Alger, Chadwick 2002. The emerging role of NGOs in the UN system. From Article 71 to a people's millennium assembly, in: *Global Governance* 8: 1, 93–117.

Alger, C.F. 2014. *Chadwick F. Alger: Pioneer in the Study of the Political Process and on NGO Participation in the United Nations*, Heidelberg: Springer.

Alter, Karen J. 2001. *Establishing the Supremacy of European Law: The Making of an International Rule of Law in Europe*, Oxford: Oxford University Press.

Alter, Karen J. 2008. Agents or trustees? International courts in their political context, in: *European Journal of International Relations* 14: 1, 33–63.

Amerasinghe, Chittharanjan F. 2005. *Principles of the Institutional Law of International Organizations*, 2nd edn, Cambridge: Cambridge University Press.

Anagnostou, Dia & Mungiu-Pippidi, Alina 2014. Domestic implementation of human rights judgments in Europe: Legal infrastructure and government effectiveness matter, in: *European Journal of International Law* 25: 1, 205–27.

Andersen, Stephen O. & Sharma, Madhava K. 2002. *Protecting the Ozone Layer. The United Nations History*, London: Earthscan.

Archer, Clive 2001. *International Organisations*, 3rd edn, London: Routledge.

Archibugi, Daniele, Held, David & Köhler, Martin (eds) 1998. *Re-imagining Political Community. Studies in Cosmopolitan Democracy*, Oxford: Polity Press.

Armstrong, David, Lloyd, Lorna & Redmond, John 1996. *From Versailles to Maastricht. International Organisation in the Twentieth Century*, London: Macmillan.

Bache, Ian & Flinders, Matthew (eds) 2004. *Multi-level Governance*, Oxford: Oxford University Press.

Baehr, Peter M. 2009. *Non-Governmental Human Rights Organizations in International Relations*, Basingstoke: Palgrave Macmillan.

Bagwell, Kyle & Staiger, Robert W. 2002. *The Economics of the World Trading System*, Cambridge, MA: The MIT Press.

Bailey, Sidney D. & Daws, Sam 1998. *The Procedure of the UN Security Council*, 3rd edn, Oxford: Clarendon Press.

Baldwin, David 2002. Power and International Relations, in: Carlsnaes, Walter, Risse, Thomas & Simmons, Beth (eds) *Handbook of International Relations*, London: Sage, 177–91.

Barnett, Michael N. & Finnemore, Martha 2004. *Rules for the World. International Organizations in Global Politics*, Ithaca, NY: Cornell University Press.

Barria, Lilian A. & Roper, Steven D. 2005. How effective are international criminal tribunals? An analysis of the ICTY and the ICTR, in: *The International Journal of Human Rights* 9: 3, 349–68.

Basch, Paul F. 1999. *Textbook of International Health*, 2nd edn, Oxford: Oxford University Press.

Bauer, Steffen 2009. The ozone secretariat: The good shepherd of ozone politics, in: Biermann, Frank & Siebenhüner, Bernd (eds) *Managers of Global Change. The Influence of International Environmental Bureaucracies*, Cambridge, MA: The MIT Press, 225–44.

Beach, Derek 2004. The unseen hand in treaty reform negotiations: The role and influence of the Council Secretariat, in: *Journal of European Public Policy* 11: 3, 408–39.

Beach, Derek 2005. *The Dynamics of European Integration – How and When EU Institutions Matter*, Basingstoke: Palgrave Macmillan.

Beckman, Peter R., Crumlish, Paul W., Dobkowski, Michael N. & Lee, Steven P. 2000. *The Nuclear Predicament. Nuclear Weapons in the Twenty-First Century*, 3rd edn, Upper Saddle River, NJ: Prentice-Hall.

Beise, Marc 2001. *Die Welthandelsorganisation (WTO). Funktion, Status, Organisation*, Baden-Baden: Nomos.

Beisheim, Marianne, Dreher, Sabine, Zangl, Bernhard & Zürn, Michael 1999. *Im Zeitalter der Globalisierung? Thesen und Daten zur gesellschaftlichen und politischen Denationalisierung*, Baden-Baden: Nomos.

References 239

Benner, Thorsten, Mergenthaler, Stephan & Rotmann, Philipp 2011. *The New World of UN Peace Operations: Learning to Build Peace?* Oxford: Oxford University Press.

Benner, Thorsten, Reinicke, Wolfgang H. & Witte, Jan Martin 2004. Multisectoral networks in global governance: Towards a pluralistic system of accountability, in: *Government and Opposition* 39: 2, 191–210.

Bercovitch, Jacob 2007. Mediation in international conflicts, in: Zartman, Ira W. (ed.) *Peacemaking in International Conflict. Methods and Techniques*, Washington, DC: United States Institute of Peace Press, 163–94.

Betsill, Michele & Hoffmann, Matthew J. 2011. The contours of 'Cap and Trade': The evolution of emissions trading systems for greenhouse gases, in: *Review of Policy Research* 28: 1, 83–106.

Bickerton, Christopher J., Hodson, Dermot & Puetter, Uwe 2015. The new intergovernmentalism: European integration in the post-Maastricht era, in: *Journal of Common Market Studies* 53: 4, 703–22.

Biermann, Frank & Siebenhüner, Bernd (eds) 2009. *Managers of Global Change. The Influence of International Environmental Bureaucracies*, Cambridge, MA: The MIT Press.

Biermann, Frank, Siebenhüner, Bernd & Schreyögg, Anna 2009. *International Organizations in Global Environmental Governance*, London: Routledge.

Biermann, Frank, Abbott, Kenneth, Andresen, Steinar, Bäckstrand, Karin, Bernstein, Steven, Betsill, Michele M. et al. 2012. Navigating the anthropocene: Improving earth system governance, in: *Science* 335: 6074, 1306–07.

Biermann, Rafael & Harsch, Michael 2017. Resource dependence theory, in: Biermann, Rafael & Koops, Joachim (eds) *Palgrave Handbook of Inter-Organizational Relations in World Politics*, London: Palgrave Macmillan, 135–55.

Blackburn, Robert & Polakiewicz, Jörg 2001. *Fundamental Rights in Europe. The European Convention on Human Rights and Its Member States, 1950–2000*, Oxford: Oxford University Press.

Blome, Kerstin & Kocks, Alexander 2009. Judizialisierungsprozesse im Menschenrechtsbereich: Erfolgsmodell EGMR, in: Zangl, Bernhard (ed.) *Auf dem Weg zu internationaler Rechtsherrschaft? Streitbeilegung zwischen Politik und Recht*, Frankfurt/M.: Campus, 229–66.

Bloxham, Donald 2006. Beyond 'realism' and legalism: A historical perspective on the limits of international humanitarian law, in: *European Review* 14: 4, 457–70.

Boekle, Henning 1998. Die Vereinten Nationen und der internationale Schutz der Menschenrechte: Eine Bestandsaufnahme, in: *Aus Politik und Zeitgeschichte* 46–47, 3–17.

Boli, John & Thomas, George M. (eds) 1999. *Constructing World Culture. International Nongovernmental Organizations since 1875*, Stanford, CA: Stanford University Press.

Bolin, Bert 2007. *A History of the Science and Politics of Climate Change. The Role of the Intergovernmental Panel on Climate Change*, Cambridge: Cambridge University Press.

Bornschier, Volker 2000. Western Europe's move toward political union, in: Bornschier, Volker (ed.) *State-Building in Europe. The Revitalization of Western European Integration*, Cambridge: Cambridge University Press, 3–37.

Bown, Chad P. & Pauwelyn, Joost (eds) 2010. *The Law, Economics and Politics of Retaliation in WTO Dispute Settlement*, Cambridge: Cambridge University Press.

Braithwaite, John & Drahos, Peter 2000. *Global Business Regulation*, Cambridge: Cambridge University Press.

Brandsma, Gijs Jan & Blom-Hansen, Jens 2017. *Controlling the EU Executive?: The Politics of Delegation in the European Union*, Oxford: Oxford University Press.

Breitmeier, Helmut 1996. *Wie entstehen globale Umweltregime? Der Konfliktaustrag zum Schutz der Ozonschicht und des globalen Klimas*, Opladen: Leske & Budrich.

Breitmeier, Helmut 1997. International organizations and the creation of environmental regimes, in: Young, Oran R. (ed.) *Global Governance. Drawing Insights from the Environmental Experience*, Cambridge, MA: The MIT Press, 87–114.

Breitmeier, Helmut 2009. Regieren in der globalen Umweltpolitik. Eine gemischte Bilanz zwischen Erfolgs- und Problemfällen, in: Breitmeier, Helmut, Roth, Michèle & Senghaas, Dieter (eds) *Sektorale Weltordnungspolitik. Effektiv, gerecht und demokratisch?* Baden-Baden: Nomos, 150–70.

Brenton, Tony 1994. *The Greening of Machiavelli. The Evolution of International Environmental Politics*, London: Earthscan.

Brühl, Tanja 2003. *Nichtregierungsorganisationen als Akteure internationaler Umweltverhandlungen. Ein Erklärungsmodell auf der Basis der situationsspezifischen Ressourcennachfrage*, Frankfurt/M.: Campus.

Brummer, Klaus 2005. *Konfliktbearbeitung durch Internationale Organisationen*, Wiesbaden: VS Verlag für Sozialwissenschaften.

Brummer, Klaus 2008. *Der Europarat. Eine Einführung*, Wiesbaden: VS Verlag für Sozialwissenschaften.

Burchill, Scott et al. (eds) 2013. *Theories of International Relations*, 5th edn, Basingstoke: Palgrave Macmillan.

Busch, Marc L. & Reinhardt, Eric 2003. Developing countries and General Agreement on Tariffs and Trade/World Trade Organization dispute settlement, in: *Journal of World Trade* 37: 4, 719–35.

Busch, Per-Olof 2009. The climate secretariat: Making a living in a straitjacket, in: Biermann, Frank & Siebenhüner, Bernd (eds) *Managers of Global Change. The Influence of International Environmental Bureaucracies*, Cambridge, MA: MIT Press, 245–64.

Busuioc, Madalina 2013. *European Agencies: Law and Practices of Accountability*, Oxford: Oxford University Press.

Butkiewicz, James L. & Yanikkaya, Halit 2005. The effects of IMF and World Bank lending on long-run economic growth: An empirical analysis, in: *World Development* 33: 3, 371–91.

Buzan, Barry, Waever, Ole & de Wilde, Jaap 1998. *Security. A New Framework for Analysis*, Boulder, CO: Lynne Rienner.

Cameron, David R. 1995. Transnational relations and the development of European economic and monetary union, in: Risse-Kappen, Thomas (ed.) *Bringing Transnational Relations Back In. Non-State Actors, Domestic Structures and International Institutions*, Cambridge: Cambridge University Press, 37–78.

Canan, Penelope & Reichman, Nancy 2002. *Ozone Connection. Expert Networks in Global Environmental Governance*, Sheffield: Greenleaf Publishing.

Carbone, Maurizio (ed.) 2010. *National Politics and European Integration. From the Constitution to the Lisbon Treaty*, London: Edward Elgar.

Carr, Edward H. 1939. *The Twenty Years' Crisis, 1919–1939. An Introduction to the Study of International Relations*, New York: St Martin's Press.

Chasek, Pamela S. 2001. *Earth Negotiations. Analyzing Thirty Years of Environmental Diplomacy*, Tokyo: United Nations University Press.

Chasek, Pamela S., Downie, David L. & Brown, Janet Welsh 2010. *Global Environmental Politics*, 5th edn, Boulder, CO: Westview.

Chatfield, Charles 1997. Intergovernmental and nongovernmental associations to 1945, in: Smith, Jackie G., Chatfield, Charles & Pagnucco, Ron (eds) *Transnational Social Movements and Global Politics. Solidarity Beyond the State*, Syracuse, NY: Syracuse University Press, 19–41.

Chayes, Abram & Chayes, Antonia 1995. *The New Sovereignty. Compliance with International Regulatory Agreements*, Cambridge, MA: Harvard University Press.

Checkel, Jeffrey T. 2005. International institutions and socialization in Europe: Introduction and framework, in: *International Organization* 59: 4, 801–26.

Chellaney, Brahma 1999. Arms control: The role of the IAEA and UNSCOM, in: Alagappa, Muthiah & Inoguchi, Takashi (eds) *International Security Management and the United Nations*, Tokyo: United Nations University Press, 375–93.

Chesterman, Simon 2003. *Just War or Just Peace? Humanitarian Intervention and International Law*, Oxford: Oxford University Press.

Chesterman, Simon (ed.) 2007. *The UN Secretary-General in World Politics*, Cambridge: Cambridge University Press.

Chorev, Nitsan 2012. *The World Health Organization Between North and South*, Ithaca, NY: Cornell University Press.

Christensen, Thomas J. 2006. Fostering stability or creating a monster? The rise of China and U.S. policy toward East Asia, in: *International Security* 31: 1, 81–126.

Christiansen, Thomas & Reh, Christine 2009. *Constitutionalizing the European Union*. Basingstoke: Palgrave Macmillan.

Chwieroth, Jeffrey M. 2009. *Capital Ideas. The IMF and the Rise of Financial Liberalization*, Princeton, NJ: Princeton University Press.

Clements, L. J., Mole, Nuala & Simmons, Alan 1999. *European Human Rights. Taking a Case under the Convention*, London: Sweet & Maxwell.

Coase, Ronald 1960. The problem of social cost, in: *Journal of Law and Economics* 3, 1–44.

Cohn, Theodore H. 2002. *Governing Global Trade. International Institutions in Conflict and Convergence*, Burlington, VT: Ashgate.

Coleman, James S. 1990. *Foundations of Social Theory*, Cambridge, MA: Belknap Press of Harvard University Press.

Colijn, Ko 1998. Non-proliferation: Reinforcing the IAEA nuclear safeguards regime in the 1990s, in: Reinalda, Bob & Verbeek, Bertjan (eds) *Autonomous Policy Making by International Organizations*, London: Routledge, 93–107.

Copelovitch, Mark 2010. *The International Monetary Fund in the Global Economy: Banks, Bonds, and Bailouts*, Cambridge: Cambridge University Press.

Corbett, Richard 2002. *The European Parliament's Role in Closer EU Integration*, Basingstoke: Palgrave Macmillan.

Cortell, Andrew P. & Peterson, Susan 2006. Dutiful agents, rogue actors, or both? Staffing, voting rules, and slack in the WHO and WTO, in: Hawkins, Darren G., Lake, David A., Nielson, Daniel L. & Tierney, Michael J. (eds) *Delegation and Agency in International Organizations*, Cambridge: Cambridge University Press, 255–80.

Cortright, David & Lopez, George A. (eds) 2002. *Smart Sanctions. Targeting Economic Statecraft*, Lanham, MD: Rowman & Littlefield.

Cox, Robert W. 1981. Social forces, states and world orders: Beyond international relations theory, in: *Millennium* 10: 2, 126–55.

Cox, Robert W. 1983. Gramsci, hegemony and international relations: An essay in method, in: *Millennium* 12: 2, 162–75.

Crisp, Brian F. & Kelly, Michael J. 1999. The socioeconomic impacts of structural adjustment, in: *International Studies Quarterly* 43: 3, 533–52.

Cronin, Bruce 2008. International consensus and the changing legal authority of the UN Security Council, in: Cronin, Bruce & Hurd, Ian (eds) *The UN Security Council and the Politics of International Authority*, London: Routledge, 57–79.

Daase, Christopher 2003. Das Ende vom Anfang des nuklearen Tabus. Zur Legitimitätskrise der Weltnuklearordnung, in: *Zeitschrift für Internationale Beziehungen* 10: 1, 7–41.

Davey, William 2014. The WTO and rules-based dispute settlement: Historical evolution, operational success, and future challenges, in: *Journal of International Economic Law* 17: 3, 679–700.

Davis, Christina L. & Pelc, Krzysztof J. 2017. Cooperation in hard times: Self-restraint of trade protection, in: *Journal of Conflict Resolution* 61: 2, 398–429.

De Grauwe, Paul 2006. What have we learnt about monetary integration since the Maastricht Treaty? in: *Journal of Common Market Studies* 44: 4, 711–30.

Deitelhoff, Nicole 2009. The discursive process of legalization: Charting islands of persuasion in the ICC case, in: *International Organization* 63: 1, 33–66.

Den Dekker, Guido 2001. *The Law of Arms Control. International Supervision and Enforcement*, The Hague: Martinus Nijhoff.

Deutsch, Karl W. et al. 1957. *Political Community and the North Atlantic Area. International Organization in the Light of Historical Experience*, Princeton, NJ: Princeton University Press.

De Wilde, Jaap 2008. Environmental security deconstructed, in: Brauch, Hans Günter et al. (eds) *Globalisation and Environmental Challenges*, Mosbach: AFES-Press, 595–602.

De Zayas, Alfred 2002. Human Rights, United Nations High Commission for, in: Volger, Helmut (ed.) *A Concise Encyclopedia of the United Nations*, The Hague: Kluwer Law International, 217–23.

Dietz, Thomas, Ostrom, Elinor & Stern, Paul C. 2003. The struggle to govern the commons, in: *Science* 302: 5652, 1907–12.

Dijkstra, Geske & Komives, Kristin 2011. The PRS approach and the Paris agenda: Experiences in Bolivia, Honduras and Nicaragua, in: *The European Journal of Development Research* 23: 2, 191–207.

Dijkstra, Hylke 2015. Shadow bureaucracies and the unilateral control of international secretariats: Insights from UN peacekeeping, in: *The Review of International Organizations* 10: 1, 23–41.

Dijkstra, Hylke 2016. *International Organizations and Military Affairs*. London: Routledge.

Dijkstra, Hylke 2017. Collusion in international organizations: How states benefit from the authority of secretariats, in: *Global Governance* 23: 4, 601–18.

Dirks, Jan, Liese, Andrea & Senghaas-Knobloch, Eva 2002. *International Regulation of Work in Times of Globalization. The International Labour Organization (ILO) in the Perspective of Organizational Learning*, Bremen: University of Bremen, Forschungszentrum Arbeit und Technik.

Dixit, Avinash & Norman, Victor 1980. *Theory of International Trade: A Dual, General Equilibrium Approach*, Cambridge: Cambridge University Press.

Donnelly, Jack 2006. *International Human Rights*, 3rd edn, Boulder, CO: Westview.

Donnelly, Jack 2009. Rethinking political structures: From 'ordering principles' to 'vertical differentiation' – and beyond, in: *International Theory* 1: 1, 49–86.

Doyle, Michael W. 1986. Liberalism and world politics, in: *American Political Science Review* 80: 4, 1151–69.

Doyle, Michael W. & Sambanis, Nicholas 2000. International peacebuilding: A theoretical and quantitative analysis, in: *American Political Science Review* 94: 4, 779–802.

Doyle, Michael W. & Sambanis, Nicholas 2006. *Making War and Building Peace. United Nations Peace Operations*, Princeton, NJ: Princeton University Press.

Dreher, Axel, Sturm, Jan-Egbert & Vreeland, James Raymond 2009a. Global horse trading: IMF loans for votes in the United Nations Security Council, in: *European Economic Review* 53: 7, 742–57.

Dreher, Axel, Sturm, Jan-Egbert & Vreeland, James Raymond 2009b. Development aid and international politics: Does membership on the UN Security Council influence World Bank decisions?, in: *Journal of Development Economics* 88: 1, 1–18.

Drezner, Daniel W. 2007. *All Politics is Global: Explaining International Regulatory Regimes*, Princeton, NJ: Princeton University Press.

Drezner, Daniel W. 2011. Sanctions sometimes smart: Targeted sanctions in theory and practice, in: *International Studies Review* 13: 1, 96–108.

Driscoll, David D. 1998. *Was ist der Internationale Währungsfonds?* Washington, DC: Internationaler Währungsfonds, Abteilung Öffentlichkeitsarbeit.

Dryzek, John S. 2016. Institutions for the anthropocene: Governance in a changing earth system. *British Journal of Political Science* 46: 4, 937–56.

Dülffer, Jost 1981. *Regeln gegen den Krieg? Die Haager Friedenskonferenzen 1899 und 1907 in der internationalen Politik*, Berlin: Ullstein.

Dunleavy, Patrick 1985. Bureaucrats, budgets and the growth of the state: Reconstructing an instrumental model, in: *British Journal of Political Science* 15: 3, 299–328.

Dunne, Tim, Kurki, Milja & Smith, Steve (eds) 2016. *International Relations Theories. Discipline and Diversity*, 3rd edn, Oxford: Oxford University Press.

Easterly, William 2005. What did structural adjustment adjust? The association of policies and growth with repeated IMF and World Bank adjustment loans, in: *Journal of Development Economics* 76: 1, 1–22.

Easton, David 1965. *A Framework for Political Analysis*, Englewood Cliffs, NJ: Prentice Hall.

Eckersley, Robyn 2010. Green theory, in: Dunne, Tim, Kurki, Milja & Smith, Steve (eds) *International Relations Theories. Discipline and Diversity*, 2nd edn, Oxford: Oxford University Press, 257–77.

Eckhard, Steffen & Ege, Jörn 2016. International bureaucracies and their influence on policy-making: A review of empirical evidence, in: *Journal of European Public Policy* 23: 7, 960–78.

Eichener, Volker 1997. Effective European problem-solving: Lessons from the regulation of occupational safety and environmental protection, in: *Journal of European Public Policy* 4: 4, 591–608.

Eichengreen, Barry 1996. *Globalizing Capital. A History of the International Monetary System*, Princeton, NJ: Princeton University Press.

Eichengreen, Barry & Frieden, Jeffrey A. 2001. The political economy of European monetary unification, in: Eichengreen, Barry & Frieden, Jeffrey A. (eds) *The Political Economy of European Monetary Unification*, 2nd edn, Boulder, CO: Westview, 1–21.

Einhorn, Jessica P. 2001. The World Bank's mission creep, in: *Foreign Affairs* 80: 5, 22–35.

Elgström, Ole & Jönsson, Christer 2000. Negotiation in the European Union: Bargaining or problem-solving? in: *Journal of European Public Policy* 7: 5, 684–704.

Elias, Norbert 2000. *The Civilizing Process. Sociogenetic and Psychogenetic Investigations*, 2nd edn, ed. Dunning, Eric, Gouldblom, Johan & Mennell, Stephen, Oxford: Blackwell.

Elsig, Manfred & Pollack, Mark A. 2014. Agents, trustees, and international courts: The politics of judicial appointment at the World Trade Organization, in: *European Journal of International Relations* 20: 2, 391–415.

Engel, Christian & Borrmann, Christine 1991. *Vom Konsens zur Mehrheitsentscheidung.EG-Entscheidungsverfahren und nationale Interessenpolitik nach der Einheitlichen Europäischen Akte*, Bonn: Europa Union.

European Central Bank n.d. *Tasks*, https://www.ecb.europa.eu/ecb/tasks/html/index.en.html, date accessed: 25 July 2018.

European Commission 2017. *Vade Mecum on the Stability and Growth Pact*, https://ec.europa.eu/info/sites/info/files/ip052_en_0.pdf, date accessed: 25 July 2018.

European Commission 2018. *DG Trade Statistical Guide, June 2018*, http://trade.ec.europa.eu/doclib/docs/2013/may/tradoc_151348.pdf, date accessed: 28 July 2018.

European External Action Service 2016. *Shared Vision, Common Action: A Stronger Europe—A Global Strategy for the European Union's Foreign And Security Policy*, Brussels: European External Action Service.

Falkner, Robert 2012. Global environmentalism and the greening of international society, in: *International Affairs* 88: 3, 503–22.

Fehl, Caroline 2004. Explaining the International Criminal Court: A practice test for rationalist and constructivist approaches, in: *European Journal of International Relations* 10: 3, 357–94.

Ferreira, Francisco H. G. & Keely, Louise C. 2000. The World Bank and structural adjustment: Lessons from the 1980s, in: Gilbert, Christopher L. & Vines, David (eds) *The World Bank. Structure and Policies*, Cambridge: Cambridge University Press, 159–95.

Feske, Susanne 1999. Der ASEAN-Staatenbund, in: Dahm, Bernhard & Ptak, Roderich (eds) *Südostasien-Handbuch*, Munich: Beck, 541–61.

Finnemore, Martha 1993. International organizations as teachers of norms: The united nations educational, scientific, and cultural organization and science policy, in: *International Organization* 47: 4, 565–98.

Finnemore, Martha & Sikkink, Kathryn 1998. International norm dynamics and political change, in: *International Organization* 52: 4, 887–917.

Forsythe, David 2006. *Human Rights in International Relations*, 2nd edn, Cambridge: Cambridge University Press.

Fortna, Virginia Page 2004a. Does peacekeeping keep peace? International intervention and the duration of peace after civil war, in: *International Studies Quarterly* 48: 2, 269–92.

Fortna, Virginia Page 2004b. Interstate peacekeeping: Causal mechanisms and empirical effects, in: *World Politics* 56: 4, 481–519.

Fortna, Virginia Page 2008. *Does Peacekeeping Work? Shaping Belligerents' Choices after Civil War*, Princeton, NJ: Princeton University Press.

Fortna, Virginia Page & Howard, Lisa Morjé 2008. Pitfalls and prospects in the peacekeeping literature, in: *Annual Review of Political Science* 11, 283–301.

Franklin, James C. 2008. 'Shame on you': The impact of human rights criticism on political repression in Latin America, in: *International Studies Quarterly* 52: 1, 187–211.

Friedrich, Carl J. 1968. *Trends of Federalism in Theory and Practice*, New York: Praeger.

Gareis, Sven Bernhard & Varwick, Johannes 2005. *The United Nations. An Introduction*, Basingstoke: Palgrave Macmillan.

Gemmill, Barbara & Bamidele-Izu, Abimbola 2002. The role of NGOs and civil society in global environmental governance, in: Esty, Daniel C. & Ivanova, Maria H. (eds) *Global Environmental Governance. Options & Opportunities*, New Haven, CT: Yale School of Forestry and Environmental Studies, 1–24.

Genschel, Philipp & Jachtenfuchs, Markus (eds) 2014. *Beyond the Regulatory Polity?: The European Integration of Core State Powers*, Oxford: Oxford University Press.

Gilbert, Christopher L. & Vines, David 2000. The World Bank: An overview of some major issues, in: Gilbert, Christopher L. & Vines, David (eds) *The World Bank. Structure and Policies*, Cambridge: Cambridge University Press, 10–38.

Gill, George 1996. *The League of Nations. From 1929 to 1946*, Garden City Park, NY: Avery.

Gill, Stephen 1989. Global hegemony and the structural power of capital, in: *International Studies Quarterly* 33: 4, 475–99.

Gilligan, Michael J. 2006. Is enforcement necessary for effectiveness? A model of the international criminal regime, in: *International Organization* 60: 4, 935–67.

Gilpin, Robert 1981. *War and Change in World Politics*, Cambridge: Cambridge University Press.

Gilpin, Robert 2000. *The Challenge of Global Capitalism. The World Economy in the 21st Century*, Princeton, NJ: Princeton University Press.

Goetz, Klaus H. & Patz, Ronny 2017. Resourcing international organizations: Resource diversification, organizational differentiation, and administrative governance, in: *Global Policy* 8: S5, 5–14.

Goldsmith, Jack L. 2003. The self-defeating International Criminal Court, in: *Chicago Law Review* 70: 1, 89–104.

Goldstein, Judith L., Rivers, Douglas & Tomz, Michael 2007. Institutions in international relations: Understanding the effects of the GATT and the WTO on world trade, in: *International Organization* 61: 1, 37–67.

Goldstein, Judith & Keohane, Robert O. 1993. Ideas and foreign policy: An analytical framework, in: Goldstein, Judith & Keohane, Robert O. (eds) *Ideas and Foreign Policy. Beliefs, Institutions, and Political Change*, Ithaca, NY: Cornell University Press, 3–30.

Goldstone, Richard 2007. International criminal courts and ad-hoc tribunals, in: Weiss, Thomas G. & Daws, Sam (eds) *The Oxford Handbook on the United Nations*, Oxford: Oxford University Press, 463–78.

Grabenwarter, Christoph 2005. *Europäische Menschenrechtskonvention*, 2nd edn, Munich: Beck.

Graham, Erin R. 2015. Money and multilateralism: How funding rules constitute IO governance, in: *International Theory* 7: 1, 162–94.

Green, Duncan & Griffith, Matthew 2002. Globalization and its discontents, in: *International Affairs* 78: 1, 49–68.

Green, Jessica F. & Colgan, Jeff 2013. Protecting sovereignty, protecting the planet: State delegation to international organizations and private actors in environmental politics, in: *Governance* 26: 3, 473–97.

Greene, Owen 1998. The system of implementation review in the ozone regime, in: Victor, David G., Raustiala, Kal & Skolnikoff, Eugene B. (eds) *The Implementation and Effectiveness of International Environmental Commitments. Theory and Practice*, Cambridge, MA: MIT Press, 89–136.

Greig, J. Michael & Diehl, Paul F. 2005. The peacekeeping-peacemaking dilemma, in: *International Studies Quarterly* 49: 4, 621–45.

Grieco, Joseph M. 1988. Anarchy and the limits of cooperation: A realist critique of the newest liberal institutionalism, in: *International Organization* 42: 3, 485–507.

Groom, A. J. R. 1988. The advent of international organisation, in: Taylor, Paul & Groom, A. J. R. (eds) *International Institutions at Work*, London: Pinter, 3–20.

Gruber, Lloyd 2000. *Ruling The World: Power Politics and The Rise of Supranational Institutions*, Princeton, NJ: Princeton University Press.

Guimarães, Joao & Avendaño, Nestor 2010. The great experiment: Testing the PRSP approach in Nicaragua, 2000–2007, in: *European Journal of Development Research*, published online on 4 November 2010, as doi:10.1057/ejdr.2010.50.

Gutner, Tamar & Thompson, Alexander 2010. The politics of IO performance: A framework, in: *The Review of International Organizations* 5: 3, 227–48.

Guzman, Andrew T. 2008. *How International Law Works*, Oxford: Oxford University Press.

Guzman, Andrew T. & Simmons, Beth A. 2005. Power plays and capacity constraints. The selection of defendants in World Trade Organization disputes, in: *Journal of Legal Studies* 34: 2, 557–98.

Haas, Ernst B. 1964. *Beyond the Nation State. Functionalism and International Organization*, Stanford, CA: Stanford University Press.

Haas, Ernst B. 1968. *The Uniting of Europe. Political, Social, and Economic Forces 1950–1957*, Stanford, CA: Stanford University Press.

Haas, Peter M. 1989. Do regimes matter? Epistemic communities and Mediterranean pollution control, in: *International Organization* 43: 3, 377–403.

Haas, Peter M. 1990. *Saving the Mediterranean. The Politics of International Environmental Cooperation*, New York: Columbia University Press.

Haas, Peter M. 1992a. Introduction: Epistemic communities and international policy coordination, in: *International Organization* 46: 1, 1–35.

Haas, Peter M. 1992b. Banning chlorofluorocarbons: Epistemic community efforts to protect stratospheric ozone, in: *International Organization* 46: 1, 187–224.

Haas, Peter M. 1992c. Obtaining environmental protection through epistemic communities, in: Rowlands, Ian H. & Greene, Malory (eds) *Global Environmental Change and International Relations*, Basingstoke: Palgrave Macmillan, 38–59.

Hafner-Burton, Emilie M. 2008. Sticks and stones: Naming and shaming the human rights enforcement problem, in: *International Organization* 62: 3, 689–716.

Häge, Frank M. 2013. Coalition building and consensus in the Council of the European Union, in: *British Journal of Political Science* 43: 3, 481–504.

Hale, Thomas, Held, David & Young, Kevin 2013. *Gridlock: Why Global Cooperation is Failing When We Need it Most*, London: Polity Press.

Hanrieder, Tine 2015. *International Organization in Time: Fragmentation and Reform*, Oxford: Oxford University Press.

Hardin, Garrett 1968. The tragedy of the commons, in: *Science* 162: 3859, 1243–48.

Harbom, Lotta & Wallensteen, Peter 2010. Armed conflicts, 1946–2009, in: *Journal of Peace Research* 47: 4, 501–09.

Harrigan, Jane & Mosley, Paul 1991. Evaluating the impact of World Bank structural adjustment lending: 1980–87, in: *Journal of Development Studies* 27: 1, 63–94.

Harris, David 2000. Lessons from the reporting system of the European Social Charter, in: Alston, Philip & Crawford, James (eds) *The Future of UN Human Rights Treaty Monitoring*, Cambridge: Cambridge University Press, 347–60.

Hartzell, Caroline, Hoddie, Matthew & Rothchild, Donald 2001. Stabilizing the peace after civil war, in: *International Organization* 55: 1, 183–208.

Hasenclever, Andreas 2001. *Die Macht der Moral in der internationalen Politik. Militärische Interventionen westlicher Staaten in Somalia, Ruanda und Bosnien-Herzegowina*, Frankfurt/M.: Campus.

Hasenclever, Andreas, Mayer, Peter & Rittberger, Volker 1997. *Theories of International Regimes*, Cambridge: Cambridge University Press.

Hathaway, Oona A. 2002. Do human rights treaties make a difference? in: *Yale Law Journal* 111: 8, 1935–2042.

Hauser, Heinz & Schanz, Kai-Uwe 1995. *Das neue GATT. Die Welthandelsordnung nach Abschluss der Uruguay-Runde*, 2nd edn, Munich: Oldenbourg.

Hawkins, Darren G. & Jacoby, Wade 2006. How agents matter, in: Hawkins, Darren G., Lake, David A., Nielson, Daniel L. & Tierney, Michael J. (eds) *Delegation and Agency in International Organizations*, Cambridge: Cambridge University Press, 199–228.

Hawkins, Darren G., Lake, David A., Nielson, Daniel L. & Tierney, Michael J. 2006. Delegation under anarchy: States, international organizations, and principal-agent theory, in: Hawkins, Darren G., Lake, David A., Nielson, Daniel L. & Tierney, Michael J. (eds) *Delegation and Agency in International Organizations*, Cambridge: Cambridge University Press, 3–38.

Hayes-Renshaw, Fiona, Van Aken, W. & Wallace, Helen 2006. When and why the EU Council of Ministers votes explicitly, in: *Journal of Common Market Studies* 44: 1, 161–94.

Heinz, Wolfgang S. 2006. Von der Menschenrechtskommission zum Menschenrechtsrat, in *Die Friedens-Warte* 81: 1, 129–44.

Heisenberg, Dorothee 2005. The institution of 'consensus' in the European Union: Formal versus informal decision-making in the Council, in: *European Journal of Political Research* 44: 1, 65–90.

Helfer, Lawrence & Slaughter, Anne-Marie 1997. Toward a theory of effective supranational adjudication, in: *Yale Law Journal* 107: 2, 273–391.

Helleiner, Eric 1994. *States and the Reemergence of Global Finance. From Bretton Woods to the 1990s*, Ithaca, NY: Cornell University Press.

Helm, Carsten & Sprinz, Detlef 2000. Measuring the effectiveness of international environmental regimes, in: *Journal of Conflict Resolution* 44: 5, 630–52.

Hernández, Gleider 2014. *The International Court of Justice and The Judicial Function*, Oxford: Oxford University Press.

Herz, John H. 1950. Idealist internationalism and the security dilemma, in: *World Politics* 2: 2, 157–80.

Higgott, Richard 2001. Economic globalization and global governance: Towards a Post-Washington consensus? in: Rittberger, Volker (ed.) *Global Governance and the United Nations System*, Tokyo: United Nations University Press, 127–57.

Hillebrecht, Courtney 2014. The power of human rights tribunals: Compliance with the European Court of Human Rights and domestic policy change, in: *European Journal of International Relations* 20: 4, 1100–23.

Hinnebush, Raymond & Ehteshami, Anoushiravan 2002. *The Foreign Policies of Middle East States*, Boulder, CO: Lynne Rienner.

Hix, Simon 2005. *The Political System of the European Union*, 2nd edn, London: Palgrave Macmillan.

Hix, Simon, & Høyland, Bjørn 2011. *The Political System of the European Union*, 3rd edn, Basingstoke: Palgrave Macmillan.

Hix, Simon, Noury, Abdul & Roland, Gerard 2006. Dimensions of politics in the European Parliament, in: *American Journal of Political Science* 50: 2, 494–520.

Höffe, Otfried 2001. Subsidiary and federal world republic: Thoughts on democracy in an age of globalization, in: Rittberger, Volker (ed.) *Global Governance and the United Nations System*, Tokyo: United Nations University Press, 181–202.

Hoffmann-Van de Poll, Frederike 2011. *A Quest for Accountability. The Effects of International Criminal Tribunals and Courts on Impunity*, Berlin: Berliner Wissenschaftsverlag.

Holtrup, Petra 2001. Das Scheitern der Klimaschutzdiplomatie, in: *Internationale Politik* 56: 6, 31–8.

Hooghe, Liesbet & Marks, Gary 2001. *Multi-level Governance and European Integration*, Lanham, MD: Rowman & Littlefield.

Hooghe, Liesbet & Marks, Gary 2015. Delegation and pooling in international organizations, in: *The Review of International Organizations* 10: 3, 305–28.

Hooghe, Liesbet, Marks, Gary, Lenz, Tobias, Bezuijen, Jeanine, Ceka, Besir & Derderyan, Svet 2017. *Measuring International Authority: A Postfunctionalist Theory of Governance, Volume III*, Oxford: Oxford University Press.

Hopewell, Kristen 2015. Different paths to power: The rise of Brazil, India and China at the World Trade Organization, in: *Review of International Political Economy* 22: 2, 311–38.

Hopmann, P. Terrence 1995. Two paradigms of negotiation: Bargaining and problem solving, in: *The Annals of the American Academy of Political and Social Science* 542 1, 24–47.

Hosli, Madeleine E. 2010. Voting weights, thresholds and population size: Member state representation in the Council of the European Union, in: Van Deemen, Adrian & Rusinowska, Agnieszka (eds) *Collective Decision-Making*, Berlin: Springer, 151–67.

Hughes, Steve & Haworth, Nigel 2010. *The International Labour Organisation*, London: Routledge.

Hüller, Thorsten & Maier, Mathias Leonard 2006. Fixing the codex? Global food-safety governance, in: Joerges, Christian & Petersmann, Ernst-Ulrich (eds) *Constitutionalism, Multilevel Trade Governance and Social Regulation*, Oxford: Oxford University Press, 267–300.

Hultman, Lisa, Kathman, Jacob & Shannon, Megan 2014. Beyond keeping peace: United Nations effectiveness in the midst of fighting, in: *American Political Science Review* 108: 4, 737–53.

Human Security Report 2010. *Human Security Report 2009/2010. The Causes of Peace and the Shrinking Costs of War*, Vancouver: Human Security Report Project.

Hurd, Ian 2007. *After Anarchy. Legitimacy and Power in the UN Security Council*, Princeton, NJ: Princeton University Press.

IAEA n.d. *Mission Statement*, https://www.iaea.org/about/mission, date accessed: 28 July 2018.

Iida, Keisuke 2004. Is WTO dispute settlement effective? in: *Global Governance* 10: 2, 207–25.

Ikenberry, G. John 2008. The rise of China and the future of the West – Can the liberal system survive, in *Foreign Affairs* 87, 23–37.

Ikenberry, G. John 2011. *Liberal Leviathan: The Origins, Crisis, and Transformation of the American World Order*, Princeton, NJ: Princeton University Press.

Ilzkovitz, Fabienne, Dierx, Adriaan, Kovacs, Viktoria & Sousa, Nuno 2007. Steps towards a deeper economic integration: The internal market in the 21st century. A contribution to the single market review, *European Commission Economic Papers* no. 271, Brussels. Independent.

Independent Evaluation Office of the IMF (IEO) 2011. *IMF Performance in the Run-Up to the Financial and Economic Crisis. IMF Surveillance in 2004–07*, Washington, DC: Evaluation Report.

Ingram, Paul, Robinson, Jeffrey & Busch, Marc L. 2005. The intergovernmental network of world trade: IGO connectedness, governance and embeddedness, in: *American Journal of Sociology* 111: 3, 824–58.

International Commission on Intervention and State Sovereignty (ICISS) 2001. *Responsibility to Protect. Report of the International Commission on Intervention and State Sovereignty*, Ottawa, ON: International Development Research Center.

International Monetary Fund (IMF) 2011. *IMF Lending – Factsheet, Online Resource*, http://www.imf.org/external/np/exr/facts/howlend.htm, date accessed: 17 October 2011.

Irwin, Douglas A. 1995. The GATT in historical perspective, in: *American Economic Review* 85: 2, 323–28.

Jackson, John Howard 1999. *The World Trading System. Law and Policy of International Economic Relations*, 2nd edn, Cambridge: Cambridge University Press.

Jackson, John H. 2004. Effektivität und Wirksamkeit des Streitbeilegungsverfahrens der WTO, in: Zangl, Bernhard & Zürn, Michael (eds) *Verrechtlichung – Baustein für Global Governance?* Bonn: Dietz.

Jacobson, Harold K. 1984. *Networks of Interdependence. International Organizations and the Global Political System*, 2nd edn, New York: Knopf.

Janis, Mark W., Kay, Richard S. & Bradley, Anthony W. 2000. *European Human Rights Law. Text and Materials*, Oxford: Oxford University Press.

Jentleson, Bruce W. & Britton, Rebecca L. 1998. Still pretty prudent: Post-Cold War American public opinion on the use of military force, in: *Journal of Conflict Resolution* 42: 4, 395–417.

Jervis, Robert 1983. Security regimes, in: Krasner, Stephen D. (ed.) *International Regimes*, Ithaca, NY: Cornell University Press, 357–78.

Jessop, Bob 2002. *The Future of the Capitalist State*, Cambridge: Polity Press.

Jetschke, Anja 2006. Weltkultur vs. Partikularismus: Die Universalität der Menschenrechte im Lichte der Ratifikation von Menschenrechtsverträgen, in: *Die Friedens-Warte* 81: 1, 25–49.

Joerges, Christian & Falke, Josef (eds) 2000. *Das Ausschusswesen der Europäischen Union: Praxis der Risikoregulierung im Binnenmarkt und ihre rechtliche Verfassung*, Baden-Baden: Nomos.

Joerges, Christian & Neyer, Jürgen 1997a. Transforming strategic interaction into deliberative problem-solving: European comitology in the foodstuffs sector, in: *Journal of European Public Policy* 4: 4, 609–25.

Joerges, Christian & Neyer, Jürgen 1997b. From intergovernmental bargaining to deliberative political processes: The constitutionalisation of comitology, in: *European Law Journal* 3: 3, 273–99.

Johnson, Tana 2014. *Organizational Progeny: Why Governments are Losing Control over the Proliferating Structures of Global Governance*. Oxford: Oxford University Press.

Johnston, Alastair Iain 2007. *Social States: China in International Institutions, 1980–2000*, Princeton, NJ: Princeton University Press.

Johnstone, Ian 2008. The Security Council as legislature, in: Cronin, Bruce & Hurd, Ian (eds) *The UN Security Council and the Politics of International Authority*, London: Routledge, 80–104.

Jones, Kent 2009. *The Doha Blues. Institutional Crisis and Reform in the WTO*, Oxford: Oxford University Press.

Jönsson, Christer & Tallberg, Jonas 1998. Compliance and post-agreement bargaining, in: *European Journal of International Relations* 4: 4, 371–408.

Jørgensen, Knud Erik (ed.) 2009. *The European Union and International Organizations*, London: Routledge.

Jupille, Joseph, Mattli, Walter & Snidal, Duncan 2013. *Institutional Choice and Global Commerce*, Cambridge: Cambridge University Press.

Kahler, Miles 1995. *International Institutions and the Political Economy of Integration*, Washington, DC: Brookings Institution.

Kaldor, Mary 1999. *New and Old Wars: Organised Violence in a Global Era*, Hoboken, NJ: John Wiley & Sons.

Kanbur, Ravi & Vines, David 2000. The World Bank and poverty reduction: Past, present and future, in: Gilbert, Christopher L. & Vines, David (eds) *The World Bank. Structure and Policies*, Cambridge: Cambridge University Press, 87–107.

Kant, Immanuel 1991 [1795]. Perpetual peace: A philosophical sketch, in: Reiss, Hans (ed.) *Kant. Political Writings*, 2nd edn, Cambridge: Cambridge University Press, 93–130.

Karlsrud, John 2015. The UN at war: Examining the consequences of peace-enforcement mandates for the UN peacekeeping operations in the CAR, the DRC and Mali, in: *Third World Quarterly* 36: 1, 40–54.

Karlsrud, John 2018. *The UN at War*, London: Palgrave Macmillan.

Katzenstein, Peter J. 1996. Introduction: Alternative perspectives on national security, in: Katzenstein, Peter J. (ed.) *The Culture of National Security. Norms and Identity in World Politics*, New York: Columbia University Press, 1–32.

Keck, Margaret E. & Sikkink, Kathryn 1998. *Activists Beyond Borders. Advocacy Networks in International Politics*, Ithaca, NY: Cornell University Press.

Keleman, Daniel R. 2002. The politics of 'eurocratic' structure and the new European agencies, in: *West European Politics* 25: 4, 93–118.

Keller, Helen & Stone Sweet, Alec (eds) 2008. *A Europe of Rights. The Impact of the ECHR on National Legal Systems*, Oxford: Oxford University Press.

Keohane, Robert O. 1980. The theory of hegemonic stability and changes in international economic regimes, 1967–1977, in: Holsti, Ole R., Siverson, Randolph & George, Alexander L. (eds) *Change in the International System*, Boulder, CO: Westview, 131–62.

Keohane, Robert O. 1984. *After Hegemony. Cooperation and Discord in the World Political Economy*, Princeton, NJ: Princeton University Press.

Keohane, Robert O. 1989. Neoliberal institutionalism: A perspective on world politics, in: Keohane, Robert O. (ed.) *International Institutions and State Power. Essays in International Relations Theory*, Boulder, CO: Westview, 1–20.

Keohane, Robert O., Moravcsik, Andrew & Slaughter, Anne-Marie 2000. Legalized dispute resolution: Interstate and transnational, in: *International Organization* 54: 3, 457–88.

Keohane, Robert O. & Nye, Joseph S., Jr. 1977. *Power and Interdependence*, New York: Longman.

Keohane, Robert O. & Victor, David G. 2011. The regime complex for climate change, in: *Perspectives on Politics* 9: 1, 7–23.

Kiewiet, D. Roderick & McCubbins, Mathew D. 1991. *The Logic of Delegation. Congressional Parties and the Appropriations Process*, Chicago, IL: University of Chicago Press.

Kilby, Christopher 2009. The political economy of conditionality: An empirical analysis of World Bank loan disbursements, in: *Journal of Development Economics* 89: 1, 51–61.

King, Gary, Keohane, Robert O. & Verba, Sidney 1994. *Designing Social Inquiry. Scientific Inference in Qualitative Research*, Princeton, NJ: Princeton University Press.

Kiss, Elizabeth 2000. Moral ambition within and beyond political constraints, in: Rotberg, Robert I. & Thompson, Dennis (eds) *Truth v. Justice: The Morality of Truth Commissions*, Princeton, NJ: Princeton University Press, 68–98.

Klabbers, Jan 2009. *An Introduction to International Institutional Law*, 2nd edn, Cambridge: Cambridge University Press.

Klein, Eckart & Brinkmeier, Friederike 2001. CCPR und EGMR: Der Menschenrechtsausschuss der Vereinten Nationen und der Europäische Gerichtshof für Menschenrechte im Vergleich, in: *Vereinte Nationen* 49: 1, 17–20.

Kleine, Mareike 2013. Trading control: National fiefdoms in international organizations, in: *International Theory* 5: 3, 321–46.

Klotz, Audie 1995. *Norms in International Relations. The Struggle against Apartheid*, Ithaca, NY: Cornell University Press.

Kolb, Robert 2013. *The International Court of Justice*, Oxford: Hart Publishing.

Kohler-Koch, Beate & Rittberger, Berthold 2006. Review article: The 'governance turn' in EU studies, in: *Journal of Common Market Studies* 44: Annual Review, 27–49.

Koops, Joachim, MacQueen, Norrie, Tardy, Thierry & Williams, Paul D. (eds) 2015. *The Oxford Handbook of United Nations Peacekeeping Operations*. Oxford: Oxford University Press.

Koremenos, Barbara, Lipson, Charles & Snidal, Duncan 2001. The rational design of international institutions, in: *International Organization* 55: 4, 761–800.

Korey, William 1998. *NGOs and the Universal Declaration of Human Rights. A Curious Grapevine*, New York: St Martin's Press.

Krasner, Stephen D. 1983. Structural causes and regime consequences: Regimes as intervening variables, in: Krasner, Stephen D. (ed.) *International Regimes*, Ithaca, NY: Cornell University Press, 1–21.

Krasner, Stephen D. 1985. *Structural Conflict. The Third World against Global Liberalism*, Berkeley, CA: University of California Press.

Krasner, Stephen D. 1991. Global communications and national power. Life on the Pareto frontier, in: *World Politics* 43: 3, 336–66.

Krasner, Stephen D. 1999. *Sovereignty. Organized Hypocrisy*, Princeton, NJ: Princeton University Press.

Krause, Keith 2007. Disarmament, in: Weiss, Thomas G. & Daws, Sam (eds) *The Oxford Handbook on the United Nations*, Oxford: Oxford University Press, 287–99.

Kristensen, Hans M. & Norris, Robert S. n.d. Nuclear notebook: Nuclear arsenals of the world, in: *Bulletin of Atomic Scientists*, https://thebulletin.org/nuclear-notebook-multimedia, date accessed: 28 July 2018.

Kruck, Andreas 2011. *Private Ratings, Public Regulations. Credit Rating Agencies and Global Financial Governance*, Basingstoke: Palgrave Macmillan.

Kruck, Andreas & Rittberger, Volker 2010. Multilateralism today and its contribution to global governance, in: Muldoon, James P., Jr, Aviel, JoAnn F., Reitano, Richard & Sullivan, Earl (eds) *The New Dynamics of Multilateralism. Diplomacy, International Organizations, and Global Governance*, Boulder, CO: Westview Press, 43–65.

Krugman, Paul R. 1979. Increasing returns, monopolistic competition, and international trade, in: *Journal of International Economics* 9: 4, 469–79.

Krugman, Paul R. & Obstfeld, Maurice 2008. *International Economics. Theory and Policy*, 8th edn, New York: Longman.

Ku, Julian & Nzelibe, Jide 2006. Do international criminal tribunals deter or exacerbate humanitarian atrocities? in: *Washington University Law Quarterly* 84: 4, 777–833.

Kucik, Jeffrey & Reinhardt, Eric 2008. Does flexibility promote cooperation? An application to the global trade regime, in: *International Organization* 62: 3, 477–505.

Kühne, Winrich 2000. Humanitäre Konfliktlagen in der globalisierten Welt und die Notwendigkeit zur Fortentwicklung des Völkerrechts, in: Menzel, Ulrich (ed.) *Vom Ewigen Frieden und vom Wohlstand der Nationen. Dieter Senghaas zum 60. Geburtstag*, Frankfurt/M.: Suhrkamp, 291–319.

Kuziemko, Ilyana & Werker, Eric 2006. How much is a seat on the Security Council worth? Foreign aid and bribery at the United Nations, in: *Journal of Political Economy* 114: 5, 905–30.

Layne, Christopher 2006. The unipolar illusion revisited: The coming end of the United States' unipolar moment, in: *International Security* 31: 2, 7–41.

Leach, Philipp 2001. *Taking a Case to the European Court of Human Rights*, London: Blackstone.

Lebovic, James H. & Voeten, Erik 2006. The politics of shame: The condemnation of country human rights practices in the UNHCR, in: *International Studies Quarterly* 50: 4, 861–88.

Lebovic, James H. & Voeten, Erik 2009. The cost of shame: International organizations and foreign aid in the punishing of human rights violators, in: *Journal of Peace Research* 46: 1, 79–97.

Lee, Kelley 2009. *The World Health Organization (WHO)*, London: Routledge.

Leitner, Kara & Lester, Simon 2005. WTO dispute settlement 1995–2004: A statistical analysis, in: *Journal of International Economic Law* 8: 1, 231–44.

Lenshow, Andrea 2010. Environmental policy: Contending dynamics of policy change, in: Wallace, Helen, Pollack, Mark A. & Young, Alasdair (eds) *Policy-Making in the European Union*, 6th edn, Oxford: Oxford University Press, 307–29.

Lenz, Tobias, Bezuijen, Jeanine, Hooghe, Liesbet & Marks, Gary 2014. *Patterns of International Organization. Task Specific vs. General Purpose*, in: Robert Schuman Centre for Advanced Studies Research Paper No. RSCAS 2014/128.

Levite, Ariel 2002/2003. Never say never again: Nuclear reversal revisited, in: *International Security* 27: 3, 59–88.

Levitt, Malcolm & Lord, Christopher 2000. *The Political Economy of Monetary Union*, Basingstoke: Palgrave Macmillan.

Levy, Marc A. 1993. European acid rain: The power of tote-board diplomacy, in: Haas, Peter M., Keohane, Robert O. & Levy, Marc A. (eds) *Institutions for the Earth. Sources of Effective International Environmental Protection*, Cambridge, MA: MIT Press, 75–132.

Lewis, Jeffrey 1998. Is the 'hard bargaining' image of the Council misleading? The Committee of Permanent Representatives and the local elections directive, in: *Journal of Common Market Studies* 36: 4, 479–504.

Lewis, Jeffrey 2005. The Janus face of Brussels: Socialization and everyday decision making in the European Union, in: *International Organization* 59: 4, 937–71.

Liddell, Roderick 2002. The European Court of Human Rights after 50 years of the European Convention on Human Rights, in: Hasse, Jana, Müller, Erwin & Schneider, Patricia (eds) *Menschenrechte. Bilanz und Perspektiven*, Baden-Baden: Nomos, 431–41.

Liese, Andrea 1998. Menschenrechtsschutz durch Nichtregierungsorganisationen, in: *Aus Politik und Zeitgeschichte* 46–47, 36–42.

Liese, Andrea 2006a. *Staaten am Pranger. Zur Wirkung internationaler Regime auf innerstaatliche Menschenrechtspolitik*, Wiesbaden: VS Verlag für Sozialwissenschaften.

Liese, Andrea 2006b. Epistula (non) erubescit. Das Staatenberichtsverfahren als Instrument internationaler Rechtsdurchsetzung, in: *Die Friedens-Warte* 81: 1, 51–69.

Lin, Justin & Chang, Ha-Joon 2009. Should industrial policy in developing countries conform to comparative advantage or defy it? A debate between Justin Lin and Ha-Joon Chang, in: *Development Policy Review* 27: 5, 483–502.

Linklater, Andrew 1990. The problem of community in international relations, in: *Alternatives* 15: 2, 135–53.

Linklater, Andrew 1998. *The Transformation of Political Community. Ethical Foundations of the Post-Westphalian Era*, Cambridge: Polity Press.

Lipscy, Phillip Y. 2017, *Renegotiating the World Order: Institutional Change in International Relations*, Cambridge: Cambridge University Press.

Lipson, Charles 1984. International cooperation in economic and security affairs, in: *World Politics* 37: 1, 1–23.

List, Martin 1991. *Umweltschutz in zwei Meeren. Vergleich der internationalen usammenarbeit zum Schutz der Meeresumwelt in Nord- und Ostsee*, Munich: tuduv.

Lister, Frederick K. 1984. *Decision-Making Strategies for International Organisations. The IMF Model*, Denver, CO: University of Denver.

Lombardi, Domenico & Woods, Ngaire 2008. The politics of influence: An analysis of IMF surveillance, in: *Review of International Political Economy* 15: 5, 711–39.

Loosch, Reinhard 2000. From 'programme 93+2' to model protocol INFCIRC/540: Negotiating for a multilateral agreement in the international atomic energy agency, in: Häckel, Erwin & Stein, Gotthard (eds) *Tightening the Reins. Towards a Strengthened International Nuclear Safeguards System*, Berlin: Springer, 23–66.

Lowi, Theodore J. 1964. American business, public policy, case studies, and political theory, in: *World Politics* 16: 4, 677–715.

Luard, Evan 1977. *International Agencies. The Emerging Framework of Interdependence*, London: Macmillan.

Luard, Evan 1982. *A History of the United Nations. The Years of Western Domination 1945–1955*, New York: St Martin's Press.

Luterbacher, Urs & Sprinz, Detlef (eds) 2001. *International Relations and Global Climate Change*, Cambridge, MA: MIT Press.

Madsen, Jakob B. 2001. Trade barriers and the collapse of world trade during the Great Depression, in: *Southern Economic Journal* 67: 4, 848–68.

Majone, Giandomenico 1994. The rise of the regulatory state in Europe, in: *West European Politics* 17: 3, 77–101.

Majone, Giandomenico 1997. The new European agencies: Regulation by information, in: *Journal of European Public Policy* 4: 2, 262–75.

Malone, David M. 2007. The Security Council, in: Weiss, Thomas G. & Daws, Sam (eds) *The Oxford Handbook on the United Nations*, Oxford: Oxford University Press, 117–35.

Mangone, Gerard J. 1975. *A Short History of International Organization*, Westport, CT: Greenwood.

Mansfield, Edward D. & Reinhardt, Eric 2008. International institutions and the volatility of international trade, in: *International Organization* 62: 4, 621–52.

Manulak, Michael W. 2017. Leading by design: Informal influence and international secretariats, in: *The Review of International Organizations* 12: 4, 497–522.

March, James G. & Olsen, Johan P. 1989. *Rediscovering Institutions. The Organizational Basis of Politics*, New York: Free Press.

Marchisio, Sergio & Di Blase, Antonietta 1991. *The Food and Agriculture Organization (FAO)*, Dordrecht: Martinus Nijhoff.

Marshall, Katherine 2008. *The World Bank. From Reconstruction to Development to Equity*, London: Routledge.

Martin, Lisa L. 2006. Distribution, information, and delegation to international organizations: The case of IMF conditionality, in: Hawkins, Darren Greg, Lake, David A., Nielson, Daniel L. & Tierney, Michael J. (eds) *Delegation and Agency in International Organizations*, Cambridge: Cambridge University Press, 140–64.

Mastanduno, Michael 1999. Preserving the unipolar moment: Realist theories and U.S. grand strategy after the Cold War, in: Kapstein, Ethan B. & Mastanduno, Michael (eds) *Unipolar Politics. Realism and State Strategies After the Cold War*, New York: Columbia University Press, 138–81.

Mathiason, John 2010. International secretariats: Diplomats or civil servants? in: Muldoon, James P., Aviel, Joann F., Reitano, Richard & Sullivan, Earl (eds) *The New Dynamics of Multilateralism. Diplomacy, International Organizations, and Global Governance*, Boulder, CO: Westview Press, 237–47.

Matsushita, Mitsou, Schoenbaum, Thomas J. & Mavroidis, Petros C. 2004. *The World Trade Organization. Law, Practice and Policy*, Oxford: Oxford University Press.

Mayntz, Renate 1977. Die implementation politischer programme: Theoretische Überlegungen zu einem neuen Forschungsgebiet, in: *Die Verwaltung* 10: 1, 51–66.

McCubbins, Mathew D., Noll, Roger G. & Weingast, Barry R. 1987. Administrative procedures as instruments of political control, in: *Journal of Law, Economics, & Organization* 3: 2, 243–77.

McCubbins, Mathew D., & Schwartz, Thomas 1984. Congressional oversight overlooked: Police patrols versus fire alarms, in: *American Journal of Political Science* 28: 1, 165–79.

McGowan, Francis 2000. Competition Policy, in: Wallace, Helen & Wallace, William (eds) *Policy-Making in the European Union*, 4th edn, Oxford: Oxford University Press, 115–47.

Mead, Walter Russell 2002. *Special Providence: American Foreign Policy and How it Changed the World*, London: Routledge.

Mearsheimer, John J. 1995. The false promise of international institutions, in: *International Security* 19: 3, 5–49.

Mearsheimer, John J. 2001. *The Tragedy of Great Power Politics*, New York: Norton.

Merrills, John Graham 2017. *International Dispute Settlement*, 6th edn, Cambridge: Cambridge University Press.

Metzger, Martina 2002. World Bank, World Bank Group, in: Volger, Helmut (ed.) *A Concise Encyclopedia of the United Nations*, The Hague: Kluwer Law International, 679–84.

Meunier, Sophie 2003. Trade policy and political legitimacy in the European Union, in: *Comparative European Politics* 1: 1, 67–90.

Meunier, Sophie & McNamara, Kathleen 2007. Making history: European integration and institutional change at fifty, in: McNamara, Kathleen & Meunier, Sophie (eds) *Making History. European Integration and Institutional Change at Fifty*, Oxford: Oxford University Press, 1–22.

Mitchell, Ronald 1994. Regime design matters: Intentional oil pollution and treaty compliance, in: *International Organization* 48: 3, 425–58.

Mitrany, David 1933. *The Progress of International Government*, New Haven, CT: Yale University Press.

Mitrany, David 1966. *A Working Peace System*, Chicago, IL: Quadrangle.

Momani, Bessma 2004. American politicization of the International Monetary Fund, in: *Review of International Political Economy* 11: 5, 880–904.

Mondré, Aletta 2009. Judizialisierungsprozesse im Sicherheitsbereich: Friedensbedrohungen vor dem UN-Sicherheitsrat, in: Zangl, Bernhard (ed.) *Auf dem Weg zu internationaler Rechtsherrschaft? Streitbeilegung zwischen Politik und Recht*, Frankfurt/M.: Campus, 119–59.

Moravcsik, Andrew 1991. Negotiating the Single European Act: National interests and conventional statecraft in the European Community, in: *International Organization* 45: 1, 19–56.

Moravcsik, Andrew 1995. Explaining international human rights regimes: Liberal theory and Western Europe, in: *European Journal of International Relations* 1: 2, 157–89.

Moravcsik, Andrew 1998. *The Choice for Europe. Social Purpose and State Power from Messina to Maastricht*, Ithaca, NY: Cornell University Press.

Moravcsik, Andrew 2000. The origins of human rights regimes: Democratic delegation in postwar Europe, in: *International Organization* 54: 2, 217–52.

Moravcsik, Andrew 2002. In defence of the 'democratic deficit': Reassessing legitimacy in the European Union, in: *Journal of Common Market Studies* 40: 4, 603–24.

Morgenthau, Hans 1948. *Politics Among Nations. The Struggle for Power and Peace*, New York: Alfred A. Knopf.

Morris, Justin 2013. Libya and Syria: R2P and the spectre of the swinging pendulum, in: *International Affairs* 89: 5, 1265–83.

Moschella, Manuela 2010. *Governing Risk. The IMF and Global Financial Crises*, Basingstoke: Palgrave Macmillan.

Mosley, Paul, Harrigan, Jane & Toye, John 1995. *Aid and Power. The World Bank and Policy-based Lending*, London: Routledge.

Müller, Harald 2010. Between power and justice: Current problems and perspectives of the NPT regime, in: *Strategic Analysis* 34: 2, 189–201.

Müller, Harald, Fischer, David & Kötter, Wolfgang 1994. *Nuclear Non- Proliferation and Global Order*, Oxford: Oxford University Press.

Müller, Harald & Schmidt, Andreas 2010. The little known story of de-proliferation: Why states give up nuclear weapon activities, in: Potter, William S. (ed.) *Forecasting Nuclear Proliferation*, Stanford, CA: Stanford University Press, 124–58.

Murphy, Craig 2006. *The United Nations Development Programme: A Better Way?* Cambridge: Cambridge University Press.

Narlikar, Amrita 2004. *International Trade and Developing Countries. Bargaining Coalitions in the GATT & WTO*, London: Routledge.

Narlikar, Amrita & Tussie, Diana 2003. The G20 at the Cancun Ministerial: Developing countries and their evolving coalitions in the WTO, in: *World Economy* 27: 7, 947–66.

Neumann, Iver B. 1996. Self and other in international relations, in: *European Journal of International Relations* 2: 2, 139–74.

Neumayer, Eric 2005. Do international human rights treaties improve respect for human rights? in: *Journal of Conflict Resolution* 49: 6, 925–53.

Newell, Peter & Bulkeley, Harriet 2010. *Governing Climate Change*, London: Routledge.

Neyer, Jürgen 2002. Politische Herrschaft in nicht-hierarchischen Mehrebenensystemen, in: *Zeitschrift für Internationale Beziehungen* 9: 1, 1–30.

Neyer, Jürgen 2004. *Postnationale politische Herrschaft. Verrechtlichung und Vergesellschaftung jenseits des Staates*, Baden-Baden: Nomos.

Nielson, Daniel L., Tierney, Michael J. & Weaver, Catherine 2006. Bridging the rationalist-constructivist divide: Re-engineering the culture of the world bank, in. *Journal of International Relations and Development* 9: 1, 107–39.

Norris, Robert S. & Kristensen, Hans M. 2010. Global nuclear weapons inventories, 1945–2010, in: *Bulletin of the Atomic Scientists* 66: 4, 77–83.

North, Douglass C. 1990. *Institutions, Institutional Change and Economic Performance*, Cambridge: Cambridge University Press.

The Norwegian Nobel Committee 2007. The Nobel Peace Prize for 2007, Oslo, 12 October, https://www.nobelprize.org/prizes/peace/2007/press-release/, date accessed: 24 September 2018.

Novak, Stéphanie 2013. The silence of ministers: Consensus and blame avoidance in the Council of the European Union, in: *Journal of Common Market Studies* 51: 6, 1091–107.

Nugent, Neill 2006. *The Government and Politics of the European Union*, 6th edn, Basingstoke: Palgrave Macmillan.

Nye, Joseph S., & Keohane, Robert O. 1971. Transnational relations and world politics: An introduction. *International Organization* 25: 3, 329–49.

Oberthür, Sebastian 2004. Verrechtlichung in der internationalen Umweltpolitik: Tendenzen, Gründe, Wirkungen, in: Zürn, Michael & Zangl, Bernhard (eds) *Verrechtlichung – Baustein für Global Governance?*, Bonn: Dietz, 119–39.

Oberthür, Sebastian & Marr, Simon 2002. Das System der Erfüllungskontrolle des Kyoto-Protokolls: Ein Schritt zur wirksamen Durchsetzung im Umweltvölkerrecht, in: *Zeitschrift für Umweltrecht* 13: 2, 81–89.

Oberthür, Sebastian & Ott, Hermann E. (in collaboration with Richard G. Tarasofsky) 1999. *The Kyoto Protocol. International Climate Policy for the 21st Century*, Berlin: Springer.

Odell, John S. (ed.) 2006. *Negotiating Trade. Developing Countries in the WTO and NAFTA*, Cambridge: Cambridge University Press.

Odell, John S. 2010. Three islands of knowledge about negotiation in international organizations, in: *Journal of European Public Policy* 17: 5, 619–32.

O'Flaherty, Michael 2002. *Human Rights and the UN. Practice Before the Treaty Bodies*, 2nd edn, The Hague: Martinus Nijhof.

Ohlin, Berth 1933. *Interregional And International Trade*, Cambridge, MA: Harvard University Press.

Ohloff, Stephan 1999. Beteiligung von Verbänden und Unternehmen im WTO Streitbeilegungsverfahren: Das Shrimps-Turtle-Verfahren als Wendepunkt? in: *Europäische Zeitschrift für Wirtschaftsrecht* 10, 139–44.

Olivier, Jos G.J., Greet Janssens-Maenhout, & Jeroen A.H.W. Peters 2012, *Trends in Global CO2 Emissions*, The Hague: Netherlands Environmental Assessment Agency & EU Joint Research Centre, http://edgar.jrc.ec.europa.eu/CO2REPORT2012.pdf, date accessed: 27 July 2018.

Ostrom, Elinor 1990. *Governing the Commons: The Evolution of Institutions for Collective Action*. Cambridge: Cambridge University Press.

Oppermann, Thomas, Classen, Claus Dieter & Nettesheim, Martin 2009. *Europarecht. ein Studienbuch*, 4th edn, Munich: Beck.

Osiander, Andreas 1994. *The States System of Europe 1640–1990. Peacemaking and the Conditions of International Stability*, Oxford: Clarendon Press.

Ott, Hermann E. 1997. Das internationale Regime zum Schutz des Klimas, in: Gehring, Thomas & Oberthür, Sebastian (eds) *Internationale Umweltregime. Umweltschutz durch Verhandlungen und Verträge*, Opladen: Leske & Budrich, 201–18.

Panel on United Nations Peace Operations 2000. *Report of the Panel on United Nations Peace Operations (The Brahimi Report)*, https://www.un.org/ruleoflaw/files/brahimi%20report%20peacekeeping.pdf, date accessed: 28 July 2018.

Panke, Diana 2012. Lobbying institutional key players: How states seek to influence the European Commission, the Council Presidency and the European Parliament, in: *Journal of Common Market Studies* 50: 1, 129–50.

Pape, Matthias 1997. *Humanitäre Intervention. Zur Bedeutung der Menschenrechte in den Vereinten Nationen*, Baden-Baden: Nomos.

Parízek, Michal 2017. Control, soft information, and the politics of international organizations staffing, in: *The Review of International Organizations* 12: 4, 559–83.

Park, Susan & Vetterlein, Antje (eds) 2010. Owning development: Creating policy norms in the IMF and the World Bank, in: Park, Susan & Vetterlein, Antje (eds) *Owning Development. Creating Policy Norms in the IMF and the World Bank*, Cambridge: Cambridge University Press, 3–26.

Parker, Robert A. C. 1967. *Das Zwanzigste Jahrhundert, Vol. I. Europa 1918–1945*, Frankfurt/M.: Fischer.

Parson, Edward E. 1993. Protecting the ozone layer, in: Haas, Peter M., Keohane, Robert O. & Levy, Marc A. (eds) *Institutions for the Earth. Sources of Effective International Environmental Protection*, Cambridge, MA: MIT Press, 27–74.

Parson, Edward A. 2003. *Protecting the Ozone Layer. Science, Strategy, and Negotiation in the Shaping of a Global Environmental Regime*, Oxford: Oxford University Press.

Parsons, Craig 2003. *A Certain Idea of Europe*, Ithaca, NY: Cornell University Press.

Paterson, Matthew 2013. Green theory, in: Burchill, Scott et al. (eds) *Theories of International Relations*, 5th edn, Basingstoke: Palgrave Macmillan, 266–90.

Pauly, Louis W. 1997. *Who Elected the Bankers? Surveillance and Control in the World Economy*, Ithaca, NY: Cornell University Press.

Pelc, Krzysztof J. 2009. Seeking escape: The use of escape clauses in international trade agreements, in: *International Studies Quarterly* 53: 2, 349–68.

Petersohn, Ulrich 2009. *Selektiver Schutz universaler Menschenrechte. Eine multikausale Erklärung des Interventionsverhaltens von Demokratien*, Baden-Baden: Nomos Verlag.

Peterson, M. J. 2007. General Assembly, in: Weiss, Thomas G. & Daws, Sam (eds) *The Oxford Handbook on the United Nations*, Oxford: Oxford University Press, 97–116.

Pevehouse, Jon, Nordstrom, Timothy & Warnke, Kevin 2004. The correlates of war 2 international governmental organizations data version 2.0, in: *Conflict Management and Peace Science* 21: 2, 101–19.

Pfeffer, Jeffrey & Salancik, Gerald R. 2003 [1978]. *The External Control of Organizations. A Resource Dependence Perspective*, Stanford, CA: Stanford University Press.

Pillinger, Mara, Hurd, Ian & Barnett, Michael N. 2016. How to get away with cholera: The UN, Haiti, and international law, in: *Perspectives on Politics* 14: 1, 70–86.

Polakiewicz, Jörg & Jacob-Foltzer, Valérie 1991. The European Human Rights Convention in domestic law: The impact of Strasbourg case law in states where direct effect is given to the Convention, in: *Human Rights Law Quarterly* 12: 3, 125–42.

Pollack, Mark A. 2003. *The Engines of European Integration. Delegation, Agency, and Agenda Setting in the European Union*, Oxford: Oxford University Press.

Pouliot, Vincent 2016. *International Pecking Orders: The Politics and Practice of Multilateral Diplomacy*, Cambridge: Cambridge University Press.

Price, Richard & Zacher, Mark 2004. *The United Nations and Global Security*, New York: Palgrave Macmillan.

Puetter, Uwe 2014. *The European Council and the Council: New Intergovernmentalism and Institutional Change*, Oxford: Oxford University Press.

Ramcharan, Bertrand 2007. Norms and machinery, in: Weiss, Thomas G. & Daws, Sam (eds) *The Oxford Handbook on the United Nations*, Oxford: Oxford University Press, 439–62.

Reinicke, Wolfgang 1998. *Global Public Policy. Governing without Government?* Washington, DC: Brookings Institutions Press.

Renteln, Alison D. 1990. *International Human Rights. Universalism vs. Relativism*, London: Sage.

Risse, Thomas 2000. 'Let's argue!': Communicative action in world politics, in: *International Organization* 54: 1, 1–41.

Risse, Thomas, Jetschke, Anja & Schmitz, Hans-Peter 2002. *Die Macht der Menschenrechte. Internationale Normen, kommunikative Prozesse und politischer Wandel in den Ländern des Südens*, Baden-Baden: Nomos.

Risse, Thomas & Ropp, Stephen C. 1999. International human rights norms and domestic change: Conclusions, in: Risse, Thomas, Ropp, Stephen C. & Sikkink, Kathryn (eds) *The Power of Human Rights. International Norms and Domestic Change*, Cambridge: Cambridge University Press, 234–78.

Risse, Thomas, Ropp, Stephen C. & Sikkink, Kathryn (eds) 1999. *The Power of Human Rights. International Norms and Domestic Change*, Cambridge: Cambridge University Press.

Risse, Thomas & Sikkink, Kathryn 1999. The socialization of international human rights norms into domestic practices, in: Risse, Thomas, Ropp, Stephen C. & Sikkink, Kathryn (eds) *The Power of Human Rights. International Norms and Domestic Change*, Cambridge: Cambridge University Press, 1–38.

Risse-Kappen, Thomas 1995. Bringing transnational relations back in: Introduction, in: Risse-Kappen, Thomas (ed.) *Bringing Transnational Relations Back In. Non-State Actors, Domestic Structures and International Institutions*, Cambridge: Cambridge University Press, 3–33.

Rittberger, Berthold 2005. *Building Europe's Parliament. Democratic Representation Beyond the Nation State*, Oxford: Oxford University Press.

Rittberger, Berthold 2009. 'Copy and paste': Parlamentarisierung jenseits des Nationalstaates, in: Deitelhoff, Nicole & Steffek, Jens (eds) *Was bleibt vom Staat? Demokratie, Recht und Verfassung im globalen Zeitalter*, Frankfurt/M.: Suhrkamp, 137–59.

Rittberger, Volker, Huckel, Carmen, Rieth, Lothar & Zimmer, Melanie 2008. Inclusive global institutions for a global political economy, in: Rittberger, Volker & Nettesheim, Martin (eds) *Authority in the Global Political Economy*, Basingstoke: Palgrave Macmillan, 11–54.

Rittberger, Volker, Kruck, Andreas & Romund, Anne 2010. *Grundzüge der Weltpolitik. Theorie und Empirie des Weltregierens*, Wiesbaden: VS Verlag für Sozialwissenschaften.

Rittberger, Volker, Mogler, Martin & Zangl, Bernhard 1997. *Vereinte Nationen und Weltordnung. Zivilisierung der internationalen Politik?* Opladen: Leske & Budrich.

Roberts, Adam 1996. The United Nations: Variants of collective security, in: Woods, Ngaire (ed.) *Explaining International Relations Since 1945*, Oxford: Oxford University Press, 309–36.

Rose, Andrew K. 2004. Do we really know that the WTO increases trade? in: *American Economic Review* 94: 1, 98–114.

Rosendorf, Peter R. & Milner, Helen V. 2001. The optimal design of international trade institutions: Uncertainty and escape, in: *International Organization* 55: 4, 829–57.

Rosenthal, Gert 2007. Economic and Social Council, in: Weiss, Thomas G. & Daws, Sam (eds) *The Oxford Handbook on the United Nations*, Oxford: Oxford University Press, 136–48.

Ross, George 1995. *Jacques Delors and European Integration*, Cambridge: Polity Press.

Rowlands, Ian H. 1995. *The Politics of Global Atmospheric Change*, Manchester: Manchester University Press.

Rudolph, Christopher 2001. Constructing an atrocities regime: The politics of war crimes tribunals, in: *International Organization* 55: 3, 655–91.

Ruggeri, Andrea, Dorussen, Han & Gizelis, Theodora-Ismene 2016. On the frontline every day? Subnational deployment of United Nations peacekeepers, in: *British Journal of Political Science*. Advance online publication. doi: 10.1017/S000712341600017X

Ruggie, John Gerard 1982. International regimes, transactions, and change: Embedded liberalism in the postwar economic order, in: *International Organization* 36: 2, 379–415.

Ruggie, John Gerard 1992. Multilateralism: The anatomy of an institution, in: *International Organization* 46: 3, 561–98.

Ruggie, John Gerard 1994. Trade, protectionism and the future of welfare capitalism, in: *Journal of International Affairs* 48: 1, 1–11.

Sandholtz, Wayne & Zysman, John 1989. 1992 – Recasting the European bargain, in: *World Politics* 42: 1, 95–128.

Schabas, William 2011. *An Introduction to the International Criminal Court*, 4th edn, Cambridge: Cambridge University Press.

Scharpf, Fritz 1999. *Governing in Europe. Effective and Democratic?* Oxford: Oxford University Press.

Scheffer, David J. 2002. Staying the course with the International Criminal Court, in: *Cornell International Law Journal* 35, 47–100.

Schimmelfennig, Frank 1995. *Debatten zwischen Staaten. Eine Argumentationstheorie internationaler Systemkonflikte*, Opladen: Leske & Budrich.

Schirm, Stefan A. 2007. *Internationale Politische Ökonomie. Eine Einführung*, 2nd edn, Baden-Baden: Nomos.

Schmitt, Daniella 2009. *Do Transitional Administrations Fail? A Comparative Study of the Kosovo and East Timor Experiences*, Saarbrücken: Südwestdeutscher Verlag für Hochschulschriften.

Schulze, Peter M. 2002. NGOs, in: Volger, Helmut (ed.) 2002a. *A Concise Encyclopedia of the United Nations*, The Hague: Kluwer Law International, 378–87.

Seidl-Hohenveldern, Ignaz & Loibl, Gerhard 2000. *Das Recht der interna- tion- alen Organisationen einschließlich der supranationalen Gemeinschaften*, 7th edn, Cologne: Heymann.

Sending, Ole Jacob & Neumann, Iver B. 2006. Governance to governmentality: Analyzing NGOs, states and power, in: *International Studies Quarterly* 50: 3, 651–72.

Senti, Richard 2000. *WTO – System und Funktionsweise der Welthandelsordnung*, Zurich: Schultheiss.

Shelton, Dina 2003. The boundaries of human rights jurisdiction in Europe, in: *Duke Journal of Comparative and International Law* 13: 1, 95–154.

Shepherd, Laura 2008. *Gender, Violence and Security: Discourse as Practice*, London: Zed Books.

Shepsle, Kenneth A. 1997. *Analyzing Politics. Rationality, Behaviour and Institutions*, New York: Norton.

Sikkink, Kathryn & Walling, Carrie Booth 2007. The impact of human rights trials in Latin America, in: *Journal of Peace Research* 44: 4, 427–45.

Simmons, Beth 2009. *Mobilizing for Human Rights. International Law in Domestic Politics*, Cambridge: Cambridge University Press.

Simmons, Beth & Danner, Allison 2010. Credible commitments and the International Criminal Court, in: *International Organization* 64: 2, 225–56.

Skjærseth, Jon Birger & Wettestad, Jørgen 2008. *EU Emissions Trading. Initiation, Decision-Making and Implementation*, Aldershot: Ashgate.

Slaughter, Anne-Marie 2004. *A New World Order*, Princeton, NJ: Princeton University Press.

Smith, Jackie, Chatfield, Charles & Pagnucco, Ron (eds) 1997. *Transnational Social Movements and Global Politics. Solidarity Beyond the State*, Syracuse, NY: Syracuse University Press.

Snyder, Jack & Vinjamuri, Leslie 2004. Trials and errors: Principle and pragmatism in strategies of international justice, in: *International Security* 28: 3, 5–44.

Spector, Leonard 2002. Nuclear non-proliferation, in: Larsen, Jeffrey A. (ed.). *Arms Control. Cooperative Security in a Changing Environment*, Boulder, CO: Lynne Rienner, 119–41.

Spero, Joan Edelman & Hart, Jeffrey A. 2003. *The Politics of International Economic Relations*, 6th edn, London: Routledge.

Sprinz, Detlef F. 1998. Internationale Klimapolitik, in: *Die Friedens-Warte*, 73: 1, 25–44.

Sprinz, Detlef F. & Helm, Carsten 1999. The effect of global environmental regimes: A measurement concept, in: *International Political Science Review* 20: 4, 359–69.

Steffek, Jens, Kissling, Claudia & Nanz, Patrizia (eds) 2008. *Civil Society Participation in European and Global Governance. A Cure for the Democratic Deficit?* Basingstoke: Palgrave Macmillan.

Steinberg, Richard 2002. In the shadow of law or power? Consensus-based bar- gaining and outcomes in the GATT/WTO, in: *International Organization* 56: 2, 339–74.

Steiner, Henry J. & Alston, Philip 2000. *International Human Rights in Context. Law, Politics, Morals – Text and Materials*, 2nd edn, Oxford: Clarendon Press.

Steinwand, Martin C. & Stone, Randall W. 2008. The International Monetary Fund: A review of the recent evidence, in: *Review of International Organizations* 3, 123–49.

Stiglitz, Joseph 2002. *Globalization and its Discontents*, New York: Norton.

Stone, Randall W. 2011. *Controlling Institutions: International Organizations and the Global Economy*, Cambridge: Cambridge University Press.

Stone Sweet, Alec 2004. *The Judicial Construction of Europe*, Oxford: Oxford University Press.

Stone Sweet, Alec & Brunell, Thomas L. 1998. Constructing a supranational constitution: dispute resolution and governance in the European Community, in: *American Political Science Review* 92: 1, 63–81.

Strange, Susan 1996. *The Retreat of the State: The Diffusion of Power in the World Economy*, Cambridge: Cambridge University Press.

Straubhaar, Thomas 2002. *Migration im 21. Jahrhundert*, Tübingen: Mohr Siebeck.

Sweeney, Gareth & Saito, Yuri 2009. An NGO assessment of the new mechanisms of the UN Human Rights Council, in: *Human Rights Law Review* 9: 2, 203–23.

Tallberg, Jonas 2000. The anatomy of autonomy: An institutional account of variation in supranational influence, in: *Journal of Common Market Studies* 38: 5, 843–64.

Tallberg, Jonas 2002a. Delegation to supranational institutions: Why, how, and with what consequences? in: *West European Politics* 25: 1, 23–46.

Tallberg, Jonas 2002b. Paths to compliance: Enforcement, management, and the European Union, in: *International Organization* 56: 3, 609–43.

Tallberg, Jonas 2006. *Leadership and Negotiation in the European Union*, Cambridge: Cambridge University Press.

Tallberg, Jonas 2010. The power of the chair: Formal leadership in international cooperation, in: *International Studies Quarterly* 54: 1, 241–65.

Tallberg, Jonas, Sommerer, Thomas, Squatrito, Theresa & Jönsson, Christer 2013. *The Opening Up of International Organizations: Transnational Access in Global Governance*. Cambridge: Cambridge University Press.

Tallberg, Jonas, Sommerer, Thomas, Squatrito, Theresa & Lundgren, Magnus 2016. The performance of international organizations: A policy output approach, in: *Journal of European Public Policy* 23: 7, 1077–96.

Talmon, Stefan 2000. Law of the Sea, in: Volger, Helmut (ed.) *A Concise Encyclopedia of the United Nations*, The Hague: Kluwer Law International, 356–66.

Talmon, Stefan 2005. The Security Council as world legislature, in: *American Journal of International Law* 99: 1, 175–93.

Tanaka, Yoshifumi 2018. *The Peaceful Settlement of International Disputes*, Cambridge: Cambridge University Press.

Tannenwald, Nina 1999. The nuclear taboo: The United States and the normative basis of nuclear non-use, in: *International Organization* 53: 3, 433–68.

Tannenwald, Nina 2005. Stigmatizing the bomb: Origins of the nuclear taboo, in: *International Security* 30: 1, 5–49.

Tannenwald, Nina 2007. *The Nuclear Taboo: The United States and the Non-Use of Nuclear Weapons Since 1945*, Cambridge: Cambridge University Press.

Taylor, Paul 1993. *International Organization in the Modern World. The Regional and the Global Process*, London: Pinter.

Taylor, Paul & Groom, A. J. R. (eds) 1988. *International Institutions at Work*, London: Pinter.

Tetzlaff, Rainer 1996. *Weltbank und Währungsfonds – Gestalter der Bretton- Woods-Ära. Kooperations- und Integrationsregime in einer sich dynamisch entwickelnden Weltgesellschaft*, Opladen: Leske & Budrich.

Thakur, Ramesh, Cooper, Andrew F. & English, John (eds) 2005. *International Commissions and the Power of Ideas*, Tokyo: United Nations University Press.

Thomas, Daniel C. 2001. *The Helsinki Effect. International Norms, Human Rights, and the Demise of Communism*, Princeton, NJ: Princeton University Press.

Thompson, Alexander 2006. Coercion through IOs: The Security Council and the logic of information transmission, in: *International Organization* 60: 1, 1–34.

Thompson, Alexander 2010. Rational design in motion: Uncertainty and flexibility in the global climate regime, in: *European Journal of International Relations* 16: 2, 269–96.

Tickner, J. Ann & Sjoberg, Laura 2010. Feminism, in: Dunne, Tim, Kurki, Milja & Smith, Steve (eds) *International Relations Theories. Discipline and Diversity*, 2nd edn, Oxford: Oxford University Press, 195–212.

Tomuschat, Christian 2008. *Human Rights. Between Idealism and Realism*, 2nd edn, Oxford: Oxford University Press.

Trondal, Jarle, Marcussen, Martin, Larsson, Torbjörn & Veggeland, Frode 2010. *Unpacking International Organisations: The Dynamics of Compound Bureaucracies*. Oxford: Oxford University Press.

True, Jacqui 2013. Feminism, in: Burchill, Scott et al. (eds) *Theories of International Relations*, 5th edn, Basingstoke: Palgrave Macmillan, 241–65.

Tsebelis, George 2002. *Veto Players. How Political Institutions Work*, Princeton, NJ: Princeton University Press.

Underdal, Arild 1992. The concept of regime 'effectiveness', in: *Cooperation and Conflict* 27: 3, 227–40.

Underdal, Arild 1998. Explaining compliance and defection: Three models, in: *European Journal of International Relations* 4: 1, 5–30.

Underdal, Arild 2002. One question, two answers, in: Miles, Edward L., Underdal, Arild, Andresen, Steinar, Wettestad, Jorgen, Skaerseth, Jon Birger & Carlin, Elaine M. (eds) *Environmental Regime Effectiveness. Confronting Theory with Evidence*, Cambridge, MA: MIT Press, 3–45.

Underdal, Arild 2004. Methodological challenges in the study of regime consequences, in: Underdal, Arild & Young, Oran R. (eds) *Regime Consequences. Methodological Challenges and Research Strategies*, Dordrecht: Kluwer Law International, 27–48.

Underhill, Geoffrey, Blom, Jasper & Mügge, Daniel 2010. Introduction: The challenges and prospects of global financial integration, in: Underhill, Geoffrey, Blom, Jasper & Mügge, Daniel (eds) *Global Financial Integration Thirty Years On. From Reform to Crisis*, Cambridge: Cambridge University Press, 1–21.

Union of International Associations n.d. *The Yearbook of International Organizations*, https://uia.org/yearbook/, date accessed: 29 July 2018.

United Nations 2004. *The Blue Helmets. A Review of United Nations Peacekeeping*, New York: United Nations Department of Public Information.

United Nations General Assembly 2005. *World Summit Outcome Document*, A/RES/60/1, http://www.un.org/en/development/desa/population/migration/generalassembly/docs/globalcompact/A_RES_60_1.pdf, date accessed: 28 July 2018.

Urpelainen, Johannes 2012. Unilateral influence on international bureaucrats: An international delegation problem, in: *Journal of Conflict Resolution* 56: 4, 704–35.

Urquhart, Brian 1995. The United Nations in the Middle East: A 50-year retrospective, in: *Middle East Journal* 49: 4, 573–81.

Vabulas, Felicity & Snidal, Duncan 2013. Organization without delegation: Informal intergovernmental organizations (IIGOs) and the spectrum of intergovernmental arrangements, in: *The Review of International Organizations* 8: 2, 193–220.

Van den Bossche, Peter 2008. *The Law and Policy of the World Trade Organization. Text, Cases and Materials*, 2nd edn, Cambridge: Cambridge University Press.

Van der Pijl, Kees 1998. *Transnational Classes and International Relations*, London: Routledge.

Van der Wee, Hermann 1984. *Der gebremste Wohlstand. Wiederaufbau, Wachstum und Strukturwandel der Weltwirtschaft seit 1945*, Munich: Deutscher Taschenbuch Verlag.

Vanhoonacker, Sophie & Pomorska, Karolina 2017. The institutional framework, in: Hill, Christopher, Smith, Michael & Vanhoonacker, Sophie (eds) *International Relations and the European Union*, Oxford: Oxford University Press, 97–122.

Vaubel, Roland 1996. Bureaucracy at the IMF and the World Bank: A comparison of the evidence, in: *World Economy* 19: 2, 195–210.

Vaubel, Roland, Dreher, Axel & Soylu, Uğurlu 2007. Staff growth in international organizations: A principal-agent problem? An empirical analysis, in: *Public Choice* 133: 3–4, 275–95.

Victor, David 1998. The operation and effectiveness of the Montreal Protocol's non-compliance procedure, in: Victor, David G., Raustiala, Kal & Skolnikoff, Eugene B. (eds) *The Implementation and Effectiveness of International Environmental Commitments. Theory and Practice*, Cambridge, MA: MIT Press, 137–76.

Victor, David G. 2001. *The Collapse of the Kyoto Protocol and the Struggle to Slow Global Warming*, Princeton, NJ: Princeton University Press.

Voeten, Erik 2000. Clashes in the Assembly, in: *International Organization* 54: 2, 185–215.

Voeten, Erik 2005. The political origins of the UN Security Council's ability to legitimize the use of force, in: *International Organization* 59: 3, 527–57.

Volgy, Thomas J., Fausett, Elisabeth, Grant Keith A. & Rodgers, Stuart 2008. Identifying formal intergovernmental organizations, in: *Journal of Peace Research* 45: 6, 837–50.

Von Hagen, Jürgen & Wyplosz, Charles 2010. EMU's decentralized system of fiscal policy, in: Buti, Marco, Deroose, Servaas, Gaspar, Vitor & Nogueira Martins, João (eds) *The Euro. The First Decade*, Cambridge: Cambridge University Press, 415–44.

Von Urff, Winfried 2000. Agrarpolitik, in: Weidenfeld, Werner & Wessels, Wolfgang (eds) 2000. *Europa von A bis Z*, 7th edn, Bonn: Europa Union, 58–65.

Vreeland, James Raymond 2007. *The International Monetary Fund. Politics of Conditional Lending*, London: Routledge.

Wallace, Helen 2010. An institutional anatomy and five policy modes, in: Wallace, Helen, Pollack, Mark A. & Young, Alasdair A. (eds) *Policy-Making in the European Union*, 6th edn, Oxford: Oxford University Press, 69–104.

Wallander, Celeste A. 2000. Institutional assets and adaptability: NATO after the Cold War., in: *International Organization* 54: 4, 705–35.

Wallander, Celeste A. & Keohane, Robert O. 1999. Risk, threat, and security institutions, in: Haftendorn, Helga, Keohane, Robert O. & Wallander, Celeste A. (eds) *Imperfect Unions. Security Institutions over Space and Time*, Oxford: Oxford University Press, 21–47.

Wallensteen, Peter & Johansson, Patrik 2016. The UN Security Council: Decisions and actions, in: von Einsiedel, Sebastian, Malone, David M. & Ugarte, Bruno Stagno (eds) *The UN Security Council in the 21st Century*, Boulder, CO: Lynne Rienner, 27–54.

Wallensteen, Peter & Svensson, Isak 2014. Talking peace: International mediation in armed conflicts, in: *Journal of Peace Research* 51: 2, 315–27.

Walt, Stephen M. 1987. *The Origin of Alliances*, Ithaca, NY: Cornell University Press.

Walter, Barbara 2002. *Committing to Peace. The Successful Settlement of Civil Wars*, Princeton, NJ: Princeton University Press.

Waltz, Kenneth N. 1959. *Man, the State, and War: A Theoretical Analysis*, New York: Columbia University Press.

Waltz, Kenneth N. 1979. *Theory of International Politics*, New York: McGraw-Hill.

Waltz, Kenneth N. 1986. Reflections on theory of international politics: A response to my critics, in: Keohane, Robert O. (ed.) *Neorealism and Its Critics*, New York: Columbia University Press, 322–46.

Waltz, Kenneth N. 1990. Neorealist thought and neorealist theory, in: *Journal of International Affairs* 44: 1, 21–38.

Waltz, Kenneth N. 1993. The emerging structure of international politics, in: *International Security* 18: 2, 44–79.

Waters, Sarah 2004. Mobilising against globalisation: Attac and the French intellectuals, in: *West European Politics* 27: 5, 854–74.

Weaver, Catherine 2008. *Hypocrisy Trap. The World Bank and the Poverty of Reform*, Ithaca, NY: Cornell University Press.

Weber, Albrecht 1983. *Geschichte der internationalen Wirtschaftsorganisationen*, Wiesbaden: Steiner.

Weinlich, Silke 2014. *The UN Secretariat's Influence on the Evolution of Peacekeeping*, London: Palgrave Macmillan.

Weiss, Thomas G., Forsythe, David P., Coate, Roger A. & Pease, Kelly-Kate 2007. *The United Nations and Changing World Politics*, 5th edn, Boulder, CO: Westview Press.

Weiss, Thomas G. & Wilkinson, Rorden (eds) 2018. *International Organization and Global Governance*, London: Routledge.

Wendt, Alexander 1992. Anarchy is what states make of it, in: *International Organization* 46: 2, 391–425.

Wendt, Alexander 1999. *Social Theory of International Politics*, Cambridge: Cambridge University Press.

Wendt, Alexander 2003. Why a world state is inevitable, in: *European Journal of International Relations* 9: 4, 491–542.

Wettestad, Jorgen 1999. *Designing Effective Environmental Regimes. The Key Conditions*, Cheltenham: Edward Elgar.

Wettestad, Jorgen 2002. The Vienna Convention and Montreal Protocol on Ozone-Layer Depletion, in: Miles, Edward L., Underdal, Arild, Andresen, Steinar, Wettestad, Jorgen, Skjaerseth, Jon Birger & Carlin, Elaine M. (eds) *Environmental Regime Effectiveness. Confronting Theory with Evidence*, Cambridge, MA: MIT Press, 149–69.

Whitfield, Teresa 2007. Good offices and 'groups of friends', in: Chesterman, Simon (ed.) *Secretary or General? The UN Secretary-General in World Politics*, Cambridge: Cambridge University Press, 86–101.

Wilkinson, Rorden 2000. *Multilateralism and the World Trade Organisation. The Architecture and Extension of International Trade Regulation*, London: Routledge.

Williamson, John 1990. What Washington means by policy reform, in: Williamson, John (ed.) *Latin American Adjustment. How Much Has Happened?* Washington, DC: Institute for International Economics.

Wilson, James Q. & DiIulio, John J., Jr. 1997. *American Government. Institutions and Policies*, 7th edn, Boston, MA: Houghton Mifflin.

Wilson, Woodrow 1917/18. *President Wilson's Great Speeches and Other History Making Documents*, Chicago, IL: Stanton & Van Vliet.

Wolf, Klaus Dieter 1999. *Integrationstheorien im Vergleich. Funktionalistische und intergouvernementalistische Erklärung für die Europäische Wirtschafts- und Währungsunion im Vertrag von Maastricht*, Baden-Baden: Nomos.

Wolf, Klaus Dieter & Zangl, Bernhard 1996. The European Economic and Monetary Union: two-level games and the formation of international institutions, in: *European Journal of International Relations* 2: 3, 355–93.

Wolf, Klaus Dieter 1981. *Die dritte Seerechtskonferenz der Vereinten Nationen. Beiträge zur Reform der internationalen Ordnung und Entwicklungstendenzen im Nord-Süd-Verhältnis*, Baden-Baden: Nomos.

Wonka, Arndt & Rittberger, Berthold 2010. Credibility, complexity and uncertainty: Explaining the institutional independence of 29 EU agencies, in: *West European Politics* 33: 4, 730–52.

Woods, Ngaire 2000. The challenges of multilateralism and governance, in: Gilbert, Christopher L. & Vines, David (eds) *The World Bank. Structure and Policies*, Cambridge: Cambridge University Press, 132–56.

Woolcock Stephen 2010. Trade policy, in: Wallace, Helen, Pollack, Mark A. & Young, Alasdair A. (eds) *Policy-Making in the European Union*, 6th edn, Oxford: Oxford University Press, 381–99.

World Bank 2007. *A Guide to the World Bank*, 2nd edn, Washington, DC: World Bank.

World Bank n.d. *The World Bank Data: Trade (% of GDP)*, https://data.worldbank. org/indicator/NE.TRD.GNFS.ZS, date accessed: 27 July 2018.

World Bank Group 2014. *A Stronger, Connected, Solutions World Bank Group*, Washington, DC: The World Bank Group.

Yamin, Farhana & Depledge, Joanna 2004. *The International Climate Change Regime. A Guide to Rules, Institutions and Procedures*, Cambridge: Cambridge University Press.

Young, Oran R. 1979. *Compliance and Public Authority. A Theory with International Applications*, Baltimore, MD: Johns Hopkins University Press.

Young, Oran R. (ed.) 1999. *The Effectiveness of International Environmental Regimes: Causal Connections and Behavioral Mechanisms*, Cambridge, MA: The MIT Press.

Young, Oran R. 2001. Inferences and indices: Evaluating the effectiveness of international environmental regimes, in: *Global Environmental Politics* 1: 1, 99–121.

Young, Oran R. 2004. The consequences of international regimes: A framework for analysis, in: Underdal, Arild & Young, Oran R. (eds) *Regime Consequences: Methodological Challenges and Research Strategies*, Dortrecht: Kluwer Law International, 2–23.

Young, Oran R. 2017. *Governing Complex Systems: Social Capital for the Anthropocene*. Cambridge, MA: The MIT Press.

Zakaria, Fareed 2008. *The Post-American World*, New York: Norton.

Zangl, Bernhard 1999. *Interessen auf zwei Ebenen. Internationale Regime in der Agrarhandels-, Währungs- und Walfangpolitik*, Baden-Baden: Nomos.

Zangl, Bernhard 2008. Judicialization matters! A comparison of dispute settlement under GATT and the WTO, in: *International Studies Quarterly* 52: 4, 825–54.

Zangl, Bernhard, Helmedach, Achim, Mondré, Aletta, Kocks, Alexander, Neubauer, Gerald, & Blome, Kerstin 2012. Between law and politics: Explaining international dispute settlement behavior, in: *European Journal of International Relations* 18: 2, 369–401.

Zangl, Bernhard, Heußner, Frederick, Kruck, Andreas & Lanzendörfer, Xenia 2016. Imperfect adaptation: How the WTO and the IMF adjust to shifting power distributions among their members, in: *The Review of International Organizations* 11: 2, 171–96.

Zolberg, Aristide R. 1991. Bounded states in a global market: The uses of international labor migrations, in: Bourdieu, Pierre & Coleman, James S. (eds) *Social Theory for a Changing Society*, Boulder, CO: Westview, 301–25.

Zürn, Michael 2000. Democratic governance beyond the nation-state: The EU and other international institutions, in: *European Journal for International Relations* 6: 2, 183–222.

Zürn, Michael, Binder, Martin, Ecker-Ehrhardt, Matthias & Radtke, Katrin 2007. Politische Ordnungsbildung wider Willen, in: *Zeitschrift für Internationale Beziehungen* 14: 1, 129–64.

Zürn, Michael, Binder, Martin & Ecker-Ehrhardt, Matthias 2012. International authority and its politicization, in: *International Theory* 4: 1, 69–106.

Index

Page numbers in **bold type** indicate figures, those in *italics* indicate tables.